PROJECTIONS 2

PROJECTIONS 2

A Forum for Film-makers

edited by

John Boorman and

Walter Donohue

faber and faber

LONDON · BOSTON

First published in 1993
by Faber and Faber Limited
3 Queen Square London WC1N 3AU

Photoset by Parker Typesetting Service Leicester
Printed in England by Clays Ltd, St Ives Plc

A CIP record for this book is available from the British Library
ISBN 0-571-16828-0

10 9 8 7 6 5 4 3 2 1

Contents

Illustrations

Acknowledgements

The editors wish to thank Isabella Weibrecht, Paul Webster, Gordon Kato, Julia Overton, Laura Phillips, Helena Gudmundson, Arielle, Mark Seldes, Barbara Nolan and DJ; and Shaun Whiteside for the conscientiousness, good humour and resilience with which he tackled the translation requirements of this book. Stills appear by courtesy of BFI Stills, Posters and Designs.

Copyright for stills are held by the following: MGM (*Knights of the Round Table*, *Ben Hur*); Kennedy Miller (*Mad Max*, *Mad Max II*, *Mad Max Beyond Thunderdome*); Warner Brothers (*The Witches of Eastwick*, *McCabe and Mrs Miller*); Columbia (*Dr Strangelove*); Zoetrope (*Apocalypse Now*); Electric Pictures (*Toto the Hero*); Mosfilm (*Mirror*); Hibiscus Films (*Crush*); New Line (*My Own Private Idaho*); Working Title/British Film Institute/BBC Films (*Edward II*); Grain of Sand Productions (*Light Sleeper*); Hemdale (*Platoon*); Universal (*The Last Temptation of Christ*, *Ulzana's Raid*); BIP (*The Farmer's Wife*); Gaumont (*The Lady Vanishes*); GFD/Gainsborough (*Millions Like Us*); GFD/Individual (*I See A Dark Stranger*, *Rake's Progress*); GFD/David Lean/Cineguild (*Madeleine*); Twentieth-Century Fox/Aspen (*M⋆A⋆S⋆H*); Twentieth-Century Fox/Lions Gate (*Three Women*); Lions Gate/Hemdale (*Images*); Svensk Filmindustri (*Persona*); UA (*To Live and Die in LA*, *Buffalo Bill and the Indians*); UA/Lions Gate (*The Long Goodbye*); Paramount (*Nashville*, *Flight of the Intruder*); Paramount/Bob Roberts Company (*Bob Roberts*); Sandcastle 5/Mark Goodman/Viacom (*Come Back to the Five and Dime, Jimmy Dean, Jimmy Dean*); William Fox (*Regeneration*); Spelling Films International (*The Player*); Little Bear/Artificial Eye (L 627); RKO (*I Walked with a Zombie*); DDA (*My Own Private Idaho*).

Photos from *Crush* by Bridget Ikin; of Gus Van Sant by Eric Alan Edwards; of Derek Jarman and *Edward II* by Liam Longman; of *Light Sleeper* by Steve Sands; of the Wooster Group by Bob Van Dantzig; of Bertrand Tavernier, and of Michael Powell and Jean-Pierre Melville by Jacques Prayer/Gamma; of *Bob Roberts* by Sam Jones.

The passage from *Sexing the Cherry* by Jeanette Winterson appears by kind permission of Bloomsbury Publishing Limited.

Fade In . . .

John Boorman

My journal in last year's *Projections* recounting my frustrations in getting projects going touched a lot of raw nerves and a few funny bones. Robert Altman told me that by changing some of the names it could have been his story. Many others responded in similar ways. Karel Reitz said we feel we have to pretend that everything is going well otherwise they think we are on the slide whereas, in truth, anguish and rejection are the common lot of film-makers. And it was ever so. D. W. Griffith had to borrow money from his actors to finish *Birth of a Nation* and spent the last thirty years of his life spurned, then forgotten, in a dingy New York hotel room. Orson Welles begged and borrowed and died leaving unfinished films. Kurosawa was driven to attempt suicide. Michael Powell became a pariah after *Peeping Tom*. Truffaut and Bergman, whose careers seemed to move smoothly from film to film, both revealed in their autobiographies their constant struggles to finance their films and the usual catalogue of betrayal and cupidity.

Yet film directors are envied and often admired. The aura they wear surely comes from the power they exercise when they actually make a movie. As someone once said, power corrupts, absolute power is absolutely delicious. Between films, or when directors can no longer make them, the mark of that power remains upon them, just as men who have known the fire of battle are set apart. David Hare wrote me after reading my journal to say that we between-film directors reminded him of deposed royalty, forever wandering the globe to be encountered in hotel lobbies and festivals. We retain the title but for most of the time we lack a kingdom.

I said in *Projections 1* that the aim of the annual is to give film-makers a forum to reflect on their concerns with as much honesty as they can muster and speak directly to their fellow practitioners. I am happy to say that the contributions in *Projections 2* – which my co-editor Walter Donohue has gathered together – offer us frankness that is sometimes brutal and an honesty which is always compelling. 'Altman on Altman' is the story of a man whose vision was banished by the mainstream but who reclaimed his crown with *The Player*, whose leading actor, Tim Robbins, made the directorial début of the year with *Bob Roberts*. Bertrand Tavernier's journal reflects his love and prodigious knowledge of the movies and his readiness to do battle with the hypocrites, the phonies and the philistines. George Miller, Jaco van Dormael, Willem Dafoe, Alison Maclean all investigate the process of movie-making with the same generosity and openness.

The refrain I hear from film-makers I meet or encounter through this publication is that they – the studios, the financiers – don't want to make the films we want to make and we don't want to make the films they want us to make. This divide grows ever wider. Are the studio executives responding to an audience whose brow gets lower by the year, or are the movies they choose to make what they (cynically) *think* the audience wants?

Jazz and the movies occurred at about the same time and quickly became the popular art forms of the century. Jazz has been eclipsed by rock 'n' roll. Could it be that the movies coming out of Hollywood – the reductive, kinetic, noisy ones that we don't want to make – are analogous to rock 'n' roll? Are the movies as we knew and loved them suffering the fate of jazz?

It is tempting to lay the blame at the door of the studios – what the world gets to see as entertainment is whatever filters through the minds of Jeffrey Katzenberg and Peter Guber. The studios argue that they are responding to public taste. Yet not only do they decide which pictures get made, but also which ones get the multi-million dollar advertising campaigns and the 1,000-plus print runs. I recall that in the early days of commercial television in Britain Lew Grade, a dominant player, was asked how he would define a prime-time programme. 'A prime-time programme,' he replied, 'is any programme I decide to put on during prime-time.'

H. L. Mencken's much-quoted dictum that nobody ever went broke under-estimating the intelligence of the American people has been holy writ in Hollywood for some time, but a rider must now be added: unless you are carrying a multi-billion dollar debt burden, which most of the studios are. Bought and sold with borrowed money in the eighties, with many executives getting an annual salary equal to the total budget of the average European film, they find themselves saddled with such bloated costs that success is no longer enough however down-market they go.

Imagine a scene that might have been in Altman's *The Player*. A producer pitches his film to a studio chief, the usual stuff: 'It's *Wayne's World* meets *Home Alone*. It's zany, but you care. You laugh and you cry too and you're scared shitless. Here's a nice family guy, a Kevin Costner type married to a Michelle Pfeiffer or an Annette Bening, three young kids. He crashes his car. They think he's dead. They revive him in the hospital but – and here's the twist – his mind gets switched with a serial killer.' The producer leans forward and in a reverential voice confides to the studio chief, 'It's a home run. This is a hundred million dollar grosser.' The chief, trembling with rage, screams back, 'Only a hundred million dollars? What are you trying to do, bankrupt the studio?'

With costs and debts being what they are, can it go on? Or is the system on the point of collapse? If it did collapse, and the supply of Hollywood movies dried up, would audiences come out to see European films and the offerings of American independents? Or would the multi-plexes close their doors?

In this edition of *Projections* we invited film-makers to speculate on what kinds of film will be made in the future. But if the future of film itself is threatened and these lunatics can no longer run the asylum, perhaps it is time for us, the movie-makers to think about taking over. To this end, the question for next year's *Projections* is: What would you do if you were running a Hollywood studio? Send your thoughts on that to:

Walter Donohue
Faber and Faber
3 Queen Square
London WC1N 3AU

1   George Miller

1 Shadow and Substance

George Miller in Conversation with Daphne Paris

Daphne Paris has been connected with George Miller and his company Kennedy Miller for some years as Script Supervisor. As such she seemed an apt choice to interview George Miller about his work, and the conditions in which it developed and thrived.

DAPHNE PARIS: *Growing up in the fifties in a small country town, how interested or influenced were you by the movies?*

GEORGE MILLER: Like virtually everyone of my generation, I was always interested in films. In my case, the only experience of the outside world tended to be the Saturday matinée. This was well before television in Australia, so the Saturday matinée was a magical event – it had an essential influence on me and on my attitude to cinema. It must be quite different now for kids. There's an overwhelming choice of information. Most of my childhood was spent playing games influenced by the cinema. I grew up in a family of boys, and there were always gangs of kids running around, all acting out the latest cliffhanger. For *Sir Galahad*, we'd do up our horses with armour, paint shields on garbage bin-lids and make jousting poles, put cans with feathers on top of our heads, pretend we were some sort of knight, build castles and so on. A childhood like that is almost an invisible apprenticeship in film-making. Also, I enjoyed drawing a lot. I used to love comic books and almost always had them hidden in the back of my text books.

DP: *But you went on to become a doctor. That's a long way from film-making.*

GM: From a very early age I decided I wanted to study medicine, so I never even imagined myself making films. But at university I did go to the cinema a lot. My twin brother John and I were at medical school together and he would tend to go to lectures while I'd go to a morning session of the movies. There were the usual film societies and there was the wonderful Sydney Film Festival, run by David Stratton, who used to bring in great, unforgettable movies. I believe the festivals had a big influence on Australian film-makers. I think Australian movies were a kind of hybrid between European and American cinema; those early Australian movies tended to have a tone that was partly European art film, partly Hollywood movie.

2   *Knights of the Round Table* (1953)

DP: *How did you become involved in film-making?*

GM: I'd finished my final exams and while waiting to take up a post in a hospital I was working as a brickie on a multi-storey hotel. One lunch time some bricks fell off the top of the building with me standing many storeys below. They missed, but it gave me a useful existential jolt. I climbed on my motor bike and rode 600 miles to Melbourne University, where I'd heard there was to be the first ever workshop in film-making. I talked my way in and for the next month got to play with the most elementary tools of film-making. That was it, I was totally addicted, as if on heroin. I used to paint and draw a lot, and what got me hooked was the plasticity of film – cutting together little pieces of time, playing with a visual and aural syntax. It was a wonderful period. My response to the medium was 'primary', like a child's, without any regard to context or outcome. I found myself entirely curious about form. The other fine thing that happened at that workshop was that I met Byron Kennedy; even though we came from different parts of the country and had a different world view, we absolutely concurred on the way films should be. We enjoyed complementary skills. Afterwards I went back to Sydney and worked for two years in hospital. During that time we started making short films at weekends.

The great thing about that era was the Film-makers Co-op. It was a kind of unofficial film school in Sydney and Melbourne, where it originated. All the film-makers, the Bruce Beresfords and the Peter Weirs, were making short films on minor grants or bits of money scrounged together. Everyone was working on everyone else's film. You'd go off and do a bit of, say, sound. Generally you'd screw it up, but at least you learnt how to do it. Or someone would need an extra camera, or an actor to do a bit part. It was a lovely time, blessed, because there was no sophistry. It was all about essence, about ideas and how to put them on celluloid. Like every industry, the Australian industry eventually matured into a very sophisticated machine, with the whole infra-structure of unions, agents, lawyers, money men, script editors, film schools and their bureaucrats, who are the exact equivalent of the studio bureaucrats. Suddenly that essential hunger for the idea was complicated and people started to be preoccupied with careers. Before the early 1980s there was no such thing as a 'career' in the Australian film industry.

DP: *So at that stage you still only thought of film as something you enjoyed?*

GM: Oh, absolutely. In fact I'm still registered as a doctor. I still don't see film as a career. For me, at least, it was always a vocation. I think it's because I never came to it formally. The fact that the first feature was so successful gave us a kind of financial independence. I never really felt I had to do anything except the next good idea that came along. It's basically what drove Kennedy Miller* too.

---

* The company formed by Byron Kennedy and George Miller in Australia which became the celebrated producer of television and feature films in the eighties.

DP: *How do you define that which drives Kennedy Miller?*

GM: Story, story, story. There's a paradox about a life in film-making – we mistake the shadow and the substance. The real substance is that intangible, fragile thing that happens between an audience and the screen. We all know that the best parts of the best films stay in the memory, they burn into the memory. In that way they shape a little bit of how we read the world. This exchange with the audience is the substance of film and everything else is the shadow. And yet the mistake we all make is to completely flip it around. The deals, the lifestyles, the studios, the film bureaucracies, the publicists and the agents and the lawyers, the actors, the writers, the directors, the technicians are all essential to the process, but you better be careful that they aren't perceived as the substance. It's particularly evident in Australia where the industry has shrunk again since the tax concessions have gone and the good thing is that people now have to look more towards the real substance – the ideas and the essential passion of us film makers to put those ideas on the screen. Now what's so scary about that is, it's profoundly mysterious.

DP: *If it's so mysterious and it's the stuff that drives film-making, how do you get a handle on it?*

GM: Obviously, it's driven by intuition more than anything else. That's why we try as hard as possible to cerebrate it, to try and figure out how some of the process works. You may never understand it, but at least if you try, it helps inform the intuition. It guides that moment of shooting or writing when you get a feeling that this is the way it should go, or a feeling for a rhythm or how you should solve a particular problem that an actor or the camera or the script is having. All that intuitive response comes from thinking about it beforehand. I always say – the intellect prepares the film and the intuition shoots it.

DP: *In 1971, the year after the workshop, you made* Violence in the Cinema, Part I. *How did that come about?*

GM: I was working at St Vincent's Hospital. In those days junior doctors would work a 90-hour week – the hospital was like a village – you'd eat there, your friendships, your life was all in the hospital – very similar to film-making, so it was great preparation. We had a long weekend, Easter weekend, four days off. I remember calling Byron Kennedy, and saying, here is an idea for a film, how much money have you got? Together we had a total of $1,500, so we said: OK we'll make this film which was a parody of all the violent films about at the time. There was *Clockwork Orange*, and the Sam Peckinpah movies, and there were think pieces in the news magazines, they called it 'ultra violence'. Of course it's a debate that has gone on forever, and will continue to go on. It was a fifteen-minute film. Now the interesting thing about that film was that it was picked up for distribution. David Stratton put it in the Sydney Festival proper as a short, and it was picked up for distribution by Greater Union, so it was blown up and shown around the country. We'd never even heard of distribution until that point. I think it was the first ever short distributed in the commercial cinema in Australia and it eventually earned a tiny profit. So we said: Well, we'll try a feature film. We were very arrogant then. That was '72, but it was '79 before we managed to make a full-length film. Meanwhile I was earning money working as a doctor and Byron was working as a cameraman on experimental films. He shot a couple of low budget features and I worked as an editor. Again virtually no money, mostly we did it in exchange for room and board.

DP: *And that film was* Mad Max *which became a big hit. Was that a complete surprise?*

GM: Yes, it was a total surprise. I didn't know much about screenwriting, and it took us about a year to do the screenplay, by the time we got it right, working on and off. And then it took us almost another year to raise the $350,000 to make it because the government funding bodies weren't interested in investing in this vulgarity. It wasn't Australian . . . it wasn't a period film, the kind of film Australians were making at that time. But for me it was pure cinema – action films truly are. I loved all the classic film chases, the chariot races in *Ben Hur*, and the classic comedies of Harold Lloyd, and particularly Buster Keaton, because it was pure film language. So we thought we'd make a film where, as Hitchcock said, they wouldn't have to read the subtitles in Japan. People didn't believe we could do it because it required lots of stunts – nobody had done anything like that in Australia at the time. I suppose, looking back on it, they were probably right and we were wrong. If someone came to me now with *Mad Max*, saying that they could make it with so little money, I'd say they're crazy.

As we were shooting it, I found the process quite shocking. I had planned out the movie in my head, I knew what I wanted to do. But I'd never really been on a proper film set before. I'd never really directed actors before and, in particular, I had never had to do action before. The crew had never done it before either. A lot hadn't even shot 35mm, they'd only shot 16mm on very low budget television. We couldn't afford one of the crews that were doing features at the time. Mel Gibson had never done a movie other than a weekend movie or something while he was at the national drama school. What I found amazing was that it was so difficult. I approached it very methodically, as if it were a surgical operation. In surgery there is a certain methodology already before you and usually when you go to look for the gall bladder you'll find it with a high degree of predictability. But films ain't like that. There's always millions of variables. Someone once described making movies as like being 'pecked to death by ducks'. Others have said the best way to approach film-making is like guerrilla warfare. I knew none of that.

By the time we finished shooting we were told that the film couldn't be edited, that it was a mess. But I knew there was a film there. We had only enough money to spend a month in the cutting room and it looked like a badly

3 *Ben Hur* (1959)

4 *Mad Max*

cut TV show – arhythmic, odd. So Byron and I took on the cutting ourselves. I set up the cutting room in the kitchen with very primitive equipment and Byron was in the lounge doing the sound. That's when I got to know the film backwards, literally, every frame of film, I'd seen it a thousand times. I cut it silent, no sound, no music. If it played as a silent movie, then I knew it had a chance of playing as a sound movie. You know your first feature is difficult to watch. All you see is terrible mistakes. You know I honestly thought the film was unreleasable. That wasn't the case, but I was able to confront the failure of the film before it was ever released, so I suppose that led me to being objective about it. And it turned us from film paupers to being very well off. At that point we'd never considered the possibility it would be a major commercial success.

DP: *And then you went on to* Mad Max II *because of the opportunity it offered to do it better?*

GM: Well *Mad Max* was a very interesting experience because a most unexpected thing happened. Here was an Australian genre picture that seems to have resonance all over the world. Like in Japan, for instance. I'd never seen a Kurosawa movie, yet the Japanese said *Mad Max* is a samurai and that's why he's successful in Japan. Someone from Iceland told me it's exactly like the wandering loner in Viking folklore. I began, for the first time, to question this process we call 'storytelling'. With my basically scientific background, I took a phenomonological view of the world, everything was cause and effect. Now I had concrete experience of what Jung called the 'collective unconscious'. That really was one of the big shocks of my life and I came to it through the practice of film-making. Here was something a lot bigger than any individual – forces deep and mysterious that drive this need we have to tell each other stories. The person who shone the great floodlight on all this was Joseph Campbell through his discourses on mythology. He went well beyond Jung or anybody else. In all time and space there is this compulsion to put ourselves into the broadest context, to connect ourselves to what came before and what will come after. And the means by which we do this most effectively is 'storytelling', whether they are religious stories or movie stories or children's stories or whether they are rituals like˙football. *Mad Max* was something that fell into that context and that allowed us to do *Road Warrior* with a bit more clarity.

DP: *That's why you started on* Mad Max II *or* Road Warrior?

GM: Well, we also had a decent budget. I have to say that it was the complete antithesis of the shoot we had on *Mad Max*. By then I knew that film-making was guerrilla warfare, that film-making was an act of will and that come what may you had to make the best of it. That was a very happy shoot. It was, I think, Dean Semler's first big feature and Mel was much more comfortable with the process of acting. By then he'd become an international movie star. It was a physically tough shoot, but we got closer to what had been conceived. It was done very fast. The writing was fast, we almost had no screenplay before we

5   Mel Gibson's first appearance as Mad Max

6   Mel Gibson as the road warrior in *Mad Max II*

started shooting it. It was very hectic, so it was a big blur of activity. We even had to cut the film lightning fast. I never saw the completed film till I saw the answer print. We had to get it out by a certain release date. *Road Warrior* went on in a way to eclipse the success of *Mad Max*, and I was more satisfied with it.

DP: *Almost immediately you embarked on a mini-series,* The Dismissal. *Why television?*

GM: Up to that point I absolutely hated television. I thought it was a mean little box, a tiny window, never engaging – mental chewing gum for the masses. But Rupert Murdoch had just bought 10 Network in Australia and offered us something we couldn't refuse. We were to do a mini-series, or any television we wanted, providing it was bold. He needed something bold to redefine the network. So we did *The Dismissal* which was six hours on the constitutional crisis we had in 1975 when the legitimate government of Australia was sacked. That was really exciting because for the first time I had to work with other directors like Phil Noyce and George Ogilvie, who had never worked in film before but had done opera, ballet and particularly theatre. He conducted those wonderful workshops where for the first time we were able to get writers and directors and actors together before the screenplays were actually written, and immerse ourselves simultaneously in the project. We could afford to do it and we had the time. The collective energy that came out was incredible.

DP: *The workshops led to a more organic progression from the writing through rehearsal and finally to the shoot. Was this very different from the way you worked with the cast on the* Mad Max *films?*

GM: Yes it was. However, *The Dismissal* workshop, mainly led by George Ogilvie, I think influenced everything Kennedy Miller did after that. The first thing is to acknowledge that the process is an organic one; that is, can't differentiate the function of the producer, the writer, the director and to some extent the actor, the cameraman and so on. The second thing to acknowledge is that everyone must have a shared vision for the ensemble to work, and finally the thing is to acknowledge that the process of film-making is not art, craft or commerce. It's all of the above. The Kennedy Miller workshop tries to take into account all of this.

DP: *Why do they work so well?*

GM: It's a question of forging a collective view. You see directors never really get to see other directors work and writers really never get to work with other writers. The director tends to spend a lot more time on a film than anybody else, except perhaps the producer, so their turnover of work is a lot less. Actors, cameramen, most crew members work with many more directors and consequently many more methodologies and styles. So it's always immensely educational for directors to work together if they have a chance. Even more so, the writer and the director. Writers, I find by and large, tend to be non-collaborative by nature. It's their instinct not to be and the tragedy of this

7   *The Dismissal*

continuous dilemma between the film writer and the director is that it is completely false; it must be recognized that the process is a continuum. It doesn't stop with the writing and it doesn't begin with the directing. I always know when I write a scene, say for a mini-series, and I hand it over to a director, that the director must process it through his or her own intuition. They're at the coal face. It's their rhythm, their 'musicality' which presides. This is not to deny the value of collaboration so long as the final arbiter is the director.

DP: *Did workshopping before you had completed scripts happen with the other mini-series Kennedy Miller produced?*

GM: Yes, on most of them. One of the big things we learnt from *The Dismissal* was that the fact we didn't have completed screenplays was a boon in disguise because it kept everyone away from the text. By and large people knew the material because it had already been written by history; it was in the recent public record. So the actors and directors were obliged to look at the characters at large. The cast brought the characters to the process, regardless of what was in the screenplay and it gave them tremendous authority. It also meant that the directors had to look to the world of the story. How do both sides of the parliament operate, how does the press gallery work? What is that unholy alliance between the press gallery and the politicians?

DP: *During* The Dismissal *you went to the States and did a segment of* The Twilight Zone *for a studio. How was that?*

GM: We were in post-production on *The Dismissal* and *Mad Max II* had come out as *Road Warrior* in the States and they were preparing to do the ill-fated *Twilight Zone* movie. When I met Steven Spielberg and Frank Marshall there were to be three episodes. They said they'd add another one for me and I thought it would be great fun. It was a short film, 25 minutes or so. They were a wonderful bunch of people, we had a lovely time. But the whole event was overshadowed by that obscene accident.*

DP: *What was it like working for a Hollywood studio?*

GM: As a film-making environment the studio system seemed benign, but I had confused it with working for Spielberg's 'Amblin' company which was quite different because they were hands-on film-makers of like mind. It made me leave my guard down for *The Witches of Eastwick* a couple of years later when I paid no attention to the production personnel who were eventually to be on the film, and that was a mistake. The so-called producers like Guber Peters were deal makers, packagers or politicians. They were not film-makers.

DP: *In the four years between* Road Warrior *and* Mad Max Beyond Thunderdome *you concentrated more on television. What attracted you to it?*

GM: *The Dismissal* was great fun and what led me personally away from feature

---

* During the filming of the John Landis segment of the film a helicopter crashed, killing actor Vic Morrow and two Vietnamese children.

films was that it was such a success in every way. Despite everyone's predictions, it was a huge ratings success and probably changed the face of television in Australia. Here was television on something ostensibly as dry and boring as the constitutional crisis and yet the whole country stopped to watch it. And for the film-makers the learning curve accelerated spectacularly. It split Kennedy Miller into two streams, one was features and the other was television. We were very lucky in Australia in that we were able to make profitable television with total creative freedom. No one vetted screenplays, casting or anything else. It was a very seductive set of circumstances where we could do what we wanted, the only stipulation being that it had to rate highly. We kept on rating highly, so that was fine. Two big influences on Kennedy Miller at the time were the arrival of Doug Mitchell and the death of Byron Kennedy. Doug became Byron's protégé and he virtually took over from Byron as the backbone of the company ever since.

DP: *During that time you were also developing* Mad Max III.

GM: Although we were deeply into television we were already committed to do *Mad Max III*, and I was, you know, grieving badly for Byron. That's when George Ogilvie came on to do *Mad Max III*. He co-directed that. We were under huge pressure, yet I enjoyed working with George so much. It was interesting because we both had twin brothers and that made it very easy for us to work together. And *Mad Max III*, my favourite *Mad Max*, was in a sense the most ambitious of the three films. Looking back on it now, we had too much story, we had enough for three or four feature films. We could have done a whole movie on BarterTown, a whole movie on the world of the Lost Children. Unfortunately, we had to skip through it too quickly, even though I think the thing that attracted me to the story was that it was completely different to the other two. They were three completely different films, the only thing in common was the character and Mel Gibson. I think the biggest disappointment that people had was that it shifted its genre. The first two established a genre, but *Mad Max III* shifted its constituency.

DP: *Will there be a fourth?*

GM: There's been a lot of pressure from a lot of quarters to do *Mad Max IV*, but unless there is a completely different way of doing the film, I wouldn't attempt it. And the world has changed.

DP: *You mean you don't think that a post-holocaust world is quite as attractive today?*

GM: It's not a place to explore. Basically it's a mythological landscape in the same way as any biblical story, or anything set in the past would be. The *Mad Max* films just happened to be set in some sort of future which is apocalyptic – which reduces human beings to some sort of more essential state, and I guess that's the function of setting them in that sort of future. The films are not in any way prophetic or anything like that, they are just terrific landscapes to set things in.

8 *Mad Max Beyond Thunderdome*: The Lost Children

9 Mel Gibson's third incarnation of Mad Max

DP: *And the world is a little bit softer now in some way?*

GM: Not necessarily softer, but there are shifts in the way we perceive and think of things. In many ways the kind of things we saw in the *Mad Max* films has almost got into the mainstream, you see them in commercials, and pop videos.

DP: *You've called the* Mad Max *films your teenage films.*

GM: Yes, a notion I took from a French critic. The great critics are always illuminators, great teachers, if you like. He said that whenever he watched the *Mad Max* films he felt like a teenager, and whenever he watched a Spielberg movie he became a child. In one way it was a double-edged sword. It was a way of saying that the films themselves aren't adult, that they are more young male teenage fantasies, and that's a valuable way of looking at them. Many times I find event television more adult, you have to watch as an adult, even if you are a teenager you need to become an adult to watch it. I think most mainstream American movies are bringing out the teenager in you, not the adult. People define them as either popcorn movies, or capuccino movies. The popcorn movies are those that we all love to go and see because they take you back to that first experience of sitting in that dark theatre at the Saturday matinée with all the thousands of other kids screaming and yelling even before the credits come up, throwing the popcorn around. And yet there are other movies, the capuccino movies, where the adult in you has to address them. Quite often they're the most powerful movies. I've got this theory now, a way of gauging movies by how long it stays with you after you walk out of the cinema. If you forget the movie before you're out of the foyer well, that's not so good a movie. Then there are those that stay in your consciousness for ever. Images from a Kubrick movie – he manages to get them in most of his movies – like Slim Pickens dropping out of the bomb bay of the aircraft in *Dr Strangelove* or a David Lean film: the entrance of Omar Sharif in *Lawrence of Arabia*. Seen once you never forget them.

DP: *Or Robert Duvall on the beach in* Apocalypse Now.

GM: Exactly. Now what is it that makes one scene – 'I love the smell of napalm in the morning' – burn into the collective memory? It's the confluence of a myriad factors: the actor, the moment within the broad context of the movie, the moment in time, and the way that it speaks to us about our time in history. They are deeply poetic. By that I mean they cram the maximum amount of meaning into the minimum units of information. Sometimes it changes you. I'll never forget the day – on this single day I saw both Robert Altman's *M★A★S★H* and *The Battle of Algiers*. I had no preconception about either film. I found both so extraordinary, that I'm sure they had a big influence on my need to communicate through storytelling. It's interesting that I never ever wanted to go back and see either of them again because I know I could never recapture how they spoke to me that first time.

10   *Dr Strangelove*: Slim Pickens being lowered over the bomb

11   Robert Duvall in *Apocalypse Now*: 'I love the smell of napalm in the morning'

DP: *Soon after completing* Mad Max III *in 1985 you started work on* The Witches of Eastwick *which was an unpleasant experience for you.*

GM: Well, *The Witches of Eastwick* was only half unpleasant. I was caught somewhere between heaven and hell. Completely paradoxical. On the one hand there was a wonderful screenplay written by Michael Cristofer, and the great privilege of working with Jack Nicholson and people like Susan Sarandon and Michelle Pfeiffer, all very gifted actors. But, with a few exceptions I had a mediocre crew and grotesque producers and studio executives. The number of times I was about to quit because, you know, life is too short . . . But I'd look at the footage and I'd say: wait a minute, there is some good work being done here. On the hell side of it, the bizarre nature of the producers and the studio brought out the worst in me. I'd suddenly become the antithesis of the way I wanted to work. Because I was a film-maker, I was always able to outflank them, but I became a very manipulative, dictatorial, cruel director, almost a cliché of the Hollywood tyrant. What scared me so much was that I enjoyed it. I enjoyed being rewarded for bad behaviour. I think it is one of the tragedies of Hollywood that the more powerful you become the greater the tendency to be rewarded for bad behaviour. In fact, the converse applies and there is a tendency to penalize good behaviour.

DP: *Can you give an example?*

GM: Well, the first mistake I made was when we scrutinized the budget and I said, I don't need a trailer, 'cause I never use a trailer, I'm always on the set or in the actors' trailers. Well, that was my first mistake because it said: this guy is open to negotiation on everything. It was interpreted as a sign of weakness, not as a sign of someone wanting to get a film made for a budget. So then everything was open to negotiation, the number of extras, the shooting time, the this the that. As a tactic, I then had to do the opposite. I reflexly went the other way demanding everything, and if it wasn't there, I went slow. So you end up with a bizarre game which is nothing to do with the process of getting a film made.

DP: *What attracted you to* The Witches of Eastwick *story?*

GM: I thought it was one of the most beguiling screenplays I've ever read. I'd just finished *Mad Max III* when Terry Semmel at Warner's had it sent to me. At the time I thought it was just a Warner's screenplay, but as each day went by there were more and more producers. I'd never met Guber Peters and I should have, and I wished people had warned me about Jon Peters beforehand but they didn't. Or I should have made it my business to find out, and I didn't. That's one of the problems. I think it's very important that, if you are to work with people, you should ask more than one person about them, try to get some sense of how they'll work. Exactly the same amount of effort you put into casting an actor you should put into the people you work with. But they sent me the screenplay and it was absolutely delightful, lovely, full of irony. A potent metaphor for the war between men and women, and to that extent it was mythological. And, most of all, it was to be light in tone. Making it became a sheer act of will. I read *The Devil's Candy*, the book about the making of *Bonfire of the Vanities* with the same crew, same writer and the same producers and studio executives as *The Witches of Eastwick*. And history repeated itself fiercely. At the time, for me, it was like this strange dream. I was setting off to run a marathon and suddenly someone is handing me seven ferrets, a snake and a bunny rabbit on a leash and saying this is what you gotta run with. It was a grotesque experience, organizationally, creatively and morally and, I don't think, uncommon for the unsuspecting.

DP: *What was it like working with such a strong main cast, Jack Nicholson, Cher, Michelle Pfeiffer and Susan Sarandon? I can imagine Susan would have raised some confronting questions.*

GM: No, my biggest problem was Cher. I was extremely ambivalent about her casting. We couldn't quite cast the third witch, as we called her, and in order to make it fit we switched roles. Susan played Cher's role, and that was not the best position for any of the actors. The three women were under siege psychologically, and they weren't helped by the producers who were extremely lacking in regard for them. But Susan and Michelle are very gifted actors and that never fails to be exciting. I'd get to the set and I'd always enjoy doing scenes with them. Cher is too much of a performer, she'd be OK in a solo effort, but it was a disaster in an ensemble.

Nick Nolte gave me a great insight, he's worked with everybody from Kate Hepburn to Eddie Murphy. He said that if a performer, such as a singer or a comedian, comes to the process of acting, then the entire production revolves around them. Of necessity they are used to being the centre of the universe. If the concert doesn't go well that day it's their fault, it stands or falls by how well they perform. It's very difficult for those people to become part of an ensemble. You take an actor who is used to the collaborative process, usually from theatre, and they are extremely adept at becoming part of and respectful of the greater work. Jack Nicholson – who had seen it all – saw part of his job as keeping the film together, keeping the company working, and keeping abreast of the work. Michelle was relatively new, she was in with some big leaguers and did remarkably well. Susan had done a hell of a lot too. And they were very gifted. Cher was still more of a performer than she was an actor and therefore her ability to work with others was, I believe, at least in that case, a lot less than desirable.

DP: *What was interesting to you about the battle between the sexes?*

GM: It was a delicious fable on the interminable war between men and women. Who ultimately is the more powerful? I think that was what originally John Updike had in mind and what attracted everybody to the project.

DP: *Who better than Nicholson to front the male cause!*

12 Jack Nicholson with the Witches of Eastwick: Cher, Susan Sarandon, and
Michelle Pfeiffer

GM: Of course! That was the biggest surprise about Jack. He is a highly evolved human being. Very sophisticated, in the best sense of the word. He is spiritual, his life is a quest. He reminds me of Tina Turner – someone who is a thousand years old and at the same time is still a child. That's Jack. There are people who are super adults. Life has always been a quest for them, and they've derived from some place where there is as much certainty as any human can have. That's what gives them the charisma.

DP: *Were the women well-represented also? Sarandon, Cher and Pfeiffer?*

DP: For someone who is a so-called movie star, Susan is totally lacking in any vanity whatsoever. I've never met a human being, let alone a movie star, who has no vanity, but she has none. She's a tremendous under-achiever as an actor. Extremely gifted, but tosses everything off. There's absolutely nothing whatsoever calculated about Susan. And you have Cher who is the complete antithesis. Everything about her, even the way she is physically, is calculated and constructed. And Michelle, again extremely gifted, extremely ambitious. So you have this strange mixture of people and you're trying to give them some common vision. Looking back on it, I was very well endowed with talent. Jack, Susan and Michelle all basically have a comedic or ironic tone. Susan and Michelle are two of the funniest people I ever met and so the odd man out was Cher.

DP: *You chose to work with Susan again on* Lorenzo's Oil.

GM: I envy Susan because she follows that Oscar Wilde credo 'put my talent into my work and my genius into life'. That was what I meant before about Tina and Jack – they've found that balance where their genius is both in their work and in their life.

DP: *With* The Witches of Eastwick *you moved away from films whose worlds were bleak and brutal to a film that's light-hearted and loving – even of the devil. Was that a conscious move?*

GM: Oh, very conscious. That was the power of the screenplay, that the devil has to be as charming as all hell. It's what the great male seducers are like. The great irony about *Witches*, of course, was that Jack was so obvious for the role that reflexly I said, no he can't be. Before I even got through the first reading of the screenplay, I started to see Jack Nicholson saying the lines. I'd never done that before. I remember saying to Warner's, he's so obvious you've got to go completely against it. I'll never forget Carol Kane, who's a friend of Jack Nicholson's, saying, Jack is one of the most gracious and spiritual people she knows and that I should meet him at least. When I did I was astonished by him. I think what gives him the charisma is that he's both masculine and very feminine, both profane and extremely sublime, all at the same moment and that's what the devil has to be. If the devil comes on malevolent, he's not going to convince anybody. But ultimately the devil is foolish, he's flawed because he's blind to the alternative point of view and that's why he's evil. I really

13 *The Witches of Eastwick*: Jack Nicholson and George Miller

thought about evil a lot during the process of making that film. It's almost impossible to define good and evil, but the closest I got to it is that the root of all evil is ignorance. In particular, if you're ignorant of the Other's place in the universe, then you are capable of evil. In order to kill somebody you must be blind to their humanity, in order to destroy someone you must be incapable of seeing them as human beings. Jack's devil was ultimately blind as to what it was to be a woman and what it was to be in love. It's a problem that men seem to have.

DP: *After* Witches *it was another four years, almost five years before your next film,* Lorenzo's Oil, *currently in post-production.*

GM: Five years. With *Witches* I lost all my curiosity for directing films.

DP: *And during those years you concentrated on producing?*

GM: What drew me back to Australia was that *Dead Calm* was having trouble. It became a plagued production and I came back to do second unit. At Kennedy Miller at the time we had *The Year My Voice Broke*, a John Duigan auto-biographical feature, in the cutting room, and *Dirtwater Dynasty*, a 10-hour mini-series shooting that was going over schedule, so I became the producer. What I enjoyed so much about the role was that I could do three or four projects at the same time – not become obsessed with any one of them, but able to guide and nurture all of them. I suddenly found myself having no responsibility, in the sense that I was no longer the director, but having a lot of fun. We were churning out a huge amount of work at Kennedy Miller.

The other great thing that happened was that I was able to devote myself more to the outside world. One thing that suddenly occurred to me in the late eighties was that there's a world out there changing at a horrific rate and, apart from anything else, film language is changing at a horrific rate. It was an astonishing era, the late eighties. The decade of the pig, as people called it. Materialism became rampant, and the kind of spiritual values for which people are searching again in the nineties – and I think as the millenium approaches they'll be looking for much more assiduously – were pushed aside. The change in what was perceived as world politics was extraordinary at that time. So I said to myself, I would not direct again until my curiosity was aroused. There was an added incentive with *Lorenzo's Oil*. Behind the film there is a substantial amount of money going into medical research and every day delayed in making and releasing it delays the time when people like Lorenzo can be helped. So I guess *Lorenzo's Oil* is my first adult film.

DP: Lorenzo's Oil, *the true story of the Odones who fight the medical establishment to save their six-year-old son's life threatened by an obscure disease, seems very different from the* Mad Max *films where the Joseph Campbell hero, a loner, is almost forced to take up the challenge. The Odones seem to be heroes of a different kind.*

GM: The truth is that only time will tell if the Odones' story is mythologically heroic in the way Joseph Campbell defined it, but I believe it has all the hallmarks of a hero journey. That is, they are the agents of evolution, they are

14 *The Year My Voice Broke*: Noah Taylor and Loene Carmen

the shatterers of their world. The world happens to be the world of their boy's illness; the landscape, one room in one house. But the story is just as epic because it follows the hero's path. They never intended to become scientists–doctors, but they were called to the adventure by their son, by the figure of their son who refuses to die. Lorenzo is their magical figure. And for that they went on a quest. They trod where no one had gone before, as scientists, and in a sense they shattered the world of their son's disease. That is the function of the heroic figure. So, in a way, they follow the heroic path much more accurately than a Mad Max figure, I think.

As I said, one's a teenage version, and the other is an adult version. That's why they are different. They look like very different films. Certainly, physically, they're tremendously different. I couldn't imagine something more antithetical to *Mad Max III* than *Lorenzo's Oil*. But I shouldn't pre-empt how the film should be read. One of the dangers of all these things, and Campbell warned against it, is to concretize, make concrete the myth. In fact, that's what destroys all religions. You shouldn't sully its poetic dimension.

DP: *One of the changes I've noticed over the years working with you is in the language you're using to talk about story and structure. You're using music and musical terms as references more often than Campbell and the legendary hero's journey.*

GM: Without wanting to reduce film to pat definitions, another useful way to think of film is as 'visual music'. Some movies are rock and roll and others are symphonic. You might argue that the *Mad Max* films are rock and roll and *Lawrence of Arabia* is symphonic. But what film, at least until it becomes interactive, has in common with music is that it is time dependent, it is tyrannized by time: the time the audience is in there; the film plays twenty-four frames a second inexorably until it's over. That's shifted a little bit now by the fact that people can fast-forward on their video machine, but essentially film has rhythmical shape and movement like a symphony. Drama has rhythm, musical rhythms – sometimes largo, sometimes sostenuto. You can apply all the terms of music to film. I think the word I probably use more than any other in the process of working in film is 'rhythm'. In writing we use it all the time, the rhythm of ideas, the dramatic rhythm. In shooting it's the rhythm of the camera, the rhythm of the cutting, particularly the rhythm of the performance. And then when you get into the cutting room, it's the most commonly used word. It's always fascinating to me when the film is finally locked off and you begin to talk with the composer, that you have the same discussions as when you started on the screenplay – you echo the essence of the film, you once again start dealing with subtext.

DP: *Are you musical? You have a reputation as a tap dancer.*

GM: My twin brother is quite musical. I'm not musically literate. One of the great privileges of working on film, of course, is that you're forced to address all these things. I realized that until I actually made my first film, I never really listened. I knew I *saw* the world, I looked, I used my ears. I'm not deaf, I wouldn't care two hoots if I was deaf, but it would be like life to me if I lost my eyesight. Byron Kennedy listened to the world, and on *Mad Max* I began to listen. Every time I walk on to location now I listen, because I want to make sure it all sounds correct.

DP: *In an early interview you talked about the importance of music, how it has to be considered from the very beginning of the project. Do you keep the soundtrack in mind while shooting?*

GM: I think you do, I think a lot of directors do. A lot of directors play music on the set, it's a great device for getting the feel for it, the mood. I notice a lot of actors quite often use music to evoke a mood. Looking back at the early films I realize just how, as a fledgling director, I made the mistake of insisting there be too much music. You feel so embarrassed about every scene that you want to support it with music just to make sure that the audience gets it, or at least bridges through. One of the first things I would do is hold back on some music, even though Brian May did a fabulous job. I just kept on saying, please put some music in there and he would say, like all good composers, you don't need it there, but he would do it anyway.

DP: *I saw Satyajit Ray interviewed on SBS the other night and he said he used a lot more music in his earlier work as a kind of insurance.*

GM: That's exactly what it is. Music is another narrator of the film, sometimes subliminal, depending on the skill of the composer. There are several mistakes that every first time feature director makes. One of them is the over-use of music. Another is that almost invariably the rhythms from slate to camera stop are too slow. The rhythms of the performance, and the rhythms within the shot are always too slow because the state of the director on the set is quite unlike the state of the audience in repose in a dark cinema. As a director on set, there's a frenzy about you or around you: activity, adrenalin, colour and movement. In the theatre there is only the screen and you're almost in a state of sensory deprivation except for what's on the screen and what you're hearing through the speakers. So one of the things you've got to do as a director is to shut everything out and focus only on what's happening through the view-finder. Probably the third mistake for a fledgling director – for the record – is not quite knowing where to put your resources, spending too much time on a scene which doesn't need it and not enough time where it is needed, like the obligatory scene, the A scene, and we still all do that as directors.

DP: *How often do you limit time on one scene for the benefit of another?*

GM: Often. I guess *Lorenzo's Oil* is a bit different in that I found that every moment really had to earn its place in the final cut. But I found myself often thinking, OK, well, it's not quite right, but I'll just move on. It's always a balance, with performance. If we go another couple of takes, how much better is it going to get or is it going to get worse? And when you have really fine

15   *Lorenzo's Oil*: Susan Sarandon, Nick Nolte, Zack O'Malley-Greenburg, Kathleen Wilhoite, and La Tanya Richardson

actors, it's great. If you can achieve it early, like Nick and Susan both get it real early, you could push for another take, but pretty soon it starts to disintegrate.

DP: *Are you happy with* Lorenzo's Oil?

GM: It gets to the stage where you can't tell, you really can't tell. All I know is that quote from Francis Coppola – 'It's never as good as the dailies and never as bad as the first cut'. It's extremely difficult to keep any objectivity. Things that were once powerful to you are just routine. I honestly don't believe the film-maker or anybody knows what the film is until it gets before an audience. The audience will tell you. All I can say is I'm very proud of a lot of the work we've achieved. I've not been part of a film before where I feel good about such a high percentage of the footage.

DP: *Is it closer to your original vision?*

GM: Yeah, closer than I've ever been before. But it's not a vision like a *Mad Max* film which comes purely out of fantasy. Even a *Witches of Eastwick* is purely out of fantasy. *Lorenzo's Oil* conforms to real life as much as possible, so in a way it was pre-ordained. I found on this film I had to resist becoming too flamboyant – it somehow diminished the truth. What I find surprising about *Lorenzo's Oil* is that, unlike just about every other story, we took almost no poetic licence. Everything that is on the screen happened without any contrivance. Unlike anything else we've done based on fact – *The Dismissal, Bodyline* – it's remarkably close to what happened.

DP: *Like* Mad Max III *you story-boarded almost all of* Lorenzo's Oil, *meticulously, planning every shot. The camera is a very important tool for you as a director.*

GM: I split film directors into two sorts, the '*mise-en-scène*' and the 'montage' director. *Mise-en-scène* directors are those who basically create a scene and then stand back and photograph it, usually on a long lens. The camera tends to be static and pictorial. For the montage director the camera becomes almost another character – it's got a very specific point of view. They're the directors that tend to use the wider lenses and move the camera a lot. It's harder to be a montage director than a *mise-en-scène* director.

DP: *I've noticed you're very specific about your choice of lens. How do you decide?*

GM: It's a struggle. I'm tempted to use long lenses, but I find most times I go 'wide'. Wide lenses approximate the visual qualities of the eye and you get more in the frame, they enhance three-dimensionality, you see what is in the background. The longer lenses shift the face, broaden the features. One thing I've noticed about movie stars is that they are invariably smaller and thinner than on the screen. There is a tendency in my film-making to work with the widest lenses, except I find it's always more flattering, more dynamic, to work the long end of the lens. But somehow it's always less realistic when you go 'long'. Directors out of what I call the TV commercial school tend to work the very long end of the lens. I think Ridley Scott is the master of that. I envy his ability to work the lens where everything is out of focus except the actors and yet somehow a visually rich world is suggested beyond it.

DP: *One of my most persistent memories from* Mad Max III *is of you spending ages moving the camera around looking for the perfect angle and sometimes ending up within inches of where we started. I remember you saying that out of all the possible angles, one was far superior.*

GM: Yeah, particularly with stunts. It's one thing to have five cameras on the stunt and it's another thing to figure out exactly where to put them. When you're doing a stunt you have to preconceive exactly what's going to happen. And yet that's the first time in the history of the universe that that exact event is going to happen, so you have to predict where it will happen. I saw *Lawrence of Arabia* the other day. On tape – God forgive me. There's a stunt where a steam train rolls on to its side and slides as it comes to a halt across the sand, with the smoke pouring out of the stack filling the screen. Now if you watch the wide shot, it's flat desert. There's no evidence whatsoever of a second camera close to where the train finally comes to rest. I wound back two or three times and I could not see the second camera and I cannot imagine that it was done twice. So how they did it I don't know, but whoever put the camera in that second spot put it in the perfect place.

DP: *On* Lorenzo's Oil *you didn't spend so much time finding the perfect place for the camera but you were always adjusting the shot ever so slightly, often adding movement, even though initially you said that you were determined to use a more static camera.*

GM: It's a compulsion of mine to move the camera, and I now know why: it enhances three-dimensionality. It puts you in the space and if you move the camera the audience becomes aware of the space, particularly in a film like *Lorenzo's Oil* which risks being a 'talking heads' movie. I don't know if you felt that when you saw it.

DP: *No, I was never conscious of it being a 'talking heads' picture – surprisingly, seeing it's essentially two people, the parents and their bedridden son in a small house.*

GM: Perhaps because I move the camera. It was the thing that first drew me to film. I was never really interested in drama or performance. It's only in recent years I've become interested in the process of acting and in fact that's become the most fascinating thing for me. The craft of film-making is interesting, but there are two great mysteries in the hierarchy of film mysteries. One is the process of the actor which goes back to our earlier talk of the shadow and the substance. It's so subtle – almost a thing of the ether – acting. What is it when you see Robert Duvall say 'I love the smell of napalm in the morning' or Meryl Streep 'I once had a farm in Africa'. What is the musicality of that, that makes it impinge on the memory? It's hard to grasp. It's deeply mysterious and also, for me, very fascinasting. Then, of course, the other great mystery is the process of writing. Interestingly enough, I see myself more as a film writer than a film-maker. It is the area which people really know least about. It's a new craft, film writing, less than a century old.

DP: *You've co-written all of your projects except* Twilight Zone *and* The Witches of Eastwick. *How do you work on the writing? Do you concentrate on structure?*

GM: Structure is all, as the great Bill Goldman said. It's one of the great truths of cinema. It's the same as the musical structure of the film, the musical architecture – if you can mix metaphors. For me every single word is important in a screenplay. Every time I've sat down with a collaborator I've said, it's not like you go and write and I review. We play out the scene, work out the syntax of each word, look at the rhythm of every line, at every comma, at the languge of the screenplay so that it conveys to the reader the dramatic flow of the story and to some extent the visual flow. I'm very bad at the process of saying you're the writer, here's a certain amount of money and time, come back to me in three weeks with the first draft and I'll edit. What that tends to do, at least to my mind, is to institutionalize the flaws of the screenplay. Quite often they're invisible, you don't pick them up till the editing room and you say, my God, why didn't we see that before. That's why I've written or co-written almost every screenplay I've done. On *Twilight Zone* I re-drafted the whole thing into a shooting story, and I worked very intimately with Michael Cristofer on *The Witches of Eastwick*. But on everything else I've been involved in the writing, even though I don't see myself as a literate person.

DP: *In an earlier interview you talked about how the protocol and functioning of the film set are the director's responsibility and that you were not only fascinated by how those little strips of film are cut together, but how you achieve those strips of film. On* Lorenzo's Oil, *I was aware of you constantly monitoring the progress of every single facet of the process. What time the actors arrived, what mood they were in, how much longer in make-up, hair, wardrobe and so on, what stage the lighting and sound were at. How important do you think it is for a director to be so preoccupied with the mechanics?*

GM: It's necessary. Film-making is the harnessing of events and rhythms. The constellation of ingredients are: the actor poised for peak performance, the mood, the camera, its moves, its focus. Everyone's authority needs to coincide. It's like an implosion, like watching some footage of an explosion in reverse – all the parts get sucked together into a whole. It's all about capturing that moment on film. If any one of those elements is off, it will destroy everybody's work. If an actor hasn't got the authority over their role, if it is not truthful, everything else might be perfect, but the moment is lost. If the focus puller's missed a mark or the sun comes out when you want cloud or someone bumps into a light and falls into the set, the moment is lost. So you have to be concerned with all those things. It's the process. You've got to be aware of it. A lot of my ADs say don't worry, leave it to us. But I want to know if there is a problem, because then I can factor it in.

Particularly with a performance piece like *Lorenzo's Oil*, it is incredibly important to know what the mood of the actor is, whether that's going to be conducive to the mood of the character. With Nick Nolte and Susan Saran-don, who are magnificent actors, you could almost predict their mood by the mood of the scene coming up. If one of the ADs said, Nick's not in a good mood today, my next thought was, what's the scene? What was interesting about Nick is that whenever we'd have arguments he would always argue in character, always with the Italian accent of Augusto Odone. It was always about progressing work and I loved him for that. So it's incredibly important for a director to know, because if for some reason there is something external that's influencing how they are on the set, that's got nothing to do with the work, well, then you'd better know about it so that you can try and mitigate it.

It's quite different from doing an action picture, where a lot of my energy goes on knowing how the stuntmen are and how safe it feels, which I personally believe is the director's responsibility. If somebody gets hurt on a film, it's the director's responsibility. If I personally believe something won't work, or some sixth sense tells me that's not going to work, I won't go with it, even though I'm not very technical where special effects or stunts are con-cerned. Common sense applies. With a special effects movie the mood of the actors is perhaps less important but in something like *Lorenzo's Oil*, it is all.

DP: *What do you think is going to happen to Kennedy Miller?*

GM: Well, the saddest thing is that Kennedy Miller won't be doing television in Australia any more. Basically, we will be doing more feature films. Essentially within Australia Kennedy Miller became known mainly as a television produc-tion company doing mini-series which rated very highly and that Kennedy Miller is gone until such time as television in Australia becomes able to support high budget television. We're in litigation against Kerry Packer as we speak because we had an arrangement to produce all the television drama for the 9 network. So that side of Kennedy Miller is gone, only because the ecology, if you like, is not right. We got into television not because we wanted to make television *per se*. We got into television because it was a way of exploring subjects you could never do on film. Now sadly that's gone.

DP: *You've produced several very successful films here. The John Duigan films,* The Year My Voice Broke, Flirting *and Phil Noyce's* Dead Calm *among others.*

GM: I'm very proud of the John Duigan films because, in their own way, they redefined the direction of Australian film. *The Year My Voice Broke* was the first of the small Australian films which really spoke out of the artist. Kennedy Miller, even if I say it myself, had the first international success in genre film with *Mad Max* and then when we did *The Dismissal* that shifted television. *The Year My Voice Broke* was the beginning of a shift in Australian film-making with a return to personal, smaller films that were not trying to compete on the international market. The Duigan films were very successful, both artistically and commercially. I'm much more proud of *The Year My Voice Broke* and *Flirting* than I am of *Dead Calm* which was more international and gave rise to

Nicole Kidman's and Phil Noyce's careers internationally. But in a sense it was a genre film following in the footsteps of what Australian films have striven for in the past. You know, drama is where you find it. It's not geographically or nationally specific, it's not defined by latitude and longitude, even though people try to define an Australian cinema or a Chinese cinema or a Japanese Cinema or a French cinema. It's where the stories are and even though it's my preference to live and work in Australia, the stories are elsewhere at this point. The next two are in Africa, so that's where we'll go.

2   The Burning Question: Cinema after the Millennium?

In *Projections 1* we asked a selection of film-makers what they would do if they had absolute freedom to make whatever they wanted. Except for a few like Kevin Reynolds – who envisioned an epic retelling of the Second World War from a viewpoint 500 years from now – most film-makers adhered to Orson Welles' dictum: 'The enemy of art is the absence of limitations.' The Taviani brothers' response was typical of the experience of most film-makers: 'The film that is closest to our hearts, we shot in four weeks, with 14,000 metres of film.'

This year we asked film-makers to imagine what kind of cinema would emerge in the next millennium. Technically, film has remained the same for 100 years. Now that is changing. Recent developments, like computerized special effects systems, use of high definition or digital processing, offer new possibilities. Virtual reality and movies that invite the viewer to participate in the plot suggest a new relationship between audience and film. *What kind of movies do you imagine might emerge in the next millennium?*

The response was . . .

Paul Schrader

I don't believe that the stories people meet to tell each other have changed since communication began. The same tales loop and circle atop each other over centuries. What does change, what runs as a relentless chronological line, is the accelerating onslaught of technology. Scientific knowledge (and all its effects) expands as exponentially as the earth's population. The arts, like all other endeavours, are subject to a decreasing half-life dictated by science. Art forms come and go. The life span of a given art form, born and given life by the technological possibilities and needs of the time, grows consequently shorter. Epic poetry lived for a millennium; 'film' will be lucky if it survives a hundred years.

Storytellers should not be particularly concerned about the death of motion pictures as they have evolved to this point. Movies have been a useful twentieth-century tool; when they are no longer useful, they will fade from view, replaced by their technological offspring.

It's not the storyteller's job to defend an art form. He has but a sentimental attachment to his tools. It's not the storyteller's job to bemoan 'progress' or resist technology. The storyteller's job is to revamp humankind's tales using new technologies, telling and retelling old truths and moral conflicts. Don't cry for cinema.

Moving pictures knocked the other arts into the twentieth century but remained in the nineteenth. The narrative conventions of cinema have, for the most part, been those of the Victorian era. This is about to change. The tools are rusting.

I don't know what new form storytelling will take. I believe it will be tied to our exploding knowledge of the brain and the processes of perception. Story-tellers of the future may work in concert with scientists to design drug entertainment. The next version of *Ulysses* may come in pill form. I only wish I could live to be part of it. Today's film-makers will glimpse this land but not enter it. The next twenty years will be years of confusion and exploration. Film-makers will be forced to choose: refine your dying art or stumble like awkward children into the new forms. Neither will be fully satisfying.

Fred Zinnemann

At the age of eighty-five I hope I may be forgiven for taking the long view: there is no way of guessing what may happen if the dance around the golden calf is not stopped. Perhaps there will be no movies. Perhaps there will be no millennium?

P.S.   I'm sorry.

Michael Verhoeven

The best films of Rainer Werner Fassbinder were his early ones – the ones filmed under the emergency of not having money. His poorest films were his finest. The more financing he had, and hence access to all the technical finesse of his time, the more sets, costume and décor were at his disposal, the more lacquered and smooth his films became.

In *Cape Fear* Scorsese shows us breathtaking film techniques. Over the roofs and landscapes shines a beautiful artificial sky. Apparently, Scorsese doesn't work with digital methods. But, even so, we have to admire his encyclopedia of the suggestive cinema. Yet what will always remain in my head is the scene between De Niro and Juliette Lewis in the dark and empty hall of the school, in which Scorsese lets two wonderful actors talk and listen to each other and lets them get very close, painfully close. Those are the most thrilling moments of the film.

It is not that I disdain the astonishing new possibilities of trick-techniques in movies nowadays. My film, *The Nasty Girl*, is full of technical effects. But I made them obvious and recognizable, and put them in a dialectical relationship to the film's story. I am very curious to work with these new digital methods in this way.

I have no doubt that virtual reality is going to change the image of film. Indeed, I believe that virtual reality will be able to convey true messages and statements about the 'real' reality of people. But these new techniques will be used in an inflationary manner. The miracles will get more miraculous, the sensations even more sensational. The wonders will be seen everywhere, on TV, on all channels, every day, until they become part of our daily routine and lose all their magic.

Then cinema will come back to the simplest things of life: a camera, two people talking, listening, getting close.

David Byrne

The next millennium is only eight years away – seven by the time this is published – so any momentous changes should already be underway. The new technical, structural, economic and political events of today should be making themselves visible by the end of the decade.

Thinking out loud – HI-8 cameras or similar equipment in many people's hands ... the Rodney King video as a prototype of future 'documentaries' ... made not by trained film-makers, but by witnesses, participants (in the case of the Rob Lowe video) and innocent bystanders. Although I haven't seen it, there is a popular TV show in Britain made by ordinary people, and America's *Funniest Home Videos* was the most popular new show in the States for a number of years (I hear that it's actually a rip-off of a Japanese show whose title escapes me).

But that's mostly about television, and you asked about film. The repercussions of all the failed blockbusters will probably be felt. Just as the Reagan/ Bush/Thatcher era is having its playback, so Hollywood and the mega-lomaniacs who sponsored and encouraged its excesses will have to deal with the results of their policies. The tendency for all business to be absorbed into huge multinational investment firms, incurring incredible debts, will reverse itself as these firms fail by the dozens – leaving their shareholders holding the bag. The only 'studio' that will survive will be wholly Black-owned and operated. Japanese cyberpunk animated characters will replace Hollywood's top stars as the most popular actors. Arnold, Bruce and Tom will be replaced with the creations of 20-year-old computer hackers. That, and films which blatantly sell something – cars, liquor, marijuana, medicines, cosmetic surgery, fashion accessories – will be the staples of mass entertainment.

For the rest of us, things will be looking up: with the collapse of the studios (or what is left of them), there will be an incredible thirst for product. Japanese Dialogue Replacement Technology will enable small-time film-makers to have their work translated perfectly into any language. There will be no more hegemony of action films over talkies in the international market. Film-makers from all over the world will have equal access to audiences – a new movie from Mali will attract as large a popular and critical following as the latest from New York or Madrid.

A new form of cheaper and faster distribution will bypass the existing conglomerates; in all forms of media. No more will the distributors have a stranglehold on who gets to see what, on which films receive advertising and which do not. There will be true democracy as regards film availability and selection. And true chaos too. The media glut will be overwhelming, and the public will eventually reject all product and there will be a return to storytelling. The world will have a brief period of ecstatic communion, of incredible and glorious communication uncensored and unaffected by the media giants, and then, completely overloaded and saturated, everyone will break off into smaller groups than ever before. The return to tribalism. And the rebirth of myth.

Jocelyn Moorhouse

If movies manage to survive as a medium, I think they will continue to reflect the fears, dreams and reality of the societies from which they are created. Technological toys will have their place in films, but will operate primarily as tools for the ever-expanding human imagination. As home-movie cameras become smaller and slicker and cheaper, then the language of cinema will be learned by children as early as the spoken word. As reality becomes more frightening, I think that computer-generated virtual reality will become an escapist, addictive, home-based toy, while movies will revert to comforting hope-filled stories, nostalgic tales of the good times gone. Once mankind has totally polluted Mother Earth and found some distant rock to colonize, museums will be established to house ancient movies that give a glimpse of earlier civilizations that existed on earth. As scientific exploration runs out of external adventures, no doubt it will turn inwards in search of the mysteries of the human mind and soul. And film, with all its corresponding techno-toys, will play a role in that.

Here is my prediction for the next twenty years. A wealthy teenager will finance and direct his own movie. It will be a mega-hit, ensuring that by the year 2012 the studios will only make movies directed by 13-year-olds. Adult directors and writers will have to find 13-year-old 'fronts' in order to peddle their works. Producers from every country will be scouting primary schools, trying to mould pre-pubescent prodigies into film geniuses. For these unfortunate youngsters, childhood will become a thing of the past. Then someone will invent the first womb camera for foetal use and all will be lost.

John Boorman

To predict the future it might be instructive to glance at A Brief History of Film. A case can be made that things have got steadily worse and will get more so.

As we know, the language of film, its grammar, evolved very rapidly in the first few years of the century. D. W. Griffith and his cameraman Billy Bitzer worked most of it out and nothing much has been added since. Titles could be easily translated into divers tongues and the new entertainment quickly conquered the world with its golden section format and its mute, sepia (sometimes tinted) otherness. Griffith believed it to be the universal language promised by the Bible that would bring about the millennium, and so did many others.

Birth of a Nation opened in a legit Broadway theatre with a full orchestra in the pit and men behind the screen making sound effects. The weeping spectators ran into the street afterwards and seized strangers to tell them of the wonders they had witnessed.

The cumbersome sound camera anchored film-makers to the studio and betrayed them into the control of the studio chiefs. The camera had lost its freedom. And yet, black-and-white film still suggested a parallel world, a dream place, a contiguous reality.

Then came colour. It painted the faces of our dream gods and goddesses and gave us a garish and gaudy version of the world we actually lived in. The race was on to simulate reality, to make film more 'lifelike'. The effect was to weaken film as metaphor.

Wide-screen formats. The theory is that a 1:2.35 ratio approximates the scope of the human eye with its peripheral vision. In practice, the viewer's eye tends to roam over the wide-screen and we have to impose strong compositions to prevent the viewer's attention from wandering.

Stereo sound systems. When we make movies we try to give the illusion of depth, but sound coming from the sides and back of the auditorium reminds the audience of the two-dimensional nature of the image. The metaphor gets weaker. Film is effective, not when it is copying life, but when it offers an experience which differs from everyday reality. A close-up on a big screen when the face is eight feet high gives extraordinary insights. The enlarging of people and objects in the cinema has been one of its great revelations.

TV and video, however, have scaled the movie down, domesticated it, tamed it. The cinema enlarges experience, TV diminishes it. A lot of directors rely heavily on TV assist when they shoot, instantly replaying each shot. I never do. I need a decent interval of time between making the shot and viewing the image. They are separate and should be separated.

The future? As technology, film is a nineteenth-century mechanical/chemical process which is clearly out of date. Images recorded digitally can achieve any quality required and those images can be altered and enhanced in every possible way, limited only by the imagination of the operator. The language of film was defined by its limitations. The new language will lack limits. Griffith's universal language may become the Tower of Babel. So far the ubiquitous TV camera has imposed only a democracy of banality on the world around us.

About virtual reality I would say only this: reality is not a virtue where art is concerned. Film has been part of the story of the optical lens. The microscope and the telescope allowed us to puncture the surface of the world. The camera lens has penetrated the human heart.

The lens itself may soon become redundant. Just as the images on the retina of the eye are converted into electrical impulses, so similar impulses may be fed directly to the brain, eliminating the camera and the eye. Once experience itself is transferable and accessible through the phone company, will that mean the end of stories and myths and metaphor itself? Will we have time for such trifles?

Philippe Rousselot*

Things change, and they change whether we notice or not. Sometimes these changes seem like earthquakes, sometimes the sliding of one plate over another is so slow that the landscape seems eternally unchanging. The epicentre of our little film-making world is Hollywood, on the San Andreas fault. It loves earthquakes, it welcomes them with admiration, respect and fear. Likewise, cinematic techniques evolve slowly and imperceptibly, but from time to time a major tremor shakes them to their foundations. Often, when the tremor has passed, the building regains its former stability and appearance.

One of these tremors occurred during the summer of 1991, in the form of a film: *Terminator 2*, followed by secondary shocks of lesser importance (two Michael Jackson shorts made using the same technique) and probably other things that I haven't had the courage to see; I prefer to feel solid ground under my feet.

The rumour before its release was that it was the best science fiction film ever made, and its audience success matched the rumour. *T2* is a hallucinatory, hallucinating film, stuffed full of remarkable and perfectly realized visual effects, which are unlike anything the cinema had made us familiar with

* Translated by Shaun Whiteside.

before; they are utterly different in kind. Since *King Kong*, the major principles of special effects had not changed; they marked out the boundaries of
our visual universe, and only the way in which they were carried out had
undergone constant technical improvements.

Here, though, there isn't anything like the old 'matte' processes, inlays,
blue screen and so on. This is a real revolution, opening doors to a new
world. Perfection. This time the effects eliminate the by-products of their
manufacture, the minor faults due to their hand-made origins – no more
problems of camera wobble, camera tilt, fringing and so on. The technology
is perfect, undetectable.

What does this revolution consist of? The conjunction of three operations:
the transfer of the chemical film image into digital data (pixels), the computer
treatment of that data and the re-transfer of those data into a high quality
film. This last operation is the one that has been perfected most recently; the
other two (electronic treatment of the image with a view to video distribution)
had been practised for a number of years.

The consequences of this are the following: any element of the image can
be given a code, and this code can be manipulated at will and *ad infinitum*.
The colour green can be told to turn red, rain to turn into snow, beauty to
become a beast.

Henceforward, it is no longer a question of applying classic 'matte' effects
– which at best are optical illusions – but rather of trading in effects, switching identities, disrupting meanings. The inanimate becomes human, and
man, in turn, is objectified. Thus, in *T2*, a hand becomes a knife-blade; in
Michael Jackson's film a black face turns white, a man becomes a woman.

Henceforward, at these electronic consoles, people and objects – reduced
to the state of pixels – will acquire equal status, democratically stockpiled in
memory, interchangeable and interpenetrable.

The film image couldn't be treated in the same way, it was different in
kind, had to be treated with care, kept in a cold room, and in spite of all the
attention paid to it, it persisted in ageing and disappearing. Now, reduced to
the state of computer data, it becomes eternal and ready for use of any kind.

The introduction of computers into this process suggests a medical metaphor: the presence in a healthy body of a virus which will turn cellular
functions to its own ends, from which point onwards we see proliferation,
tumours, cancers. *T2* has been invaded by these tumours (but no one's going
to die of this cancer, except possibly the studio). From this point on it's quite
natural for a character to turn into a set of kitchen utensils.

The wicked stepmother of the fairy tales assumed the form of a poor old
lady to deceive Snow White. Now, flesh turns into metal, a hand becomes a
knife and really kills. It is no longer appearance that deceives and leads to
death, but matter itself. Here, perhaps, we are witnessing the modernization

of myth, matter becoming empowered, the revenge of the inanimate.

If *T2* abounds in these transformation effects, this is not solely due to the lavishness of the producers, but also to the fact that there are no longer any natural limits to the extraordinary freedom supplied by technology. Once the machine had been switched on, there is no reason for it to stop. The computer variations are infinite.

Consequently, cinema is drunk on this new power, fascinated as it is with itself and its own technology. The final result certainly creates an impression of superabundance, congestion and nausea.

Once this absence of limits has been established, the eye is no longer satisfied, the mind ceases to find any nourishment. At best it remains curious, fascinated by the machine that produced the effects, rather than the effects themselves.

But what saves *T2* from being swamped by technology is the fact that this abundance is the very subject of the film. A new version of the sorcerer's apprentice, it tells the story of a new machine that knows no bounds, the story of a technological virus fighting a more highly developed virus than itself (just as *T2* is more highly developed than *T1*). There is a perfect correspondence between the subject of the film and its mode of production.

Thus the film promotes its own technology, elevates it to the level of a mythology – a mythology of the gadget, the very image of a society in love with its technology. And the film is thus so thoroughly possessed by the machine that we feel ill at ease simply for being human, for being there.

Shortly after the release of *T2*, a Michael Jackson short in turn used digital computer techniques: faces follow one another in the metronomic binary rhythm of the music. Unlike a classic dissolve, the computer has managed to cover the journey between two totally different faces. As in *T2*, the effect is spectacular, the realization perfect, the flaws invisible. But where we might expect that transformation of faces, races and sexes to produce a meaning or at least a shock, an emotion – one of those bizarre effects that the surrealists were so good at – all we have is a short-lived fascination with a new gadget, boredom in the face of something that is meaningless, but brilliantly achieved.

In fact the eye refuses to accept these images on the grounds that their transformation has been taken too far; we refuse to invest it with any meaning.

The new technologies henceforth permit the evolution of images freed from the constraints of reality, the manacles of shape, colour and perspective. (Until now, this was only made possible by cartoons.) The cinema audience needs to recognize images as real in order to accept them, and when they are too far removed from reality the audience rejects them or refuses to see them. Convention is a matter for the theatre – in the cinema the spectator wants reality and solidity: the certainty that the photographic image and reality are one and the same thing. It is the task of the image to show something that is recognizable to the audience, either in their real world or in their imagination and hence their mythology. The images in Michael Jackson's film refer to neither.

T2, on the other hand, is entirely based on ancient myths (the sorcerer's apprentice) and modern myths (technology taking over). But this is not what ensures *T2*'s success – at best it serves to back it up. The film's real success lies in an ironic and permanent destruction of reality, a killing-off of ninety-five years of real images, the de-construction of the movies. The audience is overjoyed to see a reality that breaks down and reassembles instantaneously; they are delighted by this new equality of creatures and objects, delighted that metal turns into flesh and flesh into metal. They forget the plot, the fact that the plot does not hold up, and that the same plot had already been used in the first *Terminator*. In fact, the audience is celebrating the birth of a new technology, which has taken a film and its actors hostage, and which is self-promoting.

Similarly, audiences at the end of the last century were overjoyed to witness Lumière's film of 'the arrival of a train at the station at La Ciotat' and celebrated the birth not of cinema but of a new technology. For this reason *T2* runs the risk of being nothing but an exception: the exceptional encounter between a nascent technology and a script which, using a fictional form, tells the story of its own birth. The film is a closed loop, it devours its own tail, showing the beginning and the end of a machine – symbolically, in an ocean of molten metal, with its thumb raised.

T2 will doubtless have its sequels or imitations. One fears that they will be disappointing. As for the new techniques, they will doubtless replace optical effects because of their undeniable technical superiority. Will they create a new imagination? It all depends on the virus that has been introduced into the system. The use of the computer within this technology has reintroduced the concept of artificial intelligence and could give credence to the idea that if a machine were intelligent it could develop an imagination and substitute it for our own. But even if the computer can transmute anything at all into anything at all, we'll still be able to tell a hawk from a handsaw.

I don't think the machine can be intelligent, and by the same token I don't think it can be stupid, either. Even if it contributes to it, it won't replace our imagination. But it slumbers in the heart of our mythologies. It can still make us dream, but it will not dream in our place. Technology is merely a nodal and immovable point half-way between science and poetry.

Denys Arcand

Universities are full of people worrying about the next millennium. My only concern is my next film. In this country (Canada), it is still almost impossible to get a decent soundtrack on a picture, let alone properly printed titles. So any futuristic daydreaming seems a little ridiculous.

Maybe if I lived in Los Angeles, I would see things differently. And besides, I always try to resist making bold predictions. Ten years ago the most feared sexually-transmitted disease was herpes, and four years ago the main threat to democracy was the massive power of the USSR. The main characteristic of the future is that we don't know anything about it.

Roger Spottiswoode

New technology gives people easier access to film. More movies will be seen at home – they'll be getting them down the phone lines, eventually. But I think the essential experience of watching films, collectively, won't change that much; neither will the nature of the stories films tell. But this new technology – when embodied in films like *Terminator 2* and *Total Recall* – raises a serious question: the problem of violence.

I believe what people view has a discernible effect on their behaviour. We are desensitizing people to violence and this will create repercussions echoing into the next millennium. To place someone behind a gun, encourage them to pull the trigger, and then show them that it was all right – to give an audience pleasure through the vicarious experience of killing – raises powerful moral questions. Familiarization with killing though video games, or movie games, dehumanizes people. You cannot avoid this moral dilemma by pretending that it's simply an art form.

When technology brilliantly re-creates people on the screen and then blasts them to smithereens – what does this do to the human spirit?

Richard Lowenstein

Throughout the history of human existence, the art of the storyteller and the desire to experience a story has been an essential part of our own consciousness. With media as diverse as cave paintings, oils, paint, canvas, prose, song, theatre, the written and printed word, radio, photography, cinema and television, the desire to tell and be told a story has been consistent.

Throughout this time, the basic relationship between the storyteller and the audience has remained largely unchanged. The audience's imagination has always been an integral part of the storytelling process – whatever the media. In the single image, the spoken and written word, it plays an obvious and major part in the receiver's interpretation of the story.

In cinema, the role of the imagination has been diminished somewhat. Yet, the audience's imagination has never been totally constrained by the limits of the cinema screen. The top, bottom, left and right side of the screen, the clarity of the image, along with the beginning and end of the moving picture are merely the borders where the film-maker's vision stops and the audience's take over. There are still a hell of a lot of blank spaces to fill in. This is what makes cinema a truly engrossing experience.

As technology progresses, the borders of storytelling will be pushed further and further into the realms of the imagination. The colouring-in will continue. In the years to come, new technologies will break new ground in the clarity and dimension of image and sound. High definition computers and film scanners will replace the optical printer. IMAX, Omnimax, three-dimensional images, six-track digital sound and interactive media will be tools used to push the (high budget) film-maker's vision.

The technology of interactive media, photo-realistic virtual reality will provide the audience not only with the ability to participate in the plot of their own story, but to indulge in their own dreams and fantasies – whatever their nature. The role of the audience's own consciousness and imagination, and the sociological impact of this onslaught of overwhelming completeness, is something that must undoubtedly be brought into serious question.

What will the effect on society be, if the advent of photo-realistic virtual reality causes a diminishing of fertile imagination? Will it replace the computer game as a way of keeping your children quiet: keep your children quiet by putting a virtual reality helmet on their head? How many books have been left unread in preference to a Nintendo game? Or will the ability to create your own story lines within pre-set story patterns, in much the same way as a computer game works, develop wild bursts of creativity in the audience to provide the artists and storytellers of the next generation?

Do we really need to have what dreams and imaginations are left to us in this post-TV world fed to us through high technology? Or will we find that it is an added stimulus to a culturally depressed society that will encourage the soaring of cinematic imagination.

These things may well be the new canvas, pen, paper, voice and 35mm film of a new breed of storytellers, but fundamentally I think the traditional structure of the storytelling process will remain the same, much as it has since the first cave painting, using whatever tools we can find at our disposal.

There is one thing about photo-realistic virtual reality, which as a film-maker disturbs me greatly. If the audience can walk around inside the film and its plot, looking wherever they want, where are the lights, the camera, and the rest of the crew going to go?

Some things never change.

Ron Sheldon

I have no interest in movies in which the audience can manipulate the narrative. That is the film-maker's job. I will probably, therefore, be looking for a job in the next millennium.

Vincent Ward

It is easy to see the new technology in a negative light – especially as the additional costs make the studios more blinkered about content (something I encountered on *Alien 3*.) But, somehow, I trust that advances in technology will bring audiences a fresh and richer range of experience, much as colour and sound expanded film's ability to 'see'.

In 1945 the Allies photographed the bombing of Dresden from the air, and in colour. The raid itself was a cruel anthem to technology and its recording equally so. The ability to record events – to record life and death – had expanded. And these photographs became the raw material for the small group of film-makers on *Map of the Human Heart*. We were trying to recreate the raid, trying to make our own cinematic bombing of Dresden forty-seven years later.

Ironically, while we were attempting to recreate the documentary record of the raid with models and computers, similar computers were being used to plot massed bombing attacks on Iraq. Furthermore, newer technologies were being used to enhance the photographic recordings of those raids – recordings which will be used, in turn, by film-makers seeking to produce an authentic recreation of that event, and who will have recourse to technology to achieve this, a technology developed for further military endeavours. So it goes on, and we, like latterday Red Riding Hoods, naïvely ask: 'Grandma, what do you *see*?' to a wolf who grins as he answers . . .

Monte Hellman

Science fascinates me. I've always been interested in technology and have appreciated its value in making my job easier. But in spite of recent advances, I feel that a great film will still be able to be made on 8mm – even if it is ten generations down. Technology can enhance a film, but it cannot compensate for the lack of a good performance, or an expressive face, or something essentially dramatic at the core.

Special effects can be terrific, but audiences accommodate change quickly and will become bored if the effects are there solely for their own sake. However impressive the IMAX process, if there's a terrific picture playing on television, you'll stay up until four o'clock in the morning to watch it. Ultimately, the content overrides the nature of the format.

It distresses me that fewer people go to the cinemas, that more people are watching movies at home. We are losing what is uniquely cinematic – the group dreaming experience: sitting in a dark room and reacting with others, giving ourselves over to the images on the big screen.

This is the change I most regret.

Arthur Penn

Well, here we go with another millennium. This will be the third after what's-his-name got hung out to dry. Of course, he fooled them and got resurrected after all. Leaves you wondering though – as myth or absolute fact – why we need for someone else to go through that horror to redeem us. Why don't we just redeem ourselves? What kind of God has to put his son through this elaborate and painful visit to our planet where He knows the kid will be treated like he was and then resurrects him so as to get him back home again? All to let us know that He is a merciful God. What kind of story is that?

A good story.

So, to the question: 'What kind of movie do you imagine might emerge in the next millennium?'

Well, there are going to be computerized special effects movies with high definition icing and digital processing and they are going to play around with virtual reality and the whole thing will fit right in your lap. You'll be able to feel them and smell them (but that's nothing new), taste them and probably take them to bed with you. They'll even be able to deliver splinters of the True Cross in the bottom of your popcorn.

But look at the first paragraph here. That's a story. And it will be told again and again with paradox and mystery and danger. And you can use any medium you want to tell those stories. So let's let them continue heaping technology after technology on to this medium. It will keep the homeless executives off the streets and in the studios where they belong. Busy little souls fiddling with the movie medium, and they still won't know a good story, even when it comes up and bites them on the ass. Now the poor things are struggling to cut the costs of films when the excessive costs are their very selves and their belief that huge salaries – including their own – are necessary to making good films.

Technical wizards come and go. Deconstructionists come and go, but the beat goes on.

What's the word? How does it fit into this thing I call my life? The narrative is still being spun, whether by campfires in the dwindling jungles, or in AIDS wards, or at a child's bedside. How did I get here? Where is here? Why? Where am I going? Is there any place else to go?

Maybe we might just find ourselves in there, somewhere. So tell it any way you want, virtual definition or computerized high reality, baby – it's still the word.

Jaco van Dormael

My dream as regards the new technologies of film would be a computerized special-effects system that allows you to shoot sixteen hours without overtime, a high definition system that makes the script good, and digital processing that allows you to be concerned only with the actors.

Lindsay Anderson

I have never been particularly interested in, or excited by, technological advance. By 1939, with sound and colour, the cinema had developed as fully as has ever been necessary, and it is worth remembering that *Listen to Britain* was dubbed off music and effects on gramophone records. Tape joins are certainly useful, but I understood the hesitation of the Polish film editor with whom I worked on *Raz, Dwa, Trzy*, when I presented her with the first tape joiner ever to be seen at the Documentary Studio in Warsaw, and I don't know that she did better work with it than she had done with a razor blade and film cement. It is convenient to be able to use 'rock and roll' when mixing tracks, but are the results any better today than when we had to dub a whole reel at a time? I remember the tension when, after many rehearsals, the dubbing mixer would announce: 'Let's go for a take'. Nothing today quite equals that excitement.

Good films, like works of any art, are made out of feelings and ideas and the creative impulse – what Coleridge called 'The Shaping Spirit of Imagination'. Are any film school graduates, or any Oscar or BAFTA winners, likely to make anything as lasting as *Intolerance* or *Earth* or Jean Vigo's films sixty years ago? Film schools and commercials have caused a lot of damage by their obsession with techniques. Video systems should make movies cheaper and easier to make; but sensation provides no substitute for concentration and imagination and a sense of style. Now we can have *Broken Blossoms* and *Pather Panchali* and *Fires Were Started* on our shelves. That's about as far as it goes.

So I regard 'technological advance' with scepticism. It has not made cinema easier (cheaper) to produce. Tomorrow's films will only be 'better' than yesterday's if they are made by better people. Computerized special effects systems, high definition, virtual reality etc. may provide short (but expensive) cuts and gloss. They do *not* offer new possibilities and relationships except in the most superficial way.

Anyway, the cinema is only just about to celebrate its centenary. Can we really assume that it (or the human race) will survive for another thousand years? Perhaps that would be a more profitable subject for discussion?

Nicolas Roeg

What will films be like in the next millennium? I hope they will no longer rely on formula. Or, better, that the formula will be: *there is no formula!* Nowadays screenwriters are encouraged to write in a very superficial way; each action completes the moment; each scene completes that segment; each action has an instant result. Behind each action there is a clear and specific intention: 'I will go rob a bank because the children need new orthodontistry, or because I need a new BMW.' There are no underlying 'secret' thoughts that one senses or can read or identify with. You're not even getting a glimpse of it. The fourth dimension is missing. What you see is all you get. This is strange because a human being does not exist who doesn't have a secret life running parallel with the observed existence. We are on many journeys throughout our lifetime, but we expose only one. In books, poetry and comics these other dimensions have always been explored and today are being explored even more, but there's a powerful reaction against any film-maker who attempts to expand the characters who inhabit the plot or story into anything more than a very simply motivated fiction of the two-dimensional person you see on the screen. This is doubly strange and baffling because in many ways film and the cinema are both the ideal medium and theatre for this extension of storytelling to take place. The essential difference between film and staged theatre is the movable audience. The cinema has the ability to move the audience instantly in time and place to show what's happening in the thoughts of characters almost at the same time as they are reacting and interrelating to one another. This is something unique in film. The audience is hurled in a shot to stand in between two people gazing with love or hatred into each other's eyes. Then flung outside to sit beside someone driving in a reckless and desperate way to reach the lovers before they kiss or kill each other.

My parents were born in the late eighteen hundreds and I remember as a boy, whenever I had to fill in a form with their birth dates, I felt a strange sense of distance from them, perhaps even a little embarrassment with the other boys, even though my mother was born in 1899, the last year of that century; it was still the eighteen hundreds and what a far off time that seemed. I think as film moves, in eight years time, past the magical frontier of the year 2000, when everything and everyone from this century will seem to be behind an invisible wall of the distant past, great changes in dramatic form will begin to happen.

The idea of the flat story line and what is described by present day studio executives as the three acts (or worse still what is currently becoming the 'in phrase' – 'The arc of the story and characters') will seem as rooted in the past as the theatre must have done before 'crazy' Thespis had his actors speak the lines as though it was dialogue actually taking place between the characters of the epic poems, instead of just a recitation. How baffled those ancient Greek audiences were. I can hear them now leaving the amphitheatre saying: 'What the hell was all that about?'; 'Ridiculous, too arty and pretentious ...'; 'Sure, Thespis, it was great but please let's do something a bit more commercial. Just good old entertainment – a good old epic poem that doesn't come to an end. A beautiful declamation by a poet supported by a masked chorus – something ordinary people from Sparta can understand.' How long did it take before that incomprehensible and ridiculous idea of Thespis' became what we accept today as the standard for playwriting?

Strangely, there has always been a certain subconscious reactionary running-down or retrenchment of established values as a century comes to an end and that is possibly what is happening today with film. I believe the French have a saying that: 'After great strides forward have been taken, there is always a little step back, before an even greater leap onwards.' The cinema, as with art and politics and business, is going through a very reactionary time with everyone rushing around trying to find some certain formula. There is a desperate fear of change or risk, a longing for a unified theory. Personally, instinctively, I cannot believe in a unified theory that is the completion of knowledge. I think it is a desperate thought brought about by the fear of chaos. If only there was a reason. If only it made sense for all of us. One formula that explains and satisfies everything. If that were so, then for me there would be no hope. No, because for me the world is still a quandary – there are no answers, no solutions, no rules.

Cinema is not about assurances. If mankind had ever been satisfied with rules that were categorically unbreakable, we would never have evolved, never have progressed in any form of life. However comforting it would be, I don't believe an unbreakable rule is possible in this ever-changing world. Great institutions, seemingly unassailable, collapse. Whatever empire you build, whatever band wagon you latch on to – sci-fi films, comic book films, musicals, westerns – eventually the formula exhausts itself. Nothing is forever. If there are no rules you can move out into uncharted territory, but that is what is being fought against in these closing years of this millennium – even though being launched out into the unknown is what truly excites an audience.

The cinema is a far more personal place than the legitimate theatre: a dark hall with a screen we look up at and see figures much larger than ourselves playing to each other and, unlike the theatre, with no sense of physical commitment to those who watch them, turning us into secret voyeurs. I remember seeing *Belle de Jour* at the Curzon cinema, and the sense of isolation in the audience which was composed, in large part, of couples, was very disturbing and exciting. Slowly they realized they were voyeurs of a very secret life. And as the film progressed, it had an extraordinary separating effect on these couples. People holding hands imperceptibly moved away from their partners as the film exerted its effect on them. As the audience was filing out, I got the impression they didn't want their partners to be aware of what had been passing through their own heads. Just because film is a popular cultural form doesn't mean that it can't deal with the secret emotions of people. That is what art does: it moves you privately; it's something you can find a truth in. And to make a distinction between popular cinema and art cinema is bullshit. It's all art. If it moves you to tears, to laughter, to thought – then it's art.

For me the word 'entertainment', even more than meaning a diversion, means involvement. Sometimes even bafflement, like a magic show. Somehow the commercial cinema, as it's called, has become very frightened of that aspect of cinema entertainment. To capture and involve an audience I believe the film-maker of the future will be constructing his film and characters showing many levels and sides to their lives. We will see their hidden journeys and inevitably, by doing so, the film-maker will expose aspects of his own 'secret life' – far more than he does today – and however oblique this might seem in terms of the plot of the film, I'm sure the audience of the future will have some innate sense and understanding of it. I think we are, at present, going through a phase where Entertainment is solely equated with distraction. A half-escape. When sitting in that dark hall your reactions are likely to be: 'Oh, that shot's nice . . . I wonder if I put the cat out . . . Wow, what a spectacular effect . . . Oh, shit, I forgot to make that phone call.' How different that will be in the palaces of virtual reality where the film-goer of the future will not only be in the action, but in the mind of the actors.

Cinema is also about the secret life people lead. Why shouldn't characters have complex hidden lives running parallel? Movies don't normally deal with that, but they will do. There are indications that young film-makers and writers are wanting to work this back into their films. Recently I read *Sexing the Cherry*, a book by Jeanette Winterson, a young woman whose work I've since discovered is tremendously admired by film-makers. Here are a couple of paragraphs from this book:

Every journey conceals another journey within its lines: the path not taken and the forgotten angle. These are the journeys I wish to record. Not the ones I made, but the ones I might have made, or perhaps did make in some other place or time. I could tell you the truth as you will find it in diaries and maps and log-books. I could faithfully describe all that I saw and heard and give you a travel book. You could follow it then, tracing those travels with your finger, putting red flags where I went.

For the Greeks, the hidden life demanded invisible ink. They wrote an ordinary letter and in between the lines set out another letter, written in milk. The document looked innocent enough until one who knew better sprinkled coal-dust over it. What the letter had been no longer mattered; what mattered was the life flaring up undetected . . . till now.

For years I have been struggling in film to do what this young woman does on the page and it seems to me there are times when many writers would like to use film to enhance the words.

Some years ago I was working with Colin Wilson. He had recently finished his novel *Lingard*, a very graphic and tragic story of a murderer. As we talked about the translation of word to film he told me that when he was writing *Lingard* he had visited the police 'Black Museum' for research and had looked at many photographs of murder victims taken at the scene of the crime. Then, when he had finished the book and was going over the publisher's proofs, it struck him that no matter how carefully he had written the description of the aftermath of the murder, the shock and emotional effect of the word did not compare to that of the police photographs. Not that one was better than the other, but that they excited the senses in a completely different way. He thought about it and felt that perhaps it was only to do with time. The time it took to read the paragraph of description worked in a totally different way on the emotions from the immediate response and flood of feeling he had when he looked at the photograph. He said he would have liked to somehow combine the two. I wonder now if that passing thought might not have thrown a glimmer of light on what the future of film could be. Although there is more being printed now than ever before, I think in the next century the written word will take a very minor third position to film and the recorded voice, certainly insofar as history or the novel are concerned. Cocteau thought that history is truth that sooner or later becomes a lie, and myth is a lie that sooner or later becomes the truth. I think we will see that that thought will belong to another age. History will be *viewed* and not re-viewed and written about by those who are only writing about what someone else has written about what someone else has, etc., etc. Where is the truth in that? What of myth? Well that, too, will take a bashing.

A few years before her death Sarah Bernhard, known as the greatest actress of her time, even called the greatest actress of all time, heard about this new invention, the motion picture camera, and agreed to record on film one of her greatest performances, that of *L'Aiglon*, the play about the young son of Napoleon. By this time she was already an old woman with a wooden leg and had no idea what a hunter of truth the camera is. I have seen the film of that performance and as I watched that elderly woman hobble about the stage in a young officer's uniform, I thought, poor Sarah, how could she possibly have understood the great mystery of film and its incredible ability to extend the levels of human contact and understanding. I have always felt the camera, that little dark room that images go into and are sealed on film, is the closest thing we have so far to a time machine. Today our children, sitting in front of the television set, spend a lot of their time watching dead people in old movies.

In the past few years, because of television and tape and computers, special effects have become so extraordinary, so dazzling, they have almost become the sole reason for the film to be made. I suppose with any new development in technology this is inevitable. Everybody likes new toys, especially if they are as good as the ones on offer from the effects department today. However, as with every new toy, more often than not the novelty wears off. The old teddy bear is the one to go to bed with, even if it might be sitting in a brand new space car. I think something similar will happen to film in the next millennium. Those extraordinary and brilliant effects will become tools and helpers to take the audience even further into the secret heart of the drama. But so far they're just wonderful tools that we are confused by and nervous of using in other ways than as a demonstration of what is capable of being done. With all these new toys, the cinema in which Orson Welles worked and compared to being the greatest train set a boy could ever be allowed to play with, will seem just as archaic a curiosity as that very train set itself, gathering dust in a box in the attic. Oh God! I would love to be a film-maker in the twenty-first century. And as this millennium closes I feel so trapped, as all of us are, in a time that is swiftly coming to the end of its time. The challenge of those who are still young in the twentieth century is how to bridge the gap. That moment on the strike of twelve in 1999.

Maybe the old Roman poet was closer to understanding the future and excitement of change than those of us who cling to rules to help us sleep at night. *Sed haec prius fuere. Atque in perpetuum. Ave atque vale.* But those things are past and gone. And so for ever. Hail and farewell.

István Szabó

I believe that the true and lasting value of the moving picture is the ability to show the live human face with its ever-changing emotions. If these feelings are genuine, the audience will react with compassion. Everything else can be written down, painted, choreographed or reproduced. But showing how a smile is being born, how laughter can burst forth, how desperation can be defeated by hope – these are unique moments, in each and every case different and unrepeatable, and full of secrets just like life itself.

I don't think that technical development will change the fact that the moving picture is the only suitable art to visually express changing human emotions/close-ups confronting them with the environment – nature and society/long shot. Only the style can change, the essence should remain the same: a human message.

In the next century, the only problem to be overcome will be the fact that many film-makers will speak without saying anything.

16 Jaco van Dormael

Movie Lessons

Jaco van Dormael in Conversation
with Pierre Hodgson

Jaco van Dormael was born in Belgium. He grew up partly in Germany, where his father was working, and partly in Belgium. Apart from a year in Paris, he has spent all his working life in Brussels. He has lived in the same, communally-owned building in the centre of town since he was 18 years old. He is in his thirties, married to Laurette, with two young children. Toto the Hero *is his first feature, though he has made a large number of shorts.*

Introduction   Pierre Hodgson

It was a cold day in January 1992. I arrived in Brussels at about ten in the morning. The train was late. It was almost snowing. I used to work here, ten years ago. I hadn't been back. I was struck by the faces on the Métro – there are more different races (and more different languages) than anywhere else in Europe. Despite the skyscraper banality of its Eurobanks and Euro-offices, Brussels remains a quirky town and a strong one, where the cafés stay open half the night and even in the mornings they are thick with the convivial stench of beer and smoke and steaming human beings.

I had come for a hastily arranged interview with Jaco van Dormael, whose first feature, *Toto the Hero*, was one of the big hits of 1991. It isn't often that a first feature is a big hit and Jaco was not yet accustomed to success. Come to think of it, he probably never will be. Half his head remains at home, in the immigrant quarter of Scarbeek, where he has lived in the same commune since he was eighteen; the other half talks to Mr Spielberg. This split predates his success and lies at the heart of his work, for Jaco combines a natural shyness, strong moral principles and a great, trenchant insight into the show business craft of guiding emotions. *Toto the Hero* is both an idiosyncratic, European *auteur* film and a populist comedy in the Hollywood tradition.

The film is about an old man named Thomas who recalls the salient episodes of his life from his cell in a prison-like old people's home. Thomas grew up next door to some rich neighbours whose son, Alfred, was exactly the same age as he was. Thomas has always hated Alfred and the hatred is compounded by a fantasy that he and Alfred were swapped in the hospital at birth: according to Thomas he is really Alfred and Alfred is really Thomas. In

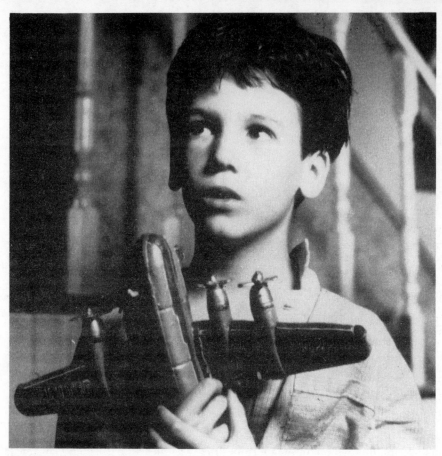

17   *Toto the Hero*: the young Thomas (Thomas Godet)

some mysterious way, their two lives remain inextricably intertwined and Thomas builds up a fierce resentment of Alfred. By old age, he is left with only one desire – revenge.

Thomas and Alfred are played by three different actors of three different ages and the whole film is constructed around the various generation gaps of an embittered old man's recall. It bears more than a passing resemblance to Dennis Potter's *Singing Detective*, which Jaco says he saw only after the script was complete.

Our conversation was conducted in French and took place before the film was released in the USA. Jaco had given, in the previous weeks and months, 350 interviews on the subject of his film. He was wary of sounding stale and he was not willing to discuss future plans. Consequently, we found ourselves talking about making films in general, about what works and what doesn't. And when we found ourselves straying on to ground covered already by Jaco while promoting *Toto the Hero*, we would skid to a halt and seek a passage into virgin territory. The result is a conversation piece necessarily irregular and scrappy in its construction, but as fresh and as true as we could make it. It aims to provide an insight into the thoughts of a singularly thoughtful film-maker.

I   The Three Ages of Film: Writing, Shooting, Editing

In the Beginning . . .

JACO VAN DORMAEL: I start with chaos, with bits and pieces. I scribble on index cards, then file them away in boxes. That goes on for months. I write a few scenes, fragments, not much more than that, shopping for images, characters, scenes. Nothing is excluded. I go off in lots of different directions, worry about all the potential avenues, so that when the time comes to narrow the scope, I have as much raw material as possible. This is not an efficient way of working. I could first devise an initial structure, then fill it out, which would be quicker. As it is, I am likely to lose my way. I never know whether I'm making any headway, or when a script is definitively finished. But my method does have one great advantage: the story appears to be writing itself. It feels natural, because when I do arrive at some sort of structure, it has been generated by the material, from within, and not imposed from without. Structure is what I'm most interested in, more than actual scenes, because the meaning of a film is in its structure, its narrative.

Finding out What a Story is About

JVD: I wrote the first version of *Toto* a long time ago, in 1982. It centred on the children, the adults did not come into it. I didn't like it, so I put it in a drawer. The story only began to grab me when there was a contrast between the different periods of the same characters' lives. I began to think: this is more like it, this confusion between past and present is what life is like. The story was still all over the place, but it did have one big connecting theme: that there is no such thing as fate. Rimbaud said: 'We slip into behaving a little less well than expected; we do things which, on the whole, we would rather not have done; and then, when our lives are finished, it turns out that it is not as we would have wished. And, of course by then it is too late.' That comes from a letter he wrote to his sister when he was thirty, dealing in arms in Abyssinia and about to have his leg amputated. He couldn't see any connection between that Rimbaud and the other one, the young poet of Charleville. I know what he means, I recognize the sensation. He means there is no such thing as fate. And that is why, in the plot of *Toto*, age matters: if we could simultaneously witness ourselves at twenty, at forty, at sixty, we would discover how it is we slip into becoming something other than what we hoped we would be.

When, in *Toto* the old man looks in the mirror and imagines what he was like forty years before, or the middle-aged man looks in the mirror and thinks back to what he was like twenty years earlier, it is the gap, the abyss of years, which matters.

Routine

JVD: I need discipline otherwise I just sit and stare out of the window. So I write for three hours a day, every day. I do this five days a week, Monday to Friday. I rest at weekends. That way, things move forward. Sometimes, I sit down to write and I think, 'today I don't know what to write' and sometimes there really is nothing in my brain so I muck around, I write the first thing that comes to me, whatever that may be. Most of the time, the script is off the road, like a broken-down car. I spend half my time under the bonnet, fixing things. My maddest ideas always come to me when things look bleakest. You pull something out of the hat to get things going again. Sometimes, there is only one sentence out of a whole day's work, out of the three pages, which is worth keeping. But then the day is worth it for that one sentence.

PIERRE HODGSON: *And do you ever laugh at what you've written?*

JVD: No. Sometimes I think it's funny, but I can't laugh. Obviously, I am hugely nervous about the way things are going. Nobody likes what they write. Anyway I have this discipline. Every Friday afternoon people come over, friends, and they read whatever I've got to give them. They're all close friends. For *Toto* there was Laurette and Didier who plays Mr Kant (the baddie supermarket owner) and Pascal, who is a friend and a scriptwriter. They all come on Friday afternoons and say: oh yes, that's good; or I see they are laughing, and I draw my conclusions. They are my audience if you like. I need the feedback. That way I am not working in a vacuum. I couldn't work all on my own, it is unbearable over a long period. After two months, you just get depressed. Either that or you are so desperate to finish you rush things. I need a lot of time for a story to fall into shape. I don't know the meaning of inspiration. Routine is all I have.

PH: *Isn't everyone like that?*

JVD: No, there are some people, I know some, who suddenly think of something and write for three days and three nights without a break, drinking lots of coffee. I cannot do that. I never think up an idea for a whole film. If I wrote fifteen pages a day, I'd throw twelve away so I might as well stick to three.

Frank Daniel

JVD: I was taught screenwriting by Frank Daniel who is from Czechoslovakia. He was head of FAMU, the Prague Film School, until 1968, when he emigrated to the United States. In New York, he opened a film school with Milos Forman called, I think, the Film Institute. Later, he became head of the film department at USC. Every summer for six or seven years, he would come over to Belgium and teach us what questions we ought to be asking about our own scripts, the common sense questions an audience is going to ask: 'What does this character want?', 'Why does he want it?'. He was never prescriptive, but he did make it plain that it was our job to know the answers – which was salutary. Usually, screenwriters avoid asking themselves anything which is going to cause trouble.

PH: *What about structure?*

JVD: He was much stricter about structure. He would make comments like the second act starts too late or this statement has to come earlier.

PH: *Was he an advocate of that American method which says after eight minutes such and such has to happen?*

JVD: Absolutely. That is how I wrote *Toto*. First act ends on page 24; page 68, beginning of the third act; a major explosion at the midpoint; set up and pay off; beats and so on. The system works because it is natural. The audience expects an event – after twenty-six minutes or between the twenty-fifth and the thirtieth minute – which changes the course of the story, and brings in act two, which is the period of conflict. If that event comes too late, the film feels slow, and if it doesn't happen at all, the audience thinks the story is incomprehensible because, from the beginning of time, that is how stories have been told. What we call the American system is only the Eastern European system. When the talkies came, Hollywood imported all these German, French, Eastern European, Hungarian writers and their rules came from Greek theatre. They are the rules of rhetoric. They haven't changed. They've merely been adapted to film. The main narrative issues remain the same.

PH: *How do your three pages a day get transformed into a structured whole?*

JVD: I look to see if any kind of pattern emerges from the raw material. I put huge sheets of paper on the wall and I start to make charts. And when a story begins to emerge, I show it to my collaborators. At that point, I write a first draft, which is the crucial phase. Changes from one draft to the next are major structural changes. I don't tamper, I always write complete drafts. *Toto* was written in seven drafts.

PH: *You must find yourself straining against the constraints.*

JVD: Not at all. They're a help. Despite its complexity, there is nothing innovative about the construction of *Toto*: the story and the style are too strange to withstand any kind of structural monkey business. In fact, the whole thing is like the *Palais du Facteur Cheval*, a crazy house built by a provincial French postman in the 1890s, which the surrealists loved because they thought it epitomized the 'automatic' principles of their art. Close up, it looks like a heap of mad, accumulated matter, but from a distance you can see the shape of a proper chateau beneath the lunacy.

The Rules of the Trade

JVD: At first I was very scornful of screenwriting 'rules', but once I started writing I found they were essential. Now I trust them, I feel confident enough to make deliberate mistakes and advertise those mistakes. Mistakes become stylistic devices when you are in a position to choose what mistakes you want to make.

PH: *I always try and think of films that don't comply with the rules of screenwriting.*

JVD: There aren't any. That is what is so astonishing. Frank Daniel is brilliant at analysing films. When he read my screenplay, he said, we're going to make *Amarcord*. What he meant by that is that we're going to make a film which seems completely crazy, but in fact is highly structured. *Amarcord* is constructed along strictly classical lines with three-act sub-plots, the main acts syncopated so the first act contains a scene from the second, the second act of story A comes before the third act of story C and so on. The story is built around a sequence of triple-act stories, a three-point rhythm contained within a superstructure which is the fête – the fête itself has three acts of course. The lesson from *Amarcord* is that you can be as complicated as you like provided you obey the rules: it is when you don't obey the rules that a story feels clumsy and unnatural.

The odd thing about Frank Daniel is that he tends to concentrate on old movies, movies from the 1940s, because the construction of those films is easier to describe, but when he screens *Amarcord* he cries. 1940s films don't make him cry.

Ken Tarkovsky

JVD: Not all films are classically constructed. Robbe-Grillet isn't. But as soon as a story is dramatized, as soon as the author is attempting to draw the audience into his story by identification with the aspirations of major characters, then the story has to be built like a Greek classical tragedy or like a comedy. That's what Aristotle says and the same rules apply today.

PH: *When you see a movie, are you aware of the construction?*

JVD: No.

PH: *You forget all the technical side?*

JVD: Yes. I watch the characters, I believe what they are going through. If it is a good film, I forget I am in a cinema, otherwise I'd be bored stiff!

PH: *Do you see more films now than when you were seventeen?*

JVD: Yes, because now I like films that are flawed. When I was seventeen I would have been bothered by the fact that a film didn't work and was badly made, or by a lopsided story, whereas now there's always something for me to learn from in the mistakes. I am more demanding in one respect now though: I demand of a film that it should say something important; I expect to come out of the cinema having had a life-changing experience or to have learnt something about life. If I don't get that I can still enjoy the movie, but it isn't the same thing. What really makes a film worthwhile is the feeling that it has introduced me to a new set of people and allowed me to share in a slice of their lives. I liked *Riff-Raff*, the Ken Loach movie. It was a life-changing experience.

PH: *Why? Did you like the way he developed his characters?*

JVD: I liked the truth of what he had to say. I liked the fact that what he is saying is crucially true and important.

PH: *Is that a question of ideology?*

JVD: I like the ideology. But what matters is the feeling that you have been in the company of a group of people who are real. It is, of course, a one-way relationship, but a meaningful one all the same.

PH: *What about Loach's other films?*

JVD: I like them too.

PH: *Anything else?*

JVD: I like Tarkovsky.

PH: *Despite the structure of his films?*

JVD: I don't know about his structure. I don't understand the structure of *Mirror*. I find it fascinating, but I do not understand it.

PH: *Have you seen it several times?*

JVD: Yes, it was showing for a week in Brussels and I think I must have gone to it every day.

Shooting is a Series of Headaches

JVD: It is in the writing and then again in the editing that a director is closest to narrative. Shooting is a series of headaches. You have to achieve a certain number of correct decisions within a fixed amount of time. Of course, I like working with actors and with technicians, but the best bit is in the dreaming. That is a quote from Pasolini. I get much more fun out of rehearsing the actors than directing them on set, because in rehearsal I can make mistakes, I can change my mind. I can when I'm writing too. A writer rereads what he has written the morning after. Same in the cutting room: you go back over what you've done once you are detached enough to know what might be wrong. In writing, editing, rehearsal you can change things. Not while you are shooting. There's always that moment when you know that a shot has got to be finished in the next twenty minutes or dropped altogether.

PH: *How many takes do you do?*

JVD: As many as I need.

PH: *Jacques Doillon, the French director, is famous for doing sixty-seven takes . . .*

JVD: I do somewhere between two and twelve. Usually the second take is the best. From then on, you're more likely to lose as much as you gain. And you lose the ability to tell whether a take is good or not. Doing lots of takes works for impulsive directors who know immediately whether a take is good or not. I am someone who needs to sit back and think.

From Writing to Shooting . . .

JVD: A writer's brain cannot anticipate every detail of performance, of an actor's physiognomy. If you could plug a lead into the writer's brain and transmit directly everything he imagines on to the screen, you'd get something much less powerful than what you get after the director has had to battle with actors, with lights and a set. Film needs the chaos of real life. You say *Toto the Hero* is very meticulous, but I actually think it is quite approximate. The emotions I am trying to describe are very precise in my mind and I hope in the audience's mind, which is what makes it a good, memorable film. But the actual sounds and images captured are approximations of life.

A film consists not in what is on the screen, but in what remains in the audience's mind when they leave the cinema. When the lights go up, at the end of a performance, the audience takes the heart of a film home. The imprecision and flaws stay behind in the empty picture palace. Of course, the audience is taking home precisely those ideas and images which inspired the writer and the director to make the film in the first place, often years before.

The germ of an idea for a film is something so imprecise it cannot be described, a portion of chaos. And the whole process of writing is one of pinning things down, of working and reworking the scenes till they distil into a set of specific characters in specific places doing specific things at a specific time.

Reading a scene one has just written is always disappointment. 'Oh, that's all it was.' Then, as you rework it, as you go into it again and again, you discover more and more of the detail and so you catch a glimpse of what it was that inspired you in the first place. Eventually, if the scene is well-written, it will contain a replica of the original emotion which first made you want to write it. And that is what you are after when you start shooting.

And from Shooting to Editing . . .

JVD: I call shooting shopping. You know what the dish is, so you go out and find the ingredients. You want them to be as fresh as possible, you want a bit of variety. You know that if something is missing, you'll have to make do with something else. But the main thing is to get all the ingredients into that shopping bag and get the shopping bag into the kitchen – the cutting room.

PH: *The film feels story-boarded.*

JVD: I draw quite badly, but drawing is the best way I know of thinking things out. Even if no one was going to see my storyboard, I'd still have one. As it is, I hand it out to the crew, which saves time because it tells everyone exactly what is going to be in shot and what isn't – or what is supposed to be in shot because, in the end, I suppose everything always turns out unexpectedly. The real reason I use a storyboard is that it represents my mental images as closely as possible. For instance, it shows the surface relationships between characters, where people should stand, how the image is going to be ordered and that in itself is a part of the meaning of the shot – it is a first step. In a sketch I can work things out ahead of time, changing my angles, or switching one character from foreground to background; I can move everything, people, furniture, the shape of the space in a second, whereas on set it would involve taking a window out and so on – it would be impossible.

PH: *Do you sketch scenes out as you are writing them or only after the script is complete?*

JVD: When it is finished. But the images are there at the time of writing as clearly as if I was sitting in a cinema describing what I was seeing and hearing. That is what a script is: it is a formal device for recording what one wishes to see and wishes to hear. When I reread a script I know the images I imagined when I was writing it and I hear the sounds I imagined too.

PH: *Do you think you could write plays?*

JVD: I have written plays, long ago. But that isn't how I like to work in the theatre. My experience in the theatre is that we always improvised, there was never an author, or at least everyone was the author, a collective author, we would improvise endless scenes and then cut away all the bad stuff till we had got it right. The process is the same as scriptwriting, except that it is collective. We would work out a story, then scene by scene develop it until it turned into a play.

PH: *There are people who make films that way, by improvising.*

JVD: I've done that, turned up the morning of the shoot with two sentences of dialogue on an index card and then taken it from there. We did it in *Toto* in the scenes in the mental home. That was one of the bits I enjoyed most, probably because I had no idea what was going to happen and I knew I was going to ask the inmates to do one thing and they would inevitably do something else which was much much better.

PH: *Those scenes feel as if they have been shot differently.*

JVD: They were. I mean, all I could do really was to roughly define a space for the inmates to occupy and let them get on with it. Of course, I told them what I was after and they produced something related, but different. Every take came as a surprise. But it all had tremendous energy. They enjoyed themselves. And it is wonderfully gratifying to have something new in every take. Actors have an enormous amount of self-control which makes it hard for them to improvise in front of a camera. It works much better with people who don't govern everything they do, like children or lunatics. With them, improvisation can be brilliant because no one is in control, least of all me. You have to be on the same wavelength as your actors. With professional actors you must be professional, you must be technical and thoughtful. Some need a lot of technical guidance; some want to be left alone; some need their hand held every inch of the way. My job is to find the key, to get on the right wavelength. That's why I enjoyed working with Célestin, the lunatic brother in *Toto*, because it meant I had to become lunatic too. The continuity girl would say you've got 40 metres left, will that do? And I would say, I have no idea. I would give directions like, 'Then you sing a song and kiss him and . . . ' off he would go and we had no idea what we were going to get. It was crazy.

PH: *Did you rehearse Célestin much?*

JVD: No, not much. It was not necessary.

PH: *How did you find him?*

JVD: I saw quite a lot of lunatics.

PH: *Would it be fair to say that you have discovered a formula in the combination of meticulous construction with moments of complete improvisation ?*

JVD: I have no idea what I am going to do next and the only thing I do know is that I would like each film to be radically different. In *Toto* I managed to cram quite a few different styles into the one film, which was good because I need variety. One of my slogans is that I most admire films when you cannot tell who directed them. I admire that because it suggests to me the style chosen was a function of what the story required and not a limitation imposed on the story by the director's subjective concerns. Having said which, people have said about *Toto*, 'What a weird film, it's so complicated', but to me it isn't weird at all because that is how I think.

PH: *But surely if a film is to be at all personal, then the director's own style must be apparent?*

JVD: OK, but you can feel a strong director behind a film, without knowing who the director is, as soon as you have seen the first three shots. Signature shots. I'd love to make films in the style of Cassavetes, I'd love to have that freedom, just to work on the actors, to shoot actors . . . that would be amazing.

PH: *Just once, as an experiment?*

JVD: At least once. My shorts are all made in different styles and I'd like all my films to be in different genres. I've made lots of documentaries, improvised films, one musical, comedy, tragedy, completely experimental things, completely incomprehensible things, just trying out new things all the time.

PH: *Do you work with the same actors? Do you have a family of actors?*

JVD: As far as I can, I work with people who are close to me because it is more fun, but I don't write for specific actors. I write for a ghost and then I try and find a body to incarnate that ghost. Once, I wrote a short for an actor and then he couldn't do it because he went off to Japan, he was getting married. His reasons were excellent, but it was horrific. I'd written the part especially for him and suddenly he wasn't available any more.

PH: *Did you make the film?*

JVD: Yes, with someone else, but it was a huge upheaval. Anyway, you have to rewrite a part when you work with a new actor. Because suddenly everything in your head changes. The actor does not own the character, but he brings himself to it and that affects the character, affects the way you can conceive the character. It is a question of balance: if the actor is tough, then you may have to tone down the toughness of the character and so on. I always rewrite the characters once I have cast them – at least the main parts. I try and make it so that that actor becomes part of the story, that he is an integral part of it. It helps the actor and it helps the film. That should be part of a screenwriter's job too, tailoring the screenplay to specific actors. At the end, the whole edifice should be so carefully put together that if one element is removed the whole thing collapses.

PH: *Does everyone on set have a copy of the script?*

JVD: Yes. And a shooting script. And a storyboard. And everyone is allowed to see the rushes. But no one is allowed into the cutting room. The cutting room is the secret place where rhythm and precision and meaning are restored. Of course, your first impression on seeing the rushes is exactly the same as when you first sat down to write the script. You think, 'Oh, so that's all it was.' Then, gradually, as you get down to work in the cutting room, as you weed things out, shorten some bits, build up other bits, as you manufacture a structure, the thing you're after begins to emerge: the thing that originally made you want to make the film, which is what the audience will take away with them – a way of looking at the world. And giving people a new way of looking at the world is what film does.

PH: *How long did it take to edit* Toto?

JVD: Six months, I think, two thirds of which was sound editing. There were two sound editors, with two assistants just for sound. Sound is tremendously important; because it is invisible, it carries a disproportionate amount of the emotion in a film. Sound is nowhere near as meaningful as picture, but it is more tangible, more sensuous. Altering sound completely alters the atmosphere of a given scene. Sound governs the degree of tension. But the viewer has no idea of the effect of sound; he or she thinks that, because he sees the picture, he is somehow in control of his reaction to it, he can check whether a door is crooked or not and so on. He understands dialogue, he can recognize music – usually – and he hears sound that is transmitting concrete information. But viewers don't 'hear' abstract sound. Perhaps, if he or she concentrates very hard, a viewer may recognize up to three distinct simultaneous sounds out of a total of twenty or thirty on a given shot. And those other sounds really matter. Imagine having an argument with someone in a room, and your voices get louder and louder and louder until suddenly someone switches the air conditioning off and only then do you realize what was irritating you so much. I have been working with the same sound engineer, Dominique Warnier, since I started making films and we have developed a common language, we both know we are after the same thing.

PH: *There is one important difference between picture and sound and that is that the viewer chooses where to look on a big screen, whereas he cannot consciously choose which sounds to listen to.*

JVD: Absolutely. And you can use sound to shift the viewer's attention from the foreground to the background or vice versa. Sound is more than what is going on outside the frame, it is also like music, providing you aren't restricted to a realistic handling of sound. In fact, proper film sound is much more complex than music because there is no tempo, no notes. The brain uses beat to process music whereas sound is too chaotic for the brain to recognize; sound is quite crazy. The emotional charge of sound comes from the fact that the brain cannot process it. In *Toto*, the first fire scene in which the two babies are swapped wouldn't have worked at all without intense sound treatment. The number of different types of sound on the tape at that point is incredible. There are about thirty different sounds involved, and they all sound like a single sound.

PH: *What sounds are they?*

JVD: Sounds manufactured by the sound engineer, or sounds he already possessed, in his sound library – as I said, we have been working together for ten years – which we then manipulated, slowed down or reversed. For instance, in the fire in the maternity ward: a blacksmith's hammer, slowed down; screaming mothers and reversed screaming mothers, who sound like ululating wolves; slow motion steps; slow motion breaking glass, which sounds like bells, and ordinary breaking glass; there's a continuous bass sound of slow motion flames, a normal sound of guttering flames and a high-pitched flicker sound as well. The aim is to have sound from the bottom to the top of the register, and to place reversed or slowed-down sounds beside real-time sounds. There is a sound of babies crying, the sound of a fire alarm, of a fire engine, of wind whistling and so on. I can't remember half of them. But each sound creates its own particular atmosphere and together they denote confusion, panic, emotional upheaval.

PH: *Does the mother, who is on screen, say anything?*

JVD: Just one scream, at the end of the shot.

PH: *When did you put Thomas's voiceover in?*

JVD: We recorded it before shooting so that we could play it back during shooting, for the actors to work with, then we re-recorded some passages after the shoot.

PH: *And when did you decide there would be voiceover?*

JVD: Very early on during the writing.

PH: *Is it part of the initial structure?*

JVD: Yes. In fact, over the baby, the voiceover was pleonastic from the start. It describes what we are seeing on camera. Because the old man is the narrator, it makes sense to begin and end with his voiceover.

PH: *How much voiceover is there in between the opening and the end sequences?*

JVD: Quite a bit.

PH: *Is voiceover an instrument of irony?*

JVD: No, as I said, over the childhood sequences, it is pleonastic. The old man's voiceover is not and so I suppose you could call it ironic, the idea being that life is pretty dull, but the person remembering it is a gas. In any case, there is a practical reason for the old man's voiceover which is that nothing happens in the old people's home: the only interesting developments are inside the character's head and that's why we need an entrée through voiceover.

A Story Emerges: Pacing

JVD: When you get into the cutting room some scenes need to be dropped because they slow the film down. Or sometimes the scene is fine, but the beginning and the end are too laborious. I know that as a writer I take too long to bring a scene to a climax and too long to finish it once it has achieved its purpose. You should go straight to the heart of a scene, cut straight to the action. Even then, the chances are it will still be too long.

There's another thing which you can only really get right in the cutting room and that is the business of exposition: when should a piece of information come? Even though you may think you've decided all that at script stage, the script conveys so much less information than the finished film that some elements of exposition are going to have to be changed. If a script had to describe everything people were going to see and hear, it would be unreadable, and thousands of pages long; there would be no rhythm to it. The way a script reads tells you the intended pace of a film. I like a page to represent about fifty seconds of film time, that's the pace I like.

PH: *Is that a fixed rule or is it just an average?*

JVD: It is a fixed rule, it's quite a lot of work. Usually people reckon on about a minute per page.

PH: *What about description? Do you give detailed descriptions of sets, sound, music and so on?*

JVD: No, most of the time I don't include descriptions of locations in the script or, if I do write them, I put them to one side and give them to the designer as notes – unless they are essential to understanding the script. For instance, if there's a shot that lasts several minutes, I am almost bound to describe the set because I want the time it takes to read the description to relate to the time the shot will last. If, on the other hand, a location is not described in the script, even though it will be shown on film, that simply means that things are moving fast at that particular juncture.

A director's style is the sum of his mistakes; the mistakes he makes regularly. They are an expression of what he is afraid of, which is a function of style too. I believe that directors who are afraid of people are more likely to use wide shots and be reluctant to have an actor face the camera directly. Some people are terrified of cutting and try to avoid doing so; they shoot in extended *plan-séquences* in an attempt to get most of the editing over during shooting.

My own phobia is pace. If I have to shoot a scene, eight weeks after shooting a related scene, I cannot spontaneously recall the rhythm we had found. Pacing is critical. You need to remember changes of rhythm, you need to know when narrative should speed up or slow down. I find myself varying the angles as much as possible so that I can delay having to deal with pacing until I get into the cutting room. The trouble with this is that sometimes multiple camera angles are wrong, sometimes you just want the story to pause for a bit and stay where it is. Then, of course, you need to use fewer, longer shots which means setting the pace on set, within the real time of the shot.

In *Toto* there is one such moment: when the two children are in bed together, bang in the middle of the film. That shot has to be held as long as possible because there is no reason to cut it, so I told the kids to hold their breath and take as much time as they possibly dared. But that's an exception. Usually I want to construct the rhythm of a scene at the editing table, because pace dictates the audience's perception of a story, it makes the emotion.

Another thing I am terrified of: being boring. That fear is another component of my style. It means I have to go very fast. I want to keep the audience on its toes, not waiting around while I harp on about something they already know.

Suppose a character has to stand up and leave. The action cannot take place in real time. It has to take place in the time it takes to realize what he is going to do. The film has to be one step ahead of the spectator's imagination, so that it drives his brain. The purpose is not to reproduce reality, but to plunge people into a narrative. The purpose is to manipulate the audience.

The faster a film is, the more direct it becomes. If a film is slow, it feels intellectual. *Toto*, shot more slowly, would have been an 'intellectual' film, for art houses only, because the slower a film is, the more time it gives the audience to watch and think and interpret; whereas by going very fast, you

18 *Toto the Hero*: brother (Thomas Godet) and sister (Sandrine Blancke) in bed together

force the brain to let go, analysis goes out the window, it's left behind, it can't keep up – and all that's left is sensual emotion and feeling. You address people's senses and affections. If anyone's going to think about the structure of a film, the director is, not the audience. The director should devise the structure so cunningly that by the time it reaches the screen, it is invisible. If an audience has to focus on structure, it won't recognize its emotions.

PH: *It occurred to me that maybe the films you personally enjoy are not necessarily fast-moving.*

JVD: That's absolutely true. The films I enjoy most are films I'm least likely to make, films I don't know how to make. For instance, I love Tarkovsky's films, I love *Mirror*. I do not understand it at all, it's completely impenetrable, I don't know why it works, I don't understand the story and yet I'm riveted. It's baffling.

PH: *Is there a particular film that made you want to make films?*

JVD: No. I have very eclectic taste, I like all kinds of things. Initially, I think, I was more interested in characters than in the grammar of film. When you first go to the movies you don't understand how a film is made, all you see is living creatures, characters, and they were what started me.

PH: *Do you smoke?*

JVD: No.

PH: Toto *feels like a smoker's film.*

JVD: I have never smoked. Once, when I was little, I made a pipe out of an old metal film box, pierced a hole in the bottom, and screwed the connecting tube for a bicycle pump into the hole. Of course, as soon as I lit the tobacco, I got a lungful of burnt rubber which put an end to my smoking habit. I must have been about twelve. But in films I love the obsessiveness of smokers. And I thought it was fun that Toto should turn into a smoker in old age having loathed smokers earlier on.

PH: *I used to smoke and I hated people who told me not to, which is something you put in your film. One of the effects of your way of writing, is that it makes for a very dense film, packed with observation, so that there is something for everyone in it. I am sure that is part of the reason for its success.*

JVD: The film is definitely a broad church, definitely chaotic and, in that respect, it is very realistic. Life is chaotic.

II   Memory, the Meaning of Life and the Storyteller's Craft

JVD: Pasolini, the Italian director who was murdered, said there were two kinds of life: life in the present-tense sense of living, when you don't know what is coming next, and *a life*, in the retrospective sense, which is a summing up of something ended. You can look back on a man's life and discern the meaningful pattern of it, because nothing new is going to come. Death orders

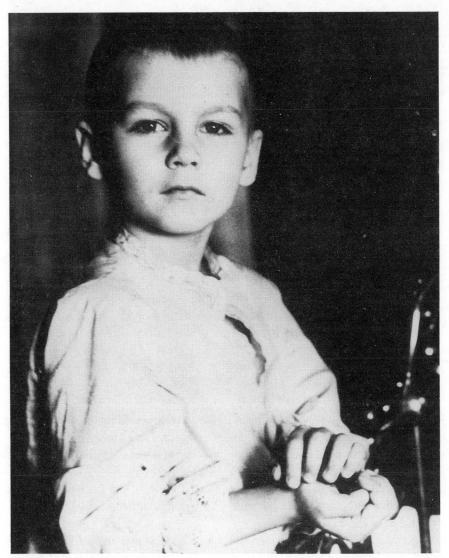

19 *Mirror*

life. And films do too. Films do not represent real, chaotic life. They represent life organized, as though by memory, into some kind of significant story. People like stories precisely because stories provide the illusion of design; they suggest that life has a point to it.

PH: *The same is true of plays.*

JVD: Yes and books and everything, they're all a way of organizing our lives. There are no gaps at the movies, no boring bits, no unnecessary business; there is nothing pointless about a film whereas, of course, life is nothing but pointless bits. You can build a story out of life, that's all. That is what Thomas does in *Toto*, he selected an hour and a half out of his life that he wants to remember. He could have chosen a different set of episodes and made a completely different autobiography. All one is doing when one tells one's own story is choosing which bits to forget about.

A story needs an ending and the choice of ending gives a story its moral significance. In *Toto* there are several endings and each ending gives the story a different meaning. What I like about multiple endings is that they raise the possibility of each potential meaning and then they say we don't have to choose, all these meanings coexist. This is a sad story, but it is very funny; a very dark tale, but an optimistic one. I find that when I am writing a very tragic scene, I start wanting to laugh; but I also find unadulterated comedy dull. Perhaps that is just the way life is, switching from tragedy to comedy and back again.

PH: *Isn't that what people mean by talent? Your talent is combining those two modes?*

JVD: It isn't talent, it is just a way of seeing things. I get it from my surroundings, from the people I live with and so on. One of my clichés, that I always put in interviews, is that films are not *by* people, but they come *through* people. *Toto* is a digest of the books I've read, the films I've seen, the people I like, the people I live with, the people I've met – my world, in other words, is processed by me and becomes the film.

PH: *So what can you say to 16-year-olds who want to go into movies? This business about talent is scary. They don't know whether they have any talent or not. They don't know what talent is. And your reply is that talent is writing three hours a day every day, whatever happens. Talent is work.*

JVD: Writing three pages a day for years, keeping on at it, is a very great talent!

PH: *Isn't it more than that? Your film isn't a hit just because you've worked hard at it. There's also an individual quality which you bring to the rest of the world and which conditions how you reflect it.*

JVD: Yes, but I think you absorb that too because the only real definition of talent is making the right choices which is an ethical thing; it's an ethic that comes from the people you live with, from your parents. If you make the right moral decisions, you are also going to make the right decisions about storytelling, about what is worth telling stories about, about what stories need to be told. The worst thing is wanting to please. If you want to please people, you're sure not to. It's like making love. It doesn't work if you try too hard. The only way really to seduce people is to be in love. A film-maker has to be in love with his story. When you are really in love with your tale, someone else can fall in love with it too, but you can only make a film because you need to tell the story, not because you want to charm other people. The thing which enables you to fall in love with a story badly enough to want to tell it is your attitude to life and what you think really matters.

PH: *Most people don't know how to be honest with themselves. Were you born with this idea of being true to yourself, not wanting to seduce, or is that kind of independence something which can be acquired?*

JVD: I don't know. I know that I live on doubt. Making films is a way of clarifying my life and using my ability to doubt to find out what matters. I always think living is much harder than making films and I know I'm better at film-making than at living. Films are easier to organize. There is in films a kind of perfect estate in which each thing sits in its allotted place. Life is much more confused. It is hard to live intensely, to be present, to be at the cutting edge and not in some never-never land of one's own manufacture. My life is not half as clear as my film. My life has less meaning or has multiple meanings. Things are ambivalent. Events are insignificant unless one gives them a significance, unless one reads them in a particular way. There is no art director in life to arrange everything nicely, no property master digging out just what you need. Everyone is the protagonist in life. We are all protagonists. An ant is its own protagonist. A bird too. Cinema is a consolation, it helps one come to terms with not understanding things which are too complicated. In a story everything is nicely obvious and meaningful: life seen from a single point of view.

PH: *That does not really apply to your film though. Does it?*

JVD: My film is a bit broader, but nothing like as broad as life. That would be impossible, how could one fit enough of life in one's head? Where is the brain that could understand life? I believe life is the exact opposite of a story: it is the absence of story. Nothing really follows on from anything else in life; stories begin and then don't end; other stories suddenly end even though they never appear to have begun; there are gaps, empty moments, blank periods, times when nothing is going on. You have to have a lot more talent to live life well than to make a film. It is hard to be happy. The art of making films is conjuring for one's own entertainment.

PH: *It is also the art of mastering memory, isn't it?*

JVD: But memory does exactly the same thing. Memory orders events in the same way as a storyteller does. Things either grab you or you forget them. You make your own story out of the things that grab you. Your head would explode if you had to remember everything that had happened to you. Anyway, you can forget things and then, out of the blue, you remember them years later, in another context, because suddenly you need them to make sense of something which has happened. Memory tries to make sense of events and it does so because we need the consolation of believing that life makes sense. That is an indispensable illusion. But only one per cent of everything that happens to a person is retained.

PH: *And things that haven't happened at all.*

JVD: Yes, that's true; fake memory is just as important as real memory.

III   Scenes from the Life of a Film-Maker

JVD: I live in a commune here and that is a great help. There are actors, costume people, a lawyer ... I have been living in this commune for sixteen years. At first we shared all our material possessions, we pooled everything we earned and those of us who were breadwinners looked after those of us who weren't making anything. There were never any problems. Living in a commune affected a lot of the decisions I made because it was like having our own social security system. If one of us suddenly got fed up with some job, he or she did not have to do it. And because our standard of living was very modest we could go on living together on that basis for a long time, sheltered from purely economic decisions.

PH: *Weren't there some people who never did any work and others who were always paying for everyone else?*

JVD: No, we never had any problems. There were no rules, no money problems, I don't think we even discussed money much.

PH: *Why did you give up this system?*

JVD: We haven't. We live in the same house with the same people. The only difference is that it is less of a commune because some of us have children of different ages, some go to bed at seven-thirty, some don't, some have to eat at eight, some go to school and so on. Synchronizing twelve different adults is much harder when there are children involved. We still try to eat together at least once a week. The oldest person in the house is seventy-three, the youngest is a 1-year-old.

PH: *How did you all come together?*

JVD: I met some of them in a circus. Some of us worked in a kids' theatre. I was eighteen when I started living with them, I worked in a theatre for kids.

PH: *Before getting into films?*

JVD: No. At the same time. I was at the INSAS (the film school in Brussels).

PH: *Is that a good school?*

JVD: I don't know what a good film school is. It's a good school because they give you lots of stock, they give you cameras; the people there are finding their way the same as you are, that's why you learn. I don't know that you can really call it teaching. Except in the script department – that is taught properly.

PH: *How does it feel to be in a position where for the first time in your life you can do anything you want.*

JVD: I did what I wanted with *Toto*. It was hard, but it was what I wanted. And I will do what I want with all my films.

PH: *But you did say you almost were not able to make it.*

JVD: That is true.

PH: *Whereas now, things are easier?*

JVD: Of course they are. Except writing a good story. That is no easier now than it was before. That will always be hard. The hardest thing of all is having a good script, harder than finding money. Even with *Toto*, finding the money was incredibly difficult, but not as difficult as writing a good script. Nor as interesting. Telling good stories is the purpose of making films, it's the only purpose.

PH: *So why not write novels then?*

JVD: I don't know how to.

PH: *Well, you learnt how to write scripts, I'm sure you could learn how to write a novel. It wouldn't take more than three years.*

JVD: True.

PH: *I am sorry to keep on at you about this, but it seems to me that at the beginning of our conversation you were slightly contemptuous of the process of shooting, as opposed to the business of screenwriting and now I am rebelling against the notion that the sole purpose of film-making is telling stories. There is a strong feeling in your film that it contains things which came during shooting, which you enjoyed.*

JVD: Ah, but when I say it is the writing I enjoy, I don't mean that I want to see my writing published, I enjoy the prospect of one day seeing my film on the screen; I want to see flesh and blood people incarnating my characters. I don't mind shooting, but I am less suited to that process because you're not allowed to make mistakes when you are shooting, you've got to get it all right in seven minutes. And if you don't get it right, you're going to carry that cross for the rest of your days. Whereas when you're writing and when you're in the cutting room, you can change things, make them better. I am not a quick thinker, taking decisions on a set is very very difficult for me. I just don't enjoy it so much.

PH: *Don't you think it is like driving, a question of reflexes and the more films you make, the more used you will become to acting quickly on set.*

JVD: Maybe. Yes, maybe. Sometimes, you're in a position to do retakes. It is true that it is only on shorts, on low budget films and first features that you cannot correct your mistakes. I hope that in the future I will be able to correct mine.

PH: *It is more than that. I think you were really talking about fear. A director is afraid on set that he won't get what he needs or what he wants or imagines. Now people know*

you can do it, and now there will be the money to correct your mistakes, isn't that
fear something which goes away. Isn't it partly, too, a question of habit?
JVD: Probably. I was more at ease at the end of the shoot than at the
beginning, but that certainly wasn't because I made fewer mistakes. I learnt
to say 'too bad!'. I didn't become a better director. A director doesn't see his
mistakes. A screenwriter does, a screenwriter can detach himself and reread
his words. A director doesn't see his mistakes till he gets into the cutting
room.
PH: *Do you use a video monitor?*
JVD: Occasionally. But it is very expensive. I think we rented one for one
week and then for another two days. A video monitor is a great help for
blocking out the scenes. I always do the blocking out so the cameraman sees
what I want without my having to go through the shot a second time with
him. The monitor gave us an extra half an hour per day.
PH: *Do you use a viewfinder?*
JVD: No, I use my eyes. Very occasionally, just when we are setting up, I'll
use the camera lens which screws into a separate eyepiece.
PH: *We haven't discussed photography at all. Do you give detailed indications about*
the light you want or do you have a general understanding with your director of
photography, as with your operator and your sound engineer?
JVD: Before the shoot, we got together to set out the kind of style we were
going to use.
PH: *How well do you know each other?*
JVD: We had made several shorts together. In this film I wanted five or six
different kinds of photography and I showed him clips from films and still
photographs and things in order to establish a kind of mutual language. We
gave each style a label. I think his main task was really to meld the various
styles I wanted together so they formed a coherent whole; they had to be
different enough to be meaningful, but not so different that they disrupted
the flow. I wanted the childhood scenes to be very bright and slightly overexposed; the scenes with the grown-ups had to be very grey and flat; and the
old man's scenes had to be very contrasty. Also the light sources had to be
low for the child, medium height in middle age and high in old age. The
camera angles are all looking up for the baby, then they gradually move
round till they are all plunging shots for the old man. When he is dead we
are vertically above him. In fact, camera angles describe an arc of 180°
according to Thomas's age.
PH: *The logic behind the camera angles is obvious, but how did you decide on the*
kind of light you wanted? That was a matter of taste was it?
JVD: Yes. But as soon as the director of photography knows what I'm after, I
leave him to it, I don't know anything about camerawork – I studied it for a
year – and I wouldn't tell him where to put his lights nor what lights to use.

My job is to look at the results, not analyse how he has reached them.

PH: *Do you see different kinds of light when you are writing the script? Is that where the choices are made?*

JVD: Yes. The simple fact of describing bright colours in childhood, of things being yellow and scarlet and blue, that it is sunny and that when he is old most of the scenes are at night, that it's raining and depressing ... the atmosphere is quite different.

PH: *What about processing?*

JVD: The only thing is that we overexposed the childhood scenes to make them warmer and to give them a sixties Kodak feel. But obviously, we couldn't take this too far or it would have disrupted the unity.

PH: *Will you make your next film in Belgium?*

JVD: My screenplays are set here because this is my world, and the ideas I have are rooted here. If I decided to accept someone else's script then I suppose the story will determine the location, whether it is in France or in the States.

PH: *And you feel you could shoot someone else's script?*

JVD: I doubt finding a good script by someone else takes any less time than writing one's own.

PH: *How much of a script do you read in order to judge it? The first thirty pages?*

JVD: Yes. You know it's of any interest in the first thirty pages. If you aren't interested in the first act, there's no reason for the other acts to be of any interest.

PH: *Are you worried about shooting in English, in a foreign language?*

JVD: The danger there is that I might miss the nuances, or that I might get stuck in a rut of clichés gleaned from years of watching American films. But the main problem is the question of rhythm. Directing an actor in your own language, you're always telling him to go faster, go faster, go as fast as you possibly can, whereas if you don't really understand what the actor is saying, the danger is you might start saying 'hang on a bit, slow down', and that is bad. I don't know how I will manage. The films will have to be very visual. The dialogue will have to be enclitic or musical.

PH: *Do you speak any languages other than French?*

JVD: I lived in Germany for seven years. I speak French, English, Flemish and German.

PH: *Comfortably?*

JVD: Comfortably enough. Actually, even in French, if I go to Paris I notice the intonations are so different that I don't catch all the nuances of the language. But I like films where the dialogue is a kind of music, not a vehicle of meaning. Those are the kind of films I try to make. And you can always hear the music of a language. I can hear the music in English. I don't think I could get all the subtleties of meaning, but when something is right, you know it is right, you can hear it. You can tell when an actor is false whatever language he is speaking, even in Polish. You know something is wrong.

PH: *Lots of directors have directed in languages other than their own.*

JVD: It can be difficult, but not necessarily damaging. I am convinced *Paris, Texas* is just as good in English as it would have been in German. Often, the reason for choosing one language rather than another is an economic one. Basically, a film should be in its author's language, but sometimes the story demands a different one. You couldn't set *Paris, Texas* between Hamburg and Berlin, it wouldn't work. It had to be set in America, and because it's in America it has to be in English. Difficult but right. An artistic decision, not an economic one.

PH: *Do you know when people are going to laugh?*

JVD: Obviously, *Toto* is meant to be funny. It is meant to be both funny and tragic. But the perception of what is funny changes radically from one country to another, so in some countries people think of it as a comedy and in others they think of it as a tragedy. For instance, I think British and American audiences expect to be 'entertained' at the movies; that's what people want, so if they start laughing at the beginning of a film, they'll go on laughing. French audiences, on the other hand, don't consider cinema to be entertainment. They think of it as culture, as food for thought. So they laugh much less. Belgians come somewhere between those two extremes.

PH: *Who do you make your films for?*

JVD: For here. For Belgium. For me and my friends, for people I know. I am not interested in addressing the world. The fact that my film has been seen all over the world is a coincidence.

PH: *If only producers could understand that, there would be a lot more good films.*

JVD: I don't think they can understand it because they'd be out of a job. After all, they want to make the films that they like – they're allowed to like films too. But the main thing about producers is that they are superstitious, they're gamblers. For example, when you're having a sensible conversation with a producer he or she will say – they all say – there's no point in having stars any more, stars have lost their drawing power, people want unknowns, they want novelty. But as soon as you start discussing a cast with them, the same producers will invariably say they want a star because 'you never know' and then they'll say it would be great if so-and-so was directing this and I hope it's going to be like such-and-such a film that was a hit, and suddenly all these perfectly sensible people become superstitious. They know you can't control success.

One of my clichés is that I don't control the audience. I don't know what is going to work and what isn't. The only thing I know is whether the film is true to what I am or not. How could I know anything else? And the funniest part of it is that producers are beginning to say, 'We need another *Toto*' – whereas the whole point about *Toto* is that it is unique. Imitations won't work.

PH: *Producers saying 'We need another* Toto' *is just the price of success, isn't it?*

JVD: I never wanted success except that everyone thinks, what if . . . ? and then if it does happen it is a real pain in the neck, it fucks everything up. Professionally, of course, success is a good thing, but only professionally. If I made a film which no one wanted to see it would not hurt me, so long as I thought the film was good. The only thing that matters is making essential films, films we can't do without. When I made shorts no one ever saw them, but I'm still very proud of them.

PH: *Are you scared that cinema is on the wane?*

JVD: It won't disappear. I am not scared of that. There will always be cinemas because there is such difference between seeing films alone at home and seeing them in public. People go to football matches where you see much less of the game than you do on TV in order to share in the *esprit de corps*. There is a gregarious instinct that makes us want to experience things with other people. That is a very strong element in the business of theatre and cinema too.

Having said which, there are some films I like watching on television because I can only see them on television and because I cannot go to the cinema all the time. Television could be great. It's a shame it is so atrociously bad. There is nothing on television, nothing at all. It is empty. I feel stupider, after I've watched television, than I did before switching it on. I feel like my brain has gone into white-out. Here in Belgium we have twenty-six channels and I can channel hop from one channel to another – we have all the major European channels – and find nothing from one end of the spectrum to the next. It is terrifying. I think the potential of television is enormous, it ought to help people communicate with each other but, in fact, it does the exact opposite. It severs communication. It stops the circulation of information. And it fucks everything up because it wastes so much of everyone's time. It devours the hours when we could all be speaking to each other and living real lives.

PH: *Do you think people will get fed up with it?*

JVD: No, I think it's going to get bigger and bigger and bigger. The thing I hate most about television is the hook. Even the news always carries a hook to make you watch the next episode, there is no difference between the news and a soap opera. They call it getting ratings and that is all it is. Ratings for what? For nothing except hooks to get more ratings. It is as if every day a voice came on and said, 'Sorry there was nothing on today, but tomorrow is going to be really great.' So everyone switches on tomorrow. The viewer spends his or her whole time waiting, waiting for something great. Television is an advertising medium. All it needs is regular viewing. So that is all it tries for.

PH: Toto *is quite a political film. It's got quite a bit of anger. And yet the politics are almost concealed, so the audience can ignore them. You loved Ken Loach's* Riff-Raff.

Do you see yourself making political films one day?

JVD: I don't see myself as having any kind of political position. It is more a question of humanitarianism.

PH: *You do believe that people are being conned though?*

JVD: I certainly do.

PH: *Is that a feeling which could come to have more importance in your work in the future?*

JVD: I don't have a high opinion of the way the world works, that is true. I think I have a split personality, though. I am quite naïve in that I tend to assume people are basically nice; but I am also disgusted by the way things are run. I am scared of power and money because of all the stupidities that people with power and money commit. Power and money are inimical to love and to pleasure. Specifically, in films, people who are motivated by money tend to make bad films.

PH: *Don't you want to get off the bandwagon, stop thinking about film for a bit, go back to the theatre or something?*

JVD: I like writing. No. I couldn't go back now. As it is, it is going to take me a long time to produce a new script. And anyway it would be stupid because getting a script is what matters and I'm incredibly slow because I enjoy it so much. I love getting up in the morning, knowing that all I have to do all day is write. That represents an enormous amount of freedom to me: organizing my dream, steadily getting it right day by day. Of course there are moments when everything goes wrong and then you start thinking 'I'm in the wrong job, I'll never make it.'

4   Searching for the Serpent: An Interview with Alison Maclean

Graham Fuller

With her scarlet lipstick and matching bomber jacket, *retroussé* nose and slit-eyed sneer, ambisexual flirtatiousness and amoral decision-making, Lane, the anti-heroine of Alison Maclean's *Crush*, is a *femme fatale* for the post-modern fallout. As played with sardonic relish by the American actress Marcia Gay Harden, she's a slippery amalgam of Melanie Griffith in *Something Wild* (herself the cartoon offspring of Louise Brooks), Laura San Giacomo in *sex, lies, and videotape*, and a boa constrictor. She's the sort of imperial bitch you find yourself colonized by in weak or neurotic moments.

That notion of colonization is central to Maclean's film. The first feature by the Canadian-born, Australian-based writer-director is a twisted fairy tale, a parable, about American cultural hegemony in New Zealand, where it was shot. Lane, an American adrift, as tacky as the signs of commerce that stud the rural routes, is recklessly driving her old college friend, Christina (Donogh Rees), a pretentious intellectual and literary groupie, to an interview with a writer, Colin (William Zappa), in Rotorua in the North Island. The car spins off the road and overturns – and Lane leaves Christina crushed beneath it as she proceeds to Colin's. There, within days, she has seduced him – she continues to toy with his emotions – and captivates his adolescent daughter, Angela (Caitlin Bossley), who finally conspires with the invalided Christina to kill the predator. The prickings of conscience come too late to rescue Lane from an ending reminiscent of that in *Black Narcissus*.

Maclean, who previously directed three shorts, including the auspicious *Kitchen Sink*, is at the forefront of a fresh wave of women film-makers from Australia and New Zealand, among them Jane Campion, Jackie McKimmie, Ann Turner, Solrun Hoass, Kathy Mueller, Susan Dermody, and Bridget Ikin, producer of both *Crush* and Campion's *An Angel at My Table*. Before *Crush* was screened at Cannes last year, Maclean had already been approached about possible employment by Disney in America. It could be a volatile mix: a director with a dark take on the downside of Americanization working at the home of theme-park Americana.

20   Alison Maclean

GRAHAM FULLER: *Tell me how the screenplay of* Crush *evolved. Did you start with a particular image or with the character of Lane?*

ALISON MACLEAN: Lane was the starting point. I wanted to do a film that dealt with a strong, complex female anti-hero, because that kind of character has always fascinated me: one of those *femmes fatales* whose sexuality is destabilizing and threatening to everyone around her – the kind who eats men for breakfast. But Lane interested me as someone who could be equally seductive to women – or, in this case, to a young girl. She has her own moral code. She's someone who doesn't put the usual kinds of limits on herself, who doesn't seem to care what other people think of her, or worry about the consequences of her actions. You may judge her for that, but I can't help admiring the daring that goes with that kind of self-confidence. When I was a teenager, it was always the bad girls I admired, because they dared to do the things I could never do. Sometimes I used to think of niceness as a kind of yoke around my neck – something I'd never be able to remove.

So I started with this character, and the mentor relationship Lane develops with the young girl, Angela. I had been thinking about this kind of thing for a while, trying to find a story that looked at the intensity of that kind of teenage infatuation with someone worldly and sophisticated and fearless. I've had certain women like that in my life, who constantly made me think, 'What would *she* do now? What would she wear, or say, or do?' It's about the influence of someone who can change your sense of self overnight through the sheer force of their personality.

GF: *Was there an antecedent for Lane in literary or cinematic terms? When you say* femme fatale, *I immediately think of* film noir.

AM: *Film noir* or a film like *Pandora's Box*. I'm fascinated by a character like Lulu because you have *totally* ambivalent feelings towards her.

GF: *I wondered where Lane's darkness came from. It's rare to see a character who makes you constantly speculate about her history.*

AM: I deliberately kept it obscure. I wasn't interested in explaining why she is the way she is. She just *is*. But you get a sense of there being a history of carelessness that's finally catching up with her. It was more interesting to me not to flesh her out too much, and instead make her more of an enigmatic, allegorical figure. In some ways it's the classic stranger-rides-into-town-and-messes-up-the-family story.

GF: *As the film proceeded, I became increasingly aware that the clues to its meaning reside in that initial conversation in the car between Christina and Lane before the crash. As the cynical American driving like a crazy woman through the commercialized New Zealand landscape, Lane is like a symbol of American cultural imperialism.*

AM: I don't think that's too much of a stretch. I didn't want to make some heavy-handed statement, but it was always a part of the original idea that she had to be an American. I mean she couldn't be Scandinavian or anything.

She's American because the film's partly about what it means to be a very tiny country that's so easily seduced by the culture and wealth of America, and which then struggles to define itself in opposition to that. Sometimes as much as 80 per cent of our news here is American; not to mention television, music, fashion and the rest. It tends to swamp the indigenous culture.

GF: *Christina speaks of the writer Colin's 'neo-parochialism'. What's meant by that?*

AM: It's a term I invented. It's a bit tongue-in-cheek. When you first see Christina in the film, she is an intellectual, an academic, and I find it amusing the way academics invent words for things. What she's saying about Colin is that he is maintaining this disingenuous image of a regional, small-town writer. But there's something trite about it because he's more sophisticated than that. He comes from a big city.

GF: *Is he a generic New Zealand writer, or did you have someone specific in mind?*

AM: He's actually an amalgamation of certain people that I've met, more than a specific writer.

GF: *The film portrays New Zealand as a rather naïve new world with dark, elemental forces literally bubbling away underneath.*

AM: There's an expression we use – usually ironically – 'God's own country'. New Zealand is a sort of Paradise in a way; it's blessed with incredibly beautiful landscape and no natural predators or poisonous snakes. Christina talks about New Zealanders having an obsession with finding the worm in the apple, searching for the serpent, as if we're uncomfortable that it's all too perfect. And maybe there's a certain truth in it, but its also just academic speak.

Apart from the Maori and Polynesians, it's a very Anglo-Saxon country; clean and well-ordered with fairly Protestant values, but there are huge tensions under the surface. I often find New Zealand cities more frightening places to be in at night than much larger cities elsewhere. It's partly the absence of people on the streets, and partly a certain aggressiveness you can smell.

GF: *You convey this uneasy peace visually, through the geography and the weather. The sky is lowering, thunder seems imminent.*

AM: But it's very exaggerated. New Zealand's a lot sunnier than that. I was very lucky with the weather on the film. I was blessed with many, many days of pouring rain, fog and wind. It became a joke with the crew that we had dry weather cover, and every time it was sunny, we'd be shooting inside. Most days we were out in the driving rain, and I was very happy.

GF: *You shot the film in Rotorua in the centre of New Zealand's geothermal activity. The terrain of the film is a mixture of geysers, lush green vegetation, and the New Zealand version of roadside, theme-park Americana.*

AM: I've always enjoyed going to Rotorua for winter holidays. It's a mad small town that's been developed and expanded for the tourist market, with great wide streets and a lot of half-empty international motels. It has a tacky side to it, but it's also a very strong Maori centre. As a Pakeha (white New Zealander), you only really have access to the tourist side of Maori culture, but you're always aware of a rich other life going on.

I was told by a scientist that it's a crazy place to build a town because it's totally unstable. You're aware of the constant pressure underground – there's a lot of steaming and hissing going on and the crust is very thin in places. It reminds me of New York, with clouds of steam escaping from the cracks in the road. It seemed like a perfect metaphor for what was happening to the characters. Did you get that it was a shot of boiling mud at the beginning?

GF: *Yes.*

AM: I love that stuff. I can watch it for hours.

GF: *It immediately makes you feel queasy because it's like sewage.*

AM: Yes, I know, and chocolate.

GF: *Getting back to what you said about Maori culture, one of your characters, Horse, the Maori nightclub singer who befriends Angela, struck me as a curious cultural hybrid.*

AM: Maybe. It's quite a complicated and at times volatile relationship between the two cultures. There's a lot of inequality, but at the same time there's a pride and autonomy in the Maori community that you don't find in the Aboriginal community, for example. The Maoris have a strong spiritual connection with the land that a lot of other New Zealanders envy. In *Crush* I wanted to show Maori culture through Pakeha eyes – so it's always coloured by that mixture of respect, fear, envy, and of course guilt – the guilt that's always present, that we've taken the land from them.

GF: *You've said that you've been influenced by Jane Bowles, and I wondered if Lane's ambivalent sexuality derived from that.*

AM: Possibly, but not consciously. I discovered Jane Bowles when I was writing the script, and she became a bit of an obsession for a while, especially after reading her biography. Her stories are deceptively non-eventful, but full of eccentric women who are often very impulsive and surprising. They're a strange mixture of the banal and the shocking and they have a wonderful drop-dead sense of humour.

GF: *The reason I ask is because there's an implication that Lane is bisexual. She causes the car crash when she takes her eyes off the road to look at an advertising mannequin of a girl in a bikini. You also hint at a sexual tension between Lane and Christina, something from their college days. Did you choose not to make that – or indeed any of the relationships in the film – explicit?*

AM: I thought it was more interesting not to spell it out. What happens to the characters has more to do with the pressures of the story than with any kind of baggage from the past. I get bored by the need in films to provide a psychological background story to explain people's behaviour. I wanted to keep a certain fable quality about it.

21 *Crush*: Lane (Marcia Gay Harden) and Angela (Caitlin Bossley) – tensions under the surface

GF: *But all fables and fairy tales are rooted in common unconscious experience. Crush could be regarded as a playing out of the Electra complex. When Lane usurps Angela's place in Colin's heart, so to speak, Angela plots to kill her.*

AM: I remember asking myself whether there was a female equivalent of the Oedipus complex. I didn't know it was called that, but I was aware of it.

GF: *Colin, the main male character, has the weakest personality. Is that because you sought to make him weak, or were you just more interested in Lane, Angela and Christina?*

AM: The women sort of wrote themselves, but I really struggled to bring Colin to life and put words into his mouth. I didn't want him to be the main motor of the story. It's complicated enough writing a script about four characters; if they're all actively pursuing their own agendas, it's almost impossible to get it to work as a story. Colin's more of a catalyst for what happens between the women. I didn't want people to think that any conflict between Lane and Christina was only about sexual jealousy – the two of them fighting over a man.

I did a directing workshop at the Sundance Institute and they cast a man to play Colin who had a stronger physical presence than the man I eventually cast in Australia. I found this actor really shifted the balance in the scenes between Lane and Colin. He took away some of Lane's power and I didn't want that.

GF: *Did you do a dry run for the film at Sundance?*

AM: Yes, I was able to work on two or three scenes, put them down on video and try them in different ways. I'd already cast Marcia Gay Harden and she was there. One of the things we talked about afterwards was that Lane shouldn't give too much away. We had to resist the temptation to soften her or try to make her more sympathetic all the time. It was a great opportunity to experiment without the pressures of shooting film.

GF: *Did you make changes to the script after that?*

AM: Not fundamentally, but some of the lines changed. There were things that the actors came up with that week that I incorporated, or changed the way I directed the performances.

GF: *When you write do you have a schema?*

AM: I'm an obsessive planner and I'm always drawing diagrams. Structure's important to me but only as a backbone, a place to start. There's something quite natural about using the three-act structure, but it always gets distorted as I go along. I only really discovered what the story was about half-way through the second draft.

GF: *How did you go about designing the look of* Crush?

AM: We used Rotorua itself as a starting point – the dull greens and browns of the landscape and that bilious yellow of the sulphur that forms a crust on the ground. That and the faded primary colours of the old motels. There's a lot about the place that makes you feel you're back in the early seventies – and that became another key to the look of the film and the way Lane dresses. I like that sense that you're not quite sure what period you're in.

GF: *Do you have fixed ideas about composition?*

AM: It changes with each film. In *Crush*, I deliberately wanted to use longer takes and a wider frame; the camera steps back a little bit. I wanted the style to be simple but hallucinatory, though in a fairly unobtrusive way. I felt afterwards that perhaps I hadn't gone far enough, that I'd been too restrained. But I find it irritating when films strain for surrealism or bizarreness for its own sake.

GF: *Why are New Zealand and Australia producing so many women directors at the moment?*

AM: I think it has something to do with it being a young, small industry that's more flexible and perhaps less intimidating than the American or European equivalent, with all its tradition and hierarchies. Because it's a young culture, you have to invent your own stories, and you gain a lot of confidence from doing that.

There's very good support for women film-makers. I've never felt any barriers there in terms of having my films funded. The shortage of films by women directors at Cannes this year was really disappointing to me. Some of the most exciting, daring films I've seen over the last couple of years have come from black or gay film-makers and I wish there was an equivalent vitality among women directors. It seems we've got past that very politically correct stage of feminism, but haven't taken many leaps since then. There are exceptions of course, and maybe it's more a problem of visibility and distribution.

GF: *What are you working on next?*

AM: I'm doing an episode for a television series on the Seven Deadly Sins for ABC in Sydney. It'll be the first time I'll have worked with somebody else's script.

GF: *Which sin is yours?*

AM: Greed! After that I want to do something that's much less domestic and more visual – not relying on dialogue as much as I did in *Crush*. I'm interested in working with genre again, like I did with *Kitchen Sink*.

GF: *When did the title* Crush *come to you?*

AM: Fairly early on. At first I called it *Crash* till I discovered J. G. Ballard's book. *Crush* was a natural progression but I resisted it at first, because it's a word I've never really liked using. But I found as I went on that the story was growing into the title more and more. Eventually, that's what it seemed to be about – variations on a crush. The essence of a crush seems to be that adolescent state of semi-fantasized infatuation – a state that's often as unreal as it is intense, and can so easily flip the other way, into its opposite.

5 Freewheelin'
Gus Van Sant Converses with Derek Jarman

22 Gus Van Sant

23 Derek Jarman

Introduction   Gus Van Sant

I first met Derek Jarman in bed. He was lounging with Andreas looking as if they had had a satisfying evening amid smoking incense and large multi-coloured dildos. Andreas was my host at the Berlin Film Festival of 1986. Manfred Salzgeber, my festival programmer, could not pay my way from Portland, Oregon, to Berlin, but had promised to put us up in an hotel or with someone who worked at the Festival – in my case it was Andreas. I had come home late that night (and in Berlin 'late at night' usually meant about six in the morning) and I stood in the doorway in my winter coat talking about some of the films at the Festival. I remember talking about Wim Wender's *Paris, Texas*, which Derek didn't like much, but which was one of my favourite films.

It was the first film festival that I had ever attended as a film-maker and for me it was a great new experience. I had seen Derek around the Festival, because he was relatively high profile, and his name carried a lot of weight with the independent film-makers. Derek was an old festival pro by that time, and the way that he worked the press and used the event not only to show his work, but to have fun, was impressive. The Festival for me was a major drain on my energy because all of a sudden I was thrown into the role of salesman, and although this was my father's occupation, I had inherited few of the right techniques. So, with little attention on my film, I made posters and tried to get as many interviews as I could – about two or three. On the other hand, Derek was fighting off the press and didn't have to work so hard at promotion because *Caravaggio* was a British Film Institute film and he had many people promoting it for him. Derek Jarman was a symbol of the future, of what my life as a film-maker would someday resemble. He was breaking new ground as an openly gay film director, and his politics and lifestyle were exciting new things to behold.

I stayed at the Festival all ten days, and by the end my head was spinning from the accumulated baggage, from days of trying to get people to buy my film and getting nowhere, fast. Or was it slow . . .

When I get to a film festival now, it is more fun, because it is no longer my job to sell the film. For you young film-makers out there who attend film festivals and feel like the only way to get further in your career is to get the film sold – good luck. I was there once and it is hard. But, there is also a romance as a young struggling film-maker that no longer exists when you get more experienced and jaded. And then you finally find out that what matters is the film, and not the sale; that you can have fun at a festival, but ultimately you shouldn't take it too hard if your film is not well-received or noticed, or whether or not you make that sale that will put your film in the profit region.

The evidence of Derek's presence was everywhere. For one thing, he came with an entourage. This was also the first time that I had ever seen a real film entourage – sort of like an Andy Warhol entourage. There were five or six good-looking guys who wore long overcoats, and were having a good time in Berlin – at Derek's invitation, I suppose. Derek was very generous in that sense. He wanted the young people to have a good time, while he did his chores with the press and otherwise stayed relatively out of eyeshot, working on his projects in his hotel room.

After that one evening at Andreas' house, Derek and I took a taxi to the Festival at about eleven in the morning. As we rode, Derek talked about the decaying British school system and British politics. And at the end of the ride, he refused to take money from me for the cab ride, saying: 'But I don't need it, Gus.' I assumed that the British Film Institute was just laying so much money on Derek, that he really *didn't* need it. But more likely, he just knew where I was coming from as a young independent. He was very generous that way. He was a good guy. He was a gay guy. And everyone really liked him and looked up to him.

And now I am talking to him about his new movie. I am in Portland, Oregon and Derek is in Los Angeles, opening his new film, *Edward II*. By this time I have made two other films besides *Mala Noche*. And also by this time I have seen many Derek Jarman films, and have been influenced by them – particularly by his *Last of England*, which reminded me so much of the underground films that I grew up watching in New York at the Museum of Modern Art, or the Anthology Film Archives or at my art school, the Rhode Island School of Design.

GUS VAN SANT: *How are you?*

DEREK JARMAN: Good, good. Where are you?

GVS: *I'm up in Portland, Oregon. I came here to make* Mala Noche *and I ended up staying here. Do you know where Portland is?*

DJ: I've been through it – I came hitchhiking down the coast in 1964.

GVS: *Wow, those were good years up here. My next film is about a hitchhiker. Were you hitchhiking in the spirit of the sixties?*

DJ: Yes. It was a mixture of hitchhiking and Greyhound. I was very young at the time, and I was one of the few English kids that got here. I got to San Francisco, and as far as Big Sur, or someplace like that . . . and I went to the Hearst Castle. On the way back I picked up a lad on a motorcycle, and we went to a Joan Baez concert in Monterey. It was an anti-Goldwater concert and I ended up at this place called The Lab, on Cannery Row. Bob Dylan was there – he was well-known, but he wasn't well-known abroad. He came on at the end of the concert. It's quite strange to think about it now. But there you are – that's history.

GVS: *Did* Edward II *open last night?*

DJ: No, it didn't open, but we gave a screening at the lesbian and gay festival here – which was strangely middle-aged, Gus. I get the impression that the idea of a lesbian and gay festival has run its course, in an odd sort of way.

GVS: *Ten or fifteen years ago, there was more energy.*

DJ: I was quite surprised, there were very few young people there. They were all middle-aged, fairly well-heeled. They were a great audience, as it turned out. It was packed out, so does one need younger people there? But I did miss them. And I missed them at the Berlin Festival this time. Maybe I'm just very old now, Gus. Fifty. You know what I mean? Somehow you come in like pop-stars; you have your time; and then suddenly you're not . . .

GVS: *What happened at the Park City festival? Was that young or old?*

DJ: Park City was much younger. Much more free-wheelingly glamorous – that's what I thought. Everyone else was complaining like crazy about Park City – Jim Jarmush and all those sort of people who come from New York. But for me it was really quite fun – it was like going into an episode of *Twin Peaks*, or something. There was a mad lady who came to collect us in her miniskirt in sub-zero temperatures and a fur coat. Without being a deserter to the cause, I think that at this moment it's much more fun to take over an ordinary film festival. I'm certain I met you at the Berlin Film Festival.

GVS: *Yeah, we met there.*

DJ: Everyone met in Berlin. It was a sort of lesbian and gay film festival without actually having the title. And I feel that that's the way of the future.

Anyway, how are you? Are you filming at the moment?

GVS: *Well, I'm working on some still photographs that I've taken over the years – they're basically casting photographs. I've created a darkroom and I've been working in there, as well as planning a film for September. Working in the darkroom is very calming. It's like knitting. It's like doing your art, but you don't have to draw or anything. You just shine light on paper, and that's how you make the image.*

DJ: It's always a relief to get back to painting. I'm not trying to set up any films at the moment. I've got a space to exhibit my paintings, at the Manchester City Art Gallery in May. I've got half the show painted. I may have to sit in the art gallery to finish some of the work off – like an artist in residence. I'll paint them there – with the public watching!

GVS: *Good idea. So, I'll start asking questions. Are you satisfied with the ways of getting money in England to finance films?*

DJ: It's complicated. After I made *Sebastian* there was a real necessity for images. Even if they weren't the right images for a specific audience, they were still needed. I created my own world making 'gay films', or films that have that sort of subject matter. I've made a lot of films because there was the space to do so, but at the same time it was very difficult to achieve decent budgets. It's amazing that even now, whenever I make a film, it's with money that's left over from everyone else. *Edward II* was made for £800,000 – I suppose that's $1.2 million. And in the same year Isaac Julien, who's a great friend of mine, was making a first feature film for more like $2 million. Even though the cash is available to me, it's also kept at arm's length. I tried for a bit more money on *Edward*, which would have given me more time, but . . . there's always the big 'but'.

Also, quite a few film-makers of my generation came to Hollywood. It seemed to be natural for Stephen Frears, or whoever, to drift there. I realized very quickly in the early eighties that that wasn't an option for me. Still, I'm very happy that the few small films that I made were made. They seem to be quite coherent, they touch on a lot of different areas. So, I can't say that I'm unhappy or frustrated.

GVS: *Your films would have been very different if you had gone to Hollywood after* Jubilee.

DJ: No way could that have happened. I think *Jubilee* upset people too much. And there was *Sebastian* in the background. I could have moved to Hollywood, but I doubt whether I would have actually been working. It would have been something like what happened to Julien Temple. He seems to be making sporadic films that don't seem to catch fire, yet he is rather talented. You wonder whether he would have made more films – on lower budgets – if he'd stayed at home. I don't think I did the wrong thing by not coming, especially if one feels that cinema is international. In a way it's irrelevant where a film is made.

GVS: *Your films have dominated the Museum circuit in America – Minneapolis, Columbus . . .*

DJ: Yes, Minneapolis in particular. That's where the films have actually had their life. They've crept into the student curriculum – which is a life. And now they go on through video. I never really feel shut out. That has never worried me.

What's fascinating is that whenever a regime is liberalizing, I seem to arrive with my films – like in Moscow last year with *The Garden*. I'm certain that was the first official performance of a gay movie in the Soviet Union. And the same thing occurred years ago in Spain when Franco died; it just happened to be the moment we made *Sebastian*. It could never have been shown before, and it came into Spain at this really good moment. So, the films have always been travelling around.

GVS: *I have a hard time seeing the world – the gay world and the straight world – through political eyes. I'm always trying to just paint a portrait; I'm not necessarily trying to comment politically. Yet I'm one of the only gay film-makers that the political cause has, and I'm called upon to make statements that I'm unable to make. Do you find that?*

DJ: Yes. I'm endlessly called upon, and what I say is: look, a film is ninety minutes and you can't possibly put the whole of history and all the variations of sexuality into just ninety minutes. I suppose people expect this, that, or the other from an image-maker. I think you're very fortunate in working here because you can put your films into the present. It's very difficult to do that in Great Britain. If I were to make a film in the same area, you could be absolutely certain that American distributors would want to have it re-voiced. That's why there's a lack of films set in the present in Great Britain.

GVS: *Because of marketability?*

DJ: Yeah, marketability. My cross is to be stuck with history in a certain way. History – if it's Marlowe's *Edward II* – can be marketed; if I had written my own script about a situation like this, no way would it have been funded.

GVS: *The American audience wouldn't buy it?*

DJ: No. They've always wanted to re-voice British films. So there's that problem. I suppose I've become more political as the years have gone by. Although I was very aware of all the gay politics that was going on, it wasn't actually central to the way I was working. That changed, to a certain extent, with the pressures of HIV in the mid-eighties – suddenly things were pushed on to some sort of front line overnight. At that moment I decided to tell everyone what was happening to me. I have to say I made that decision for my own peace of mind, not for anyone else's. I thought I'd better have this out in public. I had no way of thinking through what was going to happen, since nothing like this had happened before. There were people in the same situation as me, but not publicly. So, I suddenly found myself on the front line.

GVS: *Did you know that the* National Enquirer *had you on the front page? The headline was: 'English film director has AIDS, with no regrets'.*

DJ: It's as if I was at the end of the march, and suddenly I've been pushed up to the front. The politicization of *Edward* came out of that, and, in a way, I would like to step back from it. It would be great to wake up and say, 'Actually, I had the virus, but it's gone' – and there I'd be back at the end of the march again. In the meantime, I have to say that all this demonstrating over the last year or two has been quite fun. There have been a lot of young friends, and it's been great marching along with someone like Jimmy Somerville, who is a delightful man. So, I've enjoyed that. And I really have to do my political homework, Gus. I've got people who I ring up, and I say, 'I'm going on television now; what's the information?' It's like having a sort of speech-writer.

GVS: *Like the President.*

DJ: Yeah, I'm like the President. I say: what sort of move should I make? And they brief me.

Being a political activist is a career in a sense. But for all of us outside making artworks of one sort or another, it's more complicated. That's what I like very much about your films – they drift. They drift in the way life drifts. I like the fact that you never quite know where you're going to end up. If you think about it, any one day in anyone's life is rather like that. Your films mirror life rather accurately – the way things slide in and out and around – much more than a more tightly structured drama. Particularly *My Own Private Idaho*. I really liked it very much. It was a breath of fresh air.

GVS: *Thanks. Getting back to* Edward II, *which is based on Christopher Marlowe's play, you have said that the play still aggravates people. Do you see Marlowe as an activist?*

DJ: Yes. I suppose that's applying a twentieth-century concept to another time, but there is no doubt that Marlowe was kicking against whatever the conventions were. He was an atheist – at a time when that was a capital offence! Although people weren't often hung for it, he could have been. And, in fact, he was murdered at the age of twenty-nine.

GVS: *Do you know how?*

DJ: Very unpleasantly in a pub in Deptford. He was stabbed with a knife through the eye. I think it was politics. He was involved with the secret service. There is a whole tradition of gay men in espionage in England. People like Anthony Blunt. I suspect they were always of great value because they didn't have wives and kids to leave behind; they could be pushed into the underworld. So, Marlowe was somehow involved with all this. But we don't really know for sure.

Certainly when you look at *Edward II* as a text it's an advance on anything else – apart from the Greek plays. It's remarkable. Now I know that some people have said: Derek just turned it into an agitprop film. Actually, I didn't. All I did was to state the fact that these two guys were not just buddies, they were also sleeping together. If that makes it an agitprop film, well it is; it should be.

The real-life Edward II met Gaveston when he was sixteen and Edward was fifteen. They lived together for about ten years before Isabella came on the scene for dynastic reasons. Edward and Gaveston did fall in love and even the chronicles of the time – though they were against Edward – admitted it; the monastic chronicles stated that Edward was 'inordinately fond of sodomy'. So, there's no doubt at all about the relationship.

The real Gaveston was not at all like the film Gaveston – or even Marlowe's Gaveston. He happened to be the best athlete there was; he was a good general. But he had a pretty vicious tongue. Because of the situation with Edward, he could poke fun at all those staid people around him. He didn't spare them. Of course, he didn't endear himself to them. Edward was handsome and good-looking. I'm certain that Steve Waddington looked exactly like Edward. I cast him to the historical descriptions of Edward, not Marlowe's descriptions.

GVS: *Are there paintings?*

DJ: There are no paintings, but there are verbal descriptions. He was an outdoor boy; he spent his time hedging and ditching and working in the fields. People thought this was extraordinary. He obviously liked working alongside his men. I can just see that – a sort of Walt Whitman complex. He had red hair, and was intelligent and bright and very good-looking. I think Steven looked like a solid young king. That's why I cast him. It would have been easy to put in someone with mannerisms, someone playing a 'gay' role. But I didn't want him to do that. I just wanted him to look like a regular lad, really.

And that's exactly what you've been doing as well.

GVS: *I'm always playing with that. In* My Own Private Idaho *there was a great opportunity with Scott (the Keanu Reeves character) – this rich kid hanging around the streets. It might have worked well, and would have probably been much more realistic, if it had been played effeminately. We were considering it – and I regret we didn't try it – but in the end we played him straight.*

DJ: It does come up in your film, doesn't it? – Scott's Dad says, 'My son is very effeminate'.

GVS: *He does say that. But it's from the play (Shakespeare's* Henry IV*) and I think the character Scott's Dad is based on is referring to his son's youth, not his sexual orientation. It's that concept of the word 'effeminate'.*

DJ: It's interesting that the one criticism I received last night was from a young man in a dress. He was elegant, actually; I really liked him. He said: 'It would be great if there were characters in dresses; if all your men weren't as straight as they are.' So I said, 'Well, point taken. I'll remember that. If I make a film where it seems that should be the way it should go, I'll remember.'

It seems to me that among my generation there was a drive to make gay characters look straight or normal and not like Quentin Crisp; not effeminate or fey. Maybe that time is over and actually one should go back to that.

So, I said to this lad, 'There's space for other people to make these images'. That's what I say to people: if you disagree with the way I've imaged the world, then you must get down and do it yourself. Young kids keep on saying, 'How do you make films?' Well, you just go out and make them. Make a video tape.

GVS: *Yeah, it's so cheap now.*

DJ: You almost can't believe how cheap it is.

GVS: *For hours and hours of footage.*

DJ: Yes. If I could shut my eyes, I'd have a break from film now, for two or three years, and come up with something completely different. And make one of your films!

GVS: *Well, I was going to ask you about formats. When I saw your film,* The Last of England, *I was really blown away. It was just before I made* Drugstore Cowboy *and I thought: if I could only loosen the camera up and be as free as this film. What are your thoughts about the visual freedom of* The Last of England *as opposed to the constraints in a 35mm film like* Edward II*?*

DJ: There is a conflict, and it seems to me to be unbridgeable. You could only bridge it if you were in the Soviet Union, say, and you were Tarkovsky and they gave you a year to make a 35mm film. The pressures that we're under don't allow that kind of film-making in 35mm. It's always been a problem. My

24 *My Own Private Idaho*: River Phoenix and Keanu Reeves

25 *Edward II*: Steven Waddington and Andrew Tiernan

feeling was that with both *The Garden* and *The Last of England* I had gotten to the point I couldn't have loosened up that method of working with the Super-8 camera any more. In a way, it was done ... finished and done. So, when *Edward* came along I thought, I'm going to go for a really tight narrative, take a look over my shoulder at their faces and light them beautifully. It seemed to be the way to go.

Because of the pressures of funding, my films remained – except for the Super-8 ones – in the studio, almost ghettoized in their own visualization. It would be great to take the camera out. I would give anything to do that, to be able to get out of this sort of art ghetto that's been imposed on me, to get out with a 35mm camera, and freewheel! The wonderful thing about the Super-8 camera was that it was just hanging around ready to be used, and there are those non-narrative moments in *Idaho* – with the salmon coming up, and things like that – where it really works.

At the time of *The Last of England*, I suppose I was just telling everyone I was fed up with narrative – you know: this is much more intelligent. But then, suddenly, narrative comes back and you have to grapple with it.

GVS: *It's a format question.*

DJ: It is, really. So, I don't think it's either/or. It would be great if we could combine them both. To a certain extent that's what you've done. The great thing about film is that it carries on. I like the fact that these influences are happening. In the sixties, the influences on me were American underground cinema. No one went to see the Hollywood product. If you were an art student in the sixties, you were interested in seeing Stan Brakhage, or Michael Snow, Warhol, Bailey, Anger. All of that gang. My films came out of that – not out of whatever might have been happening in mainstream cinema. I didn't go to it and I didn't have a television until about seven years ago. Leaving home in 1960 was throwing the television away. My parting shot was: what are we going to do, watch television? So I missed everything: the space launching, the assassinations. It was great, because it made space for other things. There are too many images crashing around. In the end one has to be selective. You can't see everything.

And out of that came *The Last of England*. In my mind I haven't entirely jettisoned the Super-8 camera, although I think I'll probably work in video and transfer it. Making *The Garden* seemed to take two years and there was never any money. There were huge pressures. We would do a Super-8 shoot now and again – quite formally – and it would take months to get just a bit of money for that, to get everyone there, and the day would arrive and it would be raining. That's why in *The Garden* I used all the film lights; there was no other way that it was going to work.

So I found it a relief to do something as easy as *Edward*. It really was easy once we decided on who the characters were and we built the set. They came in in the morning, we set up our various camera moves, they went into make-up, and that was it – it wasn't a problem. In a sense it makes the film-making less interesting. There were no surprises. Not like when you're working with very low budgets. The day you say you want to have sunlight is the day you have the biggest thunderstorm in the last twenty years. You've just got to accept it. That's the thing I discovered: you just have to use whatever is there. You can write something, or have an idea – but, actually, when you come to the day it's completely different. So you have to seize the opportunity and go for it. I think that's the interesting thing about this sort of film-making – you jettison your blueprint on the spur of the moment. And if you are sufficiently in control of it you can do anything: you've got a tragedy but you make it into comedy, or the comedy goes the other way.

GVS: *One of the great things about being in control of a situation is letting go of control.*

DJ: And it's very frightening. I didn't let go in *Edward II*, of course. That was the opposite.

GVS: Thanksgiving Prayer, *a short film I made with William Burroughs, which is playing in front of* Edward II, *is very influenced by your way of making a film.*

DJ: I thought *Thanksgiving Prayer* was wonderful, and William's voice is one of the great voices of all time. Every time I hear him speak, I hang on every word.

GVS: *You did some things with him in '83?*

DJ: I filmed him. I made about twenty rolls of silent Super-8 film most of which, unfortunately, was just him talking, and I gave the film away. One reel I kept – a three-minute reel – and I made a little film out of it.

GVS: *Was that the* Pirate Tape?

DJ: Yes, that became the *Pirate Tape*. Did you ever meet Anthony Balch?

GVS: *I know the films he and Burroughs made together.*

DJ: Anthony was a great friend of mine. He died years ago. He was my introduction to Bill and *Naked Lunch*. Going back to when I was hitchhiking, back in 1964, all that sort of work was banned in England, and the real focus of my hitchhiking down the coast was to get to San Francisco to the City Lights bookshop to buy things like *Naked Lunch*. There was Ginsberg's poetry, and Michael McClure's, and all this stuff. And I came back with a thoroughly loaded rucksack on my back.

GVS: *Wow . . . Thanks for the interview, Derek.*

DJ: Thank you so much . . . and keep going.

6   Acting on Impulse:
An interview with Willem Dafoe
Graham Fuller

Introduction   Graham Fuller

Willem Dafoe is an actor of ambivalent extremes. I first interviewed him for an article in *Time Out* in 1987; looking back at it, I was struck by the number of clumsy oxymorons or dissonant expressions I'd used groping for a way to describe him: 'familiar malevolence', 'epic cheekbones', 'killer-angel', 'gargoyle beauty'. In the years since then, Dafoe's prolific screen work has built on that contradictoriness to the extent that you never quite know where you are with him. If other performers are content to fly on standard notions of Good and Evil – and sometimes we need that reassurance – Dafoe soars from a place located way above such moral absolutes. It's not a bad metaphor; he possesses the physiognomy of an eagle, played a jet bombadier over Vietnam in John Milius's hawkish *Flight of the Intruder* (1991), and can be dizzying to behold.

Dafoe's performances with the Wooster Group, the radical New York collective he has acted with for fourteen years, would be testament enough to his mistrust of dogmatic positions, but two films above the others he's made illustrate his divine mutability. As Segeant Elias in Oliver Stone's *Platoon* (1986), he protects the youngest grunts like a mother hen or even a solicitous lover: Stone has him blow dope down a gun barrel into new cherry Charlie Sheen's mouth. That's not surprising. Dafoe flirts with androgyny in his films and never subscribes to sexual sterotypes, but when the kindly Elias sets off alone, with a lopsided grin and his M-16, on a ferocious slaying mission among the NVA, you are reminded of the lethality that may lurk in gentle men. Dafoe, who was Oscar-nominated for his performance, was aware of the ambiguities at the time: 'Elias is a killer, but in this Rambo world everyone likes a killer as long as he's killing the right people. Someone once asked me, "Could you comment on the parallels between Elias and Jesus Christ?" and I said, "Wow, Elias is good man, but I don't recall Jesus blowing away the centurions before they hung him on the cross."'

The quote, of course, has a special resonance. In 1988 Dafoe realized perhaps the most religious screen incarnation of Jesus – ironically so, given the fundamentalist outrage surrounding the film's release – in Martin Scorsese's epochal *The Last Temptation of Christ* (1988). Dafoe's Christ was a questing, extemporizing man, riddled with self-doubt, dreamy but dogged, exactly the kind of conscientious messiah who might be tormented at the thought of forsaking *his* mission for the sake of Barbara Hershey's tattooed flesh and a good but futile mortal life. 'Uneasy lies the head that wears the crown of thorns' seemed to be the message of Dafoe's interpretation of Nikos Kazantzakis's Jesus; neither a Holman Hunt icon nor a De Mille monolith, still less a rad chic terrorist or an Elias on Golgotha. It was a towering achievement precisely because it made Christ sensual and frightened without being blasphemous.

Of possibly Flemish descent, Dafoe was born in Appleton, Wisconsin, in 1955, the son of a surgeon and a nurse, and the second youngest of eight. He dropped out of high school and the University of Wisconsin, travelled in Europe with Milwaukee's left-field collective, Theater X, and in 1978 joined up with the Wooster Group, initially as a carpenter and occasional actor, eventually becoming one of the seven core members, along with Spalding Gray, Ron Vawter, and artistic director Elizabeth LeCompte (Dafoe's partner and the mother of their son). Abstruse collages of live acting and video, the Wooster Group's performances push back the limits of theatre with ferocious glee, using such staples as Eugene O'Neill's *Long Day's Journey into Night* (in *Point Judith*), Arthur Miller's *The Crucible* (in *Just the High Points*), and Thornton Wilder's *Our Town* (in *The Road to Immortality*), as leaping off points for excoriating satires of social and moral dystopia. In the party scene central to *Route 1 & 9 (The Last Act)*, part one of *The Road to Immortality*, Dafoe and his colleagues – in fright wigs and black faces coursed with sweat – kicked, screamed, and sloshed beer on the stage in a frenzy of debauched minstrelsy; it was a spectacle that led to allegations of racism and the threat of slashed grants for the Wooster Group, which might have been more accurately credited with examining racial stereotypes and championing black cultural energy. 'You can interpret it of your own free will', says Dafoe. 'I think the pieces we do are strong enough to exist as an event. There's no stance – they're put together entirely as a pleasure or a curiosity.'

Dafoe has remained true to this local experimental theatre group while pursuing his career as a Hollywood movie actor, a duality that pundits often baulk at. He built his reputation playing perverse, ultra-cool villains: the taciturn, watchful leader of a rural motorcycle gang in *The Loveless* (1981); the savage, simian leader of a necropolitan motorcycle gang in *Streets of Fire* (1984); a psychopathic artist/forger in *To Live and Die in L.A.* (1985). After *Platoon*, he was back in 'Nam as an army MP tracking a prostitute killer in *Off Limits* (1988) and back in the world as a wheelchair-bound vet – a piratical cameo – in *Born on the Fourth of July* (1989). He was a by-the-book FBI man with a liberal conscience in *Mississippi Burning* (1988) and a white-stetsoned New Mexico sheriff in *White Sands* (1992) – goody-goody roles amid a Brueghelian tumult of fallen angels. He risked tactlessness, playing the Greek boxer at

Willem Dafoe: acting as alchemy

Auschwitz whose victories in the ring sentence his beaten opponents to death, in *Triumph of the Spirit* (1989); was goofy as a grinning prison warden in *Cry Baby* (1990); and memorably depraved as Bobby Peru, another Vietnam vet, with a taste for atrocity and verbal rape, in *Wild at Heart* (1990). Since his portrayal of drug delivery boy John LeTour – remarkable for its study of inertia – in *Light Sleeper* (1992), Dafoe has played a rape-trial lawyer, opposite Madonna, in *Body of Evidence* and appeared in the sequel to Wim Wenders's *Wings of Desire*.

In the following interview, which took place at the Wooster Group's Performing Garage headquarters in SoHo last March, Dafoe wrestles with the idea of acting as a craft but refuses to pin it to the canvas. It is said of fine actors that they often become their characters; it is truer to say of Willem Dafoe that, one by one, he *is* them.

GRAHAM FULLER: *What struck me most forcibly about your performance as John LeTour in* Light Sleeper *was the character's extreme passivity. Is it harder to play someone who is so passive than someone who is more dynamic?*
WILLEM DAFOE: I think that the stronger your actions are, the more fluid you are emotionally, because you're engaging your body in a physical way that allows your mind to follow. And there's something pleasant about that. I was aware of the difficulty of LeTour being very passive, because it's easy to confuse passivity with dropping out.

One of the things that I think kept LeTour active, at least in his head, what kept him from dropping out or losing energy or just imploding, was the fact that he was always looking for some sort of connection, like you often find with people who are a little unbalanced (although he himself isn't unbalanced). He is intently watching everything to find a through-line, to find a sign, to find something that will lead somewhere, something that can become fact, something he can attach himself to. Passive as he is, and though he's a voyeur – someone who serves people but has no life himself – he is still going towards something.

I can only say this in retrospect. The irony is, here we are talking about the craft of acting, and I don't think I'm an actor with a lot of craft. That's not false modesty, because I think craft is like a language or system that some people use to be interpreters or to convey something, whereas I am much more interested in just *being* the thing itself, in *inhabiting* worlds and having stuff *happen* to me.

I never think I have anything to convey. In the purest impulses – I say 'pure', although in the process of making a role you'll use whatever you can – I always seem to just want to *do* the things, have people watch me, and then, in the doing, stuff happens. In that process, a character is revealed. In *Light Sleeper*, I am John LeTour as revealed through those particular circumstances.
GF: *What's the fount of that stuff you discover? Where does it come from? Is it the unconscious?*

WD: I think so. I am interested in that, in what we can't articulate, can't design. The beauty of the creative thing is putting yourself in a place to receive the story. And you're really using your life as the raw material.

GF: *Your own life?*

WD: I think so. I mean, what your being is. Because I can't imagine being anything else. Quite simply, I look up at the screen. Who else is that? That's me.

Now, you can do whatever it takes to give you the authority to start the pretending, and that's a very important thing. I will research a role just like an actor who believes a great deal in craft, and believes that he can actually make some sort of transformation, without investing *him*self in it, you know, through observation and mimicry and his understanding of psychology. But I will only research something to get me to the place where I feel the authority to pretend. I do that particularly when I have a profession or something in a film, where it's necessary to do things with a certain ease, as if it's second nature. I think that helps you enter the story better.

GF: *Are you fastidious about research? Do you immerse yourself in background material for months?*

WD: It depends. Each time out, your function in a film is different. There are different kinds of film. The kind of reality you're trying to create depends on how the film functions.

I research in order to consider certain things. It's not necessarily an accumulation of knowledge. It's a collection of questions and curiosities that put you in a state that's approximate to the state of the person in the story. That's one aspect; the other is that I love to apply myself to researching real specific hands-on things.

GF: *You mean physical things?*

WD: Yes. They're very important. If, before I'm fully aware of it, I get comfortable doing things my body isn't normally used to doing, I find that I have created a new life for myself in a funny sort of way, just as an extreme look that you create for a character says 'mask', and through a mask you can discover things that you don't normally find out. When you look in a mirror, you don't recognize yourself, and looking different makes you feel differently.

GF: *Can you give me a specific example?*

WD: No, keep me off the specifics! Because, you know, this stuff is pretty theoretical. I can think of a direct contradiction to *everything* I say about performing, the second it's out of my mouth – that's the beauty of it. Not only are things forever shifting, but you're constantly dealing with direct opposites. You've always got a split focus that is absolutely contradictory. You're aware, but you're unaware, for example.

GF: *In* White Sands, *you play a modern-day sheriff in the American Southwest. Is that kind of role something you can slip into much more readily than, say, Jesus Christ in* The Last Temptation of Christ *or Salamo Arouch in* Triumph of the Spirit*: characters that, on paper, carry a much greater humanitarian burden?*

WD: Well, I could make the assumption that, yes, I could be this guy. You start off from a very simple place.

GF: *What did you do to get into the mood for* White Sands*?*

WD: I drove with some sheriffs in New Mexico, if for no other reason than it was fun. It may have been totally useless as research, but I'd never done anything like that and at least you come away from it with some detail that's useful. There's always little details that you surround yourself with; you're making the fiction part of your life and part of the story of the film. I like that – it's like alchemy! But it's also a contradiction: you're trying to put yourself in a place where you're receptive to the story, but at the same time you're making yourself comfortable by accumulating things that make you feel different from what you normally do.

GF: *Do you ever enter fully into the consciousness of the character you're playing?*

WD: The characters are all me, as revealed through the story. That's the way I always see it. And as soon as the story, the thing that supports the character, disappears, that character recedes back into me.

GF: *Does it ever take over from you?*

WD: No. It's a facet of me that is supported by whoever I am. It's supported by these legs, it's supported by these arms, it's read through this voice.

GF: *I'm trying to avoid making the question a cliché, but do you ever get . . .*

WD: Do I get lost in the character?

GF: *Yes.*

WD: No. Let's put it this way: part of the impulse, the desire to submit yourself to these fictional constructions, *is* a desire to be revealed in some way, a desire to have what are truly self-revelatory moments. Now, is that losing myself in the character or is that losing myself in *myself*? In any case, it approaches that blissful state of seeing or feeling in a new way.

But it's all an aspect of me, so it's an impossibility to get lost. You may have certain thoughts that you normally don't have, but those thoughts come about because an environment has been created that suggests those thoughts to you, or you *will* yourself into a certain frame of mind.

GF: *Can it therefore come equally from aspects about yourself that you don't like as much as from your good qualities?*

WD: It can be good things and bad things, or things that find their articulation in a different arena. The exhilaration that you sometimes feel when you're afforded different feelings from those you normally have, or different thinking patterns, is quite extraordinary. If I really want to stick my neck out, it's a feeling of being a medium – a sense of being a facilitator for something that's in the air. In film particularly, and somewhat in theatre, it's so collaborative that you get confused about where things start anyway.

GF: *When you get the feel for a character, do you become dogmatic about the need to bring it out?*

WD: No.

GF: *Do you fight with your directors over interpretation?*

WD: No. The biggest fight is not to get ahead of yourself. And the other big fight is not to decide on things, because you don't have to. You don't make a shopping list of places that you want to go, and then go there. Performing is all about the getting there; it's not about arriving. It's about the process of moving towards something. And this is one of those great contradictions: you have some idea where it is, but you don't know exactly what it is. I think that's what gives a character air and danger and possibility, rather than a kind of determined slogging to get to a certain point.

GF: *But what about working with directors who might see your character differently from you?*

WD: I haven't encountered that. I must intuitively pick people who know why they're coming after me. If someone wanted me to be more dogmatic, I think they'd find that I'm not as vital that way, and they will tend to re-think their own thoughts.

GF: *Because otherwise they won't be getting what they want from you anyway?*

WD: I don't know. You'd have to talk to the directors that I've worked with about that. I just have very strong instincts, and the best thing a director can do is create a world for me to enter and inhabit, and to keep me on track – that's all. My best relationships with directors have generally been ... very light touches.

GF: *Was that your experience with Paul Schrader?*

WD: Very much so. In fact, two weeks into *Light Sleeper*, he made a big deal about pulling me aside and saying, 'Look, I don't talk to you much. Don't worry. Everything is fine. I don't want to mess it up. You know this character better than I do.' Which seemed like an impossibility, because he wrote it. But the world he created was so specific – its detail was incredible. It was so free of stereotypes. From the beginning, you knew what LeTour would dress like, what the guy eats, what hours he stays up. You knew his old girlfriend, the people that he's been around for years, what books are on his bookshelf. There was a great wealth of stuff for me to consider, to help me inhabit that world. Once I was in that world, it was just about Paul watching me to make sure I stayed in it.

GF: *Do you ever feel you take wrong turns? For example, when you do a take do you know when something is not going right and you have to correct it?*

WD: Sure. Usually, when you feel something is wrong, it's because you're trying to serve something other than the story. You've gotten sidetracked. You're serving your vanity or a preconceived notion. You have an agenda. It feels bad because something feels violated then; you feel like a guy that's up on the soapbox, or a guy that's just dressing up to get love or admiration. Those *are* all parts of performing, but to think about it in those terms on a conscious level humiliates me. But if I think about it in a different way, performance is a very noble thing to do.

GF: *I once asked you if you liked seeing yourself on screen, and you said, 'Frankly, yes. It titillates me'. Do you still feel that?*

WD: I do. But it is also a pleasure because of the *distance* I have on it. Film is mediated by so many hands. When I put something out there, these other hands turn it into something else, so I can appreciate it anew. Film-making remains very mysterious and curious to me. I like it part as home movie, part as something that jogs my memory, and part because I'm intersted in the power of film and the power of collage. I have my personal memory of going into it, my personal memory of the event, and awareness of what happened after the event. And then there is this thing, this very concrete thing, this light on the screen, that's all tied to that. That whole process is pretty fascinating.

Let's put it this way. What I'm hinting at, and I think maybe what *you* were hinting at, is this: I don't feel embarrassed or vain looking at myself and enjoying it. Because it is me, but it's not me.

GF: *Some actors say 'I never look at rushes' or 'I hate seeing myself on screen'.*

WD: I don't look at rushes, but for a different reason. I don't want to react to myself, I don't want to start to shape a performance. I am still too much in love with the inarticulateness of the process! I like the blindness of putting something out there not knowing fully what it is. I also think it's important for your relationship with the director to say at some point, 'Hey, this is where my part of the game stops' – unless you're going to be involved in the editing.

GF: *Are there film performances you've done that you don't like?*

WD: Oh, absolutely.

GF: *Can you talk about them?*

WD: I don't want to talk specifically about them, because that's always struck me as being a face-saver. And sometimes the performances you don't like, other people like a great deal, and vice versa. There're lots of different ways to look at movies and I'm never sure what's a good movie and what's a bad movie. But when I'm disappointed about something, it's usually because it was a grind to make, or because I wasn't engaged in that special way that I like to be. Maybe it was clumsily handled in post-production or your co-workers disappointed you in not being rigorous or good-humoured enough, or in treating people badly. It could be a million things.

You judge the process of making a film as much as you judge the result. People ask me what is the hardest role I've done. 'Was it Jesus?' [*The Last Temptation of Christ*]. No, it wasn't Jesus, because I enjoyed that. My pistons were firing correctly, I was working with people that I admired, and we were all moving towards something. The hard ones are the ones that break down, where people are there for the wrong reasons and misunderstand each other, and nothing is really happening.

GF: *Was* Platoon *memorable, then, because of the gruelling conditions under which it was made in the Philippines?*

WD: Absolutely. It appealed to my sense of adventure, which is very important for me. I don't think I can do a film if that kind of little-boy desire isn't served.

GF: *What is your recollection of shooting* Triumph of the Spirit *at Auschwitz? Was it weird to go into the belly of the beast?*

WD: It was very strange. What went on there in the past is so far beyond our experience that you can't pretend to understand it. I get a little hesitant about saying how I felt about it out of respect to what went on before.

You are flirting with ghosts. You are flirting with something in the air, with demons that have been locked away. Even though the circumstances are very different, you are going through motions that eerily mimic what went on in the past, and I think that gets under your skin. When you're standing in formation outside the barracks, you cannot deny that fifty years earlier someone was standing in that same place, and now you're play-acting that. It's a very queasy, odd thing.

GF: *Do you ever question the morality of projects you get involved with?*

WD: Yes, all the time. But I think you've got to trust yourself instinctively. I'm not concerned with meaning. I don't know what stuff *means*. I just know I'm interested in making beautiful things and having something happen to me on stage in front of people or recorded by a camera. Personally, I do worry about the morality of a project, but, at the same time, I find myself going towards what makes me curious, and sometimes those curious things can backfire and do things you didn't intend them to. A perfect example, I think, is an action film I made that I thought was a very risky movie.

GF: Flight of the Intruder?

WD: Yes. As it was proposed to me, as I read it, it seemed like a very stark movie about these guys flying around in these machines, told to do these things. There was a queasy disconnection between what they actually did and the destruction it caused. Cause and effect had totally broken down, and I thought that that was a very modern idea of warfare. That, plus the fact that they're up in the air, was one of the reasons I wanted to do the film. I asked myself what it represented politically. At first it seemed like a sabre-rattler. But then I thought, 'No, I don't think it is.'

When it was first shown, it was too stark for the studio, and they warmed it up with some camaraderie and the kind of stuff those 1940s–1950s army films are made of. But I don't think it jogged well with the other material and, generally, it was perceived as a flag-waving, right-wing movie! People were quite puzzled why I did it. And even when I explain the film in these terms, friends look at me and say, 'Come on, don't give me that shit! You're justifying your involvement in it in retrospect.'

To answer your question, yes, I worry about the effect something might have. But, on the other hand, as an actor, I can't be too worried with what a movie is saying or I feel paralysed. I assume that people will have a different relationship to the material than I do, and they'll see things that I don't see.

GF: *What different things do you bring to working with the Wooster Group?*

WD: What we do here at the Performing Garage is pretty cinematic, in live performance as well as on video. The material is built through collage and juxtaposing things. It's not unlike film acting in that it has a dual focus. It's very dense, very designed. You've got an obligation to link up with video, to hit certain lights, to orchestrate your voice with the music. You're like a DJ up there on stage. You're mixing lots of different tracks, and you are just one of those tracks.

It's not like most theatre acting where people control their own rhythms. Here, you control your own internal rhythms, but there are so many structures outside of you that you have to link up with, then drop out from and link up with again. You're not really making your own rhythms – so it is like film acting.

For me, basically it's an abstraction until there's an audience, and whenever I start to feel the face of an audience, I don't like it. Some people get a terrific amount of energy from the audience's energy, and I respect that. It's sometimes what makes great theatre performances. But I prefer to keep it abstract.

GF: *So for you it remains a private experience?*

WD: It is. And, the truth is, the Wooster Group taught me how to perform for film. And film taught me how to perform for the Wooster Group.

GF: *How did working for film help your work as an actor here?*

WD: The thing that's very specific about what goes on here – it's a very simple notion but once you say it, it gets complex – is you learn the difference between *doing* and *showing*. I have learned to enjoy the doing much more than the showing. I think that's helpful for film, because you do want it to be a private world. You want to make a reality that this camera is peeping in on. No matter what the style of the film is, there's no way you can really play to a camera. Even in direct address, you're not playing to the inside of the camera – you're playing to four feet in front of you. You're dealing with the concrete reality that's with you.

GF: *In choosing different film roles, do you have an agenda?*

WD: I'm sure I do. I try to pretend I don't. I look at a script and I say, 'Do I want to do these things? Is this world interesting to me? Does it make me curious?' The things that I get most excited about, and I would say this is ninety-nine per cent of the time, I *need* to do. There's that kind of hunch, that kind of intuitive bite, that really gets you going.

27   The Wooster Group: Peyton Smith and Willem Dafoe in *Brace Up!*

GF: *Do you get obsessive about it?*

WD: Not specifically about a character, but I get obsessive about performing because, after all, it is accelerated living. I am still tickled to death to go on to a set. I am almost suspicious of it, that it's still so strong. It's exciting. It's always an adventure. Lots of stuff happens – stuff that I can't control, but which I am at the centre of.

GF: *You once used the word 'voodoo'. . .*

WD: The funny part is, approaching roles, performing, this process of getting up in front of a camera or people, and doing these things which I've been doing since I was eighteen years old – I'm sure there are patterns that get catalogued in your head, making you gravitate towards certain things. But I resist identifying what those things are because it would make it harder to remain open. It becomes a grind if you have to manipulate your image or your career for a certain effect. Then it loses its sweetness, its silly possibility.

GF: *Is there a danger that if you get too close to the source that it will dry up?*

WD: I don't know. I yearn to understand it as a craft, but it's an impossibility. So those secrets are safe with me, because I'll never be able to crack 'em. Often you run into actors who can tell you quite systematically how they approach something. I can't. As long as I can keep on working and feel like I am fully engaged, that I'm answering a calling, that's all I ask for. I don't need to make systems.

GF: *Somewhere out there, the media and the public and people like me have a kind of perceived image of you, an iconography based on a set of performances.*

WD: Yeah, what is that?

GF: *It's probably the fallen angel or a gentle Mephistopheles. In* Platoon, *your death as Sergeant Elias, arms outstretched in a cross, has a Christ-like supplication. Then you were Scorsese's Jesus. You must have picked up on certain symbolism like that. What do you think?*

WD: When I hear words like 'angel', 'Christ', 'fallen', 'Mephistopheles' – it's all about struggle and longing and giving-over. I believe in submission and I believe in serving the story, or serving a director's vision, because I am not an interpreter – I want to *be* the thing itself. So whether it's my personality or the kind of performing I am attracted to that results in these kinds of things, I don't know. One thing I've learned here is that submission, the act of giving over, is a great relief; it can put you on the road to new logic and new possibilities. I'm not saying I do it – *ever* – but that's what I aspire to.

GF: *Is there any role you're yearning to do?*

WD: Not really, because I'd have to picture it. I know there are certain things that I'd like to do, and there are properties that I'd like to see turned into movies. But I am not one of these guys who says, 'I'll die if I don't play Thomas Jefferson or Hamlet'. I don't think like that.

GF: *You must have the clout to get movies made, though.*

WD: But I am somewhat limited in what kind of movies they can be. I have two projects with the Wooster Group right now that I can't get funded because I'm insistent on having Elizabeth [Le Compte] direct them – partly because of that and partly because of the subject matter. One of them is about Jackson Pollock's mistress, and the perspective of the film is very much through her eyes. It drives people nuts, because if they want a film on Jackson Pollock, they want a goddam biopic!

GF: *Do you want to direct?*

WD: No, it's not my personality. It's too much responsibility, and I think you *do* have to feel compelled to express something. Me, I still like that pleasure of having the proposition of going somewhere, but not being quite sure where it is. A director has got to be concerned about the end of a story, and he's got to structure everything to get him there.

GF: *So you like being in a position where anything can come off at any time?*

WD: Well, that sounds a little *too* free. I distrust the basic idea that if you do *this*, it will get you *that*. I don't think that's a very creative proposition, to have something designed for a certain effect.

GF: *In acting?*

WD: In life as well. Of course, the most important thing is to be able to maintain a position where you can do things that interest you, and so sometimes, career-wise, I have been aware of that: if I do this, it will get me that. But you can get in trouble that way, because then your life is a series of depressing deals that robs you of any romantic notions.

GF: *One final question – and it's kind of an embarrassing one . . .*

WD: Uh-oh.

GF: *What about stardom? Do you think about that?*

WD: Sure!

GF: *Do you like being a movie star or is it a nuisance?*

WD: First of all . . . you're assuming that I'm going to be embarrassed. But this is a very complex, fascinating thing. This notion of stardom, of flirtation with stardom, of defining stardom, is relative. When you're young – you know, you're in the school play, and two or three people say you were great, and the school paper gives you a great review. If my memory serves me right, that doesn't feel terribly different than if you do a movie, lots of people see it, and you get a good review in *The New York Times*. Emotionally, it's the same thing. I'm not clear about it at all. But what are you curious about?

GF: *Well, some people allow the kudos to run away with them. How do you handle it?*

WD: I've seen ups and downs in my career. Nothing really dramatic; it's been pretty steady. But the truth is I'm always looking to the opposite side of it. When things are really going well, I get anxious about when they won't. When things are really going bad, I get an optimistic feeling about the future. It comes down to keeping your perspective and realizing there's a certain kind of consistency in your character that will stay the same, a consistency to your talent, a consistency to your intellectual prowess, your passion, or whatever. And the outside world is forever changing, so just hang on, and see it come towards you, see it run away from you, see it come towards you.

GF: *You seem to occupy a rarefied place, in that your stardom is a result of your acting.*

WD: I grew up in a very Puritan environment, and I got mixed signals, because, first of all, you were supposed to succeed, because work was a good thing. But the worst thing that you could ever do is hold yourself above other people. When I think of these things, there's a part of me that wants to be king, but there's another part of me that wants to be down with everybody. Somewhere, romantically, I look to the have-nots. The reason why I bring that up is that my life hasn't changed that much, and I continue to work here in the Performing Garage. I've got constant reminders that we're all in the same boat. I don't get an opportunity to believe my good press, even if I want to, because I've got too many people shaking me down. I am always reminded that great painters, great singers, great performers are often not rewarded. So there's a real humility, if you do get rewarded.

It's hard, because there's something too pat about me sitting here telling you that I'm interested in humility. After all, I am talking to you and we are treating this like I have something to say. So where is my humility? If I was really humble, I probably wouldn't give interviews. I think I'll forever feel like, somehow, I wandered into the film industry, and they don't really know that I wandered in. I always feel like an outsider. I don't mean that in a mean way – I generally get along very well on movie sets – but somehow Hollywood is very foreign to me. But then you're also conscious that outsiders eventually work themselves to the centre.

7 The Early Life of a Screenwriter II

Sidney Gilliat interviewed by Kevin Macdonald

Introduction   Kevin Macdonald

'This boy should go into films, George. Why, he might make as much as £10,000 a year!' Such was the advice that lead to Sidney Gilliat's first film job in 1928.

During the next decade the screenwriting duo Launder and Gilliat became synonymous with the most intelligent and witty writing in British films, scripting such classics as Hitchcock's *The Lady Vanishes* and Carol Reed's *Night Train to Munich*. In 1943 the pair turned to directing and founded their own production company, the aptly named Individual Pictures. Over the next thirty years they turned out one of the most varied and interesting – yet under-appreciated – bodies of work in British cinema: *Millions Like Us, I See A Dark Stranger, Rake's Progress, Blue Lagoon, State Secret, Only Two Can Play* and, of course, the universally popular *St Trinian's* series.

Gilliat's films are quintessentially British, drawing inspiration from what the writer-director calls 'the quirks and quiddities of the British character'. They consistently contradict the notion that the big screen and little England don't mix.

Now in his mid-eighties, Gilliat still lives in the thatched house in Wiltshire where he wrote many of his most successful scripts. Retired from films, he is working on a novel, and researching into Shakespeare's 'missing years' with volumes of facsimile documents open on a table. His love of precision, and impatience with all unsubstantiated generalizations, is apparent in the detail with which he seems to remember every day of his sixty-five years in the film business.

I   Beginnings

KEVIN MACDONALD: *Did you have a great interest in films as a boy?*

SIDNEY GILLIAT: That is an understatement. I was a devotee from the age of three or four, on my mother's knee. From about 1911 right through to the mid-twenties, I used to spend a lot of time with both sets of grandparents, who lived in what is now Greater Manchester. On my father's side they were mostly teachers, and were great film-goers because it was the new thing – and cheap. They particularly liked films adapted from well-known novels like *John Halifax, Gentleman* or *The Pickwick Papers*, or George Eliot's *Mr Gilfil's Love Story*, all of which I saw with them. I even remember *Pimple the Clown* and 'The Dramatic Describer' (a ham actor in front of the screen declaiming dialogue and describing action more or less simultaneously with the action on the screen behind him. This was unscrupulously advertised as WONDERFUL NEW INVENTION – TALKING PICTURES by our local cinema *c.* 1913. My mother asked for her money back.)

So I was brought up on films, initially as a sort of captive child audience. But at that time cinema was rather sneered at. After all the first films had been shown in 'penny gaffs'* and later mechanic's institutes, which had been built for the supposed educational benefit of the more skilled working class. The middle classes looked down on places like that and coined derogatory terms like 'flicks' and 'flea pits'.

KM: *Did your family look down on films?*

SG: No, I don't think so. The grandparents on my mother's side, who were less well off and lived in Manchester itself, were even more populist in their taste. They were not interested in literary adaptations at all. They went for Chaplin and Larry Semon, the Keystone Cops – but Chaplin in particular. I was taken to Chaplin from a very early age. I have the feeling that most of the people who looked down on it had pretensions and lived in the suburbs. If they went to the cinema they would do it surreptitiously, rather like buying fish and chips. Come to think of it, the two often went together!

KM: *So you became involved in the cinema yourself by a kind of natural progression?*

SG: Not at all. Largely by accident. My father, who was a journalist, left Manchester to work in London. By the mid-twenties he became Managing Editor of the *Evening Standard* and through that paper I would occasionally get tickets to the recently formed Film Society. I really had a passionate interest in films without the slightest thought of going into them. I became particularly devoted to the more avant-garde films, most of which at that time were French, German or occasionally Swedish; but it was always assumed that I would become a journalist like my father. In my boyhood he had given me some work experience on the *Standard*, the odd day as an office boy for the subs. Now, one of those subs was a man called Walter Mycroft and I got to know him slightly. He became the *Standard*'s film critic and correspondent – they were fairly casual about appointing film critics in those days. I don't recall what he was like as a critic, but he was certainly very good at picking up stories about stars and directors and he got to know a lot of cinema people.

---

* Penny gaffs were the earliest film theatres, often situated in derelict, insalubrious surrounds or in fair-ground tents.

KM: *And Mycroft introduced you to one of these people?*

SG: Not quite. I had been to see *The Iron Horse* – early John Ford, prior to his canonization – at my local cinema. When I got home I found Mycroft sitting there having coffee with my father. I don't think he had ever visited the house before. I burst in upon them and Mycroft, for polite conversation, said, 'I hear you've been to the cinema.' I said yes, and he asked me what I had seen, so I told him. 'Oh', he said, with a sort of 'tell me young man' attitude, 'What did you think of it?' Well, I had enjoyed it thoroughly and was about to tell him so, when I remembered that he had reviewed it rather adversely when it first came out. I was not trying to impress him – that didn't occur to me – but I didn't want to embarrass him and myself by giving a totally contrary opinion to his. So I said something lame like, 'I thought it lacked flair', or 'was wanting in panache'. He turned to my father – I remember his words – and said, 'This boy should go into films, George. Why, he might make as much as ten thousand a year.' My father looked startled, not to say incredulous. I felt partly gratified and partly guilty for my deception. (I have often wondered what would have happened had I told the truth. Would I have gone into films at all?)

Much to my surprise, my father turned to Mycroft and said: 'Would you like to take the boy with you?' It transpired that Mycroft had come to see my father because he hoped to be released from his *Evening Standard* contract to take up an offer he had had from The Gaumont Company to become a scenario editor. Before Mycroft could answer his question, my dear father turned back to me and said: 'Would you like to do it?' I had never thought for a moment of going into films. I don't know whether Father had Mycroft's compliment in mind or whether the mention of ten thousand a year occupied it exclusively, but I could read his thought: 'If Sidney goes into films I won't have to get him a job on Fleet Street.'

I looked at Mycroft. He nodded, feeling, no doubt, that it would be unwise to shake his head. I nodded too in a cramped sort of way. 'I don't mind if I do,' I said, or something similarly enthusiastic. In fact, I was absolutely terrified.

So it came about that Mycroft – who I forgot to say was a hunchback dwarf, and a man of exceptional courage in the circumstances – asked me to come along to a meeting he was going to have with Gareth Gundrey, who was Head of Production at Gaumont.

I wasn't mentally prepared – or prepared in any other way – and made a frightful mess of it. Gundrey was a tall man with grey hair, and an artificial leg which creaked a great deal. As soon as he saw me he took, not so much a dislike, as an extreme distaste to me. I don't know why, but that was the attitude of almost everyone I met in my first years in the film business. The interview lasted about five minutes. In desperation I offered to sweep the floors. The reply to any young men is always the same: 'I rather think we have someone to do that already!' Eventually, Mycroft interceded and Gundrey muttered something like, 'Well I suppose he could report on stories or something' (he almost said, 'Can you read?'). 'Do you think you could do a synopsis?' I said I could, but what of? He just waved me away and said, 'It doesn't matter, anything.' He then asked whether Mycroft would like to come up on the floor and see a film being shot, as he had to go off and see rushes. So, he walked off down the corridor with his leg creaking like mad and Mycroft took me up to the stage, where they were making a film called *Quinney's* with John Longdon, directed by Maurice Elvey.*

Elvey was dancing about a lot; he was a very literate person, but a great exhibitionist. 'Ah there you are Mycroft!' he boomed. 'Well, I think we've got a great picture here – great picture!' And there was John Longdon, about twenty-five at this time, playing Quinney at forty-five with all this make-up on, and that's just what he looked like: a 25-year-old playing a 45-year-old! As we went off the floor Mycroft said to me – I remember this vividly – 'I should take with a pinch of salt anything Elvey says.' Which proved true for the rest of my acquaintance with him!

KM: *So you started work with The Gaumont Company?*

SG: Oh no, it wasn't as simple as that. Over the next few days my father got me some of the review copies of books, and I wrote a few synopses for Gundrey. Then one evening Mycroft turned up at my father's house again. It turned out that Mycroft had got a better offer from Elstree, and he wanted the *Standard* to back him up in whatever excuse he'd have to offer for not taking up the Gaumont post. I suppose my father must have said, 'What about my son?' And Mycroft thought, 'Oh, my God! I've got to take the son too! Not again!' I was a bit of a bargaining chip. A few days later I got a message from Mycroft asking me to go along with him to Elstree. There was a press conference to discuss the studio's new programme – this was the end of 1927 – and he told me that I was to pretend to be a journalist. I must have looked the most unlikely member of the press ever, but down I went with them in a fleet of specially hired Daimlers.

No one took any notice of me all day, but I did meet Hitchcock – briefly. I spent about half an hour on the set of *The Farmer's Wife*. I remember well that the cameraman – Jack Cox – had the camera strapped to his chest and was crouching down about half height and walking down the stairs. It was supposed to be the viewpoint of the coffin of the farmer's wife who dies at the beginning of the film. This was an early Hitchcock, obviously inspired by the Germans. I was introduced to him, which didn't mean much. He was then 22 stone and twenty-eight years old.

At the end of the day I was given a lift home by Hitchcock in his Chrysler car

---

* Elvey was the most prolific and long-serving of British directors, churning out scores of mainly undistinguished films between his début in 1912 and retirement in 1957.

28 *The Farmer's Wife*: Alfred Hitchcock (seated table, left) with the cast

with Mycroft and the head of the studio, a man who rejoiced in the name of John Court Appleby Thorpe.

The next thing I heard from Mycroft was that Hitchcock thought he had a job for me – liaising between the cutting room and the floor. That meant absolutely nothing to me, except I suddenly saw myself tangled up in rolls of film and unable to get out – so I said, 'I'm very clumsy with my fingers.' Mycroft said, 'I don't think that will necessarily come into it!' Of course, looking back, Mycroft didn't have a clue either!

I should explain at this stage how British International Pictures and Elstree came into existence. It was a result of the new British quota regulations that were passed in 1927. They built this large, modern studio to make big British films on a par with the best of Hollywood. They thought that with the quota for domestic films legally fixed, and increasing every year, the future of British films was assured. They were deluding themselves of course, as we so often have.

On our first day at the studios Mycroft was as lost as me. Eventually Thorpe appeared and said, 'Have you seen your office?' Mycroft said no, and Thorpe took us to a gallery directly overlooking the main stage. (Everything was still silent of course, so you didn't have to have any sound-proofing.)

It was a tiny office with a desk, a notice board with nothing on it, a couple of desk chairs and a chair with arms that you couldn't really call an armchair. It turned out – much to Mycroft's chagrin – that no separate arrangements had been made for me and I had to sit at the other side of the same desk as him in this tiny office. I think Thorpe must have been a bit embarrassed because he shouted at me, 'Go and get a duster and clean up this desk!' That was my first job, and like a fool I said, 'Where do I find a duster?' He said, 'Use your *intinative*' – Thorpe was the absolute king of the malaprop. (The prize remark was after my time, when he'd been 'kicked upstairs'. He was making a film – *producing* it forsooth – and there was a scene with a Butler handing someone a letter and he stopped the scene and said, 'You can't do that! You can't 'ave the Butler *'anding* 'im a letter! Not in a 'ouse like this – take him out and give him a silver saliva!')

The only good thing about the office he gave us was that gallery overlooking the production floor. There could be as many as five films all in production at the same time down below and we could see everything that was going on. The different productions didn't have to bother much about each other, as long as they didn't get each other in the camera. There was always a great bustle going on, and there was usually some kind of music being played to help the artists. I remember watching Olga Tschechowa, who was in *Moulin Rouge*, emoting to the camera – looking right into it – with a string trio playing something heart-rending like 'Hearts and Flowers', to create the mood for her. Simultaneously Syd Chaplin was doing *A Little Bit of Fluff* about 20 yards away, with typical Keystone piano music . . . babababum . . . babababum! And, of course, they were never in the same key! Complete bedlam!

KM: *It sounds as though the studio was very cosmopolitan.*

SG: Very much so. All the best cameramen, except Jack Cox, were from Germany, usually UFA. Karl Freund* was photographing Dupont's *Moulin Rouge* at that time, and then there was Werner Brandes, a first class lighting man, and Theodor Sparkuhl.

It was really the most cosmopolitan period of British films – before sound came in. You could hear at least three languages all on the same stage. You would have an international cast, just as Hitchcock did in *Blackmail* – Anny Odra was Czech, didn't speak a word of English, and was playing a Cockney, but it didn't deter anybody. But when talkies came, within eighteen months to two years all that was lost. After that it was only bi-linguals and remakes of German pictures that were at all international.

Widdicombe Fair was one of the films that was being made during those first days. I remember looking down from the gallery and right below me was Charlie Chaplin visiting his brother Syd on the set of *A Little Bit of Fluff*. He was a very good comedian, Syd Chaplin. Look at *Charly's Aunt*, which he did as a silent film, or *The Better 'Ole*, which was directed by an old pal of mine Chuck Reisner, who was one of Charlie Chaplin's directors behind the camera [*The GoldRush*, *The Kid* etc.]. They were much better films technically than Charlie Chaplin's, because Charlie never learnt anything about technique.

KM: *If Syd Chaplin was so good, why didn't he carry on in films?*

SG: Syd was talented and efficient – a rare combination – but unfortunately some time after *A Little Bit of Fluff* there was an awful scandal over a girl whom he approached too enthusiastically in his dressing room, which led to a hurried departure for sunnier climes before charges could be brought. I don't think he was ever able to come back. That kind of episode was far from unknown at Elstree in those days, but it generally took a milder form.

KM: *Did the Continentals bring a degree of quality and artistry that was lacking in British film-makers?*

SG: Yes and no. The Continentals like Dupont tended to concentrate more on aesthetics and mood than on story. They wasted a tremendous amount of time just making the point that they were artists. Some of them had a marked lack of self-discipline. I'd often see the crew just standing about on *Moulin Rouge* and if you went down and asked them what was going on they'd say: 'Oh, Dupont didn't arrive on the set until ten o'clock and then decided he didn't like the wallpaper, so he asked us to change it and went away and hasn't come back yet.' He'd eventually return at about five o'clock and make everyone work until

* One of the great innovative cameramen, Freund photographed *Metropolis*, *The Last Laugh* and several of E. A. Dupont's films, among many others. He ended his days lighting the hit American TV show *I Love Lucy*.

two o'clock in the morning. That sort of thing happened only too often. So the director was, perhaps, not so much a god as the very devil. He was a law unto himself.

This sort of attitude was clearly allied to such things as Von Sternberg's wearing riding breeches, or the kind of scarf that cavalry men wore. English directors, on the other hand, generally favoured snap-brim hats or spats and tried, occasionally successfully, to look respectable.

KM: *Were the Continentals generally considered pretentious then?*

SG: Dupont was a damned good director, but he spent a lot of the time arranging delicate flowery or leafy things over his leading man, Jean Bradin, trying to get the shadows just right on his face – as if he was Garbo! *Moulin Rouge* was restored recently. Somebody told me they thought it quite a good film and I said, 'It can't be! I saw how it was filmed, it can't be! Even after the lapse of half a century!' Historically interesting, maybe. But I don't think Dupont could be called a *phoney*, since he did direct *Variety*, which I think is one of the classic German films. But I certainly felt there was a good deal of phoneyness about *Moulin Rouge*.

KM: *To get back to you. What were your duties at Elstree?*

SG: Initially, I didn't really have anything to do. I was Mycroft's assistant. I was given a few token tasks – making ridiculous lists of things for no apparent reason – and then one day I was told to go and join the reader's department. Up to that time there hadn't even been a reader's department. That Monday a woman called Mrs Boyd appeared on the scene and I was her first reader – except that she wouldn't let me read anything. At first all she would let me do was tie up parcels of the books which had to be sent back!

She eventually let me do the 'tripe pile'. It was enormous, and quite unsorted – a year's worth of unsolicited manuscripts. 'Do I write a synopsis?' I asked her, and she looked shocked. 'No, not a synopsis, just an idea of the plot.' When I said, 'What about a recommendation?' she looked as though I had said something indecent. 'No, no, no, don't do that.' In other words, I was excluded from expressing any opinion at all.

So there I was with this pile of absolutely unspeakable material. Most of it came either from mad clergymen or from illiterate, retired postmen. After a while I was able to single out the themes; reincarnation was a favourite (you could bet the clergymen would get up to that), generally in ancient Egypt – always something they knew nothing about!

KM: *What sort of status did the writers have at Elstree?*

SG: Most of the films, even the German ones that were made while I was there, didn't seem to have proper scripts – not complete scripts anyway. They were made up as they went along. On *Moulin Rouge* there was some sort of script and Mycroft tried to get me to go down on the floor and make sure they kept to it. You can imagine someone of my age saying, 'Look, it says here: "He jumps out of the window" and you have him going out of the door.' That wouldn't have gone down well! I was given the continuity sheets and had to go through them to see what departures had been made from the script. But that phase didn't last long!

KM: *Was there a writers' department?*

SG: Not exactly. There was no team of writers while I was there – that's the first ten months of 1928 – not until Monty Banks came in, followed by Tim Whelan, who was a good comedy writer. The only resident British writer I can remember was Eliot Stannard, a great character. He seemed to be writing or rewriting everything. If something went wrong on a picture, Stannard was called up – like Shakespeare would have been – and asked to come in and pep up the scene a bit.

KM: *When did you actually start contributing title cards to films?*

SG: I remember three or four films, including a dreadful one called *Toni* with Jack Buchanan. By that time Frank Launder had arrived on the scene, as had Val Valentine, and we all chipped in a few titles.

KM: *How did you go about writing titles? Did you write them after the film was made with a print in front of you?*

SG: If you were lucky. Often we'd be expected to write them without seeing a foot of the finished film. I remember on *Toni* I hadn't seen any of the film. But we had quite a lot of fun with them. I remember a couple of titles that appeared a stage later in my career. In *Red Pearls* we had a bad piece of continuity: you suddenly cut to a lavish party run by a shady financier called Gregory Marston, but there was no lead up to the party. Various titles were suggested to bridge the gap. The one that was finally used was: 'Whatever the state of Gregory Marston's finances, his champagne was undeniably sound!'

In general in those days far too many British films were standardized, full of stock characters. All of them seemed to have a big cabaret scene and the hunt met perpetually in front of the lord of the manor's mansion. A man must have been permanently employed to clean up after the horses! It all added up to built-in obsolescence.

KM: *So it was with good reason that the average cinema-goer preferred American films?*

SG: Oh, yes. No doubt about that. I think if one looks back at the whole period up to the beginning of the war, the truth of the matter was that you were only there because of the quota, which reached its extreme low point in the 'quota quickie'.* Some people thought that they were a good training ground, which may well have been true. Micky Powell made about twenty of them and really learned his trade that way.

KM: *All in all, you don't sound as though you were convinced by the output of Elstree.*

* Extremely low budget films often paid for by the foot, £1 per foot being the standard rate.

SG: Well, maybe I've been a little unfair to Elstree. I was always rude about it afterwards – mostly in private conversation. I think it was a pretty deplorable place and they later went into low-budget stuff no better than quota quickies. But it is true that in the first two years they didn't lack *enterprise*. And right up to the time of their big talkies like *Atlantic* [1929, E. A. Dupont], they did try. But when that failed, they brought their horns right in, I'm afraid, and they made little that was really notable afterwards.

KM: *Were you at Elstree when sound was introduced?*

SG: I left in November 1928, just as *Blackmail* was being filmed. It started as a silent and was changed into a talkie half-way through. What stays in my mind is how little people were talking about the introduction of sound in the studios. I, for one, maintained that talkies wouldn't come – an unfortunate prophecy! – because silent films had reached a stage where they really were, at their best, manifestations of art – like the Pabst picture, *The Love of Jeanne Ney* [1927, German], and many others. You felt film had now become respectable, had reached a high point of development both artistically and as entertainment. Talkies would only spoil the medium. I envisaged, very hazily, some kind of compromise emerging which would use music but would not necessarily use dialogue. And then it came with a bang. *The Jazz Singer*, of course, had been out in its part-talkie form even before I started my job, some time in 1927.

KM: *But did you feel at first that talkies were just a sort of gimmick?*

SG: Well, yes. People generally say that it was the second one, *The Singing Fool*, that actually started the revolution.

KM: *Did any of those early talkies convert you?*

SG: *The Singing Fool* didn't, not a bit. I hated the songs, but then I went to see, of all things, a film taken from a J. M. Barrie play called *The Doctor's Secret*, with Ruth Chatterton. Now it's totally forgotten. I suppose it had little merit, but it completely fascinated me because it was a complete thing on its own. The lighting was different from what you got on silent films because of the incandescent lamps, which they used because of the soundtrack, and that gave it a different look. I still felt that talkies had nothing to do with art, but did have something very immediate. The audience felt a part of a whole new medium. Looking back, it was probably like a photographed stage play, but when I came out of the cinema I said, 'Talkies are here and they're here to stay!' That totally forgotten film was the one that convinced me.

KM: *How did your co-workers at Elstree feel about it?*

SG: They had mixed opinions. But strangely it was spoken about as a theoretical subject rather than a practical one. Nobody really considered, in a level-headed way, how it was going to affect their job. What was going on in the top echelons I don't know, but I suppose they must have been preparing for the change-over in technology.

KM: *Many people have said that for several years talkies caused cinema to regress and that the camera virtually stopped moving – was that your experience?*

SG: I think that view is often exaggerated, but there was an element of that, which was entirely the fault of the sound men. Not only did they deprive the camera of movement, they also virtually prevented you from filming on location. When sound came in it was rather like people sitting in front of a temple in Egypt, or perhaps in Delphi, waiting for the oracle. They sat there waiting and out came someone in a white coat who talked such a tremendous amount of jargon with words like 'decibels' and 'high frequencies' and 'low frequencies' and words that are not commonly uttered in films: 'In order to achieve the maximum results we must cut off the top' or 'improve the bottom', or whatever. And the worshipper says, yes, yes, oh yes . . . and they built little temples called booths to which the camera was anchored and everyone was quite docile because this was a great new magic.

In November 1928 Thorpe finally got his way, and Gilliat was sacked from Elstree when a comment he made casually on the train back to London was overheard and reported by Thorpe's secretary. After spending a short period out of work, during which time he sold his first screen story ('to my and the public's great relief it was never made'), he joined Walter Forde at Nettleford studios working in a variety of capacities: assistant director, gagman, stuntman, actor and writer. In 1932 he had his first real screen credit – Rome Express, *one of the big hits of the year, starring Conrad Veidt. The casual direction of it gave him his first impetus towards directing. In 1934 he began his collaboration with Frank Launder and they soon earned a name as the best scriptwriting duo in Britain. In 1936, while under contract to Gainsborough, they wrote* The Lady Vanishes, *which was assigned a year later to Alfred Hitchcock.*

II   Working with Hitchcock

KM: *It seems to me that the most startling difference between the kind of films you were doing in the thirties and what you went on to do in the forties, is the depth of characterization. The thirties characters are often based on stereotype. Would you agree?*

SG: It's not so much that they were stereotypical, just that there wasn't a lot of characterization. But there are some obvious exceptions. Some comedies, like *The Libeled Lady* with Myrna Loy and William Powell, stand up very well. I saw it when it was first released and thought it was a fine comedy of its kind, but not to be taken seriously. I think that class of films stands up much better than more dramatic films because they don't really need characterization so much. You are dealing – if you like – in 'stereotypes', but they are a kind that you can play around with. *The Thin Man* (with the same pair) is a good example. The actors are able to give so much to the roles that, although they are not really characterized, you don't feel the lack of it. You might define

29   *The Lady Vanishes*: Michael Redgrave as an eccentric collector of folk tunes

30   *The Lady Vanishes*: Alfred Hitchcock with Caldicott (Naunton Wayne) and Charters (Basil Radford)

progress in that department as from (1) cardboard to (2) characteristics to (3) character.

KM: *In* The Lady Vanishes *you characterize very quickly, giving the characters a lot of interesting idiosyncracies in the opening scenes in the hotel.*

SG: Yes, that was one of the things we tried very hard to do. For instance, we invented the young man called Gilbert who wasn't in the book. We thought: 'We don't want an ordinary leading man, what can we do?' So, I thought of folk tunes.* At that time, it seemed to be wildly eccentric and perhaps a bit twee, whereas I don't think anyone would think twice about it now: it would be quite natural – someone going about collecting old tunes. But it's still really only phase (2) characteristics, not character.

That opening sequence was written much later than the original script; I wasn't free at the time, so Frank did most of it. Originally, I had written a much longer opening which took place on a lake steamer in the Balkans. I invented the Charters and Caldicott characters specifically for that scene, as parodies of the typical Englishman abroad, but we liked them so much that they ended up in the whole film – and then in several other films as well. Hitch wanted to do the whole thing in the studio, which was advisable, as by then it was winter, and someone thought of this idea of the avalanche holding up the train, so they are held in a hotel overnight. It was rather like jumping half a reel into the picture, in comparison to the original.

KM: *What exactly was the genesis of* The Lady Vanishes?

SG: The script was written in 1936, perhaps overlapping a week or two, into 1937. I started on it sometime in the latish summer here in his house. Frank joined me shortly after.

KM: *Who were you writing it for at that stage?*

SG: For an American director, Roy Neil, William Roy Neil or Roy William Neil, no one knows which! He was under contract to Gainsborough, through Edward Black, and he had one more picture to do. We only had one conference with him. I doubt whether he had ever read the subject. He certainly contributed nothing. We only had that one meeting, and then they sent this unit off to Yugoslavia and the production manager who was shooting it broke his ankle on the railway line, after which they managed to get themselves deported. All they had was a pretty terrible lake shot, for the scene I just mentioned. So, they decided to put it on the shelf and it wasn't made until nearly eighteen months later.

KM: *Did Hitchcock dig the subject up himself?*

SG: No, far from it. The history of that episode is rather interesting – quite different from what Spoto maintains. He says that Hitchcock had a new contract to fulfil at Gainsborough. The fact was – and Frank has confirmed

* In *The Lady Vanishes* Michael Redgrave plays an eccentric collector of central European folk tunes.

this – that he had two pictures still to run on his existing contract. They then brought in a policy of rigorous rationalization – redundancies without redundancy pay – and a lot of people went. Shepherds Bush, where Hitch had principally worked, was closed down. Hitch had made one of the pictures by that time, *Young and Innocent*. The Ostrer brothers who owned the outfit were, according to Frank, ready to settle Hitch's contract, pay him off and not make the last one. He was never regarded by the more commercial end of the business as particularly good box office. They told Ted Black this and he said, 'He's got one picture to do.' The Ostrers asked Black if Hitchcock had a suitable subject and Ted said, 'I think I have.' Hitch hadn't found one on his own, you see. He was working on one with Michael Hogan, but there was some doubt whether he would ever make it. And then Black took down *The Lady Vanishes* from the shelf. Hitch wanted to get away because he had another picture to do, which was *Jamaica Inn* with Mayflower, for Erich Pommer* and Charles Laughton, and then he had a contract lined up with Selznick.

KM: *That was already planned?*

SG: Yes. So I don't think he had all that much interest in *The Lady Vanishes*. He accepted it to finish his contract and went into production very quickly.

KM: *So you didn't have much contact with him during pre-production or during the production?*

SG: Well, I was working on *A Yank at Oxford* at another studio. I met him once or twice in the evening. Frank agreed some new scenes with Hitch – because Ted Black admired Hitch, they had decided to put a little extra in the budget, so they were able to extend the ending, which Frank rewrote. They also knocked off the opening, so, essentially, the parts that were 'authored' by Hitch were the beginning and the end. There were odd alterations in the middle, which Frank did with Hitch. Frank says I worked with them, but I didn't really; I spent perhaps one or two evenings, just agreeing things and talking the script over. I don't think I did any further rewriting.

KM: *Did Hitchcock always work closely on his scripts at this period?*

SG: Always – but, of course, much less so on that one, since it was already complete. Hitch, by the way, never wrote dialogue. But Hitch is a complex story in himself. He always had a very curious relationship with writers. Regrettably he was one of those – a little like Tony Hancock, but without the self-destructive impulse – who liked working with people, but didn't want them to take attention away from himself. So, he seldom or never took writing credit officially. He might be responsible for all sorts of things in the script, but he'd never take screen credit – to his credit. To his *discredit*, he would never

---

* An exile from Nazi Germany, Erich Pommer was the legendary producer of *The Cabinet of Dr Caligari*, *Dr Mabuse the Gambler*, *The Last Laugh*, *Variety*, *Metropolis* and *The Blue Angel*, among many others. He came to England in 1934 and in 1936 founded the production company Mayflower Pictures with Charles Laughton.

acknowledge the writer in any way outside that. What he gave with one hand, he took away with the other. With *The Lady Vanishes*, I think he simply regarded it as a picture to be gotten out of the way. He was quite interested in it, but not really committed. He then went on to make *Jamaica Inn*, and I was brought in to do what was supposedly a repair job because the censor in America had refused to allow a clergyman to be the villain, which is how it was in the original Daphne du Maurier novel. Before I came on the scene they had decided to make him a Cornish squire. As I said at the time, it was a great step down. In their position I would not have sent it to the censor. I would have gone ahead and made the film. It was most unlikely that they would have stopped it. As it was, we never got it right.

One day while we were working on the script at Hitch's flat, he said to me: 'I'm the only Englishman ever to have a double profile in the *New Yorker* – in two parts. And in it I am quoted as saying, "I always write 99.2 per cent of my scripts" and I want you to know that that doesn't apply to people like you and Frank, who I regard as real writers.' So I said: 'Well, thank you, Hitch.' But afterwards I thought: 'Well, poor old Charlie Bennett.' He was the author of the original *Blackmail* play, and on any showing Hitch couldn't have made it without him. He was also the credited screenwriter on *The Thirty-Nine Steps* and *The Man Who Knew Too Much*. Bennett was a personal friend, and a writer who worked with Hitch until the point where they both emigrated to America; he only wrote 0.8 per cent of all those scripts! So I was very guarded about it. When this article duly appeared Hitchcock gave me the copy to read. Then out came *The Lady Vanishes*, which from Hitch's point of view was a surprise hit. And first of all, Castlerosse in the *Sunday Express* quoted Hitchcock's 99.2 per cent remark. This was followed by the critic of the *Daily Express* – who quoted Castlerosse and applied it to *The Lady Vanishes*. So I said to Hitch, 'I think you ought to cover us over that.' And he said, 'It's not my fault.' And I said, 'I'm not saying it is your fault, but I'd be terribly grateful if you would correct it with regard to *The Lady Vanishes*.' He wouldn't do a thing.

Just after this we were at a sub-committee of the newly formed Screenwriters Association, which was convened to sort out relations with the press and deal with our own publicity. Jim Williams – a well-known screenwriter – was on the committee. He'd read the original script long before Hitch ever saw it, so when Hitch's claim was repeated in the *Daily Sketch* or whatever it was, he wrote a letter to that effect and saying that it should have been made clear that it was written by Frank and myself.

Hitchcock was much offended by this – even more so when Frank sent him a humorous telegram reading: 'I don't like OUR 0.8 per cent being belittled!' I went in to work with Hitch the next day – and when Hitch was embarrassed, or sometimes when he was acting a character, he would stand flat like this against the wall. He looked very odd and a bit sinister when he did it. He said,

'Frank has sent me a terrible letter.' And I said, 'It wasn't a letter, it was a telegram.' He was rather disconcerted and said, 'Well, he shouldn't have said things like that.' And I said, 'Well, Hitch, look at our position.'

Anyway, Hitch didn't realize that he had met his match! He responded, typically, by sending a series of telegrams to Frank from morn to dusk – you could send them any hour in those days. The first one read: 'My son Alf says the reference complained of was copied from a certain Viscount [Castlerosse], signed Emma Hitchcock.' (That *was* the name of his mother!) Two hours later another telegram arrived: 'My son Alf says that the statement made by a certain Viscount was copied from *Time Magazine* – Emma Hitchcock.' Then a third one arrived saying: 'My son Alf says that the reference in *Time* was copied from *The New Yorker* – Emma Hitchcock.' Frank rang me after the third and said, 'What do I do about this? Should I let it go or send him a civil telegram?' I said, 'I should send him a barbed one'. 'Right, I'll think about it,' says Frank. A few minutes later he rings me back and says, 'I've just sent Hitch this: "My son Frank says that he won't play with your son Alf any more because he's a big bully who steals all the marbles. Signed Ethel Launder."' Hitch pretended to be very insulted by that, but he was only getting what he asked for!

KM: *Do you subscribe to the theory that Hitchcock was emotionally underdeveloped, that he was really little more than a grown-up schoolboy?*

SG: Who knows? Psychiatrists have, to a large extent, to go by categories, and Hitch doesn't quite fit any of them. He was a very complex character, he was a very destructive character, destructive of other people. But he always had the pose of the inscrutable Buddha, which he liked to play up. He used to do a lot of that rather odd standing against the wall business when he was rehearsing certain scenes for the Laughton character in *Jamaica Inn*.

KM: *Did you have much to do with the creation of that character?*

SG: I think that was more or less common ground by the time I arrived. Hitch was fascinated by the idea of this man who would finger a beautiful piece of cambric, or silk, but would squirm with repulsion as soon as he saw the blood on it. It was a sort of elementary Jekyll and Hyde – a character who appears to be a dandy and an aesthete, but has a cold and monstrous side to him – and it worked. But then, of course, Charles Laughton had to get high-falutin' about it, had to be a character who was 'real'. (The truth about Charles Laughton as an actor is that he could be very fine indeed when he trusted his instinct, but as soon as he got a scene right by instinct – and knew it – he would then try to repeat it by intellect. Now his instinct was sounder than his intellect, but he distrusted the one and cultivated the other.) He was very fancy in the language that he used and at his instigation we got in J. B. Priestley, who wrote scenes more or less straight out of Ashden's *End of the 18th Century*, a famous source book, and completely ruined the end of the picture. If you see it on television now those sequences have been removed.

KM: *I've seen the ending in which Laughton jumps to his death from the mast of the ship.*

SG: Ah, yes, that was my ending, and one of my favourite lines; the Robert Newton character, Mr Trehearne, is looking up at him from the deck, and Laughton says, 'I shall be down to you before you are up to me, Mr Trehearne!' I liked that line! I think it had the right spirit! But originally it was preceded by a scene in which a deranged Laughton – in an enormous saloon on this small schooner – receives all the guests in his imagination: 'Ah, your grace, my dearest Georgina! AhhOhOhh!' I said at the time, when it appeared in the script, 'It's in the wrong place.' You cannot, after a chase, suddenly show a madman going through these demented performances. Anyway, by the time I'd seen it in the picture Hitch had left for America.

KM: *The version which I saw seemed to be surprisingly well structured considering what you are saying.*

SG: If Hitch hadn't had Laughton and Pommer in the background, we would have had a much more relaxed atmosphere. Between us we could have teased up a pretty good cinematic script. The trouble was that Laughton wanted the high-falutin'. He had no faith in me because he didn't know me; to Hitch he sometimes referred to me as: 'your damn writer'. This was because I objected to some things.

KM: *In spite of what you have said, Laughton did turn in a fascinating, macabre performance. I particularly enjoyed the decadent dining scene when the horse called Nancy is led into the house.*

SG: Well, that was one of the scenes that Priestley rewrote with period lines like 'Buzz the Madeira, Charles,' instead of 'Circulate the port!' He was good at that – yes, that was a tolerable scene. I wish I could remember who thought of the horse.

KM: *What was Hitchcock's view of the two films that you did with him?*

SG: *The Lady Vanishes* was a stop-gap for Hitch, a means for him to get rid of his contract. But with *Jamaica Inn* it was a loss of sympathy more than a loss of interest, due to his failing to get on with Pommer, and particularly Laughton. Lots of people panned *Jamaica Inn*, but no one's ever mentioned the real reason for its failure, which was that it started off with half the point of the leading character shorn off.

KM: *I would have thought that the darkness of the latter film, both literally and metaphorically, would have appealed to Hitchcock.*

SG: That's quite true, and with one or two exceptions I was relatively happy with the script – I wouldn't say with the dialogue, because I was still learning. But Laughton took the line that the thing was unrealistic, and said disdainfully, 'I have to feel that the character's feet are on the ground.' He had to feel the reality of it 'like the sweat in a whore's bed' – which I may say is nothing to do with *Jamaica Inn* whatsoever! He was a very pretentious man and therefore, in his own way, very insecure. I remember I had to meet Laughton and Pommer at a club after Laughton had been to an anti-Nazi meeting at the Albert Hall. He had spoken on the stage, as had a lot of other people. It was probably a week or two before Munich. He arrived with Pommer, apparently disturbed, and announced, 'I felt I had to do it, one must take the risk.' The risk he took was to speak on that platform. Well, presumably the real risk would be if the Nazis came over and won!

Well, Jack Priestley had many good points, many abilities, and many virtues, but a sense of reality was not among them. He was essentially a romanticist, and I couldn't see him adding sweat to any kind of bed. And he didn't! In fact, he added all the Regency romantic stuff, which would have been all right if it had been disciplined, but it wasn't. It's the old business of what I was saying about actors and Shakespeare: 'William, can't you write me a bit more here, I haven't got much to do ...' Laughton was exactly like that in the demented scene before he jumped from the mast.

KM: *Did Laughton actually write these extra scenes himself, or did he just suggest them?*

SG: He discussed ideas for scenes with Priestley, who wrote them for him. Priestley himself was very courteous to me and said, 'I've read the script. And I thought we had better have a brief discussion, because I don't want to tread on any toes. I like the script, it's just adding a bit of a Regency touch, you know, and a few things which I think are wrong. You've got a line, "I'll tell them off." That's a later remark, I think it's British army and much later, probably Indian Empire.' A perfectly reasonable criticism. At the same time he said to me, 'I don't want any credit other than what I do: additional dialogue. I don't want your credit.' Then, of course, Laughton wanted to give Priestley credit for more than that, just to use his name, I suspect. They had to ask my permission, because I was the designated screenwriter in the contract, and I simply replied that Mr Priestley himself had told me that he didn't want screenplay credit. I knew that if it got back to Priestley he would back me up.

KM: *Do you think that Hitchcock saw something of himself in the Laughton character?*

SG: Yes, there might be something in that. The sadistic element was certainly there. There was a character among the grotesque band of wreckers, whom Hitch invented, called Dandy. Well, he didn't so much invent him as create a part for a friend and actor he'd known and worked with called Edwin Greenwood, who was a writer, director and actor in his time and a wonderful wit. He was also a very strange-looking man with a long, long face and a very shiny bald head. And Hitch said, 'He's an ugly man Edwin, a nice man, but an ugly man. I can see him naked in this picture, or as near naked as we can get away with. I've got a nice idea: he's interested in clothes but you never see him in any so they call him Dandy.' A typical Hitch joke.

Now, when they came to do the scene, they had this big chute sending water down for the storm scene. This was in December. Previously Edwin, rather typically, had managed to contract a tropical disease without going any further east than Rome – he was a converted Catholic. They took him to the tropical medicines place and eventually cured him. He went into the film and he was there with very little on, on this biting December night. Hitch could easily have sent him home, as you didn't really see the individual characters in the middle of those rolling waves and wind machines; but Hitch went on shooting and poor Edwin went down with pneumonia and died shortly afterwards. I felt that could have been avoided and that Hitch was to blame for what happened.

KM: *Was* Jamaica Inn *your last association with Hitchcock?*

SG: Not quite. Hitch already had his contract with David O. Selznick, and he asked me to go with him to work on *Rebecca*, which was to be his first Hollywood film. During *Jamaica Inn* he'd shown me a cable he was sending to Selznick: 'I would like a writer called Gilliat to work on *Rebecca* with me.' I said, 'You can't send that. It makes me sound like the triangle player in your orchestra.' We rephrased it, so that I sounded a bit more independent. After Hitch had left for America I got an offer from Selznick, a measly offer, and I thought, 'It's hardly worth going to Hollywood for that.' So I cabled Hitch and told him and he cabled back saying: 'Don't bank on it, but think I can secure a better deal. Are you free for these dates?' I was really very reluctant. The war was on the horizon and I disagreed with Hitch over how the story should be constructed. In the book Rebecca herself never appears. That's the whole point. Well, Hitch wanted to have Rebecca in the film; he'd written a treatment with some Hollywood writer in which Rebecca was shown. I was totally against that. Anyway, I took the cable to Ted Black, who I was working for at Gainsborough, to ask his advice. He said, 'Stay and finish the script you're working on.' And I said to him: 'That's exactly the advice I wanted to hear.' So I sent a cable to Hitch saying, 'Sorry not available – studio won't release me.' And that was that, although Hitch didn't communicate with me for a long time afterwards.

Ironically enough, much later I learnt from Selznick's published memos that Selznick himself had agreed with me over the story. If I'd gone, I probably could have been Selznick's blue-eyed boy for a few months and maybe done rather well.

Instead of following Hitchcock to Hollywood, Gilliat stayed on in wartime London and solidified his writing partnership with Frank Launder. In the next couple of years they wrote more than half a dozen successful screenplays for Carol Reed and others, created a popular radio series, and had a West End comedy hit. Together they had also been founder members of the Screenwriters Association (now The Writer's Guild of Great Britain) in 1937, and took a very active role in forcing an agreement over screenwriting credits, and improving the standing of screenwriters in general. Having worked on A

Yank at Oxford *(1937)*, *on which more than twenty writers worked in London and Hollywood, Gilliat had seen the worst face of the profession. In 1942 they made their co-directional début, an eccentric Ministry of Information short,* Partners in Crime.

III   Directing in the Forties: The Golden Age

KM: *Was it by choice that you and Launder directed your first feature,* Millions Like Us, *together?*

SG: It had to do with our contracts. Either only one of us could direct or we could both do it. We decided to both have a go. Of course, we had both directed *Partners in Crime*, but that was a fairly easy job.

KM: *Did that work – directing together?*

SG: Not really, largely because I was terribly self-conscious and Frank was terribly unselfconscious so that before I could say anything, or before we could discuss it, he'd go and tell the actors what to do and I'd be left standing behind the camera. So I said to him, 'Frank, can we just have a chat beforehand and then we can decide who goes up and speaks to the actors. It looks ridiculous if you dart off and I come dashing up to your elbow to make sure you don't say anything I don't like.' But we never solved that problem because Frank would say, 'Yes, yes, good idea.' And then forget all about it. He was a great one for last-minute instructions. Many was the time when you saw Frank tip-toe on to the set with the camera running, whisper to the actor, and tip-toe out again. It didn't work because the actors would then see Frank come back to me, tell me what he had said and I would object to something that we hadn't discussed beforehand. Of course, the actors thought I was criticizing their performance.

KM: *Did you feel that you had had a good apprenticeship to become a director?*

SG: Up to a point – except relationships with actors, the actual direction of the actors, because I hadn't had Frank's experience in the theatre. And I was no great technician. In later life I'd have given almost anything to have served part of my apprenticeship in the cutting room.

KM: *Were you pleased with* Millions Like Us?

SG: Yes. Frank and I only had one serious quarrel that I can remember and that was about the sequence before the war started, the Brighton sequence. I think it is too long. Frank wasn't born in Brighton, but had spent most of his youth there, part of it in the Brighton Rep, and I think he had a terrible affection for the seaside. Originally that sequence was even longer than it is in the finished film. I always felt that it went into too much detail and incident instead of just establishing the family (what it was like then, the beaches, etc.) and then quickly coming to the outbreak of war. When it was shown at Cannes a couple of years ago it had a very good reception from people like Bertrand Tavernier, but the only criticism some people had was that it was slow off the mark.

KM: *But I liked the fact that the film isn't strictly plotted.*

31 *Millions Like Us*: before the war – on the road to Brighton

32 *Millions Like Us*: during the war – the factory

SG: Of course, it never was strictly plotted. We almost went to the length of eliminating plot – not quite, but nearly. Hence the 'cut off' nature of the end. We did think about that and came to the conclusion that it might not work but that bereavement is like that, the film cuts off where so many people were cut off. Terry Randall, who played the north country girl, lost her husband during shooting. Our production secretary also lost her fiancée during the run of the film. Both in the air force. It all had an unfortunate ring of truth.*

KM: *When you realized that you were going to get the opportunity to direct a film, did you think: now I can do the kind of stories that I want. Was it more personal?*

SG: Yes, I think we were conscious of breaking new ground in the kind of subject we were dealing with. As far as I know the only other example of a first feature at that time which had a working-class point of view was *Love on the Dole* – but that's a completely different sort of thing. You see we did an awful lot of research for *Millions Like Us*. It was originally meant to be wholly sponsored by the Ministry of Information. They had asked us to do something on the home front – the work in the factories, the woman's land army, that kind of thing. We travelled round the whole country – it was fascinating – but, of course, there was far too much material, so we had to narrow it down to one family and one factory. The factory was the real centre of the thing.

KM: *So it was a conscious decision to try and portray real people in everyday situations – the war for the average person?*

SG: Very much so. Everyday, Any-town. It was also important, of course, that it wasn't London. Up to that time the working classes – it's a horrible term – tended very much to be comic relief, or ancillaries. We felt that that class of family should be at the centre of it. They undoubtedly got the worst deal during the war. But, you know, it was difficult getting actors to play working-class characters. Very few of them were from that sort of background. Eric Portman, luckily, was a Yorkshireman from Halifax and he was a very solid actor. Then, of course, there was Gordon Jackson. He more or less played himself in the film. He says in the film that he worked in a solicitor's office – in real life he had been a draughtsman, which is why he hadn't been called up.

KM: *Having said that, doesn't it seem a little out of place to have Charters and Caldicott, your characters from* The Lady Vanishes, *appear in the film?*

SG: We were asked to put them in and we had no objection. Unfortunately Basil Radford, who played Charters, had gone into the army since *Night Train to Munich* [1940] and was so nervous when he came out that he couldn't get his lines out. I don't think they added much to the film, except that it gave us a chance to get some extra footage on crowded trains – that's part of the war we've all forgotten now – you couldn't get on a train with much hope of a seat!

---

* In *Millions Like Us* Gordon Jackson, newly married to Patricia Roc, is killed in an RAF raid. The film ends at a sing-song, with Patricia Roc trying to come to terms with his death.

33 *Millions Like Us*: the newly-weds – Gordon Jackson and Patricia Roc

34 *Millions Like Us*: Caldicott (Naunton Wayne) and Charters (Basil Radford) on the train

KM: *After* Millions Like Us *did you feel comfortable as a director? Did you plan to carry on?*

SG: I assumed I had to continue, so I was looking for subjects and it so happened that Val Valentine* came up with the next two that I did, *Waterloo Road* and *Rake's Progress*. Val was a remarkable character, he had been a song-plugger and subsequently a song writer before he came into films. He was a wonderful ideas man, but you had an awful job getting him to put anything on paper. He always told it better than he wrote it.

KM: Waterloo Road *was a big hit at the time, but it doesn't seem as successful artistically as* Millions Like Us.

SG: When it came to *Waterloo Road* I think I really lost confidence in the idea before I finished the script, and it was whittled down so much in the end that the film was about seven or eight minutes shorter than the minimum contractual length. Luckily no one ever noticed! In fact Gainsborough almost pulled the plug on it. Maurice Ostrer† and his toadies used to have a field day running our rough cuts and sniggering at them! *Waterloo Road* was my first film as solo director and I was very conscious of the fact that I was ignorant of some elementary points of direction, the camera set ups, not crossing eye-lines and what not. My cameraman, Arthur Crabtree, helped me a lot. When it was released, of course, the film broke records.

KM: *Your next two films were* Rake's Progress *and* I See a Dark Stranger, *which you co-wrote but which Frank Launder directed. The latter is more typical, being a comedy thriller.*

SG: We were great fans of *The Thin Man* series in the thirties and I think that was an influence. In *Seven Sinners* [1936], the first script we properly collaborated on, we imitated the style quite a lot. It wasn't well directed, but it's got some good things in it, some very good lines.

KM: *This type of thriller – one which has elements of comedy in it – is something that most people associate with Hitchcock.*

SG: People often say: 'That's quite Hitchcockian' or 'You've stolen it from Hitchcock.' Not so. It really came from German gothic cinema of the twenties. Hitch had worked in Germany, made his first film there and he had this gothic feeling – a rather nasty gothic feeling in his case. At that time I was very well versed in German cinema and I regarded Hitchcock's approach in *The Lodger* as 'poor man's UFA'. When I first saw it I thought, 'This is Germanic.' Frank didn't have as morbid a mind as I had, but we tended to be Germanic gothic when we came to thrillers (though lighter moments would keep breaking in – applying sudden shocks and that kind of thing, using deep shadows and

* Val Valentine (1898–1971), remembered as one of the great personalities of the British film industry in the thirties and forties, originated the stories of several Launder and Gilliat films and remained with them on a small retainer until his death.
† Head of Production at Gainsborough.

35 *I See a Dark Stranger*

pregnant camera angles. I had a great respect for German cinema.

KM: *How did you actually go about writing together?*

SG: We always talked the story over first. If we wanted to do a full treatment and it was a bulky affair, we would take it away in sections. We'd do an outline to roughly block out the story and then divide it up: 'I'll do the full treatment from A to B and you take B to C.' Then we'd pass them back to each other for revision. Once we'd started actual scripting we'd pass each sequence backwards and forwards and made the style uniform – which makes it pretty unreasonable when people say: 'Oh, that's where Sidney started and Frank left off.' Of course, there were characteristic phrases which he used, and others no doubt which I used, but by eliminating them you could make it reasonably uniform.

KM: *The German émigré Wolfgang Wilhelm also collaborated on* I See a Dark Stranger. *How did you all go about writing that?*

SG: The first stage was getting away and working quietly some place where there were no telephones – the Moorland Inn on Exmoor, near Linton. It was a rather bare sort of pub. We worked there for a few days, bicycling all over the place. We wrote in the mornings and evenings, but took the middle of the day off. And we did make quite a good progress. Wolfgang was always industrious and perhaps a bit prissy – I think he would have been more at home with the Aristotelian rules of drama! He used to say, quite rightly probably, 'You have a very good character here, an excellent character. You use her for one reel and then she's gone.' He didn't like our 'leapfrog' construction. After a time we went back to London and they used my house; I was writing *Rake's Progress* in a little alcove on the landing and they were working in the drawing room. After a time I decided to come down here to Wiltshire to finish *Rake's Progress* because the flying bombs were giving us a bit of a battering. Now, I must have worked on the script of *Dark Stranger*, since I recognize so many of the lines, but if you'd asked me before I saw the film at Cannes a couple of years ago, I would have said I hadn't done all that much.

KM: *Did you feel that you had developed a recognizable visual style by the time you came to direct* Rake's Progress?

SG: Well, I wouldn't say a visual style. A narrative style if you like.

KM: *What about the lighting?*

SG: Both *Rake's Progress* and *I See a Dark Stranger* were photographed by Wilkie Cooper. Some people have said that *Dark Stranger* was brilliantly photographed, had exactly the right atmosphere all the way through, but that the lighting of *Rake's Progress* had no particular character, that it would have been a better film had it had a more distinctive visual style. If you look at *Dark Stranger* as a cameraman you'd probably adopt the same approach as Wilkie Cooper, but if I was asked to approach *Rake's Progress*, now or any time, as a cameraman, I probably would have frowned a lot and said: 'What is the style for this film?' On reflection, I suppose it should really have had three or four different styles, according to the period and the subject matter. But I never thought of that.

KM: Dark Stranger *should obviously be dark and shadowy. As you said previously, the film was influenced by German gothic, so it would seem to demand a dark, expressionist style.*

SG: Yes. *Rake's Progress* is brightly lit on the whole, but it doesn't have a cohesive style. I think one of the troubles was that Wilkie didn't get much guidance on style from me because I was much more worried about the actors and the script than I was about the actual shape of the lighting. So between us we didn't give it enough character. I've also noticed that *Rake's Progress* does not reprint uniformly, it does not recreate the original quite in the same way as *Dark Stranger.* I don't know whether that's something to do with the original negative – it must be I suppose, because the others, like *Dark Stranger*, are of the same date.

KM: *Do you think that coming from a writer's background you were more preoccupied with dialogue and narrative than say, Powell and Lean, your peers at Independent Producers,* * *who both have reputations as visual stylists?*

SG: Well, I've never been anything like as good on the visual side as Mickey Powell, who perhaps arrived at that by his early stills training. He did it naturally. I think David Lean did it with a considerable amount of effort, but he had a wonderful sense when he finally got it right. I don't think I had that. I also have very poor visual recollection, so although I remember a face and every detail of a person's facial features, I remember much less about their clothes, or even the set that I've left at six o'clock in the evening. And when I have to remember it before I go to bed and I try to work out the shots, I get the dimensions wrong.

KM: *And consequently you concentrated on dialogue?*

SG: If you didn't concentrate on dialogue under the sound system we had with *Rake's Progress* you would have been in constant trouble because they had a system of 'favouring microphones' on toggle things. If they weren't absolutely on the actor at the right time they wouldn't get the line and they would tell you they had to retake it. Today it's easy: 'We'll just put the sound on afterwards if it isn't clear or do something with it to filter the offending part out' – but in those days you didn't know when your dubbing dates were and so you didn't know when you could post-sync or anything. You might have to wait six months. So you had to get it at the time. Consequently, the amount of attention that had to go on simply getting the dialogue on to the sound track

* Independent Producers was a loose amalgam of small, creatively autonomous production companies funded by J. Arthur Rank, comprising The Archers (Powell and Pressburger), Gabriel Pascal Productions, Individual Pictures (Launder and Gilliat), Cineguild (Lean, Ronald Neame and Anthony Havelock-Allen) and Wessex Productions (Ian Dalrymple).

was totally disproportionate. I saw boom operators on that picture write the dialogue on a piece of paper with the actors' names on it, pulling these wretched toggles and then complaining, 'We're off mike on one line', 'Why?' 'Oh, Rex coughed, and we moved over to get that. The cough wasn't written down.' It was the most impossible circumstances for an actor, especially a quick rehearser like Rex Harrison. He went off the boil quickly. Because you had out-of-date, defective or worn equipment during the war, all sorts of undesirable things happened.

KM: *Was there any real division between you and the more visually showy film-makers of the period?*

SG: Mickey Powell didn't see anything of *Rake's Progress* until the first night, but when he and Emeric saw it they said to me: 'Ah! It's a wonderful film!' I know that the David Lean group thought that it was uncinematic, a bit on the static side.

Looking at the picture now, funnily enough, I don't feel that. I think *Rake's Progress* may lack some visual high quality, which was partly a result of the equipment and the somewhat cramped studio where we shot it. But when I look at *Dark Stranger* – and I saw it only last autumn – it seems to me completely up-to-date visually and the dialogue stands up awfully well.

KM: *In our talks you have frequently referred to Shakespeare, Dickens, Thackeray. Do you feel that your films – particularly in the characterization – are carrying on a specifically English literary tradition, rather than a filmic one?*

SG: Some of my colleagues may have thought me a rather bookish character, but I don't think that applies to our films. Anyway, Frank Launder is decidedly not a literary-minded character! David Lean may have thought that we were too 'verbal', but he himself only handled one original story, everything was based on existing narrative (whereas nine of our first fifteen films as director–writers were originals written for the screen). And who were his mentors? Dickens and Coward! You can't get much more literary than that!

Colonel Kenway in *The Rake's Progress* was to some extent modelled on Thackeray's Colonel Newcome, but that was Val Valentine's conception. When I started in films I was most influenced by the German cinema of the twenties – though perhaps subconsciously in different ways by the Americans – and my early ideas were full of symbols and portents. I have, however, been a fairly omnivorous reader and ideas may well have been absorbed from the authors you mentioned. My opera libretto of *Our Man in Havana** was studded with Shakespearean references to a far greater extent than Graham Greene's book. Greene stated publicly that he 'infinitely preferred' my libretto to his own screenplay of it – not that that proved anything.

I rather think that, in common with colleagues like Hitchcock, William

---

* First performed at Sadler's Wells Theatre, July 1963. Music by Malcolm Williamson.

Rose, Balcon and Launder, I have been more influenced by what one might call the quirks and quiddities of British characters, exemplified, for instance, in remarks I heard during the London blitz when coming down here at the weekends by train. During the worst of the September 1940 blitz the most frequent topic appeared to be tomatoes – how the greenhouse remained intact with all its tomatoes still quietly ripening; or how all the glass had gone, but the fruit was still edible. This sort of thing is a long-standing British characteristic. Perhaps it is not so much the carrying on of a 'literary tradition' as a national liking for anti-climax (as in 'Master Shallow, I owe you a thousand pounds'). As a high percentage of our films were original work for the screen, we had more latitude than most to carry on such a tradition. In general, don't forget many of us were fighting to keep and put on the screen a British identity; fighting for years to keep a recognizable British head above the American flood. Nobody cares about that nowadays.

KM: *You don't feel then that the British character is somehow incompatible with film – as Truffaut notoriously remarked?*

SG: I am inclined to beg you to Truffaut me no more Truffauts. If all of Truffaut's films had been in English instead of French, and the same applied to their locations, would the critics think them as good? If you had ever been a pupil at the Lycée Français, you would certainly have been studying something called 'Civilization'. At first, no doubt, you would consider this was a study of the development of man throughout our globe, but you would be wrong. Civilization in the eyes of the French is a French affair and others barely intrude on the fringes. However, I know what Truffaut meant by what he said, and why he said it. The French have always had a more serious and adult approach to the cinema than we have had – but an astonishing amount of junk appeared in France that we never saw at all, and which was therefore never criticized in England. The French, too, were protected, by language as well as by the quota system, from the follies of making bad American imitations.

KM: *Now to get back to* Rake's Progress, *which we haven't really touched on. In many respects it is unlike a lot of your other work. It is not a thriller, or a straight comedy. I read recently in* Hitchcock–Truffaut *that Truffaut liked it a lot and thought it your best picture. And I have to say that I agree.*

SG: Are you sure that's what it said? Because I read the book and didn't notice anything complimentary. I remember reading the interview with Hitch because it touched upon *The Lady Vanishes* and it looked to me shrewdly slanted from Hitch's perspective. I don't remember how they introduced Hitch and myself, but Hitchcock said, 'Have you seen any of their other films?' And this I thought was indirectly saying: 'If you have, compare them to *The Lady Vanishes*, which I made!' Perhaps I'm being over-sensitive, but I knew my Hitchcock by then!

KM: *No, I didn't read it like that. I think he is quite complimentary about you and Frank.*

SG: I know he saw the film, though he boasted that he never saw other people's. Hitch never told me himself, but Selznick did. Selznick had seen it with Hitchcock. But as far as I can recollect Hitch never said a word to me about it. As for the Truffaut book, Joan Harrison said to me: 'Take it with a ton of salt!' And if any one knew Hitch, she did.

KM: *Well, whatever Hitchcock thought, it is an excellent film.*

SG: I felt much more committed to *Rake's Progress* than to anything I'd done, but at the same time I was terribly uncertain about it.

KM: *What do you mean?*

SG: It's the one that touches me most deeply, and so I suppose I know less about it in a way than any other of our pictures. I never quite grasped what its impact might be. When I see it, it often seems a different picture from what it was the time before.

KM: *That's the strength of a great film – that it changes with the times and keeps a certain ambiguity. It reflects the ambiguity of real life. It seems to me that Rex Harrison as Vivian gave his most emotionally true performance in* Rake's Progress. *That suavity he has normally blocks out any real emotion.*

SG: He'd never done anything like it before – or since, I believe – in films anyway. He said to me, over the death scene with his father, 'You'll have to help me, I've never done anything quite like this.' He wasn't arrogant about his performance – never. He could be terribly rude to other people, especially if they touched him. If you had to fix any apparatus on him he was abominably rude, but he was not arrogant as a performer. I said to him on that occasion: 'Let us do it for you. Just think it and don't do anything, don't focus on anything. That's why you don't know your father's died until the moment after it's happened.' And we just did that. There's a great deal of the Hollywood thing there, in the sense that a great deal of American acting is based on being relaxed, on not being theatrical – that's probably the origin of the Method, you know, to get away from standard stage performance.

KM: *I also think Godfrey Tearle is wonderful as the father – the terribly nice, totally unselfish father.*

SG: Yes, he's too nice – that's his problem. The awfully nice, awfully honourable gentleman, who is also awfully foolish ... like Colonel Newcome in Thackeray, in fact.

KM: *He always thinks the best of his son – no matter what.*

SG: Yes, whereas our instinct is that he really should have rejected him. Whenever I met Larry Olivier he never failed to mention that line when Godfrey Tearle is dying, as the result of an accident caused by the Rake, and Vivian is sitting there by his bedside. The father just looks at him and says, with the deepest concern, 'You've hurt your hand', and Vivian starts talking about something else and when he looks up his father is dead.

KM: *Yes, that moment is played just right – very low key.*

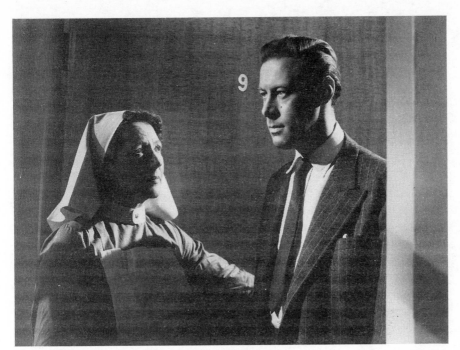

36 *Rake's Progress*: Rex Harrison at his father's deathbed

SG: Olivier said that every time he saw that, it moved him to tears. It affects me like that as well – always.

KM: *There is a great moral complexity about the film. You make the audience simultaneously like and admire the Rake, while showing him to be a callous, selfish man. There are no moral guidelines. The ambiguity of our feelings for the character is increased by the fact that we see his development, his growing up, and how he became a rake. We do not just encounter him fully formed.*

SG: One of the phrases that has been used about this picture at Cannes and everywhere else is: 'He redeems himself in the war.' Now this was something that I never even thought. He wasn't redeemed. He just did a job, that for once suited him; he liked it, it excited him. But I don't think he ever looked on himself as a hero and I tried to counter that with his last conscious act: drinking champagne that he never paid for!

There was never meant to be any justification for the character except perhaps that the circumstances before the war didn't suit him. They might have suited him fifty years before – and they surely wouldn't have suited him after the war – but *during* the war . . . that was the irony: he had to have a war to find something that he could do really well!

KM: *What was it that you captured in* Rake's Progress – *what makes it different from your other films?*

SG: Well, it affects my heart more. I can't explain why really. I suppose it must have been something real and true in the character's personality, however regrettable. It remains, I think, a one-off. Tavernier told me it was thirty or forty years ahead of its time. Though it was well received and very successful, I have always felt it's never had its due.

Launder and Gilliat carried on producing their 'Individual Pictures' for Rank until 1948. They then joined London Films where they remained until Korda's death and the dissolution of the company in 1956. Among the films they made there were State Secret, The Constant Husband, *and of course,* The Belles of St Trinian's, *the first of a series that was to make them household names: 'They were more Frank's cup of tea than mine . . . his schoolgirl daughter suggested the idea to him . . . I wouldn't like to be remembered just for* St Trinian's. *They were wonderful meal tickets for all concerned and fun to make, but people are always looking for easy labels and that irks.' During the late fifties and sixties both partners became closely involved in the running of British Lion, which Gilliat on the whole regrets: 'You couldn't run a company and do your own work; one had to go – and it was the wrong one.' One film which he did find time to make was the sublimely funny* Only Two Can Play *with Peter Sellers. For some years he unknowingly shared with David Lean a desire to film Conrad's* Nostromo: *'It would make a wonderful film – the greatest film, but it is very, very difficult.' In 1972 he directed* Endless Night, *a bizarre, dark murder story adapted from an untypical Agatha Christie. 'I felt very rusty getting back on the set, and I had a*

37 *Rake Progress*: the rake – before the war

38 *Rake's Progress*: the rake – during the war

perfectly horrible time – funnily enough back at my very first studio.' The final injustice
was discovering that the Italian translators had found a better title than his: Dopo i
funerali – Champagne! *(After the Funeral, Champagne!) He is now writing a novel*
– 'writers never retire, at least they never think *they do!'*

SG: What has changed about cinema over the years? I think one could argue
that the people have changed more than the cinema. If the cinema today is
holding a mirror up to nature, then that may well be so – in which case, God
help us all (see the remarks on cannibalism in *The Brothers Karamazov* – if we
must be literary!)

Looking back over sixty years or so, I often feel the most surprising thing in
movie development has been the virtually total lack of follow-up to René
Clair's use of music in, say, *Le Million* [1931], where Prosper's conscience
addresses him in song. I felt certain that a truly integrated use of music, a free
and natural employment of its uses and benefits, would have developed after
those early Clairs. But what have we had? Practically nothing. I always wanted
to try it, but never got off the ground. We are left with *Congress Dances* [1931,
Erik Clarell] (just possibly admirable), *Fantasia* [1940, Disney] (not really
relevant, perhaps, but a partial illustration) and what else? You can't count
musicals, which have their own standard limitations – and *Les Parapluies de
Cherbourg* [1964, Jaques Demy] is only what the botanists call a 'sport'. The
nearest approach to what I miss is perhaps *Trading Places* [1983, John Landis],
an original satirical comedy, using the complete overture to *Le Nozze di Figaro*
under the main titles and with many a subtle allusion to that score and libretto
on the soundtrack throughout the film (that is, if one knows the score). And
another piece of Mozartiana – *Amadeus* [1984, Milos Forman], of course, has
something of what I mean. But what one was really expecting and never got
was a truly original music–film. Any offers?

8   Altman on Altman
edited by Graham Fuller

Introduction   Graham Fuller

At a seminar on independent film-making held in the American Pavilion during last year's Cannes festival, Robert Altman sat like Sitting Bull at a lodge meeting of fiery young bucks. Emphatically non-idealistic about the vagaries of getting personal films made in a system hungry for homogenized product, he dispensed the kind of cold wisdom that enables an old warrior to survive many war counsels and innumerable wars: in Altman's case forty-five years in (and often out of) the American film industry. Each of Altman's fellow panellists – Stacy Cochran, Tim Robbins, Quentin Tarantino, and John Turturro – had come to Cannes with an impressive directorial début, but Altman had come with *The Player*, his twenty-eighth theatrical feature, a layered, densely allusive and beautifully crafted satire of the system in question, and the most entertaining and fêted American film of the year – you could call it Bob Altman's history lesson. Not bad for a 67-year-old director who, a few years ago, seemed destined to end his career in television, where he had spent his long apprenticeship in the fifties and sixties. That 'comeback' has now been cemented by Altman's filming of *Short Cuts*, adapted from a series of Raymond Carver stories.

If Altman had proved mercurial in the previous fifteen years, his place among the elders of American *auteurism* had already been assured by his work between 1970 and 1975, when he made *M*A*S*H*, *Brewster McCloud*, *McCabe and Mrs Miller*, *Images*, *The Long Goodbye*, *Thieves Like Us*, *California Split* and *Nashville*. This was the period when Altman developed his style of mock documentary realism, characterized by overlapping dialogue, improvisation, offhand irony, and those floaty zooms into dead space and the quick of life. Although he has drawn 'reality' into invented scenarios (think of the fake Haven Hamilton greeting the real Julie Christie in *Nashville* and then asking someone who she is), particularly in *Tanner '88* and *The Player*, it has been in filming the fictional as if it was the actual that Altman has consistently revealed the kinds of truths that have often eluded contemporaneous champions of *vérité* and hyper-realism.

The following interview is excerpted from two conversations I had with

39 Robert Altman

Robert Altman in 1992. The first took place in February at his Park Avenue office, the second in June at his Malibu beach house – a few miles up the coast from where Altman filmed Roger Wade (Sterling Hayden) walking dreamily to his death in the Pacific in *The Long Goodbye*.

GRAHAM FULLER: *Your first feature film,* The Delinquents *[1957], which is rarely seen, was shown on television last night. I watched it.*

ROBERT ALTMAN: You did? Oh Jesus, I don't think I'd have the courage to see it. It's pretty dreadful.

GF: *It's really a teen exploitation flick; certain scenes reminded me of* Rebel Without a Cause. *Was it simply an opportunity for you to direct a feature?*

RA: Oh, absolutely. That was all. I was living in Kansas City, doing the Calvin industrial films,* and I'm sure I would have done anything. A guy named Elmer Rhoden Jr, whose father owned a chain of theatres in the Midwest, hired me to do a film about juvenile delinquency. I wrote it in four to five days, staying up for two nights, drove the generator truck, and made the picture in twenty-two days or something like that. We had no money – I think the total budget was $63,000. I got paid $3,000. That whole coda at the end, warning parents about teenage delinquency, was added by somebody – I've no idea who. It was a weird experience.

Alfred Hitchcock loved the picture, and he wanted to put me under contract on the basis of it. I wasn't interested in that, but I did end up directing two Hitchcock half-hours.

GF: *Is it true that you refused to continue working on* Alfred Hitchcock Presents *because there was a script that you objected to?*

RA: Well, I did the first one – *The Young One* [1957] – which was Carol Lynley's first film. Then I did *Together* [1958], with Joseph Cotten. Then they gave me a third script, and I just thought it was bad. I went in to the producer and told her, 'This is no good. I can't do this, and I strongly advise that you don't do it because it won't work.' It turned out it was a script she had developed. That was the end. I was out of favour.

GF: *Were you confident that you would get a regular directing job in television?*

RA: I don't know if I *knew* I would, but at that time in your life you are pretty confident. I remember once I came out here and almost got a job directing the Groucho Marx TV show, *You Bet Your Life*. At one time I thought I was going to get a job directing *I Love Lucy*, but they found out very quickly that I didn't have enough experience. I would bring my industrial films with me, and I would show them to people. I carried projectors to parties and set up and generally imposed myself on people – I see myself in the young film-makers

---

* Altman worked on about 60 industrial films made by the Calvin Company of Kansas City, in the early 1950s. Many of them included dramatic sequences.

who bring their work to show me now. I don't think it was ever the quality of my films that got anybody's attention, but the persistence of this nudging. I did know a lot of technical stuff. I knew about the camera, about sound, and about editing.

On the industrials, we had to do everything, and when I began working in TV, I was able to work fast, and so they liked me. If we'd finish an episode at two o'clock, which we did many times, the crew would be put to work on another show, because they were on a full day's pay. The trick was to stay out almost all day, so we started doing reflection shots and all kinds of complicated stuff just to fill the day out. I did hours and hours of syndicated television – *The Whirlybirds* [1957–8], *US Marshal* [1957–8], *The Troubleshooters* [1959], *Sugarfoot* [1959–60]. *Bonanza* [1960–61] was the big time. I did Warner Brothers television, for which they paid only scale and was really the low-quality end, but I did it because they had a series over there called *The Roaring Twenties* [1960–61], and I really liked that. So I would go between *Bonanza* and *The Roaring Twenties*. Then I got *Combat* [1962–3] and started producing.

GF: *Were you frustrated during this period that you couldn't break into features?*

RA: Yes, but I was very content in my failure. I was not on the very top level of television directors, but I'd say I was on the second level. I was doing well and I was always totally enthused about everything I did. I would get into these projects and make mini-features out of them; I was copying features. I remember on one *Combat*, I said, 'OK, this is my *Foreign Intrigue* film.' On *Bonanza* I started them doing broad comedy in their second year.

Then I got a job at Universal as a producer–director and did an experimental film, *Nightmare in Chicago* [aka *Once Upon a Savage Night*, 1964], in Chicago. We shot the whole thing on the streets with natural light and high-speed film – that was new. Then I got fired – well, I resigned – and made a life-long enemy out of Lew Wasserman.

GF: *Do you think the improvisatory methods you later developed in features grew out of your long experience of rapid-fire, spontaneous TV work?*

RA: Everything you do today forms what you do tomorrow. In TV, I was working constantly with such dreadful scripts that I just found it was better to change them, or let the actors change them – at least make these ridiculous lines that they had to say more palatable.

GF: *You've favoured single takes, where possible, throughout your career.*

RA: I don't do a lot of takes usually. My approach to shooting, even today, is that you set up an event, you determine the perimeter of your arena, and then just shoot it. I never got into nitpicking about performances – I always felt they were better when they were a little raggedy and a little spontaneous and realistic. When I was doing *Whirlybirds*, I wouldn't even read the scripts. I had a great AD, Tommy Thompson, who eventually came back and worked with me from *Brewster McCloud* [1970] to *Popeye* [1980]. He would pick me up in a car at four thirty or five in the morning – I usually had a dreadful hangover – and drive me out to the location, which was usually an hour away out in the Valley someplace, and he'd tell me the story. The actors all knew their lines, so I never read a script. We'd just set up and do it.

GF: *Your feature career really got going with the astronaut film* Countdown *at Warner Brothers in 1968.*

RA: Yes. I got fired by Jack Warner. He was gone through the whole shoot, and he came back and viewed all the footage, and they locked me out of the lot. Bill Conrad, who was the executive producer of those low-budget projects over there at that time, called me and said, 'Don't come in tomorrow, because they're not going to let you in the gate.' I said, 'I'll go to the Directors Guild. I have the right to cut the film.' He said, 'If you exercise that, they'll just give you six days and you'll cut it, and then they'll take it all apart and nobody will look at it.' Then I went to Spain on an independent project that I thought was going to get financed, and I sat in Seville for a month and the money fell out.

GF: *In 1969 you directed* A Cold Day in the Park. *It's already characterized by what became your very distinctive fly-on-the-wall, documentary approach to fiction. How did that style evolve?*

RA: I don't really know how I got to that. That picture was always kind of in my mind. I'm sure everything that everybody does is imitative.

GF: *That style is full-fledged by the time of* M★A★S★H *[1970], which had been shopped around a lot before you came on to it.*

RA: I think I was the fourteenth or fifteenth director it had been given to. Certainly that was the story, and I think it was probably true. I had been working for years on a project called *The Chicken and the Hawk*, which was a comedy about First World War flyers. (In fact, two or three years ago I paid a writer to develop it, but I couldn't get anybody interested in backing it – I doubt if it will ever get done.) I had certain ideas about how I wanted to shoot that picture, and when I read *M★A★S★H*, I saw a way to use the same kind of techniques and style I had in mind.

I did a lot of things in *M★A★S★H*. Originally, it had only eight characters who had speaking lines, and I just filled it with people who had never been on screen before. I got them from an improvisational theatre group in San Francisco, and I had to write a line in for each one in order to get them hired. If there wasn't a line of dialogue in the script, Twentieth-Century Fox wouldn't hire them as actors. So I did a little rewrite and I was able to put all these people in as actors. I'm sure that had everything to do with the success of *M★A★S★H*. I had started doing that same kind of thing in television. I had a bunch of guys I called 'panics', who were utility actors, and I would write one line into the script for them, and hire them as a reporter or whatever, to give some sense of reality to it.

By that time I was seeing Italian films, and I was striving towards that kind of

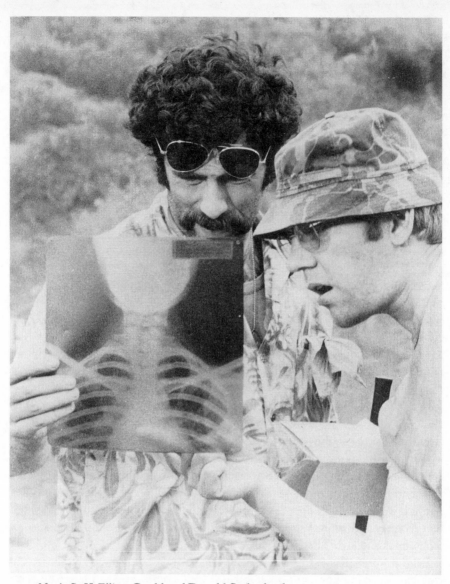

40   *M★A★S★H*: Elliott Gould and Donald Sutherland

neo-realism. It seemed to me these things should be done that way. I got away with it on *M★A★S★H*. I never would have at any other time, but there were two bigger war films going on at Fox, *Patton* and *Tora! Tora! Tora!*, and the whole studio machinery was very busy on those. *M★A★S★H* was this little $3.5 million film that was heading for the drive-ins. Nobody had any high hopes for it; there were no stars in it. I got away from the Fox lot out in the country and they didn't pay too much attention to us. I did that by staying under budget – I never let any red flags come up and so we really snuck that film through the studio system.

GF: *What elements in Ring Lardner Jr's screenplay of* M★A★S★H *had appealed to you?*

RA: I think that nobody was in that war situation because they wanted to be. Put into that arena, they did their best to survive. And mostly humour is what got people through.

GF: *But it's also a very cynical film. It's set during the Korean War, but in making it so bleak were you trying to deflate the official position on Vietnam?*

RA: Probably. I went through this whole thing without ever mentioning Korea, thinking I could slip it by. But the studio made me put that disclaimer on the front; they said, 'You've got to say this is Korea.'

GF: M★A★S★H *has been described as anti-Christian, anti-gay, and anti-women. Certainly, the humiliation of the Hotlips [Sally Kellerman] and Frank Burns [Robert Duvall] characters by Hawkeye [Donald Sutherland] and Trapper [Elliott Gould] does seem needlessly cruel. What's your take on this?*

RA: Certainly after *M★A★S★H* people said, 'You're a misogynist.' And I looked that word up and found out what it meant. But *au contraire* – my answer was and is that I'm not making this film to show you how I think things ought to be; I'm showing you the way I see them. And this is the way women were treated, this is the way gays were treated. This is what went on. The reality of that film was a reality of attitudes. It wasn't factual, but it was truthful. I was involved in all those decisions that made *M★A★S★H* seem cynical, but they had nothing to do with my own personal opinion.

GF: *Do you prefer to maintain a distance from these broader-scale pictures, like* M★A★S★H, Nashville *[1975]*, A Wedding *[1978] and* The Player *[1992], as opposed to some of the more personal films you've made?*

RA: What I see becomes personal, so I am as involved in the fabric of those films as I am in the others. The difference between those films with many, many characters and small films like *Images* [1972] and *Three Women* [1977] is just the size of the canvas. Some are small paintings, whereas others are big, broad murals.

GF: Images *and* Three Women, *which do seem to be making personal statements, focus on strong female characters. On the whole you haven't delved so deeply into the male psyche.*

41 *M★A★S★H*: the humiliation of Hotlips (Sally Kellerman)

42   *Images*: Robert Altman and Susannah York

RA: That's true. At the time, of course, I was not aware of it. I don't sit and think, 'Oh, I'll use a female character.' That's simply what attracted me. I don't know if that relates particularly to my own life or experience. I don't know where that interest in strong female characters comes from.

GF: *Is it true that these two films came to you in dreams?*

RA: Not really, although I trust my dreams. About the time I was making *M*★*A*★*S*★*H*, I got to a stage where I would consciously go to sleep with a problem and say, 'OK, the answer is somewhere in the information that's in my head; it's just a matter of getting it out – and it will occur to me.' Rarely did I have a specific dream that would answer a question, but sometimes in the next day or week, that answer would disclose itself, because it was there – trapped in my head.

Images, I think, was an imitation of Bergman's *Persona*, which I was very impressed with. I *did* dream the exterior of *Three Women*, though not its content. I was living in another house down the beach in those days, and my wife got very sick – I was very worried she would not survive. Also, I was in desperate financial shape at that time, as I find I usually am. I'd just lost a project, a broad comedy I was working on called *Easy and Hard Ways Out*, with Peter Falk and Sterling Hayden – I wanted to set it at the time of the Six Day War, but the Geffen Company told me I couldn't do it, so I passed on it.

I came home from seeing my wife in the hospital the first or second day she was in, and I was really anxious. I knew I had to get a film. I went to bed and my youngest son, Matthew, came and slept there. I had this dream that I was making a film called *Three Women*. I said to myself, 'This is really great.' I'd get up and take the yellow pad next to my bed and I'd write down something, then go back to sleep. Then I dreamed the *Three Women* cast – Sissy Spacek and Shelley Duvall, though Janice Rule wasn't in that dream – and would wake up again and make some more notes, and go back to sleep. At one point I called Tommy Thompson and Bob Eggenweiler, who was my location guy, into the bedroom, and said, 'Now, we go look for locations for this film in the desert', and I described the set – sand and desert and heat. Of course, I woke up in the morning, and Matthew was already up and out of bed and in the ocean, where he spent all of his time – and the bed was full of sand. There was no yellow pad next to my bed. So I was having dreams within dreams. I got terribly depressed because I thought, 'Oh God, that would be such a good movie and I don't know what it's about.'

But I went down and fixed some breakfast, and called Scottie Bushnell, who has worked very closely with me for years. I said to her, 'Listen, I read a short story last night that's pretty interesting', and I vamped on the telephone. I said, 'It's called *Three Women*, and it's about this woman, living in Palm Springs or some place like that, who advertises for a roommate, and a girl moves in. It's all about personality theft. These are perfect parts for Sissy Spacek and Shelley

43   *Persona*: Bibi Andersson and Liv Ullman

44   *Three Women*: Shelley Duvall and Sissy Spacek

Duvall.' Scottie said, 'Gee, can you get the rights to this story?' And I said, 'Oh, yeah.' That's how *Three Women* started, though years before, around 1959, when I was painting a lot, I had painted a picture called *Three Women*. All this stuff that spewed itself out had been inside my head, of course, all the time.

So I didn't dream the story or the plot. I dreamed the *results* of it. We sense things through our skin, smells that we don't detect, visual things that we don't think we remember, things we hear that we don't know we've heard, and temperature – and all of these things add up to a hunch. I trust hunches, because I think they are the most accurate messages we get and because they are not something you can intellectually explain. Sometimes you fool yourself, and they don't work or they're invalid. But so what? Your percentages of hits and misses are about the same.

GF: *All right, let's get technical for a moment. One print of* McCabe and Mrs Miller *[1970] I saw had a very blue tint; on another print it was kind of green.*

RA: Well, it should have been kind of yellow, blue or yellow. The prints are terrible now, although it's pretty good on laser disc. I was trying to give a sense of antiquity, of vagueness, and to make this not a life that you're living in, but a life that you're looking through.

GF: *What particularly interested you about turn-of-the-century frontier life, or was it Edmund Naughton's novel* McCabe *that attracted you?*

RA: It was a very ordinary novel about this gambler, kind of a romantic character, and this whore with a heart of gold. And then the killers came along and they are a classic trio: the Giant, the Kid, and the Half-Breed. Everything that happened was in plots that we've seen and heard a hundred times before. However, there was something unusual in that book, and I think it was probably in the scene where McCabe was talking to himself about poetry. He tells himself that he's not a poet, that he can't put things down in words. It was very moving to me, because what it was saying was that this guy didn't know anything, and knew he didn't know anything, and was justifying his lack of knowledge by the fact that he wasn't smart enough. But he did know that those feelings existed. I remember that passage very well, and that's what made the whole story for me.

The story became an easy clothes-line for me to hang my own essays on. The audience recognized those traditional things – the whore, the killers – so I did not have to dwell on them. Instead, I was able to say, 'You think you know this story, but you don't know this story, because the most interesting part of it is all these little sidebars.' The filmic approach to that occurred to me as part of telling that story.

GF: *Were you concerned to show that the West was rather different from the familiar myth?*

RA: I wanted to say that maybe it was *this* way. We do research for a Western picture through photographs or drawings that people made at that time. You

45 *McCabe and Mrs Miller*: 'The goddamnedest looking hat you've ever seen'

go through the photographic books, and you see a picture of a cowboy with a big hat. So the assumption is that everybody wore these big hats. Well, a glass plate for a camera cost about two dollars in those days, so you didn't go around and take snapshots everywhere. A photographer was very careful about what he took a picture of. My contention is that some guy comes into town, and he's got this big hat on, everybody in town runs down the street and they run to the photographer and say, 'Hey, there's a guy out there with the goddamnedest looking hat you've ever seen. Go take a picture of it.' So the photographer comes out and takes a picture of the man in the hat. I believe it was something that was very eccentric, or he wouldn't have taken a photograph of it.

GF: *But mostly they wore derbies, right? There's that famous photograph of Bat Masterson wearing a derby.*

RA: Well, most of the American West was populated by first-generation Europeans – Irish and some Italians, English, Dutch. All the clothes they had would have been European, and nobody spoke like they speak in Texas. It took a long time for the language to generate to that.

So in *McCabe* we took the vision that most of these characters were immigrants. I actually got a wardrobe of that period from Warner Brothers, took it up to Vancouver and hung it up on racks, then assembled my cast and said: 'Everybody gets to have one pair of pants, two shirts, one vest, sweater, light coat, one heavy or rain coat, one hat, and then there's objects that you can go and pick around.' So everybody picked their own wardrobe. Of course, all this wardrobe had holes in it and was tattered to make it look aged and old. From this, I could tell the personality of each actor – the guy who wanted to be the most flamboyant picked the most flamboyant stuff, and so on.

There they were all lined up with these clothes with holes in them. I said, 'Now, the needles and threads and patches are over here, and you've got two days to sew up your holes, because otherwise you'll die from cold up here. So they repaired all their clothes – because people didn't run around with clothes with holes in them – and suddenly that wardrobe became part of their characters, and they became part of the wardrobe's character. And everybody was eccentric, and yet everybody was the same.

GF: *Why was it necessary to have McCabe [Warren Beatty] ritually sacrificed at the end of the film?*

RA: Because I think he couldn't have survived. What I was really trying to say was that he won and he lost. My script and my film was originally called *The Presbyterian Church Wager*. In the book, Dog Butler [played by Hugh Millais in the film], the big guy with the goatskin coat, makes a wager with McCabe that he'll kill him. I took that out, because it became too theatrical, but we kept the essence of it – that, in gambling, you win a bet, but you also lose. I mean, everybody dies. So I just chose to end it that way. I have no idea how the book ended – I don't remember at all.

46   *McCabe and Mrs Miller*: Warren Beatty and Julie Christie

47   *McCabe and Mrs Miller*: the death of McCabe (Warren Beatty)

GF: *What were you trying to say about mythic Western archetypes with* Buffalo Bill and the Indians, or Sitting Bull's History Lesson *[1976]?*

RA: It's going the opposite way from *McCabe* – it's saying that this idea of the West is all showbusiness. When we were doing *Buffalo Bill*, Paul Newman said, 'I'm not playing Buffalo Bill Cody – I'm playing Redford and McQueen and myself. I'm playing a movie star. These are guys who are given credit for doing these super-heroic things.' But Buffalo Bill was a sham. He was originally a guy who moved cattle around, a scout for the Indians, which was just a job. Then Ned Buntline came along and started writing these heroic stories about him, and he had to play up to that role. Tom Mix, who was in the Pancho Villa wars, was probably more of a real doer of deeds than Buffalo Bill.

GF: *You seem to have consistently addressed yourself to a debunking of American myths.*

RA: It's just another look at them. They've become rigid. They don't move enough, those myths. They all become imitated to the point where they become like granite, and they're not interesting. I just want to say, 'Suppose it could have happened this way'. It's not debunking. What interests me when I start looking at a subject is that what we all accept about it probably isn't true. I'm just moving to a place where I can look at it from a different angle.

GF: *You link* M★A★S★H *together with the loudspeaker announcements;* Brewster McCloud *with the ornithological lectures of the Birdman [Rene Auberjonois];* The Long Goodbye *with the theme tune;* Thieves Like Us *[1974] with the* Romeo and Juliet *radio commentary; and* Nashville *with the canvassing of the Hal Philip Walker third-party presidential campaign . . .*

RA: Right. The H. Ross Perot truck.

GF: *What's the intention behind these devices – is it primarily to provide an ironic commentary?*

RA: It's punctuation to me. For *M★A★S★H*, I had shot all this fragmented raw material and I knew I was going to have to have punctuation, cutaways. So I came up with the idea of those loudspeakers and sent my editor, Danny Green, out to shoot them. Of course, all the sound content was put in at the editing stage. I still look for punctuation or commentary, and I find it very helpful. I'm doing it in the Raymond Carver film, *Short Cuts*, that I'm about to start shooting.

GF: *What is your linking device there?*

RA: Television – one of those guys who are station managers and give these boring political editorials – and a thing about two women musicians. Layering a movie in this way gives me more options. If something doesn't work, I can cover an awful lot of sins by using these devices. A plot, to me, is a clothes-line. For example, as I read *The Long Goodbye*, it occurred to me that Raymond Chandler's story was merely a clothes-line on which to hang a bunch of thumbnail essays, little commentaries – because that's what he was most

48 *Buffalo Bill and the Indians*: Robert Altman and Paul Newman

interested in. I thought, 'This is exactly my interest in it.'

GF: The Long Goodbye, *which was one of several Chandler adaptations to be made in the seventies, is still the only one to present a less-than-traditional view of the private detective Philip Marlowe. Were you unimpressed with the world Chandler created?*

RA: I liked Chandler's stuff OK, and Dashiell Hammett's. Marlowe is a character that didn't actually exist. He's mythical, not even based on truth. This was a script that was given to me when I was working on *Images* in London and initially I said, 'I'm not good at this sort of thing.' But Leigh Brackett, co-writer of the 1946 adaptation of Chandler's *The Big Sleep*, had written the screenplay and ended it with Marlowe killing his best friend. That I liked, and I also liked the idea of Elliott Gould playing Marlowe – although really the producers wanted somebody like Robert Mitchum. Finally, I agreed to do it with Elliott.

I never finished the book. I never understood it logically. If you really follow the plot, it isn't valid – it doesn't hold up – so I changed it. I got hold of a book called *Raymond Chandler Speaking*, which was a bunch of letters, essays and other pieces he'd written, and I gave that to all my collaborators, telling them, 'This is the book that we're making.' I took out the murder of Roger Wade [Sterling Hayden] and replaced it with him committing suicide. It's a movie suicide – I was dealing with Hollywood, *A Star is Born*. Chandler had tried to commit suicide by shooting himself in the bathtub and missed, hoping the ricochet would get him. So I tried to make the Roger Wade character Raymond Chandler in my mind.

Then I said, 'How are we going to date this film? Am I going to go back and do a period film with a bunch of 1934 Chevys in the street and all that stuff?' I didn't want to do that. Instead, I called Marlowe 'Rip Van Marlowe' and said he'd been asleep for twenty years. I tried to play up what was happening in 1973, coming off the sixties, and put him in the middle of it. It was a place in which he didn't belong. So suddenly we have Philip Marlowe in a world in which he's not even real, he's walking through it – and it's alien to him. That became the reason for doing the film and I became very excited about it. I love that picture. I think it's very close, in a physical way, to *The Player*.

GF: Nashville *has twenty-four characters. Was this an opportunity to present twenty-four little essays?*

RA: They're little soap operas that aren't particularly extraordinary on their own. They're common stories of ordinary people, but I show you such a mass of them that they comment on themselves. *Short Cuts* is the same structure as *Nashville*, basically, but the stories are much stronger and they also come from the same voice. I expect this film to be very interesting in some way, though intellectually I don't know how. I don't know what's going to come out of it; I haven't shot it yet. But I know that each individual story in it could make an

49 *The Long Goodbye*: 'I liked the idea of Marlowe (Elliott Gould) killing his best friend (Jim Bouton)'

50 *The Long Goodbye*: Elliott Gould as 'Rip Van Marlowe'

hour or a half-hour television show, or even a full movie-of-the-week if you really wanted to flesh it out, though then they wouldn't be Carver's stories any more.

It's like the blues in a way. They're all depressing stories. But just by seeing pieces of them and lifting up rooftops to look at these people, and catching a part of their behaviour, you get the essence of a full story. You get the feeling for those characters and their lives. But you never get bored with the story, because immediately I take you to another strand and you keep seeing pieces of these stories develop. Hopefully, they will all, in aggregate, present a spherical kind of structure that the audience will respond to.

GF: *Have you written the screenplay for* Short Cuts *yourself?*

RA: I wrote it with Frank Barhydt Jr, whose father had been my boss at the Calvin Company. That's how I knew Frank Jr. He came out here and edited a health magazine – it was his idea and his script that led me to do *Health* [1980].

GF: *The different plot elements coalesce very neatly in* Nashville, *even through omission. For example, when Barbara Jean [Ronee Blakley] is shot, Opal [Geraldine Chaplin] – the BBC reporter, the one person who needs to be there – is conspicuous by her absence. However, did you intend at one point to include material suggesting Opal was a phony, not really a journalist at all?*

RA: She had other scenes that didn't end up in the picture, but I don't think any of them treated her differently. We didn't make any specific indication that she was a phony. This was just something that Geraldine and I knew, and I'm not sure we even discussed it.

GF: *Why did you ask your screenwriter, Joan Tewkesbury, to include the assassination attempt on Barbara Jean? I'm interested in this because you have Lady Pearl [Barbara Baxley] talking about the Kennedy assassinations earlier in the film.*

RA: The development of the Lady Pearl reminiscences about the Kennedys came after we decided to have the assassination. I don't remember the circumstances. Joan had written this blueprint for us, based on all these characters, which really were the result of what happened to her when she went and observed Nashville for eleven days.

Then one day I was in my office – I can even remember the quality of the light – and I said, 'Let's have this woman assassinated.' Joan didn't like it, and it infuriated Polly Platt, the art director, who quit the picture because of that. But it seemed right to me; it was a hunch. I don't know where the notion came from, but I was determined to do it. And without it, I don't think there would have been a film.

Once we knew what that theme was, we were able to develop it through the other characters. Again, it's the same thing of letting there be many commentaries. Lady Pearl talking about the Kennedys was a harbinger of what was going to happen.

In *Short Cuts*, I've got two characters who will furnish all the music for me in

51 *Nashville*: twenty-four characters, 'twenty-four little soap operas'

TIMOTHY BROWN

KEITH CARRADINE

GERALDINE CHAPLIN

ROBERT DOQUI

ALLEN GARFIELD

SCOTT GLENN

BARBARA HARRIS

LILY TOMLIN

GWEN WELLES

DAVID HAYWARD

CRISTINA RAINES

BERT REMSEN

KEENAN WYNN

"Nashville", a Jerry Weintraub production of a Robert Altman film, is the explosive drama and human comedy that interweaves the lives of 24 major characters, leaders and hopefuls whose destinies are altered forever during five days in the country music capital of the world. This highly charged film is an ABC Entertainment presentation released by Paramount Pictures which was produced and directed by Altman. Written by Joan Tewkesbury, Martin Starger and Weintraub are executive producers. The music is arranged and supervised by Richard Baskin.

the picture, Annie Ross and Lori Singer, who play a mother and a daughter. This is not a Raymond Carver story; it's part of the connective tissue of the film that I mentioned earlier. Originally, I had three stories of my own that I put in *Short Cuts*, but I've cut them all out except the one about these two musicians, one of whom, the daughter, commits suicide. Everybody who has read the script says, 'This doesn't make any sense. Why did she commit suicide?' I say, 'Well, I don't think we know why *anybody* commits suicide, so I don't want to explain why in the film.' I don't even want to know why she does it, but I want the audience to furnish those reasons in their own minds. Now, I am going to get a lot of heat over this. I can see reviews right now saying, 'This is a stupid film because suddenly this woman kills herself and we never know why.' But to me it's exactly the same situation as in *Nashville*: why did Kenny [David Hayward] shoot Barbara Jean?

Right now, we have four or five assassins incarcerated in this country. With all of our technology and all of the wisdom and all of the things that we know, there's not one person who can tell you why any of those assassins assassinated or tried to assassinate the people they did.

GF: *It's been said that you are not interested in character. Looking at your films and examining the way you make them, it seems you are profoundly interested in character, but not prepared to analyse what this character is or is going to be until the actors have discovered it for themselves and let it unfold in front of the camera.*

RA: When I look at a film and I see somebody behaving in a certain way, that's what interests me. And I think the audience wants to see something that they haven't seen before, something that they can believe is true but they don't know why. That's what thrills me.

So in *Short Cuts*, I still don't know what behaviour will lead to this suicide. I've talked to Annie Ross and Lori Singer about it and they don't either yet, but something will happen. They will come up with ideas or combinations of ideas or thoughts that will *expose* themselves in their behaviour. And if this is done well enough, the audience won't feel like the suicide's come out of left field. Consequently, something will happen in the music that will start pointing arrows towards this event. Something will happen in other scenes with other actors that don't connect at all, that don't link with that, but will still form a link.

GF: *And if the actress Lori Singer explains to you afterwards the reason why her character killed herself, you are fully prepared to accept whatever it is?*

RA: She can have any opinion she wants about it, because whatever her opinion is, it's only going to be part of the answer. Because the reasons why someone commits suicide are so complex, and yet so simple – it's luck. If I have a message, it's not any profound truth, it's this: 'I am going to expose an event to you in such a way that you yourself will get a hunch that will tell you about other things in your life experience.'

GF: *It's that same sense of arbitrariness which permeates many of your films.*

RA: And this is not what you're supposed to do – this is not general drama fare. Everybody feels they have to have an explanation of why everybody does everything, and my contention is simply that that is not truthful. I don't know one person, and I don't know one person who knows one person, who is not eccentric. And if everybody is, in fact, an eccentric, then 'eccentric' is the wrong word and it can't be used!

GF: *With* Come Back to the Five and Dime, Jimmy Dean, Jimmy Dean *[1982], which I regard as the best of the stage adaptations you filmed in the eighties, you returned – albeit not directly – to the myth you'd explored twenty-five years before in* The James Dean Story *[1957].*

RA: It was a reverse angle on that, different from what you would think. I didn't have a very good feeling about James Dean because of my distasteful experience working on *The Delinquents* with the actor Tom Laughlin, who had been trying to emulate the stories he'd heard about James Dean working with Elia Kazan on *East of Eden*. My interest in making *The James Dean Story* was not in idealizing Dean, but in going the other way. The film didn't turn out that way because I'd had a partner [George W. George], and it developed more into a sentimental, soppy thing.

So when the play by Ed Graczyk was presented to me and I heard the title, I said, 'I don't want to read it, I don't want to do it, I'm not interested in James Dean.' But I agreed to read it and have actors read it, and I got interested in it because it was not about James Dean, but about the phenomenon he caused and about which I'd made a documentary. What I'm trying to say is that everything touches everything else and influences it. *Come Back to the Five and Dime, Jimmy Dean, Jimmy Dean*, on the stage or on film, would have been an entirely different piece had I not had this other experience. So really it's all one piece of work.

GF: *This notion of serendipity seems very important to you.*

RA: Yes. When I got home yesterday afternoon, after looking at a location for *Short Cuts*, I lay down and turned the television on and *Popeye* was on. I was thinking not about what was happening on the screen, but everything that happened outside of the screen, the memories that it brought back to me, and I started watching a scene where Olive Oyl [Shelley Duvall] is packing her bag and sneaking out to escape marrying Bluto. As she closed the suitcase, a piece of one of the skirts she'd packed was left hanging outside the suitcase. I grinned because I remembered the exact moment in time when we were shooting that. I'd said, 'Let's do that', because there'd been a scene in *Three Women* when Shelley had caught her skirt in a door – we did that quite often in that film. Now, nobody in the world is ever going to make that connection between those two films, nobody can know the genesis of things like that – and yet it's thick.

52 *Come Back to the Five and Dime, Jimmy Dean, Jimmy Dean*: Sandy Dennis amid Dean memorabilia

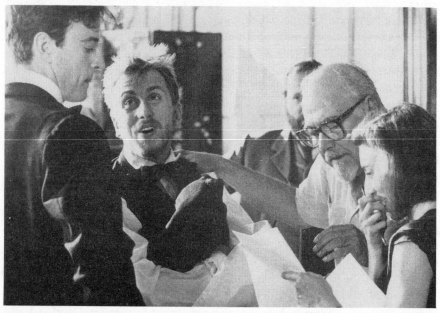

53 *Vincent and Theo*: Robert Altman with Theo (Paul Rhys) and Vincent (Tim Roth)

The presbyterian church that's at the top of the hill in *Popeye* is the same church from *McCabe*. Similarly, I took an actor, Bob Fortier, who was the town drunk in *McCabe*, the guy that did the dance on the ice, and made him the town drunk in *Popeye*, and he wore exactly the same wardrobe. These are the things that are interesting to me. I don't know whether it adds up to personal art – I guess all art is personal.

GF: *Did* Tanner '88 *[1988] grow out of the scenes with Michael Murphy as John Triplette in* Nashville?

RA: Sure it did. And *The Player* grew out of *Tanner*. *The Player* could not have existed had I not done *Tanner '88*, because it never would have occurred to me to mix real people playing themselves with fictional characters. While *The Player*'s not the same thing as *Tanner*, it *is* the same thing. You cannot pull one thing out and let it stand alone, because it does *not* stand alone. It is carrying all of the strings that are attached to all the other things in my life – and in the lives of Tim Robbins [Griffin Mill in *The Player* and star–director–author of the *Tanner*-esque *Bob Roberts*], Julie Christie [the co-star of *McCabe and Mrs Miller* who played herself in *Nashville*], and Shelley Duvall. There's no way I can avoid the sticky stuff that connects one film to another.

GF: Vincent and Theo *strikes me as one of your harshest, yet least naturalistic films. It doesn't have that documentary feel about it.*

RA: My whole purpose there was to demythify art. If I have a Van Gogh painting and I want to move it down to Christie's, six guys in white gloves and one guy with a gun will come in here to move it. But there was a time when he just painted the damn thing, and it fell on the floor, and people stepped on it or left it out in the rain. I was trying to convey that the value of art is not in its existence, but in its doing.

GF: *Going on to* The Player, *did you in any sense feel it was an opportunity to settle a score with Hollywood? When it came out, there was all that talk of it being a* film-à-clef.

RA: I have no beef with Hollywood. I never have. They have not done things that I wanted them to do, and I have not done things that they wanted me to do. I've made enemies and I don't suffer fools gracefully. It's simply that I have an interest in doing certain kinds of work that I feel I do well and it doesn't fit with their marketing plans, generally. So it's only occasionally that I am able to get a picture through the machinery. Most of the hysteria about *The Player* suggests that I'm sitting there throwing knives at a bunch of old enemies, which isn't true. I hope that the film stands on its own as a piece of work. But, in general terms, it's fraught with allegory. It's an allegory on an allegory, set inside an allegory. And the arena is something that I know fairly well. But it's no different from the museum business or the newspaper business. Hollywood is the surrogate for what I am addressing, which is the cultural dilemma between art and commerce that's taking place in this country and in most Western civilized countries.

54   The Presbyterian church

55 *The Player*: Tim Robbins as Griffin Mill

GF: *Did you feel that you were exiled from Hollywood in the eighties?*

RA: No more than I am today. I have the same projects I am trying to do today that I had last year, and the year before that, and the year before that – and nobody will fund them. A lot of people offer me *their* projects, but these aren't anything I want to do. They are not interested in what I have to say. They're interested in the fact that, oh, he's hot now, so let's get him to do something. But they want it done their way.

GF: *In the last ten years, Hollywood has seldom allowed directors, yourself included, to have any kind of artistic trajectory.*

RA: There's a scene in *The Player* where Griffin Mill says, 'I'm kind of fascinated with the idea of eliminating the writer from the artistic process.' He says, 'Now, if we can just get rid of the directors and the actors, we've really got something here.' And that's exactly what those studio guys are trying to do, though they don't even know they're trying to do it.

GF: *Are the studio types depicted in the film based on actual figures, are they amalgams of different people, or are purely fictional?*

RA: They're nobody I know. They're very generic. I made no effort to make fools of the characters themselves. Taking cheap shots is too easy. I said to the actors, 'If you're this character, think the way *you* feel the character that you've created is going to think.' Those studio people don't think they're bad guys. I tried to show that they don't turn down projects because they don't *like* an artist, but because that's what their job is. Naturally, you don't like people when they turn you down, and you say, 'Nah, they didn't get it. They're too dumb' – but that's not fair.

GF: *How did you arrive at the style for* The Player? *The beginning – when the delivery boy collapses – is reminiscent of* Nashville.

RA: I think that's just me imitating myself. The style of any film really derives from after the fact.

GF: *And then there's your homage – if homage is what it is – to* Touch of Evil *with the long opening shot.*

RA: I wanted to make that ridiculously long opening shot because so many people talk about these long opening shots as if they are some achievement in themselves. And in a way, they are, but they are all pretty pretentious – they are seldom done for narrative drive. In this case, I was trying to show the audience that this film was about movies and people who talk movies. The majority of people who see it are never gonna know that shot is eight minutes and six seconds, and it doesn't make any difference. I'm breaking linear time, but without breaking linear *film* time. It was the *effect*, cinematically, of cutting, but there was no cut in it, and it's seamless. Basically, it sets up that this is a film studio, and these are the characters, and this is the style of the film, because it's movies within movies – that's also why I had movie posters all over the place.

I have no idea how that opening shot first occurred. I never make models of sets and I never do storyboards – but I *did* have a model of that set built. I imagine I spent $5–6,000 on it, which was totally useless. I'd just sit and look at it and think, 'Where can I put people?' Then I found out that the furthest extension I could have on a dolly was 25 feet. So I had a little model of that made, then I could make little camera pivots and I could say, 'Well, from here I could go to there, but I'd have to come back here.' And I just played with those puzzles. But I never resolved them. I never came up with a plan. I got into doing the picture and then suddenly, in the middle of production, it came time to go do it – and we went over and did it. All of that pre-thinking led to what the shot finally is. Things like that stylize the picture eventually.

GF: *You once said, 'I'm trying to reach towards a picture that's totally emotional, not narrative or intellectual, where an audience walks out and they can't say anything about it except what they feel.' Is that still a goal?*

RA: I don't think I'll ever attain that. What I'm really talking about is taking the linear references out of film and having something happen that works on the individuals in the audience so that the information they get from the film suddenly invades all the information they have accumulated in their lifetime, so they can only say, 'Wow, that's so right.' It's difficult in film, where you need a narrative. You can look at a painting for a split second or you can look at it for an accumulation of time, and it's still working on you. In film, one frame has to follow the other. I think the structure of *The Player* is rather remarkable. I use one part of the film as the clothes-line to keep your attention. Hanging on that is the way the murder story is done, which is the way they are done in bad films. So I am emulating not good films but bad films, and – again – I'm hanging on that a lot of abstract thumbnail essays, so one supports the other.

GF: *I sensed that you were trying to emulate the bad film that gets made in the course of* The Player – *the* Habeas Corpus *film with Bruce Willis and Julia Roberts – and to use it as a vehicle to digress.*

RA: Yes, but the *Habeas Corpus* film was an exaggeration. It was a parody – it could never be made. The other, subtler scenes – the love scenes, the sex scenes, the interrogation scenes – were all picked off other bad movies, or even good movies. For the scene where Griffin and June [Greta Scacchi] are travelling to Palm Springs, I thought, 'I'm going to have to transport the audience with them.' So I said, 'OK, I'm going to be Ridley Scott, but I only have a day or a day and a half to be him.' So we shot it as three little commercial shots.

GF: *Both the hot-tub scene between Griffin and Bonnie [Cynthia Stevenson], his colleague and girlfriend, and the elliptical sex scene between Griffin and June give more and less than what we expect.*

RA: Paul Newman saw the film, and somebody asked him what it was like. He said, 'It's a film about how you get to see the tits of a girl whose tits you don't want to see, but you don't get to see the tits of the girl whose tits you do want to see.' I wanted to use that obligatory nudity, because otherwise the film isn't marketable. But I didn't want to put it where it should have been. So when I interviewed Cynthia Stevenson for the role of Bonnie, I said, 'Now, before we even get into what this part is about, I've got to tell you that you've got to take your shirt off.' She said, 'Nobody has ever asked me to do that before. Why?' I said, 'Because if I show you nude in a hot tub, in an unsexual situation, then I don't have to show Greta Scacchi, who the audience *does* think it's going to see nude.' I wanted to make the point that these things are done for the wrong reasons.

During the lovemaking scene between Griffin and June I didn't want to have them just screwing. I wanted it to appear that they both were very much involved and that he felt obligated to tell her that he had killed her boyfriend, and she doesn't want to hear it. Some people are going to ask, 'Did she know or didn't she?' I don't know. I don't know whether she did or not. And it doesn't really make a lot of difference. You figure out what works for you. It should always be ambiguous.

GF: *You've said that the ending of* The Player *is the same as the ending of* M★A★S★H.

RA: It is, yes. We had no ending for *The Player*, because all the endings were melodramatic, and we had to bring back the writer who threatens Griffin Mill, whom we had suddenly dismissed. Tim Robbins and I were talking about various endings, and we had many options, none of which was satisfactory. I said, 'I know this is going to come to us, so it's not a problem.' We were maybe three weeks away from shooting.

When I was editing *M★A★S★H*, I remember I had just put in those loudspeakers with the announcement of the war movies. I'd been driving through Malibu Canyon, and was just turning into my driveway when this idea came up that I would say, over a loudspeaker, 'Tonight's movie has been *M★A★S★H*, that knock-'em, sock-'em, kill-'em . . .' – and so on. And I said to myself, 'This is great. It's that idea of telling people, "The movie you've just seen is the movie you've just seen"' – that this was all a film.

I told Tim that. And about ten minutes later, he said, 'Maybe we should do the same thing in *The Player*.' And I knew immediately what he was talking about. We celebrated. We didn't actually break out the champagne, but it was that feeling. I ran from office to office saying, 'We've got the ending. Listen to this.' It was the idea that Griffin gets on the telephone with the writer, who pitches him the film we've just been watching – and it's called *The Player*. It's saying that this is a movie about itself. I want the audience to see that many of the scenes, the way the actors acted it, the way the sets were, the way it was shot was *movies*, not life. The melodrama was movie melodrama, not real life melodrama.

I've always tried to show the audience that what it's seeing isn't real – and show them the device that shows that. I'm sure that this will appear in my opera, *McTeague*. Because if I don't tell them it's an opera, how am I possibly going to succeed in making them think people behave this way – walking around singing? They don't. So something has to mirror that. I think every film I do is like that. It's making something spherical rather than linear. The more and more of this I do, the more I want it to be like you're inside a universe, you're inside a sphere. There isn't any end and beginning to it.

GF: *Tell me a little bit about* McTeague.* *Is it from Frank Norris's novel?*

RA: Yes, and, of course, Erich Von Stroheim shot that entire book when he made *Greed* [1924]. It's a very operatic story. When Von Stroheim made it, he went to San Francisco and shot the cars and people in the street, so he wasn't accurate to the period of the novel. My wardrobe and the physical look of the stage set of *McTeague* is more authentic to California in 1908 – still, most of the images and the tone of the opera are from that silent, black-and-white film, because when I look at *Greed*, I know more about those characters than I do when I read Frank Norris's book. So that has to have an influence on me – and I also *want* it to have an influence on me. I have no idea why, except that it seems to make a vague connection with what *my* history is.

GF: *Perhaps it's because you and Von Stroheim each had a contentious relationship with the Hollywood studio system. Do you see yourself working within the studio set-up again?*

RA: I doubt that will ever happen, because I have certain demands that I think they are not going to meet. I'm sixty-seven years old. I wonder: where am I going to be ten years from now? I'm going to be seventy-seven. That's pretty old. So what have I got? Six, seven pictures left. I don't want to make a film just for the sake of landing a job. And unless I feel that I will have fun with the shooting of a film, and afterwards, when you kind of smile and say, 'We really did a good job on that,' then I don't want to do it.

* *McTeague* opened at the Lyric Opera of Chicago on 31 October 1992.

9   Bob Roberts
         Tim Robbins

Introduction

About two months before we started shooting *Bob Roberts* a person very close to me, a person I have known since I was a child, reacted in a strange way to the information that I had been given the go-ahead.

'You shouldn't do it.'

'What are you talking about?'

'It's a weird time right now.'

It was. We had just been through the 'experience' in the Gulf and our television sets were giving us continual images of victory, of feel-good Americana parades, and of reruns of celebrity-support-the-troops videos. There even was the obligatory 'Bob Hope Welcomes the Troops Home Televison Special' complete with bad jokes, sexy gals, movie stars, and what – in a strange, surreal moment – appeared to be some kind of verbal soft shoe with those two feel-good guys, Dick Cheney and Colin Powell.

I thought this war stunk, from the beginning. Like a lot of people in this country, I did not buy into this as a necessary war. I hoped for reason and prayed for peace and watched futilely as impotent Democrats and partisan Republicans allowed this exercise in presidential power politics to happen. And when it came time to speak out, I was intimidated by the voracity and intensity of the drumbeating as the tribal elders from NBC, CBS, ABC, CNN, and PBS called the nation to war. The question posed to the many became: 'Do you support the troops?' not 'Do you support our policy?' People resoundingly said yes, we support the troops, how can one not support the troops?

I began getting phone calls to participate in 'bi-partisan' support-the-troops videos. I got letters from right-wing pundits 'suggesting' that I back off from protest as this was a time for unity. I was told by people I trust in the industry that my protesting against the war might have career ramifications. I called friends in the industry to join me in Washington to protest against the war. No deal. 'I'm not touching this one.'

I've never felt so alone as I did then. I was lucky to have a household with a dear friend who shared my fears, but together we felt insane, as if there was something we'd missed. All of my anxiety disappeared when we arrived in Washington on 29 January. There were hundreds of thousands of people from thousands of miles away in all directions, converging on the start of this march, having travelled for hours to affirm their sanity, to shout, and to vent their anger. 'I am not insane. This is a corrupt war. It will not stand.'

I remember feeling that although we were a minority, there was a moral certainty there. These were intelligent people all taking a risk by being there, and I realized it would be only a matter of time before the tide shifted. I marched, linking arms with parents of Gulf War soldiers. I held a flag. I held it proudly. It was our flag to protect, to fight for in our way – uncompromised by the media, at least for the present. The next day the media would compromise our actions. What was 400,000 became 75,000. What was a remarkable display of courage and conviction became a blip on page 17, buried in the recesses of the papers of record with a picture of one of the fifty pro-war maniacs shouting at a long-haired man.

Had I not gone to Washington, I don't know if I would have been able to answer my friend's concern about doing *Bob Roberts* now, in 'scary times': 'Sounds like it's the perfect time for it.'

Those that love war, that see military action as legitimate foreign policy, do not have the support of the American people. We are not a war-loving nation. The war lovers are the few. What the few do have is a way of, as Noam Chomsky puts it, 'manufacturing consent', through a facile, impotent media which allows the question to be: 'Do you support the troops?' instead of 'Do you support our policy?' A media that allows itself to be restricted, monitored and intimidated by its government is not a 'free' press and is certainly not fulfilling its role in a democracy.

We were filming in Avila, Pennsylvania one day. We had festooned this town with yellow ribbons for a drive-by bus shot. An older gentleman came up to one of the crew members and asked what we were doing. Unwilling to get into a political debate in the middle of what by all rights could have been called Bush country, the crew member said, 'We're doing a film about Desert Storm.' The man stood a moment then said, 'Desert Storm was a scam. A way for Bush to keep his friends rich.'

I have faith in the American people. I have had the good fortune to go out into it. I have seen some dark shit, some racist bile, but I have also met a lot of good people who are committed to their families and know how to love. Given the information, they would not support unneeded violence.

I set *Bob Roberts* in the fall of 1990 because I want to remember that time: it was an extremely significant time when we saw quite honestly how willing the news media is to go along with, and be the lap dog of, government. It is because of this corruption and complicity that Bob Roberts exists and is able to rise to power.

All this said, we set out to do a caustically funny film. The contributions were many from a hardworking crew and actors all working for less money than they are worth. Gore Vidal lent us his wonderfully insightful words and gave our spirit of mischief and irreverence a great validation by his presence. I have great faith in laughter – it is a great companion to fear and a much-needed release in times of such absurdity and madness. Enjoy.

INT. CONCERT HALL SCRANTON. NIGHT
We hear rhythmic applause. Clap clap clap clap. An audience is restless.
   BOB ROBERTS, *in silhouette, holds a guitar and walks confidently, calmly from his dressing room flanked by three* ASSOCIATES (CLARK ANDERSON, FRANKLIN DOCKETT *and* BART MACKLEROONEY) *dressed very Ralph Lauren.*
   We hear the ASSOCIATES *speaking.*
ANDERSON: Cobra Two, Cobra One, this is Whitey One, it's showtime.
DOCKETT: West quadrant secure, Whitey Two moving into East quadrant.
ANDERSON: Here we go.
   (*Title Card:* OCTOBER 1990
   Title Card: PENNSYLVANIA, USA
   A vibration of energy, excitement as BOB *and his* ASSOCIATES *come to the lip of the wings and stop.*
   Title Card: BOB ROBERTS
   Title Card: A DOCUMENTARY BY TERRY MANCHESTER
   'Bob Bob Bob' chant continues loudly. The audience is almost out of control. Bob takes the stage and . . . pandemonium.
   Song: COMPLAIN.)
BOB: (*Sings*) Some people will work,
         some simply will not
         But they'll complain and complain
         and complain and complain and complain

         Some people must have,
         some never will
         but they'll complain and complain
         and complain and complain and complain
   (*The song continues as we dissolve into:*)

EXT. HOTEL PARKING LOT. MORNING
On a leafy hillside covered in dew and a rising sun, a strange, surreal duel is taking place. BOB ROBERTS *and* CLARK ANDERSON, *both dressed in white, fence furiously with foils.*
   Over this we hear a montage of voices:
MAN: Bob Roberts is a stalwart American.

MAN: Bob's a championship swordsman.

MAN: Bob is a tireless worker.

WOMAN: So full of life and energy.

MAN: Bob is a man of vision.

(BOB *jumps off the hill towards camera.*)

MAN: He's a dynamic personality.

MAN: Bob is a people person.

MAN: A unique individual.

MAN: He's one of a kind.

WOMAN: He's a people person.

MAN: Bob is prime cut, first-rate, Grade A.

WOMAN: He's a genius. He's an' inspiration.

MAN: He's a man of the people.

WOMAN: I love Bob Roberts.

MAN: Bob is a paragon of virtue.

MAN: He's a people person.

MAN: He's a mover and a shaker.

WOMAN: He's the leader of a generation.

MACGREGOR: (*Off screen*) Mr Hart and I are finishing up on our T-bones when all of a sudden a young man with a guitar starts singing a song, right in the middle of the restaurant . . .

(*The source of the last voice,* CHET MACGREGOR, *Bob's Campaign Manager, stands in front of 'The Pride', Bob's tour bus. Standing next to him is* LUKAS HART III, *Bob's Campaign Chairman. We can hear* BOB *and* ANDERSON *fencing in the background.*)

. . . This is happening in Brophy's, now, and this sort of thing just doesn't happen . . .

HART: Here was a man that not only had a brilliant mind, and a wonderful wit, but could also sing.

MACGREGOR: And he finishes the song, and tremendous applause and then boom, out the door, he's gone. And I look at Mr Hart and I say, 'What was that?' and he says, in his own inimitable way, 'That, my friend, was a gold mine!'

(*We cut back to the fencers, furiously going at it.*)

TERRY: (*Voice over*) And then?

MACGREGOR: And then it happened.

(BOB *wins the match, rips off his mask and gives a victorious yell.*)

TERRY: (*Voice over*) He became a star.

MACGREGOR: That is correct.

TERRY: (*Voice over*) Overnight.

MACGREGOR: That is correct.

HART: He's a tremendous talent.

(MACGREGOR *starts for the bus,* BOB *pulls out on a motorcycle.*)
An artist in the true sense of the word.
MACGREGOR: And the next Senator from the great state of Pennsylvania.
(As BOB *rides off, we hear his voice, muffled by the helmet:)*
BOB: Seize the day!

EXT. INTERSTATE HIGHWAY. MORNING
The bus glides through the last breath of the morning led by BOB ROBERTS, *our hero,*
dressed in white fencing gear riding a customized Harley Davidson Chopper.
   COMPLAIN *continues:*
BOB: *(Sings)* . . . I spend all my time
         drunk in a bar
         I want to be rich,
         I don't have a brain
         so give me a handout
         while I complain.

EXT. INTERSTATE HIGHWAY. DAY
BOB, *on his motorcycle, and 'The Pride' drive down the highway. The camera follows*
the bus as it passes, then finds TERRY MANCHESTER *standing in front of a log cabin.*
He holds a microphone and speaks directly into the camera.
TERRY: Bob Roberts, fencing enthusiast, poet, folksinger, businessman,
         Senatorial candidate . . .

INT. TERRY'S VAN. DAY
Through the windshield of Terry Manchester's van, we see the back of Bob's bus and
the words 'Vote Bob'. TERRY *speaks in the foreground.*
   TERRY, *our host for the documentary, is an English journalist–documentarian in*
his early forties, all business and few smiles, good at his craft. He does not have the
'glitz' of a television journalist, there is no pretence of show business in him. His clothes
look as if they've been slept in and his grooming is, for want of a better description, lax.
TERRY: The controversial, yet extraordinarily popular entertainer first
         appeared on the music scene three years ago with his début album, 'The
         Freewheelin' Bob Roberts'.
         (Insert: album cover 'The Freewheelin' Bob Roberts')
         Despite being assailed by the music critics as a corrupt, unfair diatribe
         against the sixties, the album, remarkably, soared to number 23 on the
         Billboard Charts.
         (Insert Billboard *headline 'Roberts Selling Brisk in Key Markets')*

EXT. CHILDREN'S HOSPITAL SCRANTON. DAY
'The Pride' pulls up at the entrance of the Scranton Children's Hospital. We catch Bob

Roberts exiting the bus preceded in rapid formation by his trusted associates. They are all impeccably dressed, groomed and coiffed; serious young professionals, shrewd and relentless, rising stars in the corporation that is Bob Roberts. They are:

CHARLES 'CHET' MACGREGOR, *the eldest, a twisted genius with Kennedy charm. He is the direct liaison between* BOB *and* LUKAS HART III, *and Bob's Chief Advisor and Campaign Manager. The master of the 'Spin'.*

CLARK ANDERSON, *a tall red-headed man with dangerous eyes and impetuous physicality. An associate of Bob's, he is his closest friend, fencing partner and stunt coordinator.*

DELORES PERRIGREW, *beautiful, a conservative woman with lots of brainpower and savvy. She writes Bob's speeches.*

FRANKLIN DOCKETT, *a whitish black man. He is also a bodyguard, as well as Bob's personal trainer.*

BART MACKLEROONEY, *bodyguard, business whiz, zealot.*

BOB *and his* ASSOCIATES *are greeted by the* HOSPITAL STAFF. *Most of them are fans and embarrassingly familiar.* TERRY *stands in the foreground.*

TERRY: Backed by a team of novices, without the support of a major record
    label, relying on word of mouth and his own team of businessmen and
    associates who seem better suited to a townhouse than a tour bus, Roberts
    creates a niche for himself in a business that at first had contemptuously
    rejected him.
    (Insert: album cover 'Times are Changin' Back')
    His follow-up album, 'Times are Changin' Back', peaks at number 3.
    Quite an achievement for a journeyman folksinger that *Spin* Magazine
    once called a crypto-facist clown.

INT. CHILDREN'S HOSPITAL. DAY
'Just Say No'-style banners hang in prominence along with campaign posters and banners which read: 'Bob For Senate' and 'Vote Bob'.

BOB *and* HART, *followed closely by the* ASSOCIATES, *are greeting people.*
SECURITY GUARDS *are screening the press with uni-code scanners as they enter.*

We move closer in to reveal a man arguing with a SECURITY GUARD. *We cannot hear him at first. Then we see (and hear)* BUGS RAPLIN, *a nervous man in his thirties (who we will get to know well in this documentary), who is still young enough to believe anything and will stop at nothing to find the truth.*

BUGS: This is a press conference.
GUARD: Yes, that's true, but you have the wrong pass.
BUGS: I don't see the problem here.
GUARD: The problem is you need to go to the police department and get the
    proper pass.

INT. HOSPITAL CORRIDOR. DAY
The camera tracks backwards as we watch a crowd of press people and hospital officials and staff following the candidate and his entourage. BOB *is flanked by* DR CALEB MENCK *and* LUKAS HART III.

A quietly intense man, LUKAS HART III *walks with* BOB ROBERTS, *photographers seizing the opportunity to photograph the two of them together.* HART *is the brains behind the operation. Despite his smooth appearance, he is a shrewd shark of a man, a clever manipulator of the media and a ruthless businessman.*

TERRY: (*Voice over*) On July the 4th of this year, Bob Roberts announced his candidacy for the US Senate seat in Pennsylvania. This documentary chronicles the man and his quest for election.
(*Everyone stops for a photo op.*)

BOB: Eight years ago, I had had enough. I had . . .

INT. LARGE DINING HALL. CHILDREN'S HOSPITAL. DAY
'Just Say No' banner. 'Roberts For Senate' posters.

BOB *speaks to the children and administrators as* LUKAS HART *stands next to him.*

BOB: . . . seen the dreams of a generation squashed by an evil menace. An evil menace called drugs. I made up my mind there and then to dedicate my life to seeing that this problem end in our lifetime.
(*The audience applauds.*)
I contacted my friend, Lukas Hart, and I enlisted his help. And it is because of Lukas Hart's diligence and efforts that eight years ago Broken Dove was born.

INT. HOSPITAL. CHILDREN'S WING. DAY
During the last part of Bob's speech we see BOB *sitting, guitar in hand, informally singing to a room of pyjama-clad children who smile as they sing along. The song is an up, cheery tune: 'Skip to Malou'.*

BOB: (*Off screen*) Broken Dove is hard at work fighting the war on drugs but it will take time. We must start the war early, ladies and gentleman. We must start the war with our children, at home and in our classrooms!
(*We see one of Bob's* SECURITY MEN *at work.*)

LITTLE GIRL: (*Off screen*) Hey, mister, can I see your gun?
(*She approaches* DOCKETT.)
Can I see your gun?

DOCKETT: What makes you think I have a gun?
(*The music continues as:*)

INT. HOSPITAL. CHILDREN'S WING. DAY
BOB *plays 'Cops and Robbers' with a group of sickly children playing, cajoling, running. The children laugh. They love* BOB.

In another corner of the Children's Wing, we see LUKAS HART, CHET
MACGREGOR, TERRY *and* DR CALEB MENCK *speaking privately. We cannot hear
them, but Terry's camera moves in close.* HART *motions towards the camera.*

HART: (*To camera*) That's enough.

MACGREGOR: (*To camera*) Come on over this way. There's some great shots
with the kids.

    (*He leads the camera to* BOB *and the children.*)

    The camera pans back to BOB *and the children. Bob has fallen. He is shot.*)

BOB: You got me. Good work kids. I'm dead.

    BOB *nods and walks towards the camera.* MACGREGOR *makes introductions.
An attractive, well-dressed woman greets* BOB *with a kiss. This is* POLLY
ROBERTS, *his wife.*)

MACGREGOR: Here's Mrs Roberts. Mrs Roberts, Polly.

    (POLLY *kisses* BOB.)

    Polly and Bob, why don't you guys take a picture with the kids.

    (*They sit down for a picture with the children, turn towards the camera and
wave, smiling broadly. The happy couple.*)

MENCK: (*Off screen*) Bob is a tireless worker, unbridled energy. As his doctor, I
know. I tell him to slow down but he won't listen . . .

    (*We cut to* DR MENCK. *He speaks directly into the camera.*)

    . . . without his organization Broken Dove, this clinic, would not exist.

    (*Back to* BOB, POLLY *and the children. They are posing for the cameras.*)

MACGREGOR: (*Off screen*) And now, I want you all to say, 'Vote Bob'.

ALL: Vote Bob!

    (*Cut to:*)

INT. LARGE DINING HALL. CHILDREN'S HOSPITAL. DAY

'Just Say No' banners. 'Roberts For Senate' posters.

    BOB *and his* BAND *play on the stage where we just saw him speak.*

    Song: WHAT DID THE TEACHER TELL YOU.

BOB: (*Sings*) What did the teacher tell you
        in school today,
        in school today.
        What did the teacher tell you
        in school today, my child?
        Said, 'It's a crime to say a little prayer'
        Said, 'God is no longer wanted here'
        That's what the silly teacher
        told you in school

    (*We see the audience in the hospital, mostly consisting of non-comprehending
children.*)

    (*As the song continues, we cut to:*)

INT. PHILADELPHIA APARTMENT. DAY
TERRY: Robert Roberts Jr was born January 3rd, 1955 . . .
> (*Insert: black-and-white baby photo of* BOB.)
> (*Off screen*) . . . in St Vincent's Hospital, Philadephia . . . (*On screen*) In his
> early years, Bob lives on a commune in rural Pennsylvania.

INT. PHILADELPHIA APARTMENT. DAY
A woman in her late fifties, dressed simply with no make-up. CONSTANCE *is honest,
direct and smiling through her real belief.*
CONSTANCE: It was an idealistic attempt . . .
> (*Insert: black-and-white photograph of* BOB *as child with commune dwellers.*)
> . . . This was the late fifties, pre-hippie. We tried to establish a community
> based on the idea of collective responsibility.

INT. ROBERT ROBERTS' HOME. DAY
BOB SR: It was a crazy idea, nuts. It was an unrealistic environment for a child
to grow up in.

INT. PHILADELPHIA APARTMENT. DAY
CONSTANCE: We moved to Philadelphia when Bobby was three.
> (*Insert: film of Bob's childhood house.*)

INT. TELEVISION STUDIO NEWS SET. PHILADELPHIA. DAY
A LOCAL NEWS ANCHOR *glamorously reports the news:*
ANCHOR: It'll be cold today, chilly, chilly, chilly, as the leaves of Autumn make
way for the chill wind of winter. Early snow was reported in some
mountain regions, but don't dust off the skis yet folks, here in Philly it's a
brisk 43. And that's the news at the top of the hour. And now, our own
Kelly Noble interviews Senatorial candidate Bob Roberts.
> (*Simultaneously, we hear a verse from 'What Did the Teacher Tell You':*)
BOB: (*Voice over*) . . . If you don't agree
>   You've no right to object
>   We all must be politically correct . . .

INT. TELEVISION STATION. DAY
*A comfortable 'Live at Five' atmosphere. This is the 'Good Morning Philly' television
show:*
> Long shot: BOB *is being miked by a technician.*
A STAGE HAND *adjusts a microphone on* KELLY NOBLE, *a black female reporter.
She readies herself. In the foreground there are monitors with close-ups of* BOB *and*
KELLY.
KELLY: Personally, I must say up front before we go on the air that I am not a

fan of your music. I find it offensive, and, I'm sorry, I wouldn't vote for
you if my life depended on it . . .
(*The* DIRECTOR *of the television interview show gives the high sign to* KELLY
and she begins the interview.)
Good morning, Philadelphia. Our guest today is Bob Roberts,
Pennsylvania Senatorial candidate and folksinger. Our viewers are
curious about where it all began. Where did it start for you?
(BOB *is immediately guarded, almost antagonistic.*)

BOB: Where did what start?

KELLY: Well, was it a small colonial home with a mom in a yellow starched
dress and a dad in a seersucker suit?

BOB: You're speaking of my upbringing?

KELLY: Yes, your upbringing.

BOB: Well, Kelly, I came here to talk about the issues, but I will happily
indulge your personality search.
(*Insert: The* STATION MANAGER, MACGREGOR *and* HART *watch the
interview from the side.*)
I was born and raised lower middle class right outside the City of
Brotherly Love, Philadelphia, Pennsylvania. My father was a fry-cook, my
mother, a peacenik. I had no brothers or sisters. Make your judgements if
you must.

INT. PHILADELPHIA CLASSROOM. DAY

TEACHER: He was a model student.
(*Insert: photographs of* BOB *in Grade School, a brooding, serious kid.*)
So full of life and energy. Some of the other kids didn't like him very
much. Oh, but I did. Very much.

INT. PHILADELPHIA APARTMENT. DAY

TERRY: Increasing restlessness and trouble with authority figures and
classmates create problems for Bob in high school and by his senior year
his grades have fallen.
(*Insert: newspaper headline 'Teenager Missing, Feared Dead . . . Parents' Plea:
Bob Come Home'. Pull back to reveal picture of teenage* BOB.)

INT. CONCERT HALL. PHILADELPHIA. NIGHT

We see BOB *on the stage. He is rapping to the audience, tuning his guitar:*

BOB: I know what it's like to be without a home. I was homeless when I was
seventeen. Get this straight, Jack, I didn't ramble I didn't roam. Nosiree,
no boxcars or park benches,
(*We pan across a sea of faces as they listen intently to their hero,* BOB
ROBERTS.)

no panhandling for me. I went straight to work. Earned enough money out on my own to enroll myself in a school of my choice, a school I wanted.

INT. CONSTANCE ROBERTS' APARTMENT. DAY

CONSTANCE: That's not quite true. Bobby enrolled himself in military college by forging my signature on a check of mine.

INT. ROBERT ROBERTS SR'S HOME. DAY

Insert: photograph of BOB *in military school uniform.*

ROBERT SR: (*Off screen*) He was happy there. He said it was because he needed discipline, more structure in his life. He felt we offered too much freedom.
(*Insert: newspaper headline: 'Teenager Reappears'. Pull in on quote: 'Parents are Potheads Claims Wayward Son'.*
(*On screen*) And do you know what? He was right.

INT. PHILADELPHIA APARTMENT. DAY

CONSTANCE: I was trying to instill different values in him than the ones he has now. Let's just leave it at that.
(*We get the feeling she wants to say more, but doesn't.*)

INT. TELEVISION STUDIO. DAY

The interview continues: during the following we cut between different views of the interview, viewing much of it through monitors in the studio, in the foreground and background.

BOB: The sixties are, let's face it, a dark stain on American history. At no other time has lawlessness and immorality been so widespread.

KELLY: You are speaking of Watergate and our invasion of Cambodia.

BOB: No, no, I'm not. I see, I'm speaking of you, I'm speaking of lawlessness and immorality with regard to drug use and sexual practice.

KELLY: Excuse me?

BOB: Disregard in the press for the sacred institutions that have made this country what it is today.

KELLY: Is social protest disregard for our laws and institutions?

BOB: Certainly it is.

KELLY: And yet it is a guaranteed right in our Constitution.

BOB: So is burning the flag. Need I say more?

KELLY: Yes, you need say more. Or are we to believe that what Bob Roberts wants to see in America is a compliant . . .
(*We see the* STATION MANAGER, HART *and* MACGREGOR *discussing the direction the interview has taken.*)

... and silent public which respects the wishes and actions of its
presidents, no matter how immoral or illegal?

BOB: Are you a Communist?

KELLY: Excuse me?

INT. CONCERT HALL PHILADELPHIA. NIGHT

Bob's rap continues:

BOB: Self determination. The choice to be what you want to be. And I wanted
to be ... rich.

(*The* AUDIENCE *laughs, and applauds,* BOB *starts playing a song.*)

TERRY: Roberts graduates from Westmoreland Military Academy with
honours in 1977, and is selected as a candidate for a masters degree in
business at Yale University. In 1980, Roberts graduates from Yale and
begins his phenomenal rise on Wall Street.

(*Song:* THIS LAND WAS MADE FOR ME.)

BOB: (*Sings*) Grandma felt guilty
       'bout bein so rich
       And it bothered her
       until the day she died
       But I will take my inheritance
       And invest it with pride
       Yes invest it with pride

(*After the first verse, the song continues under:*)

INT. TELEVISION STUDIO. DAY

The interview continues.

Nearby, HART *and* MACGREGOR *are talking to the* STATION MANAGER. *The*
STAGE MANAGER *is frantically cueing* KELLY *to wrap it up.*

BOB: You have just said that our chief executives are immoral criminals.

(HART *leads the* STATION MANAGER *off.*)
I take offence at that. Deeply. I am an American that believes intensely in
morality. And I believe in the sanctity of the office of the presidency. I
trust that the American public do not share your cynical anti-American
views and will cast their votes accordingly, with pride and conviction.

(*The theme music is cued and the monitors cut to the* ANCHOR.)

ANCHOR: Thank you Kelly and Bob Roberts for that thought-provoking
dialogue. 'Good Morning Philadelphia' will be back.

(*The camera pans back to* BOB *and* KELLY, *now off the air.* KELLY *continues
the conversation as they get up and move away from the set.*)

KELLY: I certainly hope not, because it seems you would like Americans to cast
their vote based on hatred and ignorance.

(*The camera pulls back to follow as* BOB *and* KELLY *move off the set towards the waiting entourage.*)

BOB: What is that? You are taking sides ma'am. You are abusing your responsibility as a journalist.

KELLY: I am offended by you, sir. If I ignore my feelings, I'm taking your side.

BOB: Yet, isn't your job one of objectivity?

KELLY: You're not talking about objectivity. You're talking about ignorance.
(*Sees* DOCKETT.)
Is he yours? (*To* DOCKETT.) Hey, brother, does getting in on the ground floor mean checking your skin at the door?

DOCKETT: Wait a minute, can't black people have more than one opinion?

KELLY: Oh, you're still black?

DOCKETT: Yeah, I'd like to think so. I guess we all have to adhere to the same militant black party line.
(*As* KELLY *walks down the studio hallway the* STATION MANAGER *begins to yell at her.*

KELLY: (*Off screen*) I don't want to hear it.
The camera pans back to BOB *and* MACGREGOR, *who are speaking with the* ANCHOR.)

BOB: You do such wonderful work on the news.

ANCHOR: Oh, do you think so?

BOB: Always watch ya.
(MACGREGOR *pins a 'Vote Bob' button on to the Anchor's jacket.*)

MACGREGOR: You're now a member of our campaign team.

BOB: There's a Vote Bob button for you.

ANCHOR: All right. I'm honoured. Do you think I could get another one for my son?

MACGREGOR: Of course, we'll send you several.

BOB: Take care, Dan.
(BOB, MACGREGOR *and the entourage leave.*)

ANCHOR: Take care. You're welcome here any time, Bob. Good luck on the campaign trail.
(*The* ANCHOR *watches them leave.*)

ANCHOR: Great.
(*Bob's song continues under the following:*)

INT. STUDIO DRESSING ROOM. DAY

KELLY *in her dressing room, fed up. We see her reflected in her own mirror, with* TERRY *in the background.*

KELLY: Bob Roberts is yet another of that faction that lives to destroy whatever good came out of the sixties, to rewrite the history of this important period. A period where the American people actually were informed and aware and realized they had a voice. They demanded that a war end. Bob

Roberts is Nixon. Only he is shrewder, more complicated, this Bob Roberts. Now here is a man that has adopted the persona and the mind-set of the free-thinking rebel and turned it on itself. The Rebel-Conservative! *That* is deviant brilliance! What a Machiavellian poseur!

INT. CONCERT HALL. PHILADELPHIA. NIGHT
Bob's song continues. The AUDIENCE *joins in, singing along.*
BOB *and* AUDIENCE: This land is my land
>   This land is our land
>   You gotta be proud to be
>   In the land of the free
>   This land was made for us
>   This land was made for me.
>   (*The* AUDIENCE *erupts again and begins chantin 'Bob!'* BOB *waves – salutes – from the stage.*)

INT. STAGE DOOR, SCRANTON. NIGHT
BUGS RAPLIN, *the reporter who was denied access at the hospital, paces nervously near the stage door waiting to interview* BOB ROBERTS.
     BOB *exits the hall with his entourage and heads for the tour bus. In the background we hear the crowd still cheering.* BUGS *attempts to talk to* BOB.
BUGS: Mr Roberts? My name is Bugs Raplin. I'm from *Troubled Times Journal*.
>   I was wondering if it might be possible to arrange an interview.
BOB: Certainly. My pleasure. Chet?
MACGREGOR: Yes, certainly, here's our number, you can contact our
>   campaign headquarters.
>   (*The entourage gets on the bus.* BUGS *looks at the card.*)
BUGS: Yeah, right.
>   (*The camera follows the entourage on to the bus.*)

INT. TOUR BUS. NIGHT
As we enter, BOB *goes into the back room and starts reading the* Wall Street Journal.
ANDERSON: (*Off screen*) OK, let's fire it up!
>   (MACKLEROONEY *goes straight to a terminal and places a call to Tokyo. He speaks for a while in Japanese, then puts his hand over the receiver and reports back to* BOB, *who is reading in the background.*)
MACKLEROONEY: Nikei is up twenty-four thousand, forty-one, forty-five.
>   (*George Bush–Saddam Hussein–troops footage makes way for a report on* BOB *on the WAPW Scranton Action News. We go in full-screen on the television. The camera pulls out from the television periodically to reveal the* ASSOCIATES *in rapt attention to the television screen. The newscasters* CHUCK MARLIN *and* CAROL CRUISE, *with reporter* ROSE PONDELL, *are presenting news about*

BOB *and his opponent for the Senate seat,* SENATOR BRICKLEY PAISTE.

CHUCK MARLIN: Thank you, Carol. Senator Brickley Paiste was on the campaign trail yet again yesterday. Paiste sampled homemade goodies while visiting the Local Ladies Auxiliary in Dusquesne . . .

(*Insert: Video of* PAISTE *eating blueberry pie.*)

CHUCK MARLIN: Paiste then presided over the dedication of the Steam Torpedo Monument in Pittsburgh.

(*Insert: video of* PAISTE *dedicating a torpedo.*)

PAISTE: I think it highly suitable today, as war clouds once again are upon the horizon, that we dedicate this steam torpedo as a symbol of the thirteen million of us that fought in World War II.

CHUCK MARLIN: Carol?

CAROL CRUISE: Thanks, Chuck. Senator Paiste's opponent Bob Roberts is creating quite a sensation in his Pennsylvania Election Tour, playing to sold-out audiences, from Scranton to Pittsburgh. The candidate was in town today, paying a visit to the local Menck Clinic. With the story, Rose Pondell. Rose?

(*Insert: on monitor, hospital media footage of scenes we saw earlier.*)

ROSE PONDELL: (*Off screen*) This is the Menck Clinic in Scranton, a clinic set up with money raised by Broken Dove, Senatorial candidate Bob Roberts' private relief organization.

(*We see* ROSE PONDELL *standing in front of the stage at the hospital where* BOB *had played earlier.*)

The Menck Clinic and Broken Dove honoured Bob Roberts this afternoon in a ceremony at the clinic.

(*Insert: shot of* BOB *and* LUKAS HART *at the children's hospital.*)

HART: . . . honouring you as 'Patriot of the Year'.

(*Applause. We see a close-up of* BOB *smiling and waving with* POLLY. *On the television we see* DR MENCK.)

MENCK: Bob has a great vision for the future of our country and a great vision for the future of the children of our country. He is the only man to vote for.

(*On the television we see a group of fans including three young teenage boys,* ROGER, CALVIN *and* BURT, *some with flags, in line outside a venue.*)

ROGER: (*On TV*) He's amazing. He's a poet, and a genius.

ROSE PONDELL: It is clear to all present here that drugs are a tough problem and that a tough man is needed to tackle that problem. From all indications, Bob Roberts just might be that man.

(*We cut to wide shot on the bus, revealing the entourage watching the monitor.*)

With the Roberts campaign in Scranton, this is Rose Pondell, WAPW Action News.

MACKLEROONEY: (*Off screen*) Fabulous package, Bob!

ANDERSON: Excellent!

PERRIGREW: Excellent, Bob.

CAROL CRUISE: Thank you, Rose. Chuck?

CHUCK MARLIN: Thank you, Carol. Recent polls show incumbent Senator
Paiste in the lead over Roberts by ten percentage points. But sources in
the Roberts campaign say that Roberts will be a strong finisher. I could
use a strong finisher myself sometimes, Carol, how about you? (*Laughs.*)

CAROL CRUISE: (*Laughs*) More news in a moment.

(*As the report ends,* MACGREGOR *emerges from the back of the bus with a phone
in his hand, giving a thumb's up.*)

MACGREGOR: Mr Hart loves it!

MACKLEROONEY: What about Bob?

MACGREGOR: Bob loves it, too.

TERRY: What is Lukas Hart's connection with Bob's success?

MACKLEROONEY: No connection.

PERRIGREW: Lukas Hart is helping send Bob Roberts to Washington.

EXT. PARKING LOT. MORNING

BOB *and* ANDERSON *fencing in a parking lot. A steel mill and a barge in the
background.*

The match continues furiously. We intercut between the match and MICKIE, *the bus
driver.*

MICKIE: They do this every morning. This could last for hours. This throws
me behind schedule. And it pisses me off. I'm the one that gets the
speeding tickets, not him. But I really don't give a shit. I just try. I do the
best I can.

EXT. HIGHWAY. DAY

BOB *in fencing gear, rides his Harley, which roars down the interstate.*

ANCHOR: Good Morning, Philadelphia. Senator Brickley . . .

(*Insert: newspaper photo of* PAISTE *with a teenage girl. Pull back to reveal
headline: 'Paiste in Teenage Liaison'.*)

. . . Paiste angrily denied allegations today regarding a report that ran in
the *Pittsburgh Post Times* accusing him of an extramarital liaison with a
campaign worker.

PAISTE: (*On TV*) The girl in question is a friend of my granddaughter and had
the entire photograph been shown, you would have seen my
granddaughter sitting in the back seat of the car. I deeply resent this
slander and you can be sure that I'm going to find out who's behind it.

ANCHOR: Overnight polls show that Senator Paiste's lead has slipped
considerably and is now ahead of Roberts by only a narrow margin.

EXT. INTERSTATE HIGHWAY. DAY

'The Pride' glides through the leaves of autumn. On the sides of the tour bus there is artwork and the words: 'Vote Bob' and 'The Pride'.

MACGREGOR: (*Off screen*) We are doing very well in every area of the state. The key thing I think is that we're doing well in the depressed areas. And these areas have been hit very hard. They're very depressed economically. Plants have closed. Supporting industries have closed.

INT. THE PRIDE TOUR BUS. DAY

MACGREGOR: People don't have jobs. They can't afford to feed their families. They're foreclosing on their homes. Something has to be done for these people. And Bob's going to do it.

(*A cacophony of activity. The entourage are all on various telephones, dealing manically.*

BOB is talking rapidly on a state of the art mobile phone with a headset. After making each order he glances at a computer monitor manned by DOLORES PERRIGREW as the next stock option is called up.)

BOB: Clark, check the security coordinates. We're going to be there in a minute.

PERRIGREW: Call, uh, um –

BOB: Henry.

PERRIGREW: Henry at CNN.

BOB: (*To DOCKETT*) Fifty thousand.

(*A shot of PERRIGREW working frenetically on a monitor with a stock option read-out.*)

PERRIGREW: What's the stop loss on the bean crush?

MACKLEROONEY: Five thousand at six!

DOCKETT: Next!

(*BOB again, on his mobile phone:*)

BOB: We want out. There was a fax on that.

MACKLEROONEY: I sent a fax on that.

BOB: Read your faxes, Lavalle, or you'll be on a slow boat to Tiananmen Square, understand?

(*PERRIGREW laughs. Over the following, we hear TERRY in a voice over:*)

TERRY: Bob Roberts is a living tribute to the possibilities of the American dream. A self-made man at the age of thirty-five, he is rumoured to have a net worth of something over forty million dollars. Today, I'm waiting to meet Bob Roberts in the sanitary confines of 'The Pride': his functionally designed, two-room trading floor on wheels.

BOB: What's next? Oh, Jimminy, do I have to do everything? Do some homework for goodness sake. Get some information. Keep your nails clean. All right, that's it. Right.

MACKLEROONEY: Your fax, Clark. (*He gets up and crosses to the front of the bus.*)
ANDERSON: Thanks, Bart.
    (CHARLES MACGREGOR *leans out of the back section of the bus, a private office. He looks concerned.*)
MACGREGOR: Bob, Mr Hart on two.
BOB: I'll call him back.
MACGREGOR: That's a code yellow, Bob.
BOB: Be right there.
    (BOB *turns to* TERRY, *who waits politely.*)
    Sorry. Ever since this Iraq business talking with your broker is like talking to a rambling, insecure child.
TERRY: Oh, really?
ANDERSON: Who was that?
BOB: Lavalle.
ANDERSON: He's gone.
PERRIGREW: Oops, there goes the pool.
DOCKETT: There goes the house in the country.
    (*They all laugh.*)
TERRY: Tell me something, the world market's been in a tumultuous state for the last three years, ever since the Crash of '87. How did you do? Did you lose money in the Crash?
MACKLEROONEY: (*Sarcastically*) Yeah, right.
DOCKETT: What's funny?
BOB: (*To* DOCKETT) Back to work. (*To* TERRY) The slow lost money in that crash. Smart money got out before the junk bond hit the fan if you know what I mean. Granted, that information was up to the minute gold-plated information, cost me considerable effort and diligence, and if I had been out when those calls came in, I would have been screwed, but I am a smart businessman. A wee and dee, if you will. I know the market importance of paging systems and mobile phones. What's getting everyone nervous nowadays is their lack of control of the political situation overseas. You can't readily obtain that type of information. But you can stay in touch and – I'm not going to say too much. There are things you can do. There are ways you can read the world. And what I read excites me, quite frankly.

INT. ALLEY. DAY
A music video for the song 'Wall Street Rap'.
    An MTV-style title reads: 'Bob Roberts "Wall Street Rap" Times are Changin' Back Pride Records'.
    BOB ROBERTS *stands in the alley holding big cards with words (lyrics) printed on them* à la *Bob Dylan in the 'Subterranean Homesick Blues' film.*

DOCKETT *and* MACKLEROONEY *stand off to the side, speaking on mobile phones, in front of a pile of bags of money.*

Nine DANCERS *in business shirts and ties and black skirts dance behind* BOB, *who turns cards, revealing words from the song, and tosses them aside one by one.*

Song: WALL STREET RAP.

> Michael takes a loan from
> a midwestern S&L
> He puts the money down
> a quick dryin' inkwell
> Takes a loss, gets cross,
> walks to the corner store
> Pulls a knife, calls his wife,
> can't take it anymore
> Look out Joe,
> how far will it go?
> Take away the fire
> and where does the water flow?
>
> Jerry's in the attic
> messin' with the static
> Junior's on the telephone,
> nothing problematic
> Julie's selling T-bonds,
> her bill is turning over
> John is building walls
> manipulating a takeover
> Look out Joe,
> How far will it go?
> Take away the fire
> and where does the water flow?
>
> Get tough, get right
> try to get some sleep at night
> Try hard, get harder,
> love to win, live to fight
> Own the town, love the best,
> don't share the treasure chest
> If you cheat, get away,
> lead 'em down an alleyway
> Look out Joe,
> how far will it go?
> Take away the fire
> and where does the water flow?

Look out Joe,
how far will it go?
Take away the fire
and where does the water flow?

(*As the* DANCERS *dance off,* DOCKETT *and* MACKLEROONEY *each grab a bag of money and follow the* DANCERS. *The song ends and* BOB *stands staring into the camera.*)

INT. BOB ROBERTS' TOUR BUS. DAY

BOB: Now is the time to invest. We mustn't be intimidated by Third World madmen. We must stay strong and market confident. Reluctance feeds the aggressor. Or as we say on 'The Pride', 'If you're afraid of an active market . . .'

BOB *and* ENTOURAGE: 'You're a dead man'!

ANDERSON: Perrigrew, prepare to dock! Let's lock and load!

BOB: There'll be a resolution in the mid-East and a bull market before you know it, mark my words. Thank you for your time.

(BOB *leaves suddenly, moving towards the door of the bus.*)

ANDERSON: Cobra, Whitey one. We're on the move.

(ANDERSON, DOCKETT *and* MACKLEROONEY *exit first, followed by* BOB *and then* MACGREGOR *and* PERRIGREW. *The camera follows.*)

EXT. FREEDOM HALL HARRISBURG. DAY

BOB *and the entourage continue towards the backstage door.* BOB *signs some autographs, but is still on the phone.*

BOB: Lukas, we're rocking and rolling on the campaign. Rocking and rolling.

ANDERSON: Everybody to the right, please.

(BOB *listens as he moves towards the stage door. The camera moves, with* BOB *and the others in the background.* FANS *approach and take pictures.* BUGS RAPLIN *approaches.*)

BUGS: Mr Roberts. Mr Roberts. I contacted your campaign office and they told me I had to be connected to a major news network or newspaper in order to get an interview.

BOB: Well, that's ridiculous. You talk to Chet MacGregor back there and he'll take care of it.

(BOB *and most of the* ENTOURAGE *start to enter the building.* MACGREGOR *motions for* MACKLEROONEY *to take* BUGS' *name.*)

MACKLEROONEY: What is your name?

BUGS: Bugs.

MACKLEROONEY: Bugs?

BUGS: John.

MACKLEROONEY: John.

BUGS: John Alijah Raplin.

MACKLEROONEY: John Raplin. Publication?

BUGS: *Troubled Times*.

MACKLEROONEY: There'll be a pass waiting at the door tonight. (*He smiles and enters the building quickly.*)

BUGS: Yeah, sure.

INT. BACKSTAGE GREENROOM. LATE AFTERNOON

The camera starts on a Robbie Conal vision of BOB, *a grotesque image, with 'Time is Money' on the top and 'Time for Bob' written on the bottom.*

The camera pans to reveal: BOB, PERRIGREW, DOCKETT *and* MACKLEROONEY *all seated, having finished off a sushi lunch.* MACGREGOR *stands in front of a selection of campaign poster mock-ups.* ANDERSON *is at a desk in the background, on the phone. They are laughing at the poster.*

MACGREGOR: It scares the hell out of me.

BOB: Oh, my goodness. I don't think so, Chet.

MACGREGOR: Of course not, it's a bad idea. You wanted to see it through.

PERRIGREW: Mr Hart thinks we should just stick with the Bob Roberts in the red, white and blue. Simplicity, strength.

MACGREGOR: Well, I tend to agree with Mr Hart. This one is just too basic, too simple. This one severe, strong. I like it, but it's too strong. And this one's a nightmare. It scares me.

BOB: I know. I tend to agree with Mr Hart as well. Stick with the current campaign, red, white and blue. Bart?

MACKLEROONEY: Absolutely Bob.

BOB: Dockett?

DOCKETT: Straight up, Bob.

BOB: Terry, what do you think?

TERRY: Me? I think there's no question. That's the one.

BOB: (*To camera*) What about you? You. (*Smiles.*)

TERRY: Nigel.

(*The camera moves up and down in agreement. Everyone laughs.*)

MACGREGOR: The nodding Nigel. Thank you. All right, next up. Our new television commercial.

BOB: Oh, terrific.

MACGREGOR: All right, guys, get out of the way. Bob, you sit here. Scat, Bart.

MACKLEROONEY: Sorry.

MACGREGOR: It's fifteen seconds. It makes its point strongly. Starts airing tomorrow. (*He puts on the VCR. The commercial starts.*)
(*Insert: TV commercial. On the television, we see a black screen. Music. A flower gently swaying in the wind in front of a sunrise. The slogan, 'For a New*

Day', appears. Then, abruptly, with a surge of music: 'Vote Bob' appears in front of the sunrise.)

BOB: What do you think, Bart?

MACKLEROONEY: I love it, Bob.

BOB: Dockett?

DOCKETT: Chilly most, Bob.

BOB: (*To* PERRIGREW) What did he say?

PERRIGREW: 'Chilly most'.

BOB: What the heck is that?

DOCKETT: Cool.

PERRIGREW: It means terrific, Bob.

MACGREGOR: Glad you like it. Now we have two more spots in production. We'll be able to view them at the end of the week. Now next up, we have the Mayor's wife right outside, lovely lady, wants to see you. And three boys who want to say hello to Bob Roberts.

BOB: Oh, my pleasure.

MACGREGOR: Right this way.

(*As* MACGREGOR *leads* BOB *and* PERRIGREW *out,* ANDERSON *speaks to his security.*)

ANDERSON: Cobra Two, we're on the move.

(*As they exit the dressing room, we see:* MRS DAVIS, *the Mayor of Philly's wife, beaming, as do the three young teenage fans:* CALVIN, BURT *and* ROGER. *They are almost speechless in his presence, young Bob disciples. Their uncomfortable shuffling and embarrassed demeanour is quite funny to look at.* BOB *immediately presses the flesh.*)

BOB: Hello.

MRS DAVIS: Hi.

MACGREGOR: Mrs Davis. This is Bob Roberts.

MRS DAVIS: We're so happy to have you here. We are so proud to play your music in our home, sometimes I play it when I'm alone but don't tell my husband. (*She laughs.*)

    Anyway Frank and I both agree that you are an excellent example for the youth of this country. We wish there were more singers like you, and we intend to vote for you.

BOB: Oh, thank you.

MRS DAVIS: We're so tired of Brickley Paiste and all his philandering. Anyway, this is my son, Roger and his two friends, Burt and Kevin.

CALVIN: Calvin.

(*The three teenage boys,* ROGER, CALVIN *and* BURT, *shuffle nervously, heads bowed, eyes averted in the presence of their hero.*)

ROGER: Pleased to meet you sir. We got all, both albums. Hi.

CALVIN: Yeah. Hi. Nice to meet you sir.

BURT: Hey. Hi. Ho. Yeah. Yeah. Yeah.

(*We see* BOB *smiling, almost laughing at this nervous adulation.*)

ROGER: We got a band. We actually, we play some of your songs. We play 'Retake America' and 'This Land was Made for Me'.

BOB: You have a band? What instruments do you play?

ROGER: We all play guitar.

MRS DAVIS: I must admit that when young Roger first wanted his guitar my husband and I were fit as birds . . . but my husband trusted his son would take the lessons of the Lord with him no matter what instrument of the devil caressed his hand.

ROBER: You inspire us a lot to do stuff. You're great.

CALVIN: Yeah, you know. We wish that there was, you know, stuff. Like you know like there was, if there was, you know when I heard that, wow, you know. (*He is losing it. He's drooling.*)

BURT: Are there any more stuff? When's the new album?

BOB: Election Day. We're releasing it Election Day.

(MRS DAVIS *cuts in.*)

MRS DAVIS: Mr Roberts has to be on his way.

(BOB *and* PERRIGREW *begin to go.* MRS DAVIS *walks with them. The* BOYS *follow.*)

MRS DAVIS: What are the songs about?

BOB: Various things. The Congress. Liberals. Iraq.

BURT: Yeah, we heard about that.

CALVIN: What?

BURT: Iraq.

CALVIN: Yeah, we heard about that. I hope we kick their ass.

(*A pause.*)

Yeah.

BURT: Yeah.

CALVIN: Yeah.

MRS DAVIS: So do I. Do you think it will be necessary to use force?

BOB: We must be strong and resolute, whenever democracy is threatened, Ma'am. We want to avoid violence by any means, but I'm afraid it might be necessary. Hussein's a madman. Excuse me.

(MACGREGOR *steps in.*)

MACGREGOR: You'll have to excuse us now, Bob has a show to get ready for, you know.

MRS DAVIS: Of course. Bob Roberts, it has been a pleasure meeting you. I just wish there was a way I could vote for you a hundred times.

BOB: There is, actually.

MRS DAVIS: Really?

BOB: Yes. (*Pause*) Just kidding.

INT. BACKSTAGE CONCERT HALL. HARRISBURG. NIGHT

It's just before the concert. The camera moves backstage and finds Bob's band in prayer.
MACGREGOR*'s face appears in the camera, and leads it away.*
MACGREGOR: Let's not shoot this. Come on, come on over here with me.
>   (*Insert: photo of* BOB *and* HART.)
BUGS: (*Off screen*) In order to under-

EXT. THEATRE. HARRISBURG. NIGHT

BUGS RAPLIN *stands across the street from the theatre.*
BUGS: -stand who Bob Roberts is, you have to understand who Lukas Hart the
>   third is. Lukas Hart is a spook, one of the Langley crowd new guard. Hart
>   has been living in the shadows for years. He was a lieutenant. Vietnam.
>   Special Forces. Worked on the infamous Phoenix Program. Transferred
>   to South American operations. Helped overthrow Allende. Messed
>   around in Central America, probably popped a coupla heads – boom
>   boom – set up an organization called Broken Dove which supplied
>   transport planes to US government operations. Got his hands real dirty
>   during Iran–Contra but the Senate washed them clean.
>   (*Insert:* LUKAS HART III *testifying before the Iran–Contra investigation.*
>   SENATOR BRICKLEY PAISTE, *questions him.*)
>   *Title Card:* IRAN–CONTRA HEARINGS JUNE 1987
HART: . . . I can't recall.
PAISTE: You 'can't recall', I see. Did you or your organization Broken Dove
>   have anything at all to do with the transport plane that was downed in
>   Nicaragua on May 23, 1987?
HART: Sir, the plane was contracted to fly humanitarian supplies into
>   impoverished regions in Southern Honduras. Broken Dove is a private
>   relief corporation.
PAISTE: So you had no knowledge of the guns that were on that plane?
HART: No sir.
PAISTE: But the three men were all close business associates of yours?
HART: Rest their souls, yes. These were patriots acting on their own volition,
>   their own beliefs.
PAISTE: Can you sum up these beliefs for us?
HART: That the US Congress was restricting the growth and safeguard of
>   democracy in Central America. That the actions of these men, although
>   against the Boland Amendment, were nevertheless on the side of
>   goodness and decency.
PAISTE: I have a copy of an FBI report regarding traces of cocaine found on
>   one of the transport planes.
>   (*Sound of a gavel being struck.*)
SENATOR HAYDN: Mr Chairman. This is sensitive material that will be dealt

with in closed session.

CHAIRMAN: We had an agreement about this.

HART: This is not an investigation. This is just another example of the depths
to which the US Congress is prepared to sink. This is a travesty.

INT. BACKSTAGE DOOR. THREE MILE ISLAND. NIGHT

TERRY: (*Off screen*) But the charges against Broken Dove were found to be
groundless and the organization was completely exonerated.
(*In the background we see* ROGER, BURT *and* CALVIN *in a shoving match with
a* PROTESTOR *outside the concert hall.*)

BUGS: The whole investigation was a sham. They discovered a secret
government of liars and drug smugglers, didn't do a thing about it.
Slapped these traitors on the wrist. Big deal. The story died in the major
press. It's idiots like me who keep investigating who find out just how
deep it goes. I am meeting a contact later who claims to have evidence that
connects Broken Dove to a failed Savings and Loan. Can you believe it?
This could be big. Gotta go.

SENATOR HAYDN: (*Voice over*) I cannot believe the lies and innuendo that you
have been the victim of. It is clear that you had no involvement with this
escapade and that we are wasting your time. I am sorry.
(*Insert:* LUKAS HART III *at Iran–Contra Hearings.*)

HART: I appreciate that.

HAYDN: Is there anything that you would like to add, Mr Hart?

HART: These allegations are erroneous at best, always have been, always will
be. How much more of this fiction does my family have to suffer. God
knows, I would have thought that I had done enough by now to make my
position on narcotics perfectly clear.

INT. CONCERT HALL. THREE MILE ISLAND. NIGHT

BOB *and* CLARISSA FLAN, *a folk singer, singing. A title identifies* CLARISSA *as Miss
Broken Dove 1987.*

Song: DRUGS STINK.

BOB: (*Sings*) Drugs stink
they make me sick
Those that sell em
and those that do em
String em up
from the highest tree
Without a trace of sympathy

Drugs stink, drugs stink
Be a clean living man

with a rope in your hand
Drugs stink, drugs stink
Hang em high
for a clean living land

Pot headed wierdos, sex deviates
Dancing fools your day is done
It's time to leave
the face of our earth
Dope smoking morons,
dirty hippie freaks

Drugs stink, drugs stink
Be a clean living man
with a rope in your hand
Drugs stink, drugs stink
Hang 'em high
for a clean living land

EXT. INTERSTATE HIGHWAY. DAY
'The Pride' on the road. We hear a TV news programme theme, then cut to see it on the
screen with newscaster CHIP DALEY.
CHIP DALEY: Despite recent economic indications showing a stagnant
    economy, at least one business is showing an increase in profit: ribbon
    manufacturers are showing a tremendous increase in demand as
    Americans everywhere are showing their support of our troops in the
    Persian Gulf.
    (*Insert: newspaper headline 'Paiste Stung by Rumor' over a picture of Paiste.*)
PAISTE: Well, Mr Bob Roberts has suggested that he . . .
    (*Insert: newspaper headline 'Paiste Weak on Defense, Roberts Says', then pull*
    back to reveal entire front page of the Pittsburgh Post-Times *'Saddam Must*
    Be Stopped' 'Public Split on the Use of Force')
    . . . knew which way I was leaning on the question of war in the Middle
    East and I'm totally opposed to it. Oh, it's the enemy of the month club
    again.

INT. BRICKLEY PAISTE'S OFFICE. DAY
TERRY *is interviewing* PAISTE.
PAISTE: Saddam Hussein, I believe is, what is he, the most evil man, what did
    the President say, since Adolph Hitler. Before that was Noriega, he was
    the most evil man since Fu Manchu, and then there was Khadafi, and
    then there's Castro. And these figures are thrown out to the media and
    made into great monsters. Why? Because we must justify the military

budget. In order to do that, you must have enemies. So we blow up these
local thugs into these huge, Hitler-like figures and pretend it's World
War II all over again.

INT. BOB ROBERTS' TOUR BUS. DAY
Again, a cacophony of activity. BOB *and the entourage are all on various telephones,
dealing manically.*
MACKLEROONEY: Do not pin your hopes and dreams on transport planes.
    They're only going to build transport planes if the shooting war is
    prolonged . . . Well, something tells me that it is not going to be another
    Vietnam . . . A little bird tells me this.
BOB: Was it Hart, Dockett?
ANDERSON: C'mon, Get it, get it! The North side corridor isn't clear . . .
DOCKETT: . . . Six thousand and twelve. Next, sell 25,000.
MACKLEROONEY: Trust me. Hang on to those puts. Hang on . . . How can I
    help you – Vote Bob?

EXT. ALTOONA TOWN HALL. DAY
*In an establishing shot we see people of all types waiting to get in to the town hall. On a
banner we see: 'Broken Dove presents: Miss Independence, PA – Freedom from
Drugs'.*
    Title Card: BEAUTY PAGEANT ALTOONA PENNSYLVANIA

EXT. ALTOONA TOWN HALL. STAGE DOOR. DAY
BOB *and entourage arrive. Waiting at the stage door are* ROBER, BURT *and*
CALVIN, *the three boys* BOB *met backstage the previous night. They are giggling
nervously.*
ROGER: Bob, that was the best.
BURT: That was amazing.
ROGER: Excellent.
BOB: (*As he walks by*) Thanks.
CALVIN: We love you, Bob.
    (*The entourage enters the building.*)
ROGER: Ah, cheez whiz, Calvin. Don't be a fag.

INT. ALTOONA TOWN HALL. DAY
The manic reporter we met earlier, BUGS RAPLIN, *meets the entourage as they enter
through the stage door. They move away from* BUGS, *but he follows. The tension is
high. The camera stays primarily on* RAPLIN.
BUGS: You support the political action group, Broken Dove?
BOB: Yes. Proudly. Broken Dove in an organization that works effectively to
    keep children off drugs.

(The entourage have entered a dressing room full of beauty pageant contestants and their mothers.)

MOTHER: Wrong room.

ANDERSON: Sorry.

(The entourage excuse themselves and continue down the hallway.)

BUGS: Before its current incarnation as an anti-drug organization, Broken Dove bought transport planes that were involved with the smuggling of drugs.

BOB: That is completely absurd and subversive, and old news. Broken Dove was already exonerated of these ridiculous charges by the United States Senate. Thank you for your time.

BUGS: Recent evidence, however, suggests that these planes were purchased with money from a low-income housing loan given to your organization by West Pennsylvania Savings and Loan, a now-insolvent thrift.

BOB: What are you saying?

BUGS: You took money meant for housing to buy planes to smuggle drugs.

BOB: That's completely ridiculous. Chet, did you hear that?

MACGREGOR: Yes.

(The entourage passes a contestant practising her flute.)

BUGS: Then where is the money from those loans?

BOB: Building houses.

BUGS: Where exactly are these houses?

(They are now in the Men's bathroom. They exit and continue on, desperately searching for the right door.)

Do you feel any responsibility for the illegal activities carried out by the groups you support?

BOB: I told you already that Broken Dove was exonerated of these charges.

ANDERSON: *(Off screen)* Left.

BOB: Why would you ask a – Didn't you hear me? Why would you ask a question like that? What would motivate that?

BUGS: I am talking about new evidence connecting Broken Dove to the failed S and L.

BOB: What is your question?

BUGS: What?

(The entourage have entered a boiler room where a contestant practises the drums as another dressed as Bo Peep does vocal warmups.)

BOB: Ask the question. What is the question?

BUGS: A group you support was recently implicated . . .

BOB: Yes. And?

BUGS: And how do you explain . . .

(Another wrong door.)

BOB: And what? What is meant by the word 'implicated'?

BUGS: To suggest. To connect.

BOB: To suggest, not to prove, not to indict.

(MACGREGOR *comes into frame.*)

MACGREGOR: Are you making allegations that you are willing to back up in a court of law?

BUGS: Allegations?

MACGREGOR: Because the camera has just documented all of this on film.

(BOB *looks at the camera. Smiles.*)

Haven't they?

BUGS: I don't think you're being fair.

MACKLEROONEY: You don't think he's being fair?

BUGS: No, I don't.

MACGREGOR: Where is your evidence?

BUGS: I have here a sworn affidavit –

BOB: I don't think you are showing even the slighest respect, and more importantly you are abusing your responsibility as a journalist.

ANDERSON: Shut off the camera, please.

BOB: No, no. Leave it on. Leave it on.

(*They have reached another room where there is a Japanese candle dancer and five contestants practising a tap dance.*)

BUGS: Is being responsible as a journalist to ignore the issues, to gloss over the facts, to paint only favourable portraits?

BOB: No. Responsible journalism is objective. The interviewer does not bring his own opinions into the interview. He is objective.

ANDERSON: Bob, this way.

(*But it is the wrong way. A mime enters briefly into frame.*)

BUGS: I feel I am being objective. I've asked you a question and you have evaded it.

BOB: I've evaded nothing. You've asked an incredibly slanted question based on lies and conjecture and I have responded with an answer appropriate to that kind of yellow journalism.

(BOB *has stopped. They have found their way.*)

BUGS: And that answer, if I get it correctly, is?

BOB: The answer is I don't talk to liars and I don't talk to gossip mongers. Now, this interview is over. Thank you for your time.

MACGREGOR: OK, turn the camera off now, please.

MACKLEROONEY: OK. Let's go. Hey! The interview is over. C'mon.

BOB: Bart, Bart, would you please escort this gentleman to the door, if you can find it.

(MACGREGOR *turns his attention to the camera.*)

MACGREGOR: (*To camera*) OK. That's enough.

(*The camera sees* TERRY, *who quickly shakes his head. It continues running, shifting down.*)

BUGS: Mr Roberts, is it true you referred once to crack as being 'the great equalizer'. Are you callously suggesting that crack serves to reduce the African-American population and destroy its community. Mr Roberts!
      (MACGREGOR *looks at camera.*)

MACGREGOR: We had an agreement about this. Bob says cut it off, you cut it off?

TERRY: It's off.

MACGREGOR: Underst – All right, thank you.

BOB: (*To* ANDERSON) What the hell is this? (*To* MACGREGOR) Is that off?

MACGREGOR: Yes it's off – Isn't it off?

TERRY: Yes.

BOB: (*To* ANDERSON, *furious; another side of* BOB) What in the hell is this? This is a meltdown! Where were your men, Clark?

ANDERSON: We took the wrong door.

MACGREGOR: Clark, this can't happen. It can't!

DOCKETT: (*Off screen*) You were supposed to go where? You were supposed to meet me upstairs. You have to learn to listen to me, man. This is not – We can't do this. We have a campaign we gotta win, understand?
      (BOB *motions for* MACGREGOR *to go towards the camera.*
      We go to black.)

INT. ALTOONA TOWN HALL. NIGHT

BOB *sings, while the* CONTESTANTS *parade along the runway.*

      Song: BEAUTIFUL GIRL.

BOB: She's a beautiful girl,
            as pretty as a picture
            She's a day in May,
            as real as today,
            She's got to be a girl

            She's a beautiful girl,
            a face full of flowers
            A dynamite dame,
            she's destined for fame
            She's got to be a girl
      (*We see* RITA, *the obsessed female fan, with her head in a Bob Roberts poster.*
      PERRIGREW *is in the wings watching.*
      During the instrumental portion of the song, an ANNOUNCER *introduces each of the* CONTESTANTS *separately and they each wave and smile.*

ANNOUNCER: (*Off screen*) Ladies and Gentlemen, the finalists are: Miss Crucible. Miss Broken Dove. Miss Three-Mile Island. Miss Pittsburgh.

Miss Road-Kill. Miss Philadelphia.
(*The song continues under.*)

INT. ALTOONA TOWN HALL. NIGHT
BOB *and the entourage exit the maze of hallways.*
MACKLEROONEY: Goodbye, Mother.
(*The camera follows as they reach the stage door. With them is* JENNIFER *and*
NICOLE, *contestants from the beauty pageant.*
Just outside, in front of the bus, BUGS RAPLIN *awaits. As the entourage moves*
through the waiting crowd of fans, and nears him, he steps up.)
BUGS: Mr Roberts, you are a traitor, a drug smuggler. And you're gonna pay,
you're gonna pay!
(BUGS *is pushed out of the way violently by* ANDERSON *as the entourage*
continues, silent. They enter immediately into their bus. We turn to see BUGS,
still outside the open bus door, yelling.)
BUGS: You sold out your country, Mr Roberts, and I'm gonna get you! I'm
gonna get you!
(*The camera turns back towards the back of the bus to reveal* RITA *standing in*
the back of the bus still with the Bob Roberts campaign poster around her head.)
OBSESSED FAN: You're looking at me, Bob! You're looking at me!
(*As* DOCKETT *and* MACKLEROONEY *rush her off the bus, she continues*
calling to BOB.)
OBSESSED FAN: I'm sorry, Bob. I'm sorry!
(*They throw her off the bus and* BUGS *is still outside, yelling.*)
BUGS: I'm gonna get you, Bob Roberts! I am going to get you!

INT. 'THE PRIDE' TOUR BUS. NIGHT
We see a report on the television. Two anchors, CHIP DALEY *and* TAWNA TITAN,
are delivering the news, and in the middle of a laughing jag they can't help.
CHIP DALEY: A recent report on homelessness by the Coalition for the
Homeless estimates that over – I can't read that – Americans live without
homes and a lot of Americans live below the poverty level. At a press
conference today, Senator Brickley Paiste addressed the problem.
PAISTE: I've just been discussing the Paiste Amendment, which I shall
introduce into the Senate the following week which will earmark two
hundred million dollars for the homeless throughout the country. Where
does the money come from? Well, it's the famous Peace Dividend which I
hope very much the President will not transform into an investment in
war.
(*We reveal the entourage minus* BOB *watching the monitors. The two contestants,*
JENNIFER *and* NICOLE, *are with them.*
The following dialogue happens over the following news reports:)

ANDERSON: . . . is that you blow smoke just before the election on an issue. He knows he can't get this bill passed.

DOCKETT: Sure he knows.

ANDERSON: No one can get the bill passed.

MACKLEROONEY: . . . it comes from the pockets of unemployed defence workers.

(*A news report on* BOB ROBERTS *at the Beauty Pageant comes on to the television.*)

MACGREGOR: Here it is. Sssh.

TAWNA TITAN: On a lighter note, the Miss Independence Beauty Contest was held tonight at the Altoona Town Hall. Contestants came from throughout the state vying for top honours and the chance to represent Pennsylvania in the national finals. Current Senatorial candidate Bob Roberts was there lending his support for the contest. And the winner was Miss Crucible.

(*We see* MISS CRUCIBLE. *She is African-American.*)

CHIP DALEY: Bob Roberts' anti-drug organization, Broken Dove, sponsored the pageant, which has donated its proceeds this year to a program for drug education in the schools. Tawna?

JENNIFER: . . . you talk a lot about your childhood.

MACGREGOR: You do? That's exciting.

NICOLA: She had really great rhythm.

JENNIFER: You know she told me she's never even had fried chicken before.

(*Everyone laughs,* DOCKETT *shifts uncomfortably in his seat.*)

MACKLEROONEY: Well, what do you know?

TAWNA TITAN: Recent polls show Bob Roberts jumping ahead of Senator Brickley Paiste in their race for the Senate as Paiste can't seem to shake the accusations of sexual misconduct that hit his campaign last week.

REPORTER: (*Off screen*) Senator Paiste, have the allegations hurt your campaign?

PAISTE: (*In hallway*) Of course not, this is America. Virtue always prevails.

EXT. HIGHWAY. DAY
'The Pride' roars down the road.
Title Card: PITTSBURGH, PA
Insert: We hear a serious instrumental theme and see the graphic: 'Pennsylvania Senate Campaign Debate'. And we cut to:

INT. DEBATE HALL. NIGHT (VIDEO FOOTAGE)
An historic hall set up for a debate. Two podiums flank a table at which a MODERATOR *is seated.*
BOB *stands at one podium, at the other incumbent* BRICKLEY PAISTE, *the other candidate for Senator.*
The debate is already in progress and PAISTE *is answering a questions posed by the* MODERATOR.

MODERATOR: Senator Paiste, recent reports suggest that the Roberts
 campaign has been behind the leak of the story regarding yourself and a
 teenage campaign worker.

BOB: That is a lie.

MODERATOR: Mr Roberts.

PAISTE: The whole thing is a lie. I've already explained that the girl in question
 is a close friend of my granddaughter and I was driving them both home. I
 am also distressed that a 16-year-old who has done nothing wrong should
 be so publicly vilified. As for Bob Roberts, I could imply guilt by
 association, which I think you would like me to do, but I won't. Because I
 do not believe and I have never believed in negative campaigning.
 (*We cut between the two candidates, highlights of the debate.*)

BOB: Ladies and gentlemen, why can't you get ahead? Why can't you have the
 home of your dreams? The fast car? A nice vacation?

PAISTE: Let's tackle the homeless problem. Let's tackle childcare, healthcare.

BOB: Why has your American dream been relegated to the trash heap of
 history? I'll tell you why, because of the wasteful social programs of
 Brickly Paiste.

PAISTE: Let's put people back to work. Create jobs, encourage industry. I can
 see a brighter future but we have to work hard and, dare I say it, sacrifice.

BOB: And I remind the public that Brickly Paiste still has not told us how he
 will vote on the use of force in the Persian Gulf.

PAISTE: We need a strong America, dedicated to issues that matter. We need
 to care about people.

BOB: Let's cut taxes! Let's make it possible for the working man to keep the
 money he earns.

PAISTE: Because that's what politics is really about: reality, not image.

BOB: Vote for me and I will bring the values of the common man to bear in
 Washington, DC. I will bring youth and experience and passion and
 belief.

PAISTE: So let us be real together.

BOB: Thank you for your vote.
 (*Applause from the audience, we see* BOB *and* PAISTE *cross to the centre and
 shake hands. Then* POLLY *and* LUKAS HART III *join their man on stage. They
 all wave confidently.*)

INT. BRICKLY PAISTE'S OFFICE. DAY
TERRY *interviews* PAISTE.

PAISTE: I was quite disturbed during our famous debate, if it could be called
 that. A series of photo opportunities is perhaps more precise. I get
 vibrations from Mr Bob Roberts of a very disturbing sort. I haven't any
 idea who he is. I haven't any idea what he's like. I don't think I'm

supposed to have any idea. I know that he proved to be a master of pushing racist buttons, and sexist buttons, this and that. The politics of emotion. He's very good at that. What's behind it? I don't see anybody at home. But I will say that once or twice, in the course of our debate, I detected a slight whiff of sulphur in the air.

INT. CONCERT HALL, PENN STATE. NIGHT
BOB ROBERTS *sings a duet with* CLARISSA FLAN.
Song: DON'T VOTE.
BOB *and* CLARISSA: I'm a bleeding heart
    let's give money away
    To lazy people in the slums
    I'm a bleeding heart
    Let's eliminate our nuclear bombs
    Arabs can be . . . our friends . . . Right.

    Don't Vote
    if you believe in that
    we'll be fine without you
    It's plain to see
    what you believe
    will lead to anarchy

    So if you're hanging to the right
    You can vote for me
    It is your God-given right
    From sea to shining sea

    What's right is right
    what's left is wrong
    Who'll dare to sing this song
    C'mon and join this mighty train
    and all the free will live again
    C'mon hop and sing this song
    together we'll be strong
    And vote
(Intercut with the song is the following scene:)

EXT. CONCERT HALL. PENN STATE. NIGHT
BUGS *again. he speaks faster than humanly possible.*
BUGS: I've been up all night. I had to meet the deadline. Lead story. 'Bob Roberts and S&L' by Bugs Raplin. And I quote – this based on a source I spoke to last night. October 22, today's: an unidentified source involved

in the West Pennsylvania Savings and Loan disaster told this reporter that in 1987 an organization called Broken Dove procured real estate loans under the pretence of building housing for the homeless and proceded to use the money to buy transport planes for private enterprise. Active board members at the time included businessman Lukas Hart III and senatorial candidate Bob Roberts. Roberts and Hart ripped off Savings and Loans to buy planes. The money meant for low income housing went to buy planes to smuggle drugs.

TERRY: This is an astonishing accusation.

BUGS: This is the smoking gun. He's going down for this one.

BUGS: If the majors pick up this story, I'll be very surprised. I don't expect that they will. But I have a contact at a TV station in Harrisburg. Maybe he'll run it. This could be big. I gotta go.

(*He motions to the paper in* TERRY's *hand.*)

Hey, you keep that.

INT. CONCERT HALL. PENN STATE. NIGHT

Most of the audience applauds wildly.

BOB: How about a big hand for Clarissa Flan?

(*The audience applauds and* CLARISSA *leaves the stage joyous.*)

Thanks, Clarrie. This next little ditty is dedicated to . . .

VOICE: Bob stinks!

(*About five of the audience members, all dressed in white, are chanting 'Bob Stinks! Bob Stinks!'. Bob sees them, looks straight at them and says:*)

BOB: This next little ditty is dedicated to you!

Song: COMPLAIN.

(*He sings*)

Some people must have
some people have not
and they complain and complain
and complain and complain and
complain

Some people will work
some simply will not
But they complain and complain
and complain and complain and
complain

Like this: It's society's fault
I don't have a job
It's society's fault
that I'm a slob

I've got potential
no one can see
Give me my welfare
and let me be me.

Hey bud you're living in
the land of the free
No one's gonna hand you
opportunity
(*The live performance begins to intercut with* PROTESTORS *outside.*)
Some people must have
some never will
But they complain and complain
And complain and complain and
complain

EXT. CONCERT HALL. PENN STATE. NIGHT

PROTESTORS *intercut with the song above.*

PROTESTOR 1: Bob Roberts doesn't represent the common man, he represents
   big business.

PROTESTOR 2: ... contemptible yuppie scum ...

PROTESTOR 3: It's all about 'me' and *his* money. And that's why I'm out here,
   it's the only natural thing to do.

FEMALE PROTESTOR: He talks about traditional American values as if he
   defined what they were. As if traditional American values meant greed,
   distrust and avarice.

PROTESTOR 1: He passes the buck of blame on to the silent, who he knows will
   not respond. According to Bob Roberts, the disenfranchised are the
   problem, the reason for the mess we're in. Kind of like blaming the woman
   for the rape or the dead for the murder.

FEMALE PROTESTOR: The way that I learned about traditional American values
   were that they had something to do with altruism, equality and kindness.

PROTESTOR 3: Forget human rights, forget women's rights, forget helping the
   homeless, let me tell you that. All that's going to go away. They're going to
   take all the money that everybody makes and they're going to use it for their
   own benefit. And that's what's going to happen.

PROTESTOR 1: Bob Roberts is not for the people. He's for himself and the
   people who have made him powerful.

PROTESTOR 3: I mean, he reminds me of the roast beef, you know, at the
   butcher shop, up front, the good piece of meat that they bring out for the
   big and the powerful, whoever they are. But underneath that beef,
   something smells, let me tell you.

EXT. CONCERT HALL. PENN STATE. NIGHT
An altercation is underway between Bob supporters (including the BOYS*) and some of the* PROTESTORS.
BOB SUPPORTER: You guys are both commie liberals.
PROTESTOR: What are you doing? You're so young.

INT. 'THE PRIDE'. NIGHT
CLARISSA *plays a song softly.* BOB *is working on a laptop computer.*
CLARISSA:
>   We are marching always forward . . .
>   Never slow to fall behind
>   A day of triumph in the mind . . .
>   We are moving towards
>   a great day

(The camera pans around to see MACKLEROONEY *and* PERRIGREW *sleeping.* DOCKETT *is on the phone, speaking German.*
On the television we see George Bush, then Saddam Hussein. The camera pans back to BOB *and* CLARISSA. *A news report comes up on the TV.)*
TAWNA TITAN: At the top of our news, violence broke out during a Bob Roberts concert at Penn State University tonight. Sources say that between twenty to thirty students began verbally abusing the popular singer-candidate midway into the concert. As they were being removed from the hall the protestors attacked security guards and a mêlée ensued. Sources close to the candidate say that he is unharmed but quote 'upset at the preponderance of radicals on college campuses today. The sixties are over', said Roberts.
CHIP DALEY: I couldn't agree more, Tawna. Polls released today indicate that Brickley Paiste is running neck and neck in his race against the folksinging politician Bob Roberts. Paiste has been hurt recently by rumours of an affair with a teenage campaign worker, Tawna. Although he has denied the allegations, Paiste has not fully recovered in the polls.
(We pull back from the TV to CLARISSA *and* BOB, *now both singing.)*
CLARISSA *and* BOB:
>   We are marching for the children
>   We are marching for the poor
>   Now we're marching for self-interest
>   We will march forever more

(We see DOCKETT *put down the phone and rub his eyes. Cut to:)*

EXT. PARKING LOT. DAWN
BOB *and* ANDERSON *fencing again. Insert: television news report.*
CAROL CRUISE: A bombshell dropped overnight, Chuck, and the morning

finds us with a story destined to prove troubling for the Bob Roberts campaign. From our sister station in Harrisburg, correspondent Rock Bork.

(Insert: TV news report outside demolished building.)

ROCK: I am standing in front of what once was the West Pennsylvania Savings and Loan which, until last year, was a viable functioning thrift. Only a year ago federal regulators closed the bank and began an investigation of improprieties involving misuse of funds. Tonight comes information that Lukas Hart III, Bob Roberts' campaign chairman, may be subpoenaed to tell the regulators what he knows about an organization called Broken Dove and its involvement with unpaid housing loans.

EXT. PARKING LOT. DAWN

MACKLEROONEY *and* DOCKETT *are scoring the match and speaking to* TERRY. *Behind them, reflected in the chrome of the bus, we see a reflection of* BOB *and* ANDERSON *fencing.*

MACKLEROONEY: Hello, reality check. Broken Dove ripping off S&L's? *The* Broken Dove for whom altruism far surpasses net worth?

DOCKETT: Broken Dove whose donations to hospitals work effectively to keep youngsters off drugs?

MACKLEROONEY: Accuse your enemy of your own worst crime.

DOCKETT: A dictum of disinformation.

MACKLEROONEY: Credo hippocretus.

DOCKETT: Pot calling the kettle black.

(The match continues: TERRY *interviews* MACGREGOR *in the foreground.)*

MACGREGOR: You know Terry, most political campaigns would pale in comparison, but this one is a peach.

*(*BOB *has lost the match. As everyone rushes about, preparing to leave,* MACGREGOR *keeps talking.)*

It's like a vicious, hard-fought game, you see. Close to the final minutes, then absolute chaos reigns. And then one team explodes, right through the proverbial roof, as it were. The dust settles, the blood is flowing. It's a massacre.

*(*BOB *climbs aboard his motorcycle, starts it.)*

But that one team is jumping up and down with big, silly grins on their faces. That's gonna be us, Terry. Fun, that's what it's all about. Fun. There's nothing like the unbridled fun of a hard-fought campaign.

*(*BOB *peels out dangerously, the back wheel slides out, he wrestles to compensate but the bike goes out of control and he goes down, the bike skidding into the dirt.* ANDERSON, MACKLEROONEY *and* DOCKETT *run to* BOB, *the camera following.* BOB *is slow in getting up.)*

MACKLEROONEY: He's down.

ANDERSON: Seal the wound! Seal the wound!

DOCKETT: Call an ambulance!

BOB: Get your goddamn hands off me, you fag . . .

> (*He gets up.* PERRIGREW *and* MACKLEROONEY *arrive. Everyone walks towards the bus.*)
>
> Put your guns away . . .! (*To* ANDERSON) You get on the goddamn bus. Security's falling apart. Bush league, pal. Bush league. Get the goddamn camera out of here!

ANDERSON: Everybody on the bus!

MACGREGOR: Terry, ride behind in the van. We'll see you in Bethlehem,

EXT. INTERSTATE HIGHWAY. DAY
'The Pride' in motion through a beautiful backdrop of nature.

INT. BEST CHURCH. DAY
We are in a large congregational hall. A Spiritual Revival is in progress.

> BOB *is finishing a duet with* EDNA, *a black born-again gospel singer. Behind them on the stage is a choir in robes and an organist who is 85 years old.*
>
> *The preacher is* REVEREND PETE BEST. *His sermon is intercut with the song.*
>
> *Song:* TIMES ARE CHANGIN' BACK.

BOB *and* EDNA:

> We shall not be moved,
> we shall not be moved
> We shall not be moved today
> Our minds are quick
> and our hearts are smooth
> We shall not be moved today
>
> Times are changin' back,
> Times are changin' back
> Times are changin' back today
> Deep in my heart I do believe
> Times are changin' back today.

REVEREND: Today children, I'm talking hypocrisy . . . Hypocrisy that winds itself down, every day from Washington DC . . . The hypocrisy of an organization that calls itself the US Congress. The hypocrisy of an investigation that seeks to implicate patriots, our dearest friends, in the constant struggle to make this land a pure one once again. Lord pave the way for a rebel's path to Washington. Make the road a smooth one for Bob Roberts, a man who can clean up the devil's mess in our Capital. Say Amen!

CONGREGATION: Amen!

REVEREND: Say AMEN!
CONGREGATION: AMEN!
REVEREND: AMEN!
CONGREGATION: AMEN!
> (*We see* BOB. *He is deep in thought, somewhere else.*)
> (*Insert: television news report.*)

CAROL CRUISE: Despite his efforts to rise above what may or may not be the truth, trouble seems to be following the Roberts campaign. Chuck?

CHUCK MARLIN: Yes, Carol, it seems more bad news has come for Roberts. This morning it was announced that Lukas Hart III, Bob Roberts' friend and campaign chairman was subpoenaed today to appear before the Senate Subcommittee investigating the West Pennsylvania Savings and Loan scandal.
> (*On the television,* LUKAS HART *appears outside a courtroom, briefcase in hand and surrounded by a team of lawyers.*)

HART: Partisan manoeuvring, unsubstantiated innuendo. These allegations are hogwash. The timing is obviously meant to hurt us, but there's not a chance it will, the voters are gonna see straight through this pathetic attempt to derail our campaign. Thank you.
> (*As he walks away from the reporters,* HART *shoves violently at the lens of the camera.*)

CHUCK MARLIN: The subpoena has come as a shock to the campaign and campaign staffers fear a slippage in the polls. Despite Hart's denials, this could spell trouble for the Roberts campaign. Carol?

CAROL CRUISE: More news in a moment.
> (*Insert: television commercial. Sound of a phone ringing. We start close on the receiver in a trash can, then follow the cord up to a desk. All the lines on the phone are lit up, ringing. The desktop is littered with paper and a scribble on the blotter reads: 'I Love Teens'.*
> *Someone is sleeping on the desktop, his head resting on a porno magazine.*)

MAN: (*Off screen*) The current Senator of Pennsylvania believes in giving free rides to welfare recipients. The current Senator of Pennsylvania believes in giving unqualified men and women jobs that could be yours. The current Senator of Pennsylvania voted to give himself a pay raise last year. Paiste. As he sleeps, we live his nightmare. Wake up. Vote Bob.
> (*A super reads: Paid for by Citizens for Bob Roberts*
> *Insert: newspaper headlines: 'Investigation Rocks Roberts Campaign' and 'Paiste Retakes Lead'*)

INT. TELEVISION STUDIO. DAY
We are at a rehearsal of a sketch on the hip urban rustic set of 'Cutting Edge, Live'.
TECHNICIANS *and* ACTORS *mill about. Three cameras sit idle.* TERRY, *the* GUEST

HOST, *the* WRITERS *and producer* MICHAEL JANES, *a hip, mid-forties man dressed in the latest pastel casuals, discuss the show.*

TERRY: (*Off screen*) One week before the election, amidst controversy and declining polls, the Roberts campaign travels from Pennsylvania to New York City.

MAN *and* WOMAN ACTOR: Can't touch dees!

GUEST HOST: Immigrants.

TERRY: (*Off screen*) Bob has been invited to perform on the highly rated television show 'Cutting Edge Live'. The top-rated show reaches twenty million people nationally, one million in Pennsylvania alone.

MICHAEL: We hope, we hope.

GUEST HOST: Not – not in a real interesting way. More like at the expense of the immigrants.

WRITER: No, no – immigrants love the Kornhausers.

MICHAEL: I think we have to be at the expense of somebody.
  (*While the staff of the show are discussing the sketch which has just been rehearsed, the* DIRECTOR *notices* BOB's *presence, greets him and gets the producer's attention.*)

DIRECTOR: Excuse me, Michael.
  (BOB *and* POLLY ROBERTS *are introduced to* MICHAEL *by* MACGREGOR. *They shake hands. Also present is* CAROL, *the producer's assistant and the self-appointed conscience of the show. They are unaware of the camera's presence.*)

MICHAEL: (*Shaking hands with* BOB) Bob, how are you. Oh, it's nice to see you.

BOB: It's good to see you, too.

MACGREGOR: This is Polly Roberts, Michael.

POLLY: A pleasure.

MICHAEL: Hello, how are you? I'm Michael Janes.

BOB: It's such a pleasure for us to be here, I can't tell you what big flans, er, fans we are of the show – I'm so nervous, I guess –

DIRECTOR: Nothing to be nervous about.

BOB: It's an honour to be here, it really is.

MICHAEL: It's an honour for me to be here, I guess. This is my assistant, Carol.

BOB: Hello, Carol, it's a pleasure.

CAROL: Yeah.

BOB: My wife, Polly.

MICHAEL: And our guest host is . . .
  (MICHAEL *turns to introduce the* GUEST HOST *to* BOB, *but the* HOST *has walked away.*)

DIRECTOR: Working on his lines –

WRITER: – Kornhauser –

DIRECTOR: – immigrants –

BOB: I love the Kornhausers, it's my favourite. 'Can't Touch Dees!'

ACTOR: He knows it.

BOB: Is the Lobster Family going to be on?

DIRECTOR *and* WRITERS: Oh, yeah, absolutely.

BOB: Polly's favourite is the Lobster Family. Sorry to interrupt, carry on.

(BOB, POLLY *and* MACGREGOR *leave.*
The GUEST HOST *immediately approaches* MICHAEL.)

GUEST HOST: Michael, Michael, Michael?

MICHAEL: Yes?

GUEST HOST: What's up with Bob Roberts?

DIRECTOR: Musical guest.

GUEST HOST: You said to me that KRS–1 was going to be the musical guest.

MICHAEL: Right, right. And they're sick –

WRITER 1: – in LA –

DIRECTOR: – standards . . .

MICHAEL: . . . they're in LA, I think,

DIRECTOR: . . . standards . . .

MICHAEL: No, they're sick. They got sick in LA, and they couldn't make the
plane, I think they called before. I think it's an ear thing and they can't fly
because, you know, I mean, they might not be able to hear, and . . .

WRITER 1: Pressure . . .

DIRECTOR: Standards.

INT. TELEVISION STUDIO. DAY

The GUEST HOST *is taping a promo spot for 'Cutting Edge Live'.*

BOB *stands off to his side, waiting to be introduced,* MICHAEL JANES *stands in the
background, watching the monitor, and the three* WRITERS *prompt the* HOST.

DIRECTOR: In five, four, three, two.

HOST: Hi, c'mon and join us for 'Cutting Edge Live' and watch me grovel
before the video altar, with a special guest who I thought was going to be
KRS–1.

WRITERS: 'Can't touch dees!'

HOST: Stop saying that, I'm not going to say that.

MICHAEL: Good. I loved it. How'd we do on time? How'd we do?

DIRECTOR: That was good for time.

MICHAEL: Good for you? You sure?

DIRECTOR: That was good for time, except he didn't say 'can't touch dees'.

MICHAEL: Oh that's fine, we'll do it later. Bob, if you would just strum a little
bit . . .

BOB: Sure.

(BOB *introduces himself to the* GUEST HOST, *who reluctantly shakes his hand.*)

MICHAEL: And if you'll say the first part over again, I'd love to do a, you know, a very pulled together one with the two of them. And they have to stand together.

DIRECTOR: All right, here we go. This is promo number two.

BOB: You want me to say 'can't touch dees'? Absolutely. It would be my pleasure.

DIRECTOR: Promo, number two in five, four, three, two . . .

HOST: Hi – I'm sorry. I'm sorry. I'm leaving. You can come and talk to me, or not. I just got to take some time . . .

BOB: 'Can't touch dees'.

MICHAEL: I liked it, I thought it was good.

BOB: That was it? That was, a . . .

MICHAEL: I dunno, I liked it. Worked for me.

DIRECTOR: You liked it?

(Cut to:)

INT. BRICKLEY PAISTE'S OFFICE. DAY

The PAISTE *interview continues:*

PAISTE: Offhand, I would not say that being a professional singer is the best background for a legislator of the United States, but I believe if Mr Bob Roberts' background, if it is true that he has had some experience with the CIA, then he comes better prepared than most people do to the Senate, with the knowledge of what the real government of the United States is, which is the National Security Council. This was created in 1950 by Harry Truman, and the country is governed by the National Security Council, which is the Defence Department, the CIA in combination with the great makers of weapons around the country. So, he's already had some initiation into true power.

INT. TELEVISION STUDIO. DAY

A rehearsal is in progress. Three WRITERS *and the* DIRECTOR *watch.*

Close-up of BOB *watching the rehearsal, expressionless. The weight of the campaign hangs heavy over him.*

HOST: In the beginning our great company provided appliances for the neighbourhood. We heated your home, refrigerated your food, and improved the quality of your life. We prospered and you loved us. And we grew into a large multinational corporation. In fact, we own this very network.

(Meanwhile, MACGREGOR *and* PERRIGREW *are going over details of Bob's performance with* MICHAEL JANES *and* CAROL.)

MACGREGOR: 'Don't Vote' and a new song.

CAROL: New?

PERRIGREW: Brand new.

CAROL: 'Don't Smoke'. That's what we agreed on I believe. Yeah, yeah, yeah, 'Don't Smoke' and 'Prevailing Tides'. Michael?

(*We cut back to the* HOST.)

HOST: Our chief source of income, however, is the arms industry. Yes, we rely heavily on those fat government contracts to make these useless weapons of mass destruction. (BOB *and* POLLY *watch, unamused.*) And even though we have been indicted and convicted for fraud several times, you don't hear too much about our bad side because we own our own news division.

MACGREGOR: Bob doesn't care about what we agreed on. He made it quite clear to me, when last we spoke, that he feels very strongly about the new material, that he feels it should be said right now, and he will not back down.

(*The camera is tight on a TV monitor. The* HOST *glares into the lens.*)

HOST: So chances are pretty slim that you'll hear reports of our environmental mishaps or the way we bust those unions. We even have a highly rated Saturday night show that the public buys as entertainment with a leftist slant.

(MICHAEL *takes control of the situation.*)

MICHAEL: You know, I'm really sorry, but we actually have a policy on 'Cutting Edge' that no new material is ever performed until it is proven to work. You know, this is live television. This is not a party.

(*We see the* HOST *on stage surrounded by the* WRITERS *and* DIRECTOR. *Trouble is brewing.*)

WRITER 2: It doesn't work.

WRITER 3: It's not funny.

DIRECTOR: You can't do that. It's self-hating. It's shooting your paycheck in the foot. It's crazy. It's self-destructive. And it's not funny.

HOST: I think it's funny.

WRITER 3: Yeah, but you don't have to come to work here next week.

WRITER 1: Look, we all wanna change the world, but we want to do it slowly, and keep our jobs, too, if that's OK.

WRITER 2: Can we just rehearse the lobster sketch?

(*The argument is getting heated.*)

CAROL: I personally find him repulsive. I fought his appearance on this show from the word go. But the network has new owners and they like Bob Roberts. They like a lot of things we don't like. But they're the boss, right? They can tell us Bob's on the show, but guess again, you've got to be crazy if you think we're going to let that fascist yuppie go on live television and just sing whatever he wants to.

MICHAEL: Carol. Would you please calm down?

MACGREGOR: This conduct is quite unprofessional. Let me assure you of
    something, Michael.

MICHAEL: Yes?

MACGREGOR: Bob told me personally he will walk off this show if he isn't
    allowed to express himself freely.

CAROL: Let him walk.

(MICHAEL JAMES *becomes aware of the camera and the gathering interest of the*
    crew.)

MICHAEL: I think we're going to go to my office and we're going to talk about
    this privately.

MACGREGOR: Fine.

MICHAEL: Carol, I want you to call Bonnie immediately and have her place a
    call to Lukas Hart.

CAROL: How do I find him? What jail is he in?

MACGREGOR: Now that was uncalled for!

CAROL: Oh, yeah? Excusez-moi!

MACGREGOR: That's totally uncalled for! She is a loud, abrasive woman!

CAROL: Oh, shove it.

MACGREGOR: And she's rude!

HOST: It is not funny!!!

(*Cut to:*)

INT. HALLWAY OUTSIDE TELEVISION STUDIO. DAY

The DIRECTOR *is speaking to* TERRY.

DIRECTOR: It's been a real crazy week, full moon and all, I dunno, we're an
    hour away from air and, uh, I can't find the host. Michael?

MICHAEL: Where is he? Where is he?

DIRECTOR: I dunno.

MICHAEL: Yeah? Well, that's not an answer. Find him, now!

DIRECTOR: Yeah!

MICHAEL: What are you guys watching?

WRITERS: The news.

MICHAEL: What news? Real news? Well, why don't you do something fucking
    productive, all right?

CAROL: Michael, Michael. It's taken care of.

(PERRIGREW *walks at a brisk pace with an agitated look on her face. She sees*
    MACGREGOR.)

PERRIGREW: I told Bob the network wants a copy of the lyrics. He won't give.
    And he's ready to walk.

MACGREGOR: Mr Hart's on his way down, I think we're going to be OK.

INT. TELEVISION STUDIO. NIGHT

Hand-held camera. The show is in progress. The strains of the final moments of a comedy sketch is heard.

'KORNHAUSERS' (THE ACTORS): Can't touch dees!!!

> (*Laughter.*
>
> *The* 'KORNHAUSERS' *high-five. Applause. Theme music.*
>
> BOB *jumps up on the stage. The response is mixed. Some polite applause, some jeering.*)

BOB: I was going to sing a song tonight called 'Don't Smoke', but in the spirit of live television, I'd like to sing a song I just wrote, a song about courage and conviction in these troubled times.

> (BOB *starts a reel to reel tape machine. The intro begins. Music starts. Bells. Choir. Song:* RETAKE AMERICA. *As the musical intro begins we see the camera pan off of* BOB *to find* CAROL *walking out of the studio.*
>
> *The camera follows* CAROL, *who walks furiously towards the control room.*)

CAROL: That son of a bitch.

BOB: (*Sings off screen*) There's a man for all seasons

> There's a man with a plan
>
> Who's got the courage to take
>
> An honest stand. Me.

> (CAROL *walks down a hallway, the camera following.*)

BOB: (*Off screen*) America is a work of art

> And I thank the Lord
>
> For America.

> (CAROL *enters the control room where* CHARLIE *is chief technician.*)

CAROL: Cut it off. Go to black. Go to commercial, Charlie. What's going on, Michael?

> (CHARLIE *ignores* CAROL.)

MICHAEL: Calm down, Carol. (*He sees the camera.*) Get the camera out now.

BOB: (*Sings off screen*) Retake America

> for your little ones

CAROL: What is this? You lied to me, Michael.

MICHAEL: The network wants it on, Carol.

> (*Behind* MICHAEL *we see* BOB *in a monitor:*)

BOB: (*Sings*) They will look back with pride

> At the things you've done

CAROL: You can't fuckin' do this.

MICHAEL: The network reviewed the material and they want it on.

BOB: (*Sings on monitor*) You don't have a choice

> Come election day

CAROL: Oh, how dare you? This is obscene. It's a fucking commercial for a

fucking political candidate. You've got nothing left, Michael, you're
nothing but a fucking shell with goo inside.

MICHAEL: Are you having your period?

BOB: (*Sings on monitor*) Only one man understands
    The American Way

CAROL: Shit.

(CAROL *turns past camera and leaves the control room. The camera quickly
follows her as, incensed, she walks behind and underneath the bleachers holding
the studio audience.*)

BOB: (*Sings off screen*) America is a work of art
    And I thank the Lord for America
    Retake America.

CAROL: Cocksucking Nazi. Fuck you.

(CAROL *cursing, yanks at some electrical wires. Having disconnected some, the
audio is greatly diminished, we hear feedback, chaos.* CAROL *comes out from
underneath the bleachers heading toward the stage.*

The monitors go to black, then a preset graphic. Panic among the CREW *as they
look to correct the malfunction.* BOB *stops playing. The feedback stops and over
the PA comes the* DIRECTOR's *voice.*

Technicians scramble around. BOB *sits angrily waiting as this theatre unfolds
before him.* MICHAEL JANES *steps onstage.*)

CAROL: What happened??

MICHAEL: You get out. You get out now. This is it. You're through, you are
    finished!

CAROL: Boo hoo hoo.

MICHAEL: You get of here now!

CAROL: No problem.

MICHAEL: Now! Move it! (*To* DIRECTOR.) Ready with the lobster sketch?

MICHAEL: Bob, I'm really so sorry. I want to apologize to you right now. I'm
    very sorry. Very, very humble apologies. You're going to be on the show
    again. And everybody, I'd really love to give a nice round of applause,
    please, to Bob Roberts.

(*The* AUDIENCE *applauds.* BOB *gets up from his stool and walks off the stage.
The camera follows* BOB *out of the studio, passing actors dressed as lobsters.* BOB
is angry, his entourage by his side.

*The Lobster Family Theme. Applause. We hear the dismal sketch beginning in
the background.*)

INT. HALLWAY. DAY
BOB *goes through the studio doors.*
BOB: Where's Polly?

HART: She stayed behind to watch the Lobsters, Bob, she'll join us at the hotel later.

DOCKETT: We're coming out.

(BOB *reaches the elevator where a crowd of people wait to see celebrities.* BUGS RAPLIN *is there and yells out.*)

BUGS: Mr Roberts – Mr Roberts! Did you read my article, Mr Roberts?

(RITA *the obsessed fan suddenly steps up and plants a kiss on* BOB. *As* MACKLEROONEY *hustles her away, two gunshots ring out.*

Before we know what is happening, the camera is bumped, all hell breaks loose, the camera is jostled about again, people are yelling, screaming, panicking. ANDERSON *and* LUKAS HART *have tackled someone.*)

ANDERSON: Get the gun. Get the gun.

MACKLEROONEY: Where'd he go? Who was it?

PERRIGREW: Oh my god. Bob. Bob!

(*The camera comes back to* BOB, *who lies on the ground motionless,* PERRIGREW *beside him, holding his hand.*)

PERRIGREW: Bob. Bob. Get an ambulance!

MACKLEROONEY: Get out of the way! Get back! Get back! Give him some air! Jesus.

(*Chaos.*)

HART: I've got him!

(*The camera swings around to see a man we recognize. It is* BUGS RAPLIN.)

BUGS: What? It's not me. No.

(LUKAS HART *has a chokehold on* BUGS *from behind and keeps him restrained.*)

HART: Check his pockets, Clark.

(ANDERSON *discovers a gun in one of the man's pockets.* HART *moves towards* BOB.)

HART: He's losing a lot of blood. We can't wait for an ambulance. Let's take him in my car. Hurry. Give me a hand.

(HART, MACGREGOR, DOCKETT, MACKLEROONEY *lift* BOB *and take him down an escalator.*

We see glimpses of BOB's *frightened and confused face. . . .* PERRIGREW *in tears.* CALVIN, BURT *and* ROGER *run along with the crowd.*)

INT. LOBBY TELEVISION BUILDING. NIGHT

The camera runs out to find BOB *being put into Hart's car. The doors close and Hart's car pulls away.*

Our camera grabs a taxi and follows.

(*Cut to:*)

EXT. MID MANHATTAN PRESBYTERIAN HOSPITAL. NIGHT
BOB *is hustled out of the car.*
   The camera follows as he is carried towards an Emergency door.
NURSE: You can't come in here.

EXT. MID MANHATTAN PRESBYTERIAN HOSPITAL. NIGHT
TERRY *is getting some footage of the candlelight vigil for* BOB.
BIF (A FAN): This is how it happened: I was waiting for Bob when all of a
   sudden, gunshots, seven or eight of them. I quickly jumped on top of him
   to protect him. That's when I saw them – the Arabs – seven or eight of
   them. I found the main guy, disarmed him, knocked him unconscious,
   while the other guys were running away . . .
   (*A* POLICEMAN *approaches* TERRY.)
POLICEMAN: (*Off screen*) Terry Manchester?
TERRY: Who wants to know?
POLICEMAN: Don't get smart with me. You Terry Manchester?
TERRY: Yes, I am.
POLICEMAN: We understand you were filming during the shooting.
TERRY: Yes.
POLICEMAN: We'd like to look at that footage. It might provide us with some
   evidence.
TERRY: The footage is in my van. I'll get it for you.
   (TERRY *moves off, followed by the* POLICEMAN.)

EXT. MID MANHATTAN PRESBYTERIAN HOSPITAL. NIGHT
RITA *sits on the steps, crying.*
The BOYS *are in deep mourning.* CALVIN *and* ROGER *hug. They all cry.*
ROGER: (*Off screen*) If he dies, I swear to God, I'm going to find that guy.
   (*A* RELIGIOUS ZEALOT *dressed in a hospital gown under his coat holds a cross
   in front of his head and walks towards the camera.*)
RELIGIOUS ZEALOT: Please Jesus, please Jesus, please Jesus – save Bob, save
   Bob.

INT. MID MANHATTAN PRESBYTERIAN HOSPITAL. NIGHT
A press conference is in full swing. REPORTERS *jockey for position, scream out
questions, flashes from cameras are continuous throughout. A* POLICE SPOKESMAN
addresses the throng.
POLICE SPOKESMAN: At 12:17 a.m. this morning, Pennsylvania Senatorial
   candidate Bob Roberts was shot as he was leaving the 'Cutting Edge Live'
   television show. He was shot twice at close range with a 22 calibre pistol.
   His condition has been listed as critical.
REPORTER 3: Is there a suspect in the shooting?

POLICE SPOKESMAN: Yes, we have a suspect in custody. He is under
    interrogation at the present time.
REPORTER 2 (*Off screen*): Who is it? What is his name?
POLICE SPOKESMAN: (*Off screen*) I cannot reveal that information at this time.
    (*We see a replay of the shooting.*)

EXT. MID MANHATTAN PRESBYTERIAN HOSPITAL. NIGHT
As we pan from the doors of the hospital we see that the vigil is now still.
    One WOMAN *is singing* PREVAILING TIDES.
WOMAN: . . . Theirs is a fool's game
        and those that play
        will find their hands tied
        and their hearts dry
        Prevailing tides
        will drown you
        unless you learn
        to swim against them . . .
    (*The bodies all seem to be crowding into a centre point.*
    A news anchor, ERNESTO GALEANO, *is doing a live report from the vigil.*
    As we get closer to the ball of people we realize that they are all listening to
    something and discover it is a portable television on which GALEANO *is seen. The*
    BOYS *are there.*
ERNESTO GALEANO: Well, he's in a serious condition, Jack. And they don't
    know if he'll live or not. Just minutes ago we learned the name of the
    suspect from Frank Ryan of the NYPD. His name is John Alijah Raplin,
    nicknamed 'Bugs'. He's an ethnic male approximately thirty-five years
    old. Not much else is known about the suspect at the present time, but we
    do know that they'll be moving him shortly from the 33rd Precinct for
    further questioning. This is Ernesto Galeano reporting live from Mid
    Manhattan Presbyterian Hospital.
    (*Pandemonium in the vigil crowd as the report ends.*)
VIGILANTE 1: Where's the 33rd precinct?
MANY VOICES: Sssh SSSSSSSHHHHHHHHH!!!
    (*Pandemonium breaks out again.*)
VIGILANTE 1: Alijah. He's an Arab.
VIGILANTE 2: His last name's Raplin.
VIGILANTE 1: Half Arab.
CALVIN: Where's the 33rd Precinct?
VIGILANTE 4: 58th and Third.
ROGER: Let's go.
BURT: Who's going? Let's get that guy.
    (*Different factions set out.*)

VIGILANTE 3: 58th and Third. They're moving him. Let's get him.

CALVIN: Let's Go!!

VIGILANTE 4: They're releasing the assassin! Let's Go!

>   (CALVIN, ROGER, BURT *and about a fourth of the vigil take off down the street. Vigilantes. Cut to:*)

EXT. THREE BLOCKS LATER. NIGHT

The group has become a mob. A man with long hair approaches, unsuspecting; the LIBERAL.

>   *The mob surround him, taunt him.*

BURT: You don't deserve to live in this country, you piece of Arab trash!

VIGILANTE 4: Fuckin' Arab!

VIGILANTE (BIF): Fuckin' Liberal!

VIGILANTE 3: Kill the Arab!

VIGILANTE 1: Fuck you, you fuckin' Arab!

CALVIN: You're gonna die!

>   (*Fists hit him from all angles. The* SOUND MAN *from the documentary team goes in to break it up and gets hit himself.*
>
>   TERRY *joins in trying to reason with the mob, also gets hit.*)

VIGILANTE 3: Get out of here, there's a camera!

>   (*After some chaos, the mob disperses, running down the block. The* LIBERAL, *badly beaten, staggers off in the other direction.*

LIBERAL: (*To the mob*) Fuck you, Man! Fuck!

TERRY: (*Off screen*) Did you get that?

EXT. 33RD PRECINCT. NIGHT

The mob arrives at the Precinct.

>   BUGS RAPLIN *is surrounded by police and is being escorted into a police van. The security is tight and we, at a distance, only catch a glimpse of him. A violent display by the fans, who yell obscenities and throw objects at the suspect.*

VIGILANTES: Kill him!!!

EXT. MID MANHATTAN PRESBYTERIAN HOSPITAL. NIGHT

News reporters and crews mill about.

>   *A group of one hundred or so fans keep a candlelight vigil in the cold. The vigilantes, now calmed, stand at the foot of the stairs in front of the hospital and sing 'Times are Changin' Back'.*

>   *We pan tightly across their faces. They are mostly young, they are truly grieving. We see* CALVIN, ROGER, *and* BURT, *Bob's fans from Philadelphia, and* BIF, *the deranged fan with the boombox.*

>   TERRY *is interviewing* RITA, *whom we saw on the bus and at the shooting. She sits in a ring of white candles.*

RITA: I'm evil, I killed him. It was my fault. I'm bad luck. He said I could kiss him.

TERRY: (*Off screen*) Who? Who said you could?

RITA: One of the Bob men. The men with the black strings in their ears.

(*Insert: footage of shooting*)

RITA: (*Voice over*) He said 'you can kiss Bob'. He said 'Bob wants you to give him a kiss,' and I kissed him, and he was shot.

EXT. MID MANHATTAN PRESBYTERIAN HOSPITAL. NIGHT

PERRIGREW *comes out of the hospital. She is nervous. There is blood on her dress.*

PERRIGREW: I just came for some air.

TERRY: How is Bob?

PERRIGREW: He's gonna live. Thank God.

TERRY: Yes. My God.

PERRIGREW: He probably won't walk, for a while. But he's gonna live and that's what counts.

TERRY: You've all had a very rough evening. I'm sorry we have to bother you.

PERRIGREW: Oh, that's OK. No mind. I'm going to go back up. (*She leaves. Before we cut we see* PERRIGREW *look back towards the camera.*)

INT. HOSPITAL. NIGHT

A press conference. DR CALEB MENCK *and the* POLICE SPOKESMAN.

POLICE SPOKESMAN: Ladies and gentlemen, we have a doctor here who can shed some light on Mr Roberts' medical condition. Dr Caleb Menck.

DR MENCK: I am Bob Roberts' personal physician. I flew up from Philadelphia the moment I learned of the shooting. Mr Roberts' condition is critical. One of the bullets regrettably entered the spinal column at the L5 vertebra, paralysis has incurred in both of his legs.

REPORTER 3: Mike, Mike. Is there any truth to the rumour that the assassination attempt was filmed?

POLICE SPOKESMAN: Uh, yes, the, uh, there was a documentary film-maker present at the scene of the crime and we are now in possession of that film.

(*Pandemonium breaks out at the new information.*)

REPORTER 2: Does the film identify the assassin?

POLICE SPOKESMAN: I have no answer for that particular question at this time.

(*Insert: footage of the shooting*)

The film is being analysed frame by frame. We will inform you as soon as we know.

EXT. MID MANHATTAN PRESBYTERIAN HOSPITAL. DAY
CHET MACGREGOR *stands on the hospital steps.*
MACGREGOR: Well, there's no question it was Raplin. I was standing right
   behind him. I saw him shoot Bob.

EXT. MID MANHATTAN PRESBYTERIAN HOSPITAL. NIGHT
We see LUKAS HART *outside the hospital, surrounded by bodyguards, cameras and*
REPORTERS.
HART: The fact that men like Raplin exist shows what you get with a liberal
   agenda. You pump people full of drugs and pipe dreams and what
   happens? They come gunning for people like Bob. But those folks don't
   realize something. You can't kill the truth. Bob Roberts is not going to be
   stopped by any bullet. He'll be back and man, you better watch out, 'cause
   he's headed straight for Washington. And that's all I've got to say. Excuse
   me, I have to go pray. (*He walks towards his waiting car.*)
REPORTERS: Mr Hart! Mr Hart!

EXT. LOWER MANHATTAN CORRECTIONAL FACILITY. DAY
Hordes of REPORTERS *gather around* MACK LAFLIN, *the court-appointed attorney*
for BUGS RAPLIN.
LAFLIN: The film offers no concrete evidence of any kind regarding my client.
   Mr Raplin asserts that the gun was placed on his person at the scene of
   the attack, that he was set up.
REPORTER 4: Who did it then, if not Raplin?
LAFLIN: That is not my job, sir. That is for the police to find out. I am merely
   representing the accused.
REPORTER 5: Is it true that the assassin was a card carrying member of the
   American Civil Liberties Union?
LAFLIN: I do not know and if he was, so what?
REPORTER 4: Will Raplin be released?
LAFLIN: No, there are witnesses who assert they saw him pull the trigger. He
   is being held in custody without bail. That'll be all for now, thank you very
   much.
   (*Insert:* BOB's *face on the cover of* Newsweek, Rolling Stone, People, Time.)
   (*Insert: newspaper headline 'Polls Show Senate Race Even'*)
TERRY: (*Voice over*) After the attack on Bob's life, the media outcry is
   unprecedented. His face echoes across the American landscape on the
   covers of magazines, in newspapers, and on television specials. He is
   proclaimed 'an American hero', a 'martyr of the New Right', a 'crippled
   prophet of the future'.

EXT. MID MANHATTAN PRESBYTERIAN HOSPITAL. DAY
The YUPPIES *still gathered in vigil are erupting in cheers of 'We Want Bob!'.*
TERRY: (*Voice over*) One week after the shooting, word comes that Bob will be
    released and transported to Pennsylvania by medivac helicopter in time
    for the election.
    (*Title Card:* ELECTION EVE
    One fan, BIF, *racing through the crowd:*)
BIF: They seen him from the back, he's coming from the back, he's coming
    'round from the back way!
    (*The* YUPPIES *run towards the rear entrance as do the highly excitable press and
    assorted paparazzi.*)

EXT. MID MANHATTAN PRESBYTERIAN HOSPITAL EMERGENCY
ENTRANCE. DAY
Orderlies are lowering BOB, *strapped to a gurney, into the back of an ambulance as
reporters and fans alike call out to him. The entourage and* POLLY *are by his side.*
    BOB *flashes two 'V's for Victory'.*
TERRY: Bob!
    (BOB *is in the ambulance and the door closed behind him before anyone can ask a
    question.*
    MACGREGOR *smiles at the camera and gives a thumbs up.*
    RITA, *the Obsessed Fan, rushes the ambulance, too late.*)
RITA: Bob! Bob!
TERRY: (*Off screen*) What are the possibilities of recovery?
DR MENCK: (*Off screen*) Well, like I said, it's up to the individual. After surgery
    and extensive rehabilitation he could begin to move his toes in a couple of
    years and be walking four or five years after that.
    (PERRIGREW *hangs back, sullen and serious.*)

INT. MENCK CLINIC. DAY
DR MENCK: To tell you the truth it will be a miracle if he ever walks again.

INT. RESTAURANT. DAY
TERRY *and* MACK LAFLIN.
LAFLIN: As you've been denied access to him, Mr Raplin has asked me to
    convey his feelings to you. First he asserts his absolute innocence, given
    that due to a restrictive palsy in his right hand he would have never been
    able to fire the weapon in question. Second, he would like to express
    again his beliefs that Roberts is involved with dirty dealings involving
    guns, drugs, and Savings and Loans and lastly, and most importantly, he
    would like to say that as a witness to this incident he saw the gun fired
    twice into the ground, not at Bob Roberts.

TERRY: (*Off screen*) What?

LAFLIN: Mr Raplin contends that Bob Roberts was not shot that evening.

EXT. BRYN MAWR GATE. NIGHT

Title Card: ROBERTS' ESTATE, BRYN MAWR, PA

We see evidence of a new vigil, sleeping fans, posters, candles.

A FAN *is watching a television report (from 'Good Morning Philadelphia') on a portable television:*

ANCHOR (DAN RILEY): Charges were dropped today for lack of evidence against businessman Lukas Hart III in the Senate investigation involving the West Pennsylvania Savings and Loan scandal. The case, which gained momentum with new evidence last month was said by committee chairman, Henry Haydn, to be, quote: 'Utter contrivance, and ludicrous fantasy'. (*Insert: Newspaper. We start on a map of Pennsylvania with poll results by district panning up to reveal a picture of Bob Roberts in a wheelchair, confident with a 'V for Victory' salute. Also, a picture of Paiste with a headline reading 'Roberts Healthy, Vows Victory' and 'Paiste Confident as Election Nears.' Over the previous we hear:*)

ANCHOR (DAN RILEY): Meanwhile, tensions continue to mount in the mid-East today. Recent intelligence suggests that Iraq is very close to developing a nuclear bomb. Sources say that Saddam Hussein could have a nuclear device in a matter of months.

EXT. ROBERTS' ESTATE. NIGHT

TERRY: (*Voice over*) On election day, his new album entitled . . .

    (*Insert: album cover – 'Bob on Bob'*)

TERRY: (*Voice over*) 'Bob on Bob' is released and debuts with a bullet at number two on the charts. His video and single, 'I Want To Live', go to number one.

EXT. ROBERTS' ESTATE GATE. DAY

The vigil continues. On BIF*'s boombox we hear the instrumental introduction of the song 'I Want To Live'.*

    'I WANT TO LIVE' – *Music Video:*

    Insert: an MTV-style credit reading: 'Bob Roberts "I Want to Live" Bob on Bob, Pride Records'.

EXT. HILLSIDE. DAWN

In a murky grey light on top of a grassy hill, next to a magnificent elm tree, we see a revolutionary war fife, drum and flag corp marching.

    We intercut between images of BIF *and the* BOYS *at Bob's gates and images of dead yuppies on the hillside of the video.*

We follow them and find BOB ROBERTS *and* LIBERAL *standing back to back. A drum is beating slowly, a guitar is heard.*

BOB: I want to live

chances are I will.

In the hearts and minds

of those that care

Of those that hold their banner high

Of those with pride

(BOB *and the* LIBERAL *begin pacing off.*

The pacing BOB *in revolutionary garb is no longer singing, but we occasionally cut to* BOB *in his concert wardrobe, standing behind a floating window frame, singing, with the duel in the background.*)

I want to live

beyond my years

In Elysian Fields . . .

Where poets wrestle with injustice

Where my heart could rest

Where my words would never die

(*At the count of nine,* BOB *turns from his pacing to fire at the* LIBERAL, *but sees the* LIBERAL *only holding a quill.* BOB *turns his back on the* LIBERAL *and facing the camera, gun resting on his shoulder, sings the next verse.*)

BOB: Take me to the heart

of this beautiful land

And walk with me

down its fine white roads

Of justice and supremacy

of roads built by you and me

(*During the last lines, the* LIBERAL, *behind* BOB's *back, pulls out a portable missile launcher, readies it, and points it at* BOB. *At the end of the last line, and just in time,* BOB *turns and unloads his dueling pistol into the* LIBERAL, *who falls dead.*

BOB *behind the floating window frame again playing harmonica.*

As the song finishes, the DEAD YUPPIES *slowly rise, resurrected, and begin marching down the hill.*)

EXT. ROBERTS' ESTATE BRYN MAWR GATE. NIGHT
The fan, ROGER, *holds his guitar.*

ROGER: It's as if he knew what would happen to him. I mean we have to use the word 'prophetic'.

EXT. ROBERTS' ESTATE. NIGHT

The vigil continues. Several FANS *stand and gather around Bif's portable radio.*

TACK MANNERS: (*On radio*) This is Tack Manners, APW News.

YUPPIE: Wait. Listen.

YUPPIE: Here it is.

> (*The* FANS *all rush towards the radio.*)

TACK MANNERS: Voters throughout the state of Pennsylvania have been
turning out in record numbers tonight to cast their votes in a Senatorial
race that has been full of controversy and drama. Brickley Paiste and Bob
Roberts have been running neck and neck all night, but in the last five
minutes, APW News has learned that a winner has been declared. With
98 per cent of precincts reporting, Brickley Paiste shows 48 per cent and
Bob Roberts 52 per cent.

> (*An exultant cheer rises up from the crowd. Their cheers of 'Bob! Bob! Bob!' fade
> into the cheers of campaign workers as we cut to:*)

INT. ROBERTS CAMPAIGN HEADQUARTERS. NIGHT

The cheers subside as LUKAS HART *begins to address the crowd.*

HART: Thanks are due a lot of people but I would like to take a moment out of
this festive celebration and remember a good friend of ours who lies at
home tonight. A man who was shot for having the courage to take a stand,
a young man who speaks his mind for a better America. Let's all bow our
heads and pray for the safe recovery of Senator Bob Roberts.

> (*The camera pans across the crowd. A reverent silence fills the air.*)

BOB: (*Voice over*) Are we on?

> (*We pan to see a bank of large-screen televisions. On them,* BOB *appears, lying in
> bed,* POLLY *at his side.*)

BOB: (*By satellite from home*) Thank you, ladies and gentlemen. Thank you,
Lukas. I am truly honoured to be selected as the next Senator of the great
state of Pennsylvania. I hereby humbly vow to serve you, the people, to
best of my ability, as long as God will allow. Polly and I thank God and
thank you for this wonderful opportunity. We won't let you down.

> (*Wild cheering as* BOB, *the victorious candidate, waves and salutes from his bed
> at home. Balloons, noisemakers, pandemonium.*)

INT. BRICKLEY PAISTE'S OFFICE. DAY

PAISTE: You know, it's almost exactly thirty years since I came to the Senate. It
was 1960. Jack Kennedy had been elected President. 'We're going to get
America moving again'. There was going to be a new frontier. And the
world was going to be a better place. Well, the new frontier turned out to
be Vietnam and we sort of fell off the edge.

> (*Insert: television report. The 'Good Morning Philadelphia' logo and theme lead*

into a report (*complete with footage*) on the crisis in the Persian Gulf.)

ANCHOR: Our top story this hour: With the agreement yesterday among the
   five permanent Security Council members, the broad coalition the
   United States has mustered against Iraqi President Saddam Hussein has
   crossed a crucial threshold, authorizing the use of military force. The
   United States has won the backing of the Soviet Union, China, Britain
   and France for a UN resolution threatening to use 'all necessary means'
   to drive Iraq from Kuwait if it does not leave by January 15.

EXT. ROBERTS' ESTATE. DAY

TERRY, *inside his van, pulls up the driveway of Bob's house.*

TERRY: (*Voice over*) Six weeks after the shooting we receive a call from Chet
   MacGregor. Bob Roberts wants to see our footage of the tragic incident
   at the 'Cutting Edge Live' television show. We have transferred the film
   to videotape and are just arriving at Fair Acres, Bob's palatial estate at
   Bryn Mawr, in suburban Pennsylvania.

INT. ROBERTS' ESTATE. DAY

A servant dressed in white picks up discarded napkins and exits.

   MACGREGOR *dances with a* YOUNG WOMAN.

   BOB *sits in a wheelchair, staring off into space.* POLLY *next to him, opening
letters and cards. The entourage is there, with their dates.* DOCKETT *plays the piano
and they all sing 'Joy to the World'.*

   BOB *comes to, and continues reading a card he has just opened. The carol
continues.*

   DOCKETT *continues playing a jazzy, instrumental version of 'Joy to the World'.*
BOB'*s wife,* POLLY, *speaks for the first time.*

POLLY: Oh this is precious. Bob, sweetie, look at this. It's from a little girl in
   Stowe, Vermont. 'Dear Bob, even though it's not Valentine's Day . . .
   will you be mine? signed, Amy Biddle Richman. Age seven.'
   (*She hands the card to* BOB.)

BOB: Oh, that's sweet. Look at that. See that? (*He shows it to the camera,
   smiling.*) Why don't we send a letter back to her. Dear Amy, your kind
   valentine has made this difficult transition a great deal easier. Be good in
   school and don't do crack. It's a ghetto drug.

DOCKETT: (*Off screen*) Straight up, Bob.
   (*They all raise their glasses.*)

BOB: To Amy and all the future soldiers throughout the land.
   (*They all clink glasses.*)

INT. ROBERTS' ESTATE. DAY

BOB *sits in a wheelchair in front of a television, his back to camera.*

Around him, the entourage, their dates and POLLY *sit, still reading from cards and letters.*

BOB *stares at the large television, a remote control in his hand. On the screen we see footage of the assassination, over and over, backwards and forwards in slow motion as* BOB *searches for something.*

Meanwhile, people read aloud from cards.

ANDERSON: 'Make America great for Christian people and walk again, too, God bless, Dorian Graff, Millersville, Pennsylvania.'

MACKLEROONEY: Somebody got off an early Christmas card . . . 'We wish you a Merry Christmas and a year filled with song, and where the body is there will the vultures be gathered. Love, Billy LaRay.'

MACGREGOR: Here's one from the whole board of directors at Interunus, 'Dear Bob, we here at Interunus wish to extend our support. Best wishes for your complete recovery. As you may know, Interunus is a Fortune 500 company specializing in waste management and genetic engineering. Our philosophy here is much in tune with yours and, in fact, we play "This Land" as an anthem before – '

BOB: (*Pointing*) You see, there it is, there. The gun, right there.
(*We see a still frame from the assassination. Bugs Raplin is there. The image is blurry. Do we see a gun?*)

ANDERSON: (*Off screen*) Yeah.

MACGREGOR: (*Off screen*) 'We play "This Land" as an anthem before all of our board meetings. The best to you and yours, God bless you Bob.'
(*Now, we hear* PERRIGREW *reading a letter. Something is wrong with her. Aside from being drunk, she is distant, removed.*)

PERRIGREW: May he rot in hell . . . vengeful sword carry that terrible man that shot you to the pit of hell for eternity. Signed, James McCaw, Boston, Mass. P.S. Do more songs like 'Don't Smoke'.

MACGREGOR: Ah, more champagne.

PERRIGREW: Well, I'm going. Goodbye all. (*She starts to leave.*)

MACGREGOR: (*Up, after her*) Delores, maybe you'd better lie down for a while.

PERRIGREW: I'm tired of this shit.
(MACKLEROONEY *and* ANDERSON *go after her.*)

TERRY: Is there something wrong, old boy?

MACGREGOR: Well, she's been working very hard, Terry, and I think she's had a bit of the bubbly.

ANDERSON: (*Returning*) She could never say no to the Perignon.

EXT. PRISON. DAY
Title Card: LOWER MANHATTAN CORRECTIONAL FACILITY.

BUGS RAPLIN, *surrounded by police, is brought out of the prison and placed in a police van.*

Several press photographers and TV news REPORTERS *try to push their way towards him as do hundreds of angry* YUPPIES, *who yell at him.* ROGER, CALVIN *and* BURT *are there.*

ROGER: You're dead!

(RAPLIN'*s attorney* MACK LAFLIN *is surrounded by* REPORTERS.)

REPORTERS: Mr Laflin! A few questions!

LAFLIN: Yes, if I may. It appears the gun in question was placed on my client's person by a third party present at the time of the shooting.

REPORTER 5: How do you know that?

LAFLIN: Fingerprints indicate that the gun was fired by Mr Raplin's right hand. Mr Raplin cannot pick up a fork, let alone fire a gun with his right hand. He has constrictive palsy which cripples motor functions in that limb. And furthermore, there were no powder burns of any kind on any of his clothing.

REPORTER 4: Why has he been held in custody this long, then?

LAFLIN: You tell me.

INT. PARKING GARAGE. DAY

We see PERRIGREW *walking towards her car.*

TERRY: (*Off screen*) Delores, Delores.

PERRIGREW: I can't talk to you, Terry.

TERRY: Have you left Bob? Are you no longer working for him?

PERRIGREW: That is correct.

TERRY: What happened?

PERRIGREW: It was a mutual decision. I felt it was time to move on. (*She gets into her car.*)

TERRY: I don't believe you.

PERRIGREW: I'm sorry about that.

TERRY: Raplin's been released. They found he couldn't have fired the gun. Is there something we should know? (*She drives away.*)

INT. BUGS' APARTMENT. DAY

A distorted mirror image of BUGS. *Twisted and dark, the reflection gives way, as we pull back, showing that we have been looking at his reflection in the dead screen of a television. The camera continues until it finds* BUGS' *real face, then holds on a close-up.*

BUGS RAPLIN *looking much the worse for wear of his past three months in jail, smokes a cigarette and talks nervously.*

BUGS: You see, the truth of this is that American taxpayers have been paying for covert war. Illegal, covert war waged in countries we haven't even heard of. Central America, thousands have died, Chile, Indonesia, Africa. Up until now Americans paid for these wars every time they did cocaine or crack or heroin or any other drug smuggled in by these self-proclaimed patriots. But now, now we have a situation where *all* Americans will soon pay for these smugglings of drugs in the form of taxes to bail out failed Savings and Loans. Savings and Loans that misused people's funds and provided money to illegal covert drug smuggling operations. And surprise! We find ourselves with a seemingly insurmountable drug problem.

INT. AIRPORT. DAY

Title Card: JANUARY 15, 1991 WASHINGTON, DC

The camera, from the front, follows BOB, *being pushed through the airport. The bodyguards keep reporters and fans at a distance. The entourage* (*minus* PERRIGREW), *led by* HART, *surround* BOB *and* POLLY.

DC REPORTER: How do you feel, Bob?

BOB: Great. There's a new breeze blowin'. A new day dawnin'.

DC REPORTER: Any comment on the release of Alijah Raplin?

BOB: Well it's obvious that the legal system is too lenient on criminals in this country. As a United States Senator, I will see to it that this leniency ends in our lifetime and criminals like Raplin get their just do.

DC REPORTER: Have you been to Washington before?

BOB: Yes. But this time is special.

HART: It's a new town now.

TERRY: (*Off screen*) Why is that, Mr Hart?

HART: Because Bob Roberts is here to stay. Excuse us.

> (*Flashbulbs explode as the entourage continues.*
> *Insert: Newspaper. We start on a picture of* BOB *with a headline that reads 'Washington welcomes Rebel'. We pan up to see a pie chart on support for the impending war in the Gulf and the lead headline which reads, 'Senate OKs Force in Gulf.'*)

INT. BUGS' APARTMENT. DAY

Same as before. A nervous, smoking BUGS *talks to the interviewer.*

BUGS: The reason Iran-Contra happened is because no one did anything substantial about Watergate. And the reason Watergate happened is because there were no consequences from the Bay of Pigs. They're all the same operatives, didn't you notice? The foot soldiers in the Bay of Pigs, the plumbers that got busted at Watergate, the gun-runners in Iran-Contra; all the same people, same faces. Now it doesn't take a genius to figure out the connection here. A secret government beyond the control of the people and accountable to no one. And the closer we are to discovering the connection, the more Congress turns a blind eye to it. 'We can't talk about that in open session', they say, 'national security reasons'. The truth lies dormant in their laps and they stay blind out of choice. A conspiracy of silence.

INT. BRICKLEY PAISTE'S OFFICE. DAY

PAISTE: I think the entire Congress is quite aware of the National Security Council and its powers and its functions and the fact that this is a National Security State and less and less of a representative one. But, it's, you know, you know the story of the frog in the pan of cold water. You throw a frog into hot water and it'll jump around and suffer greatly and die. If you put the frog in a pan of cold water and you put that on the stove and you heat it to the boiling point, the frog doesn't stir. He doesn't feel it, he doesn't notice it, and at the end of it, he's dead. These things happen incrementally, they're gradual. Are we complicit? Yes, we are. Are we revolutionaries? How do you do it once you're here?

INT. BUGS' APARTMENT. DAY
Same as before.

BUGS: There are no Mr Smiths in Washington. Mr Smith has been bought. Just a bunch of dealmakers. No visionaries. No one really concerned with the disenfranchised. Just a secret state of business liaisons out of control. So out of control that they're willing to send American soldiers to war to protect their prurient business interests.

INT. HOTEL BALLROOM. NIGHT
A black tie inaugural gala is in full swing:
   The guests consist of Financial Supporters, Dignitaries and Military Personnel and their Wives.
   BOB *and his band, in black-tie attire, are on stage performing.*
   We move through the room until the camera is close on BOB.
   Song: THIS WORLD TURNS
BOB: Walls may come down
         but what is let in?
         Godless men, Godless men
         They'll take the jobs
         of the decent ones
         And wait for the day
         that their leaders
         Will make you their slaves.

         This world turns
         its back on God
         We must fight to protect Him

This world turns
its back on God
We must die to join Him

The desert teems
with dangerous schemes
Godless men, Godless men
They take the innocent
and stroke their face
And wait for the day
that their oil
Will make you their slaves.

This world turns
its back on God
We must fight to protect Him
(*The entourage and* POLLY *are seated at a table.* MACGREGOR *flashes a smile and a thumbs-up.*)
This world turns
its back on God
We must die to join Him
Meet fury with fury,
belief with belief
God against the devil,
an eternal fight
March on, march on,
brave young men
Our prayers go with you
to the holy land

This world turns
its back on God
We must fight to protect Him
This world turns
its back on God
We must kill to join Him
(*The camera catches something, we do not see exactly what and it zooms in quickly to the bottom half of* BOB ROBERTS. *We see* BOB's *foot tapping, once, twice. Then it stops.*
The AUDIENCE *applauds wildly.*
BOB *looks into the camera.*)

INT. BUGS' APARTMENT. DAY
Same as before.

BUGS: No poll will tell you the truth. The corporations and big business that own the networks and major newspapers, they won't tell you the truth. It's not in their interest to tell you the truth. The truth is too dangerous to them. If you want the truth in this country, you have to seek it out. You must be vigilant, unrelenting, uncompromising. I will get Bob Roberts. I don't need a gun to do it.

EXT. WATERGATE HOTEL. NIGHT
Our intrepid team stands outside the hotel interviewing CALVIN *and* ROGER, *who has 'Bob' tattooed on his forehead. They hold candles. They are clearly obsessed; dangerous-looking future leaders. Near them are other obsessed fans. The boys talk to* TERRY.

ROGER: . . . and I finally found it. I scooped up Calvin, he had all the candles ready. I was the first to find out, though.

CALVIN: He's in that room up there. I saw him in the wheelchair earlier. He waved. I couldn't believe it. I think he recognized me.

TERRY: Which room?

CALVIN: Two up, three to the left. The curtain's closed now, it was open before.

ROGER: So, how's the documentary going?

TERRY: Well, I'm learning a great deal about Bob Roberts.

ROGER: Yeah?

CALVIN: You know, you're lucky. You're lucky to be spending so much time with Bob Roberts.

TERRY: I don't know if I'm lucky.
(*The camera begins panning towards the window.*)

ROGER: What do you mean?

TERRY: I don't know if I really like him. I don't know if he's healthy for your country.
(*The camera locates the window.*)

TERRY: (*Off screen*) Why do you like him?

CALVIN: (*Off screen*) Because he's righteous. And he sticks up for you.

TERRY: (*Off screen*) In what way does he stick up for you?

ROGER: (*Off screen*) He believes in America. He believes in making money, being rich. He's not one of those sensitive liberals that make you feel responsible for everything that's gone wrong.

TERRY: (*Off screen*) Have you heard about his connection to the failed S & Ls and his involvement with drug smuggling?

ROGER: (*Off screen*) No.

CALVIN: (*Off screen*) Yeah. Yeah, I heard about that. That's bullshit.

TERRY: (*Off screen*) It may be.

ROGER: It's the press. They always lie.

TERRY: That may be as well.

> (BURT *comes running up, newspaper in hand.*)

BURT: Roger! Calvin! Roger, Calvin! He's dead! He's dead. They got him.

TERRY: Who's dead?

BURT: Bugs Raplin. He's dead. You guys, he's dead!

CROWD: All right!

> (*Everyone cheers.*
> *The song 'We are Marching' plays under the following:*
> *The camera stays on the crowd for a while, then pans up to the window and sees a figure walking across the room and turning the light off.*
> *We see* CALVIN *looking up, smiling.*
> *We see* BIF *dressed in Revolutionary War gear, sitting in a wheelchair. He looks up and smiles.*)

INT. TERRY'S VAN. NIGHT

TERRY *drives past various DC sites.*

> *On the radio we hear a report.*

RADIO: . . . was shot at 6:30 this evening at close range by a man describing himself as a member of 'The Arm of Justice', a radical right wing group dedicated to undoing injustices of the criminal system. Outside the 3rd Precinct in downtown Philadelphia, the as yet unidentified man yelled at reporters and police saying that he is one of many throughout this country and that his action is the beginning of a new era for justice in the United States. Mr Raplin died at 8:30 this evening after a prolonged attempt to revive him failed. Raplin, who suffered from cerebral palsy, was released last week from police custody and cleared of any connection with the attack on folksinger Bob Roberts. Raplin, a self-professed radical, leaves no surviving family.

> (*During the following part, we arrive at the Jefferson Memorial and we see* TERRY *go in.*
> *We angle up to the epitaph carved in stone and, during the following, pan across it slowly. The epitaph reads:*
> '*I have sworn upon the altar of God eternal hostility against every form of tyranny over the mind of man.*')

A United Nations delegation led by Secretary General Javier Perez de Cuellar left Baghdad last night after a last minute attempt at diplomacy with Iraq. The Iraqis have steadfastly refused to withdraw from Kuwait as the mandated deadline approaches tonight at twelve o'clock midnight. President Bush said yesterday that every attempt at diplomacy has been exhausted and that there will be no linkage and that the job of repelling the aggressor has reached a crucial stage. On Capitol Hill today, the Senate voted overwhelming to support the President if force becomes

necessary. Two weeks ago 48 per cent of Congress had voted against the use of force in the Persian Gulf. Democratic Majority Leader George Mitchell said today that, since the war appears imminent, it is important that we stand behind the President. An overnight poll released this morning shows that the American people have shifted their opinion and now are supporting the use of force in the Persian Gulf. Two weeks ago, 58 per cent opposed intervention. Tonight, on the eve of war only 48 oppose the use of force the poll says.
VOTE.

Bob Roberts was first shown at the 1992 Cannes Film Festival where it was part of the Directors' Fortnight section of the Official Selection. The cast includes:

BOB ROBERTS	Tim Robbins
BUGS RAPLIN	Giancarlo Esposito
LUKAS HART III	Alan Rickman
SENATOR BRICKLEY PAISTE	Gore Vidal
CHET MACGREGOR	Ray Wise
TERRY MANCHESTER	Brian Murray
DELORES PERRIGREW	Rebecca Jenkins
FRANKLIN DOCKETT	Harry J. Lennix
CLARK ANDERSON	John Ottavino
BART MACKLEROONEY	Robert Stanton
CLARISSA FLAN	Kelly Willis
ROGER	Jack Black
BURT	Matt McGrath
CALVIN	Matthew Faber
CHUCK MARTIN	James Spader
CAROL CRUISE	Pamela Reed
DAN RILEY	Peter Gallagher
TAWNA TITAN	Susan Sarandon
CHIP DALEY	Fred Ward
HOST OF *CUTTING EDGE*	John Cusack

with the Actors Gang

Costume Design	Bridget Kelly
Production Designer	Richard Hoover
Editor	Lisa Churgin
Music	David Robbins
Songs	David Robbins and Tim Robbins
Director of Photography	Jean Lépine
Executive Producers	Ronna Wallace
	Paul Webster
	Tim Bevan
Producer	Forrest Murray
Screenplay	Tim Robbins
Director	Tim Robbins

Bob Roberts is a Polygram/Working Title (US) production in association with Barry Levinson and Mark Johnson/Live Entertainment.

56 Tim Robbins as Bob Roberts

57 *Bob Roberts:* in front of and behind the camera

I Wake Up, Dreaming:
A Journal for 1992
Bertrand Tavernier

Prologue

I've always been frightened of starting a private diary. It's as if the words, once written, might throw a harsh light on what I'm struggling so hard to keep in the shadows. 'In Lyons, we never lie, we conceal,' my father said in a documentary I made about him.

Some months before John Boorman asked me to be his successor as the diarist for *Projections*, I had a call from Gilles Jacob. He wanted me to contribute to a collection of articles and personal accounts by directors whose films had been selected at Cannes. I was about to start work on a new film, *L 627*,* and I expressed a few doubts, in view of my timetable and state of mind. He swept them aside with the unshakable faith and optimism that everybody seems to have when they're not four weeks away from the start of a shoot. He had a brilliant idea to put a stop to my shilly-shallying: 'All you have to do is keep a journal of the shoot. It might even help you.' Won over by his enthusiasm, I agreed; and the anxiety caused by this commitment, whose text was due for delivery the following month, was thus added to all the feelings that come at the end of pre-production.

I tried. God knows I tried – often, at about one o'clock in the morning – to jot down my feelings. But in the heat of a battle to obtain a permit from property developers to erect an important set – that of the DPJ† – on an empty lot on the Quai Kennedy, I must have lost all sense of time, because when I told Gilles I'd finished, he told me it was too late. Those notes, which I want to use as a prologue to this diary (and so that Gilles will know I was telling the truth) are an account of the war that I'd begun to wage on all manner of fears: the fear that giving material form to my feelings and sensations, transcribing them, would deprive them of all mystery, all real existence – as if writing closed off the horizon, as if it short-circuited the imagination. Fear, too, of once again confronting the anxiety of a production, of overspecifying the aims and becoming prisoner to them. I prefer not to know where I'm going or what I'm looking

---

* The title refers to an article in the criminal code relating to drug offences.
† *Division de Police Judiciare*: a division which controls three arrondissements.

for on the expedition that is the shooting of a film. As Soulages said, 'It's only when I find it, that I know what I'm looking for.'

First of all, a word about *L 627*, which came into being thanks to my son Nils. After *La Passion de Béatrice* and *Une affaire de femme* by Chabrol, he had been given one of the leading roles in *Sale comme un ange* by Catherine Breillat, a fascinating film which breaks with any kind of morality, and has an authentically disturbing bleakness. Nils played a plain-clothes policeman – a foolhardy young braggart who is not particularly clever. In preparing for this role he had spent a month and a half living with the police, and had made some friends, one of whom he spoke of with such enthusiasm that I was keen to meet him. Michel Alexandre was an investigating officer (in France this is the lowest grade; there is no chance of promotion before the age of thirty-eight, short of retaking an exam and, therefore, giving up the street for more than a year) who had been in a drugs unit for thirteen years, stalking dealers on the *'voie publique'**. He was passionately fond of his job, and what he told me at meetings set up by Nils excited me so much that I asked him to collaborate on a screenplay describing the daily life of the police unit. He accepted. I questioned him about it, and every time he hit on an interesting fact I asked him to jot it down. Very soon I had more than 400 pages – a sequence of facts, situations, anecdotes shedding light on all kinds of contradictions, anxieties and frustrations. In short, a whole complex social fabric that is seldom tackled or analysed in film.

From that starting point, I tried to find a light, open and undemonstrative dramatic line, dictated not so much by psychological motivations as by the nature of the job itself. I needed a structure that did not seem 'constructed', which would remain 'accidental', raw.

Once that line had been determined, we had to write the actual screenplay and mould the characters, synthesizing both fictional elements and research materials, without recourse to a plot, or narrative twists; doubts and emotion would be laid bare. I knew I had to introduce constant changes in tone (as in *Coup de torchon*),† move from violence to drollery, from sheer emotion to nerve-shredding harshness, from the interrogation of a junkie to practical jokes worthy of *M*A*S*H*.

This approach gave rise to a whole series of reflections and questions about the relation between fiction and documentary, truth and realism; aesthetic problems: how to light the streets of Paris at night, to photograph faces in cars; I had to avoid the overly descriptive. For once I would have to be swift and fleeting, forgetting the astonishment I often felt during the months I spent

* Police jargon (untranslatable).
† *Clean Slate.*

exploring the world of the police, those nights spent rambling through the streets. What I'd felt and learned must not come across, in my direction, as a series of discoveries. It was imperative that I should not have the eye of a police investigator, of a journalist or an explorer. The direction had to correspond exactly to the point of view of my hero, Lulu.

The essential question arises: how do you express routine and habit, essentially anti-dramatic notions which are organic to this job? How do you film a job so it becomes the only source of dramatization?

A few visual groundrules are established: *respect* the different colours of street lighting (yellows and blues), not correct or soften them; *eliminate* as far as possible any descriptive shots and particularly any framing that over-dramatizes an action; *stay* with the cops and see what they see when they tail or pursue suspects; *never* leave the point of view of the pursuer; *refuse* all stylistic effects inherent in the thriller genre; *stick* to the characters, follow their rhythm, reflect the routine and unstable nature of their life, and think at the same time as they do. A difficult choice, because the audience has a thousand formal, ideological references in its head – American references in particular: promotion of individualism, rejection of collective spirit, predominance of plot. I want to overturn these references.

Most importantly, *avoid all judgement, all kinds of paternalism*, and respect the rages and moods of Lucien Marguet – Lulu.

First of all, find a face for Lulu. Forget the model he's based on (my co-screenwriter: Michel Alexandre). Keep only his essential traits. I discarded the idea of giving him a beard. Since Claude Miller's film is running late I'm not going to have the actor I chose – Didier Bezace – until very shortly before we begin shooting, so there'll be no time for him to grow a beard. On the other hand, this morning, while filming the final tests, I was delighted with the idea of curling his hair. His moustache and glasses give him a working-class look.

The film needs a face that is unknown – one free of references – someone unfamiliar to (maybe having seen Didier less than the other actors will be just as stimulating in the end). Of the six actors who make up the police unit, one (Philippe Torréton) has no film experience; two have very little and never in these kind of parts (Didier Bezace and my companion Charlotte Kady); and two are being cast against type (Jean-Roger Milo and my son Nils).

Initial contacts

For a number of weeks I've been organizing meetings between the actors and certain open and responsive cops from division headquarters. Philippe Torréton spent a night on the beat with them, and Charlotte followed a whole case, even to the point of being present at the questioning of Zaïreans arrested for drug smuggling and fake IDs. 'Without realizing it, I found myself joining in, and suddenly heard myself asking questions,' she told me. Comment from one

58 *L 627*: Bertrand Tavernier with co-screenwriter Michel Alexandre
(the model for Lulu)

59 *L 627*: Bertrand Tavernier with Lulu (Didier Bezace)

of the policemen: 'She keeps her eyes open. She doesn't miss a thing.' I don't need to push Nils, who is thoroughly familiar with this world.

I ask them to listen to the words, the accents, the language, and, at the same time, to practise the more mundane tasks: typing, writing a report, all the everyday, routine, exhausting activities that films normally leave out.

First day of training

The scenes involving arrests and interrogations are rehearsed without Nils and Didier. Jean-Roger Milo, who has volunteered to play all the suspects, gets hurled to the asphalt in the courtyard and on to the office floor a good twenty times without a word of complaint. But they can't get the cuffs on him: his wrists are too big. I'm impressed by Torréton's speed, Charlotte's concentration, Jean-Paul Comart's goodwill and, of course, Milo's strength.

Second day of training

This time with Nils and Didier. It's held in the now-abandoned premises of the old Ministry of Environment. Smail Melki, playing a dealer, is thrown to the ground five or six times. Once again, a problem with the handcuffs, which don't fit the suspect properly (a difficulty confirmed by Michel Alexandre). Since this sequence is to be filmed with a hidden camera we have to go through the various problems this might cause, and try to come up with solutions.

Milo tells me he wants to break down a door during the film. I tell him that's 'movie' stuff – you only see that in films; policemen, who are more cunning than that, use a pass key. To prove his point, Milo offers a demonstration. He disappears into the minister's office. As I know what he's like, I ask everybody to get out of the way. Suddenly, the huge padded door flies off its hinges and crashes into a pillar. A long respectful silence. Milo turns around as if it was no big deal and says, quite naturally: 'There, I just wanted to show you.'

First day of rehearsal

In a big bare warehouse of the Ministry the production designer, Guy-Claude François, has drawn on the floor the exact dimensions of the two pre-fabs he has designed as the offices for the squad. I shift things around, switching the tables. The actors all take their places and familiarize themselves with their props and the distances between the various pieces of furniture. It's the first time I've organized real rehearsals before a shoot. (For the sequences in the Grézaucourt tunnel in *La Vie et rien autre** I brought the actors to my flat and we tried to work out their characters' biographies.) Here, I have to organize ensemble sequences of collective life, to make clear to the actors the problems

---

* *Life and Nothing But.*

of working in a tight area and familiarize them with the cramped spatial arrangement of the pre-fabs.

From the very first scene, the squad starts coming to life. My feelings from the first two days reading the script are confirmed. The various personalities are already causing sparks. Didier, just like his character, watches, registers, assimilates. He is lagging behind the others in his research, but makes up for this by entering into the core of the screenplay. Philippe Torréton has found exactly the right tone, and is starting to improvise. He's extremely quick; once he comes into contact with objects and characters, the ideas start bursting out of him. I may have to hold him back. Jean-Paul, who is just right, takes more time finding his bearings. He likes to proceed by trial and error. Charlotte explodes with spontaneity. She's clearly delighted to come out with expletives, to break away from her image. She has analysed the component parts of her character very well, and incorporated what she has seen very intelligently. Nils is equally reassuring. What he does is the opposite of what he did as a cop in Catherine Breillat's fine film. Milo does not give his all at rehearsals, but the changes he suggests are often hilarious. Sometimes he tends to miss the point, and doesn't always seem to understand the comic aspects of his part. I'll have to keep an eye on him.

During a break, we watch a video of a deal filmed by Michel Alexandre from a surveillance van: dealers on the Rue Pajol, an envelope of crack changing hands. Nerves, anxiety. Milo: 'So much hassle over such a tiny journey.'

Images come back to me: a young junkie collapsing into the gutter on the Rue Myrrha, a girl trying to apply make-up to her confused eyes. I've set out on my own strange journey.

All the actors tell me the rehearsals have gone very well, and that the day has calmed their anxieties. Is that a good thing? I'm worn out. But later on this evening I have to show Albert Mathieu of Canal Plus the final cut of my documentary about the Algerian War, *La Guerre sans nom*.*

The film is well-received, and I'm showered with compliments. When we get to the matter of length I'm afraid I will lose my cool. I insist that the film has to be the same length on television as it is in the cinema, saying that I only make films for me and two or three other people (which isn't quite true). They want to take out the Grenoble demonstration so that the film will 'start with more of a shock'. I refuse, out of respect for the people concerned, and because it anchors the film within a precise French context, one that has never been shown before. When he mentions programming slots I repeat that I don't make films to fit into slots. It's up to him to find slots for my films. I don't care if I seem arrogant to him.

I have a conversation with Alain Resnais who tells me he was bowled over by

* *The Undeclared War.*

the film and stresses the importance of the Grenoble demo sequence. I arrive home exhausted.

Second day of rehearsals

In the morning I rehearse a scene where the police break into a squat, finding a black woman high on crack, with her baby. I film tests with three black actresses. The second is so true that the actors are petrified. They stop, speechless. ('Absolutely true to life,' Michel Alexandre says to me.)

In the afternoon, we set up the two most difficult scenes in the brigade's office: a lot shifts in tone, violent confrontations, a lot of people in a tiny set. Between set-ups, everyone goes back to their typewriters, or they learn to seal the evidence, weigh out quantities of drugs, make *cocottes*, the little paper bags that dealers use for one or two grams of the drug.

Two days before shooting

I visit a few locations and see two flats. One is for Lulu; it's not bad if we can smarten it up a bit. We have to make sure that it isn't too grand for Lulu – usually in French cinema financial considerations go by the board when it comes to décor. Another one for Toussaint, a Corsican stoolie who is a drug addict; it's too grand, even if filmed in semi-darkness.

I screen Robert Aldrich's *Ulzana's Raid* for Nils, pointing out the fine performance by Bruce Davison, his shocked and astonished response to the violence of the world. It's a film that I find increasingly impressive, increasingly moral, every time I see it. The American critics who laid into *Dances with Wolves* would have every right to do so if they had defended Aldrich's film. In the evening I see part of the restored version of *All Quiet on the Western Front*. A number of daring and inspired shots reveal a real passion and an incredible energy on Lewis Milestone's part. Why did I want to see this particular film again? Milestone's direction, with its lack of fluidity – each shot, each scene is done on its own – is far removed from what I want to do, but its obstinacy, its determination to impose ideas and opinions against the studios (a great deal was cut after 1933, such as that long scene between the young German hero and a dying French soldier in a shell-hole) moves me and gives me strength. A bit of strength.

Day before shooting

Rest. Concentration. I reread essays by Vialatte, Jules Renard, Tristan Bernard to get some quotes to put on the call sheets. Each day at the end of the call sheet there are word games, gossip, crosswords, etc. The whole crew participates.

60 *Ulzana's Raid*: the shocked and astonished Bruce Davison with Burt Lancaster

First day of shooting (night)

We're shooting on Rue Myrrha, with a hidden camera in the surveillance van, the 'submarine',* set up by the art department. Terrible heat. I'm drenched with sweat, and so is the cinematographer Alain Choquart. I have asked the fifty extras chosen by Bobby Pacha to make their way slowly into the street. Some of them have been milling around for an hour. None of them knows where the camera is. They look so real that on two occasions during dinner the police came to ask them for their identity papers. They tell me later that they have been offered every drug imaginable. For two hours cast and crew pass among them unnoticed despite a few blunders with the walkie-talkies. But eventually we get spotted. The tension mounts. We just manage to get the last shots as two people try to force their way into the van.

Without rehearsing, we got out into the street with our hand-held cameras to do a few shots of Lulu walking. It's even more tense, but Didier isn't too conspicuous. A big black man accosts me: 'Who says you're making a movie? I can't see the lights. Where are the lights? You can't make movies without lights.' We make off as quickly as we can.

In Montreuil, a power cut blacks out the three streets where we're filming –

---

* French police slang for an unmarked car or van specially converted to watch without being seen.

act of fate. Wasted time. Impatience. Anger. We've got to shoot a scene where three police cars tail a taxi – the ultimate horror. Each set-up takes hours and raises technical questions about the distance between two vehicles when one is tailing the other. Truth comes up against the contingencies of cinematography: respect reality, and you risk not being able to see the back of the car that you're following, especially since I want to keep to the point of view of the pursuers.

During the first takes I decide that the cars aren't far enough apart. Alain doesn't agree. Unfortunately the rushes will prove me right. The second part of the scene goes much better. These are frustrating sequences for the actors, who virtually become drivers and feel they don't get to do any genuine acting. And yet I don't mind them getting into their parts like this, doing difficult physical scenes that test their limits. It helps to shake up their psychological bearings. We're an hour behind schedule and there are still two shots to do. In addition, Milo has an eye infection. He's suffering physically and psychologically, so I try to comfort him. I'm dissatisfied.

Second night
Another scene where the group tails the Zaïrean drug dealers.

The first part of the evening – a dialogue in the 'submarine' between Nils and Lulu – goes well. As always, Nils rehearses too much and tries to load the lines with too many meanings. As a result, he appears to be commenting on the scene. I do three takes, one after the other, without cutting – which surprises him. In the second scene I change his lines after five takes and he gets a lot better. On the whole, he's just right. It's hard to tell about Didier. When the boom operator, Jean-Michel, wanted to fit him up with a radio mike he got a bit stroppy, which allowed 'Unc'* to tell him straight out: 'They told me you are a difficult bugger, but you've got a great voice. I just hope you're not one of those actors who rely on props.' Unc whispered to me, 'Remember Harvey Keitel'.†

I flounder badly during the second part. I'm unable to do the shots we'd planned for the Porte de Bagnolet because of Milo's eye, but instead of catching up with the shots I should have done yesterday, I decide to do the end of the sequence even though it's supposed to be set at dawn. It takes an hour for the team to rig up the Citroën, to find a way to conceal the sound men for a shot where the two actors have their backs to us. That's the awful thing about shooting inside cars – I hate camera cars even more, and using back-projection here is out of the question.

---

* Nickname of Michel Desrois, the sound recordist on all my films, except *Un dimanche à la campagne*.
† During the shooting of *Deathwatch*, Harvey Keitel – though loved by the crew – surprised everyone by the large numbers of questions he asked before each scene, and by the demands he made about the props.

The sun rises during the third shot. I'm furious with myself. The producer in me has overridden the director.* By filming the arrival of the 'submarine' in an establishing tracking-shot, I've abandoned the point of view of the police and the shot looks immediately more banal. It feels as if I wasn't controlling this sequence so much as sealing the gaps.

Third night

Exterior. Cours de Vincennes. Pouring with rain. We shoot between showers. I add a few lines of dialogue to explain Milo's still swollen eye. The actors lose their concentration. After four takes Jean-Paul Comart has lost his edge. I intervene a bit too brutally, but the result is excellent. The same for Charlotte, who is remarkable in the last takes. When it comes to the off-screen radio voices, Milo – who is in the Renault – is bad at using the walkie-talkie, leaving too many silences or else saying whatever comes into his head, and as I'm in the 'submarine' with Didier and Charlotte, I can't speak to him directly and have to resort to the radio. I feel cut off from him.

It's raining so heavily that we stop for two hours. Once again I have the feeling I'm being bullied by external circumstances. Impatience. Discouragement. I find the extra selected by my assistant, Tristan Ganne, worthless, completely off the mark. He seems distanced from the film. A dozen times I'm on the point of giving up for the night – especially since it's a difficult scene: during a stakeout, the head of the team plays a stupid joke on a prostitute who takes her clients into the pavement pay toilets: he sprays in a long jet of tear gas which forces them out weeping. (During the pre-production nights I saw prostitutes working like that: one client every twenty minutes.) We manage to get the scene started; a real prostitute is watching and she immediately says, 'But that's a cop's trick'. A few minutes after, two prostitutes fight over a space (600 francs a night and you get access to the toilets). One of them sprayed mace in the other one's eyes and she was screaming with terrible pain. She hides next to me in the 'submarine'. I have her taken to the canteen for first-aid treatment.

In any case, Choquart's camerawork is splendid: mixtures of colour, daring and non-realist uses of light and shade. The framing's great too: sharp, lively, acute. However, I'm worried about over-dramatizing the sense of waiting, the boredom, the routine.

Fourth night

The first sequences. Two cops on a stakeout are waiting for one of their informers, a Zaïrean named Willy. I've spent days trying to find the opening shot, and all of a sudden here it is. Something Jacques Tourneur once told me:

---

* I have co-produced all my films since *Des enfants gâtés* (1977).

'Don't know your set too well; allow it to take you by surprise, to inspire you.' That's what happened when I saw the little band of graffiti artists running through that big deserted square. I realized that the only way to shoot it was with a fixed, wide-angle shot and I threw out the tracking shot I had planned during pre-production.

Didier Castello, a young black actor with no previous film experience and whom I spotted in a good play by Xavier Durringer, is absolutely right. His meeting with Lulu, their dialogue under the *porte-cochère*, is a real joy to behold. 'Unc' comes up to me and whispers, 'He's really good.'

As on previous nights, we come up against derelicts, alcoholics, people crazed with loneliness. To get rid of a troublemaker, the local cops step in with unimaginable brutality. He shows up again a couple of hours later, bloodied, complaining he's been beaten up. I'm really ashamed, and I spend part of the night talking to him. My co-producer, Frédéric Bourboulon, has chewed out Tristan, who seems to be pulling himself together.

Fifth night

Same atmosphere, plus bikers, playing records as loud as they'll go. The previous night I avoided trouble by changing streets at the last moment, but this time we have to negotiate. Albane, the second assistant, and Catherine, the location manager, get varied responses: sometimes insults, sometimes demands for money, but then one of the bikers offers them a Coca Cola, adding, 'If anyone in the neighbourhood complains, a bunch of us'll lay into them and they'll soon stop blabbing.' A horrible gang mentality that you come across in all social classes – I saw plenty of it in college.

At the end of the night I feel I'm short of a shot establishing the arrival of Willy: a link between the exterior and interior of the 'submarine', the people who are watching and the ones being watched.

Second week, Monday

Twelve hours in the Métro. I come out, drained. Very difficult shoot on two platforms with hundreds of extras, several bit parts, Métro trains arriving, people crossing the tracks, and the main characters scattered all over the station. As always the promises made by the Paris Transport system during pre-production aren't kept. The power can be cut off on only half of the tracks, which makes the shot we had planned very dangerous. I abandon it so as not to endanger the actors and accept instead a different concept – proposed by Choquart – which proves very efficient. The Métro is jammed for half an hour, and the trains either can't move or set off in the wrong direction. Anger curiously clears the air.

Jean-Roger Milo still has the eye infection, plus a terrible toothache. He came to my flat very early in the morning (I'd slept only four hours) to explain the situation, and I entrusted him to Nils, who took him to see a doctor. He has taken some antibiotics and drunk a bit of wine. As a result he's not quite with it – and not with us; he doesn't understand any of his directions and exaggerates his gestures. He doesn't remember how to use a walkie-talkie, his identification with the character is becoming too real, and he muddles all the dialogue by overstressing things and talking at cross-purposes. He's obsessed with arresting one of the dealers, though I try to tell him it goes against what's in the script. He nods, and then, during one take, he charges off before I even call 'action', surprising the dealer, pinning him to the platform, and breaking his watch. I yell at him violently in front of everybody, telling him he's letting down a hundred people. Aware of his reputation for violence, I'm putting a lot on the line. Make or break. Make, in the end, except that in the other takes he doesn't stop when we cut and runs into the tunnel to catch the black dealer, who hightails it for République.

I'm afraid I may have overdone it with Milo, but Nils, who knows him well, reassures me. On the positive side, I've found Charlotte very efficient and real during moments of high tension. Her reactions to the radio mess-ups caused by Milo's character are both violent and contained. Very organic. She isn't skating over the surface of her character – very important when you're playing a pretty, sexy and lively female cop. The emotion will come later. No problem.

Tuesday

I'm very concerned about Milo, and even think about replacing him when I summon him to the location. I tell him, in no uncertain terms, how disappointed I am, how he's betrayed the trust I placed in him. I remind him that when nobody else wanted anything to do with him, because of his reputation for instability, I tried to help him by giving him bit-parts in *Un dimanche à la campagne** and *La Vie et rien autre* – parts which also freed him from the stereotypes he'd been locked into. *L 627* is his last chance. Today he's touching, lucid and articulate; he swears to stick with me for the rest of the film saying: 'I want to make this journey with you.' I also remember that he helped Nils a few years ago when my son had a drug problem. Milo is quite a character and I have a lot of affection for him. During pre-production he talked to me about his loathing of drug dealers. One day Milo learned that the kid brother of one of his best friends was selling drugs. He dragged him to a car park, bought everything he had and shot-up in front of him. Potentially fatal. To put him off. 'I did it again a few times. I wanted him to see what it did to me. He's stopped dealing now.'

First scene with Lara Guirao, who plays Cécile, the young drug addict and prostitute who informs for Lulu: she is true, moving. It's a pleasure to film her. She seems to inspire Didier, who is more open with her than he is with the other

* *Sunday in the Country.*

actors. They are so good, I do very few takes and finish early – for the first time.

In the evening, in a sordid setting (Boulevard des Maréchaux), the shoot is physically tiring but stimulating. We're wading through muck, the electricians are pulling their cables through a sea of used condoms – they're even sticking to the paws of the production manager's dog. All the actors are terrific. Didier plays the sub-text very well. Lara is sharp and Charlotte is brimming over with ingenuity and humour. Frédéric Bourboulon returns from seeing the rushes we shot in the Métro. He reassures me. He seems to mean what he says, but he may simply want me to sleep, unlike the previous night.

Wednesday

I'm not reassured by the Métro rushes. Milo – would you believe it! – is going to be fine, particularly if I rewrite the preceding sequences. But I may have to redo a few shots, those that depart from the original concept, those that are not filmed from the point of view of the cops. How could I have let that happen? Due to my preoccupations with the Métro, and with Milo, I lacked the necessary concentration.

Terrific day. I feel as though I'm perfectly in control of the scenes without being disturbed by anything – technical or otherwise. I'm winning the battle against time.

The lunch with Lulu and Cécile, and the street scene afterwards go remarkably well. I'm starting to get over my nervousness. Didier starts embellishing his character. He's finding his bearings.

Thursday

We move on to Guy-Claude's sets for the first time. I feel completely drained, and can't find the inspiration for the first shot. Admittedly, the room is small, and there are a lot of things going on that I need to co-ordinate, such as the discovery of Cécile being questioned by a West Indian cop, whom I want to appear dignified. After a lot of trial and error and some help from Choquart, a complicated tracking shot is set up. The rest of the day goes very well, although Lulu's entrance worries me somewhat. After thirteen films I sometimes feel more ignorant than I was at the beginning of my career. In those moments I am determined not to repeat myself or to fall back on a mechanical craftsmanship. I want to shoot each scene as if it were the first day on my first film.

Here again I'm very happy with the actors and extras. I ask two young actors, playing cops at the end of a corridor, to talk about their holidays, a campsite in the Ardèche. It works straight away and changes their attitude. I hear one of them announcing: 'I prefer Les Sables d'Olonnes' – a name I hadn't heard for twenty years. These lines send Unc into raptures.

Didier suggests a clever little change to the dialogue. In the scene with the client who's been fleeced by Cécile and who hesitates about filing a complaint because he's married, Didier, instead of saying, 'Me, too,' comes back with, 'Is there a problem?' It's better, subtler, and makes Lulu look craftier.

Third week, Monday
Back to headquarters. Two shots with the steadycam go very well. The rest is more uncertain. In the next scene, an actor is paralysed with fear. I try to change his lines, let him improvise, but nothing works.

Tuesday
During the night I decide to reshoot yesterday's scene before even seeing the rushes. I choose a new actor and rehearse it with him throughout the day. The rest of the shoot goes magnificently. I gain two hours which enable me to reshoot part of the previous day's sequence – only part of it because my assistant made a mistake and sent off two of the extras involved.

After three takes of a scene between Didier and Philippe Torréton – two of which are good – I get them to do a take using rap to surprise the technicians. And without telling the two others, I ask Jean-Claude Calon, playing a civil servant, to sing his lines as in a film by Jacques Demy. Choquart collapses behind his camera, and Unc looks at me, dumbfounded. But the joke certainly diffuses the tension and relaxes Didier, who needs reassuring. He's troubled by the fact that his character should emerge more through his professional activities than through psychology. Exhaustion and fatigue are the big psychological factors. He's afraid of the others stealing his scenes, and distrusts reaction shots. Like many theatre actors. I tell him that during the first weeks of *L'Horloger de Saint-Paul*,* the whole crew was saying that Rochefort was stealing the film from Noiret. Which was untrue. Noiret played each scene in an economical way, knowing that he was carrying the emotion in the film. I try to persuade Didier to go along with my way of working: rehearsing before make-up, which means that he has to turn up very early. But it's a method that enables you to pick out the main threads very quickly, incorporate new ideas and changes, and while the actors are being made up, it lets us do the lighting or change the sets or the props, and, thus, gives us more time to shoot the scene. 'But it's not the actors you're helping, it's the technicians.' I try to show him that the two are linked, that if we have more time it's the actors who benefit, since we've already sorted out the technical matters. He doesn't seem too convinced. Curious for a theatre director who is said to be very demanding when he's rehearsing others.

---

* *The Watchmaker of Saint-Paul.*

Wednesday

I abandon this shooting diary. It's impossible to write, even at weekends. I remember Fritz Lang saying to Pierre Rissient: 'I don't see how you can write a diary like Truffaut did for *Fahrenheit 451* while shooting. It's impossible. Or else you make a very bad film.'

And *Fahrenheit* has never struck me as one of Truffaut's best.

November

I've just received John Boorman's journal and devour it in a single evening. Every page is provocative and stimulating, whether he's talking about his dealings with the Disney executives (oh, that fabulous line of Jeffrey Katzenberg's, talking about *Where the Heart Is*, which every director lured to Hollywood ought to learn by heart: 'The trouble is, it's still a Boorman film. It is not a Disney film'); mentioning Lee Marvin or Michael Powell (an admiration we share), his mixed reactions to *Goodfellas*; the problems he has in setting up a new film. I'm bowled over by the account of his last meeting with David Lean. How could you ever forget that heartbreaking statement of victory, which Lean muttered to Boorman shortly before he died: 'Haven't we been lucky: they let us make movies.' And when Boorman answered: 'They tried to stop us', he added: 'Yes, but we fooled them.' This quotation is almost a link, a relay-baton passed between us. It should be adopted as a motto by all screen-writers' and directors' associations in the world.

The very fact of making a film is a triumph every time: over fashionable ideas and genres, over pressure from the 'decision-makers', who in France are now more likely to be distributors, or people from television. *La Vie et rien autre* was initially turned down by all the French channels apart from Canal Plus and it was only thanks to the tenacity of my producer René Cleitman (helped by a very favourable reader's report by Gilles Jacob) that we were able to 'persuade' Antenne 2 to co-produce the film. Even within his group, Hachette, René was violently attacked, and I'll never forget the Director-general of Europe 1 coming to beg me to abandon a project he deemed morbid, uninteresting and sinister, 'specially for a young audience'. I tried to explain that I wouldn't show any corpses, only the reactions of the characters searching for them, that in many scenes, energy, vitality, even humour would triumph over morbidity, that this search for the dead was intended as a vindication of life. To each explanation he replied, in a sinister voice, 'That'll be even worse.'

When the film was completed we invited the directors of Antenne 2, our co-producers, to a screening. Only the accountant turned up.

All my films were difficult to finance as well. Irwin Winkler took more than two years to package *'Round Midnight*, and succeeded only because the budget was restricted to 3 million dollars. *La Guerre sans nom* was only made possible thanks to Canal Plus, because Albert Mathieu, the programmer, had been through the war as a conscript and René Bonnel had spent his adolescence in Algeria.

The moment I return to this journal, I find myself in the opposite situation to Boorman's. I'm up to my eyes in work. I'm checking the sound mix of the four-hour *La Guerre sans nom*. It tells the story of the Algerian War through interviews with former conscripts and 'recalled' soldiers from Grenoble (young men who had already done their military service, and who were 'recalled' to serve for six months). No volunteers, then, no professional soldiers or senior officers: a conscript could not advance any higher than Lieutenant. And we've left out any archive or newsreel footage, anything 'official'. We have only used amateur photographs taken by our witnesses. My co-author Patrick Rotman and I wanted to give a voice to people who had been silent, who had been excluded from history; to bring back to life a forgotten memory; to try to understand the state of mind of those twenty-year-old Frenchmen who were sent, often against their will, to fight a war that they didn't much understand. I have a sense of continuing *La Vie et rien autre*, taking a historical fact and studying its effects and consequences: the exciting, painful footage often bowled us over. We would never have imagined that this memory was still so alive, still so close to the surface; that so many of our witnesses would break down in front of the camera, particularly the ones who were politically educated, like the communist sentenced to two years for insubordination, who then had to spend sixteen months in Algeria and who suddenly burst into tears, saying that he'd been a coward, and that he should have gone over to the FLN, or Dr Sikirdjii, who was so moved he could barely tell us how the soldiers of the ALN saluted him when he left his dispensary.

At the same time I'm editing *L 627* – the shoot was exhausting, disturbing, fascinating – while returning to my duties at SACD [Society of Dramatic Authors and Composers]. And on top of that I have to correct the mistakes in the first edition of *50 ans de cinéma américain** (which I wrote with Jean-Pierre Coursodon), because the second edition is about to be published. We're responsible for some of them (we turned Oliver Stone into an Englishman), but most were done by the copy-editors – a few display an incredible lack of knowledge: the 'Tennessee' of Tennessee Williams was adorned with a question mark and the query: 'Is this a Christian name?' A most splendid howler occurs in the essay on Charles Laughton in which, with reference to the wonderful cinematography of Stanley Cortez, 'German Expressionism' has become 'German Impressionism'.

I've just come back from a five-day holiday in Florence, a city that I love and

---

* Éditions Nathan, Paris, 1991.

wanted to show to Charlotte. We meet up with Sabine Azéma and Alain Resnais, who's being honoured by the Florence Festival. After being intimidated for years by his (and my own) shyness, I've recently discovered in Resnais an incredibly humorous and sensitive man. His knowledge is incredible. His curiosity is insatiable. He's interested in everything, with a phenomenal memory that is precise and organized. You get the feeling that everything with him will be neatly classified and labelled – articles, documents and comic-books – but that doesn't mute his passion or his appetite. He speaks with the same delight about an opera, a Lee Falk comic-strip, a 1932 film by William Wellman or an Italian dessert.

In the Uffizi, the paintings by Paolo Uccello that I wanted to show Charlotte are unfortunately not on display because they're being restored, but she's delighted to discover the Giottos, the Fra Angelicos and the fine Caravaggios. I take Resnais to a video shop where we buy some Italian films, including the fine *Tutti a casa* by Comencini. Unfortunately we don't find any Fredas (*I miserabili, Beatrice Cenci*), or Cottafavis (*Traviata 53, Milady et les mousquetaires,* nor *I nostri sogni*), which I would have liked to introduce him to. During the sixties I fought a great deal for those two directors, who became friends of mine. Freda even gave me my first work, after my two sketches:* the screenplay and dialogue for *Coplan ouvre le feu à Mexico*, an extremely bad film made in three weeks, but a good training exercise. I had to rewrite the dialogue among other things, because Freda had changed some of the scenes, making his actors say 'Bla Bla Bla Bla Bla', like all Italian directors, and refusing, after a quarrel with the producer, to tell me about his changes.

I hired him as a second-unit director on *La Passion Béatrice*† and he helped me to create the feeling of a whole church using only a black cloth into which he cut a window.

As for Cottafavi – a man of refined elegance – he is the president of the Festival jury and gives the prize to a very personal and exciting film by Nico Papatakis, *Les Equilibristes*, a rigorous and uncompromising portrait of Jean Genet, admirably interpreted by Michel Piccoli.

During a dinner Cottafavi, as dazzling as ever, launches into a long metaphysical digression. How sad it is that his best films are so little known; their lyricism is a match for Sirk. The Festival organizer, Aldo Tassone, tells me that Cottafavi did not choose to specialize in melodramas and historical stories. In 1949 he had made a very ambitious film, *Fiamma che non si spegne*, which was utterly spurned by the left-wing critics because the hero in this Resistance story was a *carabiniere*, and because a German officer was shown as a human

---

* A sketch is an episode in a film made of several stories: *O'Henry's Full House, A Story of Three Loves, Trio, Quartet*, etc.
† *Béatrice.*

being who refused to execute hostages. A manifesto was signed by all the best-known journalists excluding Cottafavi from the neo-realist movement and condemning him so violently that he had to take refuge for twenty years in cinema of the most commercial kind – melodramas, costume dramas. Then, after the commercial failure of the *100 cavalieri* (his most personal project), he retreated to television, where he directed some ambitious adaptations of classical plays, notably a moving version of *The Trojan Women* in modern dress. He shot it as if it was the last dress rehearsal, taking part in the show and inserting pauses between the acts, during which the actresses smoked cirgarettes or made phone calls.

He was not rehabilitated until this summer, at the same time as Freda, at the Locarno Festival, which had organized a triumphant double retrospective. One of the most famous and intelligent Italian critics, Tullio Kesich, even came to kiss his hand to apologize for what he had done forty-one years previously.

30 November

Screening in Billancourt of the rough cut of *L 627*. It's far too long (2 hours 46 minutes), the almost inescapable price for avoiding linear drama and using a style that includes plenty of improvisation and change. I hate being the prisoner of a plot, confining myself to a rigid structure more or less inspired by the theatre. I've always been disturbed when the Americans talk of their films in terms of different acts, and I've never seen a trace of it in Ford or Walsh. I like a dramatic line to be determined less by the plot than by the feelings of the characters, their inner life. I like the story to go wandering. When I work on a screenplay I refer more to music – and jazz in particular; more to novels than to theatre. I like the movement of a film to have the same changes of rhythm, the same hesitations as the characters; I want the audience to discover things at the same time as the characters do.

This sometimes imposes a structure that looks as if it's hesitant, particularly for the first reel. The beginnings of my films have always been haphazard, zigzagging, even uncertain. The dramatic conflict, and especially the reasons for that conflict, appears only later on. In *La Vie et rien autre* the audience discovered those 'landscapes after a battle' at the same time as Philippe Noiret and Sabine Azéma – France in 1920, a country that could bring the characters together or tear them apart. This open, linear writing sets me apart from the French cinema of the fifties, which certain critics insist on associating me with because I chose to work with Jean Aurenche and Pierre Bost.* Yet *they* were open to all experiences: it's Aurenche who taught me how to write for pleasure,

---

* Aurenche and Bost were screenwriters who often worked in tandem, most notably for Autant-Cara.

scene by scene, letting myself be guided by the characters, forgetting all the rules.

After the screening, I feel pleased with the energy *L 627* generates. There was a lot of laughter; the zany, derisive, grating effects paid off. My co-scriptwriter of *La Vie*, Jean Cosmos, is especially generous in his praise. He finds the dialogue juicy and very authentic, the actors splendid, beginning with Didier Bezace, about whom all agree. Jean speaks to me at length about Charlotte, about her radiance, her rightness, and about Nils whom he finds touching. He suggest a few cuts, but not many because, as he points out, the dramatization consists of an accumulation of mundane details, and 'the more you take the screenplay towards a story-line, the more you weaken your theme.'

There are hundreds of modifications to make; during the screening I suddenly realized how I should have done such-and-such a shot or scene and came up with the bit of dialogue that seemed missing all along. I envy American directors and their re-takes. But that's not the solution to everything: Billy Wilder told me that he suddenly came up with a brilliant idea for the end of *The Apartment* – seven years later!

In the scenes where the suspects are being tailed, we'll have to cut the shots that abandon the point of view of the characters. This aesthetic principle imposes a style of its own, and we have to remain true to it. The shots I re-took in the Métro work very well. During the film I thought about Labarthe's quip that the two big themes of cinema are education and fatigue. *L 627*, like *La Vie et rien autre* and *'Round Midnight*, contains both at once. Apprenticeship really acts as a motivating force in many of my films – the apprenticeship of a beginner or of a man shaped, broken, defeated by the habits of life or the constraints of creation. In this film I'm pleased with the important role assigned to the job, which conditions or creates the dramatic events.

Throughout the whole, the actors are really tremendous, even the smallest bit-parts (there are more than seventy). The performers all blend in with the settings, which wasn't always easy given the cramped spaces in which we filmed. Truffaut once told me that you have to make an aesthetic wager before every film. In this case it meant shooting most of the scenes in tiny settings (car interiors, vans, offices 20 feet by 6, little hotel rooms). The wager was kept, and that gives the film a tone that I find different and exciting.

5 December

I take Charlotte and Philippe Torréton off to see Walsh's *The Regeneration* (1915) at the Cinemathèque, a masterpiece that I was introduced to by William Everson. The realism in some of the scenes is startling, particularly the depiction of the young hero's family, which anticipates the Stroheim of *Greed*. The direction of the actors (and, as often in Walsh, of the actresses) is

61 Walsh's *Regeneration* (1915)

startlingly modernist. Charlotte points out the amazing resemblance between the lead actor and Brando in *On the Waterfront*, even down to his clothes. Walsh uses flashbacks and camera movements, especially one that became one of his favourite stylistic devices: tracking in on a person walking towards the camera. The frenetic rhythm, as nervous as it is in his Warner films, astonishes Philippe and Charlotte, who get the feeling they're watching a Scorsese. You only have to compare *Regeneration* to other films made that same year to see how original Walsh was.

7 December

For issue number 1,000 of *Point* news weekly, devoted to the defence of 'writing', the editor Pierre Billard asks me for a piece on 'The Relationship between Word and Image':

The *moral force* of writing has been glorified, with a furious and anxious urgency, in a recent film by a notable director, Wim Wenders. In *Until the End of the World*, he tells us that an image that is not supported by a story will be distorted, corrupted, alienated; that words can act as an antidote to dissoluteness, to the excessive consumption of images. To Max von Sydow's 'Give me a camera and I will possess man and his dreams', he seems to reply with a line of one of Conrad's characters: 'Give me words and I will conquer the world.'

This cry of alarm will seem paradoxical only to superficial minds, the people who have always made an academic distinction between cinema and literature, image and word, or the aficionados of 'pure cinema'* – an idea that has always struck me as wildly alien, even rather worrying ('pure' as in alcohol, 'pure' as in race?). It's tempting to reply that the great films are all hybrids.

Filming also means being able to film words. In the work of some great film-makers – Guitry, Rohmer, Mankiewicz – you might replace 'also' with 'especially'. This has often confused the critics. Even the greatest of them, such as Truffaut.

Everyone remembers Truffaut's virulent and sometimes unfair article attacking 'French quality cinema'. In a famous comparison, often repeated, he contrasted a scene that he (rightly) admired in *Under Capricorn*, in which Michael Wilding stretches his jacket behind a window-pane so that Ingrid Bergman can finally look at herself (since the house where she lives has no mirrors), with the sequence in *Les Orgueilleux†* in which Michèle Morgan dictates a telegram to her husband and, being short of money, deletes the word 'tenderness'. He thus contrasted two kinds of cinema, one based on 'an idea of *mise-en-scène*', and the other on a 'scriptwriter's idea', image versus text. His preference was quite clear.

This overly polemical comparison has always struck me as somewhat contrived, given that one scene is silent and the other spoken, and I wonder if we might not reverse the arguments. What annoyed me in the sequence from *Les Orgueilleux* was its rather heavy and explanatory direction. You need only imagine what Hitchcock would

* This phrase was used by French critics to refer to films where everything – content, ideas, vision – is expressed through the direction.
† *The Proud Ones.*

have done with a scene like that without changing a word. 'Delete tenderness' spoken by Ingrid Bergman or Grace Kelly would have assumed a radically different meaning because it would have been *filmed, lit, framed* differently. As to the idea in *Under Capricorn*, perhaps it was in the novel?

When I met Hume Cronyn, a fine actor and occasional scriptwriter – the scriptwriter of *Under Capricorn*, in fact – I asked him where Hitchcock got this fine sequence. He blushed and said, 'I can credit Hitchcock with 80 per cent of the ideas you see in the films on which I worked with him, but I can lay claim to that one. It wasn't in the book. I based it on a personal memory and Hitch adored it.' So it was a scriptwriter's idea after all, based on a written text, transcended by an inspired and creative *mise-en-scène*, that Truffaut was contrasting with another scriptwriter's idea, this time illustrated but not recreated by the director. The very opposite, in fact, of what Truffaut wanted to demonstrate.

As we can see, the relationship between writing and image is complex. Complex and often stormy. Filming words also means knowing that there are words and phrases that can't be filmed. A long time ago I had a discussion with a friend, Philippe Fourastié, the director of *La Bande à Bonnot*, who has since died unnoticed. He wanted to adapt Céline's *Journey to the End of the Night*. Opening the book at random, I read: 'New York is a city that stands up straight. There it was, good and stiff, not the slightest bit droopy, frighteningly stiff.' And I added: 'You want to film that? Off you go, then, and good luck.'

If there are words that can't be filmed, there are also words that you can't do without, words that become embedded within you, that pierce and flay you, dictating the rhythm of a shot or a sequence, even forcing you to make the film.

The films I've made have sometimes been born out of an image: a tramp vainly trying to shield himself from the sun (*Le Juge et l'assassin*),* a black saxophonist sitting millions of miles from anywhere, on a bed in a seedy hotel room ('*Round Midnight*), an eclipse of the sun (*Coup de torchon*). But the reason for their existence, the thing that would hurl me into an adventure lasting almost two years, could also come from the written word. I might fall head over heels in love with a sentence: 'All sorrows look alike' (*Un dimanche à la campagne*) or 'I don't think I'm intelligent', which a little girl says to her teacher in *Une semaine de vacances*.† I knew straightaway that I was going to make that film. In *Coup de torchon*, it was the desire to translate, through film-making, those abrupt passages in italics that Jim Thompson was fond of, where the story yields to metaphysics, where the ground seems to open beneath the feet of the characters.

I find this balance between 'the weight of words' – not necessarily dialogue – and 'the shock of images' in all the films I love. It amounts to a discipline, a constraint, a protection. If you try to break it, to overcome it in favour of a flood of commercial images you risk destroying 'the stuff that dreams are made of', as Bogart said at the end of *The Maltese Falcon*. Cinema itself.

8 December

Screening at the Marignan Pathé of Alain Corneau's film, *Tous les matins du monde*. I come out enraptured by the ambition of the project, the rigour of a

---

* *The Judge and the Murderer.*
† *A Week's Holiday.*

treatment rent with explosions of feeling, the intelligence of the film's intentions. It may be a coincidence, but like two other major French films this year,
Pialat's *Van Gogh* and Rivette's *La Belle Noiseuse*, Corneau is dealing with
creation and its torments, the scars it leaves on everyone concerned, the
passion and pain that it can create. Like Van Gogh, like the painter in *La Belle
Noiseuse*, Monsieur de Sainte-Colombe wounds his friends, his family, cuts
himself off from the world and from fashion. What is, for Van Gogh, the
consequence of his genius becomes, in Sainte-Colombe, a rule of life, a
metaphysical stance. He himself constructs his own loneliness, communicating
with his children only through music. I, too, have felt that when dealing with
jazz musicians during the filming of *'Round Midnight*: they chiefly talked by
playing; words, everything else, were almost superfluous. Incidentally, these
jazzmen are not very different from baroque musicians; the ornamentation
with which baroque players embellished phrases in ways that were not always
written down are very much like improvisations according to harmonic grids.

Corneau, like Rivette and Pialat, allows us to feel the physical violence
produced by creation. When the Martin Marais character finishes conducting
a piece, he is exhausted – just like Piccoli or Emmanuelle Béart after a long
sitting in *La Belle Noiseuse*.

It's interesting to note that these three films should come into being during a
period of crisis in French cinema, and that they have no equivalent in American cinema, unless it is perhaps *Barton Fink* or Scorsese's brilliant sketch for
New York Stories. It is true that the Americans have often been uneasy with the
theme of creation. Their defiance, their fear of intellectualism, has often led
them to portray creators and artists as if they were normal people, as unin-
tellectual as possible, who laugh at the interpretations other people place on
their works. The ones who transgress these taboos are shown as depraved,
dangerously sick people whom society has to eliminate (they were generally
played by 'educated', often English, actors such as Claude Rains, James
Mason or Vincent Price). A character like Lermontov in *The Red Shoes*, at once
tyrant and victim, consumed by his passion and his demanding nature, hardly
has an equivalent in American cinema, and neither does Powell and Pressburger's film, the dramatic movement of which depends entirely on the
violence inherent in artistic creation.

Also important in *Tous les matins du monde* is the beauty of the digital sound
and the way it is used; it reinforces the film's subject matter and avoids any
stereo gimmicks. I just wonder whether Corneau could not have amplified his
theme by permitting himself, during the last third of the film, a single lyrical
tracking shot like the one in Mizoguchi's *Ugetsu*, or Satyajit Ray's *The Music
Room*, to interrupt his sequence of static shots (there are only two tracking
shots, one tracking in, one tracking out from a painting), the rigorous Jansen-
ism of which finally strikes me as just that bit too theoretical. But this minor

qualm is swept aside by the extraordinary emotional power of the confrontation between Jean-Pierre Marielle, a gruff bear of a man, lonely and unpredictable, whose sense of Shakespearian madness is finally being put to good use, and Gérard Depardieu. Either way, a film that had me in tears.

10 December

Screening of the film produced by Béatrice Soulé for Amnesty International and made by thirty different directors, all of whom wanted to defend a political prisoner. In each film a prominent person (politician, intellectual, actor, actress, etc.) reads out a letter calling for the liberation of a prisoner. Even before she was awarded the Nobel Prize, I had chosen Aung San Suu Kyi as the subject, and Anouk Grinberg, an actress who bowled me over in Bertrand Blier's *Merci la vie*. I didn't want Anouk simply to read out a formal statement, so I asked her to write it herself. She took the task very seriously, and the result surpassed my expectations. What she wrote was considered so violent that Amnesty demanded that it be watered down. I told her to include that in her letter. So, the film starts with her admitting that she had written a first letter, but then had torn it up because it was too naïve, too extreme, adding, 'I'm not used to writing to generals'; then, after pleading with the dictator of Burma, she spoke directly to Aung San Suu Kyi. I shot the film on the stage of the Bouffes du Nord theatre, where the colour of the walls and the atmosphere recall certain Hindu temples. Anouk is amazing, full of conviction, sincerity and rage. Curiously, cut all together, these thirty films are neither exhausting nor depressing. Some of them radiate a rare degree of emotion: especially those by Jacques Doillon, Raymond Depardon, Jane Birkin, Chantal Ackerman, whom I congratulate at the end. All she could find to say was, 'You seem to be astonished that it worked'; then she explains to me that she thought her optical sound was so bad that she couldn't concentrate on the other films – a reaction that was so narcissistic it made me laugh. Some people will never have anything good to say about anybody.

But the worst thing was something Alain Resnais showed me: an article by Pierre Murat in *Télérama* creating a contest among the thirty films, with prizes for Male and Female Actors, for Best First Feature. Why not include a prize for the Most Moving Victim, or an Oscar for the First Prisoner Freed? You have to be completely cut off not only from politics, but from life in general, to come up with ideas like that.

11 December

Three times a month, at ten o'clock on a Wednesday morning, there is a meeting of the board of directors of the SACD, a venerable institution

founded by Beaumarchais to defend the rights of theatrical authors who lived
at the whim and financial beck and call of actors – particularly in the Comédie
Française – who literally robbed them of their earnings. To impose that law it
took no less than three regimes: Royalty (Louis XVI), Revolution (the Convention), and finally Napoleon. As one can see, authors' rights were a difficult idea
to push through.

Likewise, the concept of 'author', particularly in the new art forms. During
the twenties film-makers wanted to join the Association and encountered a
mixture of hostility and scorn. Screenwriters might be admitted, at a pinch, but
certainly not directors. The playwright Henri Bernstein railed against the
people he termed 'crank-turners'. By a funny coincidence, his name has
recently been rescued from oblivion by one of those very same 'crank-turners',
Alain Resnais, with his adaptation of *Mélo*. Today cinema and television
screenwriters and directors sit side by side with theatrical writers, composers
and choreographers, all fighting together to protect authors' rights. A battle
which is very vital today, particularly when one considers that many countries
still refuse film-makers the status of artistic creators: England, of course, and
Germany, but also Russia – the country of Eisenstein and Dovzhenko, as well
as wonderful film-makers like Barnett and Donskoï – and the USA.

It was during these working sessions that I met Jean Cosmos, whom I asked
to co-write *La Vie et rien autre*, and Louis Ducreux, the old painter in *Un
dimanche à la campagne*, who never opened his mouth. At first I thought that his
silence was due to some ailment or shyness, but he told me wickedly that he
held his tongue so that he would never be asked to join a Commission.
Recently, he's been looking very tired. His eyesight has grown much worse,
and when we last had dinner together I had to walk him to his door.

Apart from the SACD, I'm a member of the SRF (Sociéte des Réalisateurs
de Films) and ARP (Association des Réalisateurs Producteurs); I sometimes
envy film-makers like Resnais, Rivette or Rohmer who refuse any kind of
militantism, preferring the Olympian heights. It makes life simpler and takes
less time. But I tell myself that I wouldn't make the films I make if I gave up all
this work.

There are a number of rivalries between these organizations – the ARP is
chiefly pragmatic, the SRF moral and the SACD legalistic – which blur
together when the battle heats up. We all find ourselves on the same side,
facing distributors, the government, Brussels bureaucrats. We are a long way
from the stupid schisms between the Screenwriters' and Directors' Guilds in
the USA.

Let's not forget that the 'Directors' Fortnight'* at Cannes was set up by
Director of the SRF. The members of the ARP, thanks to Claude Berri,

---

* A unique initiative, it was set up originally to show those films refused for the main competition.

created SofiArp, a banking organization that helps to finance films as long as the screenplay is approved by a Commission which includes a number of film-makers. Two initiatives out of a thousand which show that French film-makers have taken some control of their destiny, rejecting both isolation and protectionism.

This morning we learn that major new changes are threatening French television, and therefore cinema, because the television channels are, almost compulsorily, co-producers of our films. The private channels and particularly Channel 5 want to reduce the quota of French and European production and get a second commercial break during films. It is worth bearing in mind that the fifth channel was created on the instructions of François Mitterrand for the worst electioneering reasons, with minimal obligations. This criminal initiative destabilized the entire audiovisual landscape, and revealed the stupidity and incompetence of politicians who claim to take an interest in television only to exert even greater control over it. Sweet-talked by Berlusconi, supported by the head of the Italian Socialist Party, Craxi, Mitterrand and Fabius thought they were creating a channel that would support their party. Once he had it, Berlusconi quickly took as his partner Hersent, the head of *Le Figaro* and a right-wing figure who controls half the French press. Once again the socialists were the dupes.

A few years later they seem ready to start all over again! Mitterrand, who refuses to acknowledge his blunder – his betrayal, in fact, of film-makers (most of whom voted for him) – wants to defend that fifth channel, which in the meantime has been bought by a friend of his, Lagardère, the head of Hachette and Matra, thanks to pressure from the Elysée Palace. After only a few months the finances were in a terrible state, and in view of the huge deficit, Lagardère wanted the law to be modified in order to show more foreign series, American ones in particular, and produce fewer original programmes.

If Lagardère got this dispensation, the regulations governing the other private channels would explode in turn. The situation risked being disastrous. This ridiculous project had the support of one of Mitterrand's ministers, Georges Kiejman, who, when he was a lawyer, had been rather good at defending directors against the caprices of power and censorship. This reversal reminds me of a phrase of Victor Hugo's: 'Some people are born to serve their country, others to serve at table.'

At the end of the session, the SACD decides to send a communiqué to all politicians exposing the threat to French culture. Likewise, the SRF sends a shattering letter which compares the contamination of the nation's minds by a flood of corrupt images to the contamination of those who contracted AIDS through blood transfusions. The violent simile has its effect. In the end, the second commercial break is not adopted.

12 December

New rough-cut screening of *L 627*. I've restructured the sixth reel, which has been giving us the most trouble – there's always one problematic reel in every film. It consists of a whole series of shots, moments describing the everyday life of the group. I like these little montages where the plot disappears behind emotional or funny touches, but they're a nightmare for the editors. Armand Psenny, who worked with me on all my films until *Daddy Nostalgie*,* called them 'Bouvier passages', after the murderer in *Le Juge et l'assassin*, whom I showed wandering about, murdering people and going mad in dozens of different landscapes.

The reel in question looked better but it isn't perfect. I'm still having trouble with the scene where they're tailing some Zaïreans, which was so hard to film.

I've got rid of other scenes, notably a visit of Lulu's to an informer friend, a sick old Corsican to whom he gives a dose of heroin as a woman (his wife or sister) nods her thanks. It was something of a nightmare finding this location. I wanted a large, high-ceilinged room, virtually empty except for some totally unlikely objects (I asked to have kilos of sugar piled up). Actually, I was looking for the kind of apartment typical of Lyon, both large and sinister. The ones I was shown were too beautiful. Suddenly, on the eve of the shoot, the designer Guy-Claude François had the idea of using the production offices, which he arranged overnight.

Because of all this work, I hesitated about cutting the scene. I notice that sequences where the locations are hard to find, the settings difficult to visualize, are often the first to be go in the editing.

Colo† is moved by the film, its violence and sense of immediacy. Pierre Rissient is also full of praise, talking to me at length about the actors – all of whom he found excellent – the inventive dialogue, the often-astonishing sense of truth that each scene generates, and of the very physical work of Alain Choquart, who is both director of photography and cameraman. 'I've seen few recent films that have given me such a sense of life today,' he tells me. He was expecting more of a *film noir* in the style of Anthony Mann's *T Men* – something I was never after. When I expressed my fears about Le Pen and the far right appropriating the film for their own political ends – most of the dealers are black or North Africans since that's what I saw during the six months of writing and the three months of preparation – he's flabbergasted. To him, neither the film, nor the protagonist, are racists. On the contrary.

Walking from Billancourt to the Porte Saint Cloud, Colo – who senses the danger better – tells me that the way to avoid it would have been to cheat, by watering down the subject-matter or by catering to a salon of left-wingers.

---

* *These Foolish Things.*
† My ex-wife and brilliant scenarist of *Une semaine de vacances, Un dimanche à la campagne, Beatrice*, and *Daddy Nostalgie.*

14 December

I devour the biography of George Cukor by Patrick McGilligan,* author of a masterly book on Robert Altman. An irreproachable, fascinating book, very well documented without ever slipping into facile anecdote or superficial judgement. McGilligan interestingly mentions Cukor's homosexuality, and the part that it played in his career (it was the reason why he was fired from *Gone with the Wind* – an event which reveals the antisemitism of Gable and Fleming and a large number of people in Hollywood) without ever falling into voyeurism or sensationalism. I've learned dozens of things: that Cukor wanted Cary Grant for *A Star is Born*, that Bresson and Dreyer wrote asking him to help them find work in Hollywood, that Katharine Hepburn wrote the script of *Travels with my Aunt*. And then this surprising discovery: Cukor may be the only director of his calibre who never originated a single personal project. That isn't true of Ford, Hawks, or Walsh, Dwan, Tourneur, Minnelli, or even Mitchell Leisen. The book makes me want to go back and watch the Cukor films I love: certainly not *The Women* or the stiff, impersonal collaborations with Selznick, but *Sylvia Scarlett* (about which Katharine Hepburn says a lot of silly things in her memoirs), *Holiday*, *Adam's Rib*, and the very underestimated *The Marrying Kind*, a realistic black comedy ahead of its time, which contains one of the most spectacular changes of tone in the history of cinema: going, in the same scene, from domestic comedy to personal drama when Shelley Winters – while playing a ukelele in the park – suddenly realizes that her child has drowned.

15 December

I spend an astonishing evening with Marcel Clouzot, the younger brother of the director of *Quai des Orfèvres*. An incredible bibliophile, he shows me an original edition of Racine annotated by the author, and a Greek manuscript that belonged to Montaigne. Because he loved *La Vie et rien autre*, after dinner he shows me a 'little' film he made on video – which lasts three hours twenty minutes! The main subject is extraordinary. It deals with an investigation carried out by Clouzot into the tragic fate of a young poet who died at Verdun during the First World War. This poet was very close to his parents, particularly his mother. Clouzot discovered letters and photographs revealing a romantic, and apparently platonic, love affair between them. Despairingly over the death of this friend, his mother immediately wanted another child, whom she called Marcel after the poet, and who now wonders about the man to whom he imagines he owes his life. Clouzot discovered letters from the poet's

---

* *George Cukor*, St Martin's Press (US), Faber and Faber (UK), 1992.

fellow soldiers – extraordinary letters, some ten pages long – written by peasants and workers in very fine French (which says a great deal about public education then). He discovers the poet's log book at the Bibliothèque Nationale and is thus able to reconstruct his last days. In the forests around Verdun, which I visited in the company of Philippe Noiret and Sabine Azéma each Sunday while working on *La Vie et rien autre*, he managed to locate the trench where the man who was responsible for his birth met his end – a beautiful subject for a film: this inquiry undertaken fifty years later, this fascination of a man for a hypothetical, emblematic 'father'.

28 December

In the production of *Les Voeux du Président* at the Théâtre de l'Aquarium, Jean-Louis Benoit not only delivers yet more evidence of his talent and inventiveness, but also rediscovers one of the chief aims of the theatre (often forgotten by contemporary writers): the ability to talk about the present-day world, the men and ideas that govern our lives, and to do it with irony, disrespect and lightness – as Sacha Guitry was always saying, a lot of 'serious' writers confuse 'deep' with 'hollow'. The spirit of Aristophanes, Molière, the Brecht of *Arturo Ui*.

The idea behind the play is admirably simple: Jean-Louis Benoit has taken the addresses that François Mitterrand has delivered on television every New Year's Eve for the past seven years. Without altering so much as a comma, he changes the setting, imagining the President of the Republic knocking on a door, inviting himself into a family home and, before the holiday dinner, reciting his speech to the assembled family. Each of the seven scenes begins with the life (and quarrels) of the family, which gradually undergoes a kind of breakdown. Initially welcomed as a hero, Mitterrand slowly turns into the kind of person who is constantly interrupted and ignored, who isn't even offered a drink. One year the burglar alarm prevents him from coming in and he begins his speech outside, behind a window, while the daughter of the house exclaims, 'He's so brave . . . It's minus five out there . . . Maybe we should rub him down.' The resulting disparity produces a vengeful, extraordinarily funny and corrosive play: a political observation on style, the way in which words, broken promises, tokens of self-congratulation, repeated warnings of difficulties to come, gradually lose their meaning, and become a series of verses whose order is simply changed round from one year to the next, a cynical litany cut off from reality. The last speech (the play was written during the Gulf War, while Mitterrand was doing very well in the polls), delivered in a dark, abandoned house by a Mitterrand with a mouth full of crabmeat, has a darkness, a violence, that sends shivers down the spine. It is the just revenge of an artist, an intellectual, on a man who has betrayed artists and intellectuals, who has sold them out so as to be able to enjoy power – even in opposition to his own party.

29 December

While working on the editing of *L627*, I'm suddenly racked by doubt. I get the feeling that none of it works, that I've failed to capture my subject. An arrest near the Place des Fêtes Métro station particularly comes as a shock. There are too many shots. Because I filmed this sequence with two cameras the editor, Ariane Boeglin, has cut together all the interesting shots and all of a sudden we've lost the point of view, the line of force, the sense of urgency in the scene, which has now become superficially spectacular – the very thing I was trying to avoid.

2 January 1992

For the tenth time I see Jacques Tourneur's *I Walked with a Zombie*, in a splendid print. As admirable as ever. The film of a poet and an architect, as Manny Farber used to say to me. Of a musician too, so well does the whisper of voices seem to match the lighting. With each viewing, the mystery deepens. Tourneur succeeds in giving form to anxiety and mystery, in creating a ghostly climate, even in the Americana films: in *An Education of the Heart*, a story of an athlete's decline, presumably far from his own preoccupations; *Stars in My Crown*, a low-key chronicle of small-town life seen through a child's eyes; the dark and unsettling *Easy Living*.

4 January

I spend a good part of the day with my composer, Philippe Sarde. We have known each other since Claude Sautet's *Les Choses de la vie*,* for which I was press attaché, and he has worked on four of my films. He's written memorable scores every time, especially the concerto for diatonique accordion and orchestra for *Le Juge et l'assassin*, which he wrote before we started shooting, and which I used on set to provide a rhythm for the shots and camera movements, and to guide the actors.

An extraordinary character, he spends his life holed up in a sort of Ali Baba's cave where you have to weave your way among computers, synthesizers and consoles, constantly at risk of bumping into a state-of-the-art projector with dolby sound, of stumbling into televisions or telephones still in their boxes. There's something wonderful about this indescribable mess; smoked

---

* *The Things of Life.*

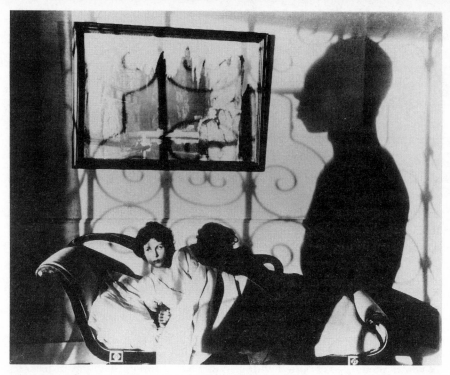

62   Tourneur's *I Walked with a Zombie* (1943)

salmon leftovers lie on a magnificent piano, hundreds of videos of old films (I catch sight of Gréville's *Menaces*, Raymond Leboursier's *Le Furet*, one of the most obscure 'turkeys' of the fifties, and *Le Dernier des 6* by Lacombe) are piled up beside huge stacks of records and CDs of his scores.

I bring him two videos (*Caprices* by Leon Joannon and *Le Sang à la tête* by Gilles Grangier), and, as a gesture of gratitude, he offers me a fax machine! He's always been insanely generous. He spends money without a thought, compulsively buys three of everything. He used to be like that with food; twenty years ago he and his brother, Alain (who is producer of *L 627*) were the models for Marco Ferreri's *La Grande bouffe*.*

When he likes a film, Sarde is a terrific person to work with, quite apart from his composing abilities. Very sensitive to the actors, the dialogue, the point of the direction, he brings a keen intelligence to his discussion of the editing, questioning the order or length of the shots; in most cases he's right, suggesting brilliant changes. One scene in *Un dimanche à la campagne*, the dance sequence, caused us a number of problems. It was over-edited. Sarde, by getting rid of most of the shots, and leaving the scene as a five-minute sequence, gave it an organic, musical rhythm. In *L 627*, his sharp eye enabled

* *Blow-Out.*

me to carry out a large number of changes. I have never encountered this quality in any other composer.

When he opens the door, Sarde may be fully dressed or in his pyjamas with a two-day growth of beard. This time he's in pyjamas, but clean-shaven. I bring him a few records, notably the ones I used as the temp music for the working print. I try to find the concept, rhythm, and style of the music during the writing of the screenplay.

For *L 627* I started with a process of elimination: no two-four rhythm, or instrumental solos. I wanted a compact sound, a clash of styles, constant changes of tempo and tonality, a mixture of the most diverse instruments; I suggested to a delighted Sarde that we should use a viola da gamba, saxes, bass clarinets, jazz drums, African percussion instruments (in order to recreate the atmosphere of violence and instability); to combine the harmonies of Guillaume de Machault, Kurt Weil, Nino Rota, Philip Glass with Senegalese rhythms; to set baroque sonorities against a waltz in a kind of Carla Bley arrangement. The music needed a pulse – the pulse of the main character, constantly on the move – based on unpredictable changes of tempo or unexpected rhythmic harmonies.

Sarde, who describes himself more as a musical screenwriter than as a composer, was enthusiastic about these options, which, for him, followed the ethical approach of the film. Seeing it again, we both agree about the sequences that require music, apart from one: when Lulu and his wife are working on the wedding videos. Philippe is sure that this scene will be 'lit' from within if we give it a musical counterpoint. On the other hand, he's violently opposed to including a song by the group Super Diamono de Dakar whose music I've used in the work print. He thought that their repetitive, two-four rhythm robs the film of its excitement and gives it unpleasant connotations. I also get the feeling that he doesn't want somebody else's composition in the middle of his score.

6 January

I see *Mozart in Gascony*, a beautiful little film by Jean-Claude Bringuier. Bringuier is a remarkable documentary film-maker whose films are not as well known as they should be. I've been a fan of his for years. He's got a knack of unearthing unforgettable characters, like the old women in *Les Cavaliers de Luneville* remembering the 1914 war.

There's a depth of feeling in Bringuier's work which brings to mind a writer who isn't as well known as he should be either: Georges Navel. Here's the opening passage of a book called *Travaux*:

My mother was forty-seven when I was born, so I can only think of her as a maternal figure, a woman measured not in terms of physical beauty or attraction, but for her kindness, her warmth, her kitchen fingers. I was her thirteenth child and to me she was a perpetual sixty-year-old, never one of those toothless old harridan grannies, sitting all day long, their hands a fidgety knot in their laps.

If they had born children, women in our village were called La Mere, not Madame, and all Meres were alike: wrinkled and well versed in tears, with garlicky hands as tough as leather. My mother had done her share of crying and it showed in the watery gaze of her spectacles, but the rest of her face, from her forehead to her lips and voice, was always at the brink of a smile.

I wonder whether Navel has been translated into English, and whether Bringuier's films have been broadcast by the BBC?

8 January

Dinner with the jury that has just awarded Jean-Pierre Coursodon and myself the Simone Genevois Prize for *50 ans de cinéma américain*. The dinner was held at the Table d'Anvers, a marvellous restaurant run by two brothers, Christian and Philippe Conticini. The former, the head chef, is lean; the latter, the *chef-pâtissier*, is somewhat more corpulent.

Simone Genevois, who, with her husband, André Conti, finances the prize, was a famous actress whose career ran from the silent period into the early days of the talkies. Most importantly, she played the lead in *La Merveilleuse vie de Jeanne d'Arc* by Marc de Gastyne (1928), which was made the same year as Dreyer's film on the same subject, and which disappeared from the annals of film history for that very reason until Kevin Brownlow rediscovered it. It's a remarkable, sometimes truly inspired film. The early part – the daily life of Joan and her family in a country devastated by war, with his powerful shots of exhumed soldiers describing the horrors they've seen, horrors that de Gastyne evokes with a rare violence and acuteness – is surprising in its intensity, its dramatic economy. If the trial, which chiefly avoids tawdry religious imagery, suffers from comparison with Dreyer, the siege of Orléans, on the other hand, creates an epic feel that is almost unique in French cinema, a lyricism that ends in the admirable moment where Joan, facing the battlefield covered with the dead and wounded, suddenly realizing that she is the cause of these atrocities, abruptly bursts into tears. The extremely modern sobriety of the acting – particularly Jean Debucourt as Charles VII – and the vibrant spirituality, the luminous intensity of Simone Genevois, whose large eyes seem to hold within them all the beauty of the sky, have a great deal to do with the emotional impact of the film.

Among this jury I'm happy to meet again critics like Jean-Paul Torok, who wrote the first passionate defence of *Peeping Tom*; film historians like Claude Beylie, a specialist on Renoir, Ophuls and Pagnol; directors like Alexandre Astruc and Claude Sautet. They seem to have found the book exciting, informative, enthralling and, most of all, lively. They fire questions at me about whether I've had the chance to see certain very obscure films, Ulmer's Yiddish movies, and especially the incredible 'turkeys' of Edward D. Wood jr, the immortal director of *Plan 9 from Outer Space*. For anyone unaware of this extravagant *auteur*, here's an extract from our entry on him:

Wood jr, Edward D., 1922–78
The list of his films may be short – only eight (including his last, a hardcore porn movie, *Necromancy*, which must not be confused with Bert I. Gordon's film of the same name, released the same year) – but, spanning thirty-one years, it is a career that has a kind of Bressonian rhythm. It is true that one of his films was released *twenty-three years* after it was shot (which must be some sort of record), having been left in a lab for lack of funds, and that *Orgy of the Dead* was rediscovered only very recently despite having been made in 1966. This somewhat distorts the historical perspective, and reduces Wood's true creative period to one of nine years, between *Glen or Glenda* and *The Sinister Urge*, also known by the title of *The Young and the Immoral* (which more accurately conveys the message of the plot, namely that pornography leads to juvenile delinquency).

This brief career didn't prevent Edward D. Wood jr from becoming – sadly, posthumously – a cult director in the United States, since *Plan 9 from Outer Space* has been hailed as 'the worst film of all time', Wood himself carrying off the prize of 'worst director'. These awards provoked the exhumation of a body of work that previously his admirers (and he himself) were only able to see at around three or four in the morning on television. His work has become one of the flagships of the video catalogues, in the 'cult classic' category. His greatest glory came in the form of a major software package launched by Bell, entitled *Plan 9* after his masterpiece (see the *Guardian*, 20 July 1990). This shows a certain sense of humour on the part of Bell's designers when one considers the unbelievable technology of the film: the flying saucers are shaped pieces of cardboard thrown in the air; when they circle around their planet the wires and cables are clearly visible.

It must be said that everything in Wood's films exudes a sense of extravagance, starting with the shooting that he often supervised dressed as a woman (he boasted that he was the only marine who landed at Anzio wearing women's undergarments). During the filming of *Plan 9*, Bela Lugosi, a great friend of his who had 'acted' in two of his films, suddenly died after two days' filming (according to Harry and Michael Medved, most of Wood's shots had shown Lugosi trying on his vampire's cape). Rather than start over with a different actor, the director chose instead to keep the test shots, which he then distributed throughout the edited version. Consequently, we see Lugosi putting on his cape several times and walking towards the camera with a grandeur worthy of the mime Etienne Decroux in Prévert's *Voyage surprise*. For the other scenes Wood used a double, an unemployed chiropractor who was taller than Lugosi and with hair of a different colour. He gave him one direction only: whatever happened, he was to keep his arm and his cape held in front of his face. This causes some hilarious lapses of continuity, since the character – from one shot to the next – suddenly grows six inches taller. This daring direction destroys in the most modern fashion all the Hollywood rules of 'movie making'.

10 January

Dinner at Michel Ciment's with Jerry Schatzberg, a film-maker whom he defends passionately, and rightly so. I'm not about to forget the shock of discovering *Puzzle of a Downfall Child* and *Scarecrow*. Jerry has problems financing his personal projects in today's Hollywood system – doubtless because he's incapable of turning out one of those products designed to flatter and titillate an audience under the age of fifteen. His direction is never exploitative, he doesn't try to 'sell' feelings, incidents, horror, sex or worthy sentiments, unlike those movies that appear to be a series of commercials. His treatment of violence in the excellent *Street Smart*, an extremely moral film, was at odds with a predominant American atmosphere that seems to have contaminated even the Scorsese of *Cape Fear*.

A number of days later I see Schatzberg again to discuss the subjects he would like to deal with. For one of them I advise him to use Dennis Potter as a scriptwriter, and then I organize several meetings for him with René Bonnell of the French TV channel Canal Plus and René Cleitman of Hachette Première. I have the feeling that Jerry will find people in Europe more open, more understanding of his ambitions.

Europe should be helping not only each of its national film industries, but also film-makers whose careers have been obstructed in their own country. In order to achieve that, we will have to overcome the idiotic and criminal ignorance of some politicians, some governments, who don't seem able to understand that an image is not only an image, or a cultural fact, but an instrument for selling food, cars, clothes, music, a way of life – an ideology. The Americans have understood this for a long time, and every treaty or commercial agreement with a country – specifically, a Third World country – always includes a clause selling – or imposing – hundreds of hours of films or television material. Or they are given free – as bait.

In Brussels or Strasbourg, whenever we sent a delegation of film-makers, scriptwriters and producers, we found ourselves face to face not with film directors, but with Carla Hill, a representative of the executive office of the White House, and Jack Valenti, the man who wrote to Lyndon Johnson about *The Green Berets*: 'As far as Vietnam is concerned, John Wayne's views are right.' When we talked about quotas, they started yelling about protectionism and censorship. (We were suggesting a 50 per cent share for American cinema. In the States, European films have a 2 per cent share. Who's more protectionist?) They also threatened reprisals where car and perfume imports were concerned. The same threats about protectionism and censorship were made by President Bush on television to the Turkish Prime Minister in September 1991 when Turkey's film-makers suggested a clause reserving 25 per cent of programming for national products. All in the name of liberalism. When I see English or Dutch politicians believing – as Valenti and Hill insinuate – that 'liberalism' and 'liberty' are synonyms (the liberty of a fox in a chicken coop), I feel like killing them. They're selling out their economy, their country, their culture to the Americans. And I'm sure that most of them are so ill-informed about cinema as a medium, so ignorant, that they don't even need thirty pieces of silver to do it.

We need not only regulation, but real European production and distribution bodies (for both cinema and television); some countries will have to stop leaning towards the States and complying with American diktats (I'm thinking about Luxembourg, which seems to want to become Europe's Panama – fair enough, there aren't any artists there), and apply genuine authors' rights, recognizing the director as an author. In order to achieve this there will have to be many more discussions and debates. We will have to try to help one another. Our survival depends on it.

14 January

I meet Serge Toubiana and Michel Pascal, who are working on a documentary on Truffaut, with whom I had long and passionate relations. When he was a critic on *Arts* magazine I read him faithfully and even wrote to him a few times, particularly when he ripped *The Searchers* to pieces. I can still remember three films that he defended vigorously, and which I have never managed to see: *South Sea Sinner* (Bruce Humberstone), *No Sad Songs for Me* (Rudolph Mate), *High Lonesome* (Alan Le May).

Truffaut even invited me to watch him shoot *Les Quatre cent coups*,* which I saw on its opening day at 2 p.m., as I did *Tirez sur le pianiste*,† skipping classes in philosophy and law respectively. My first disappointment came with *Jules et Jim* (my opinion hasn't changed after seeing it again recently); then, reading the memoirs of Henri Jeanson, I was shocked by what he really did to Jean Aurenche and Pierre Bost, whom he tore apart in a well-known article.‡ Jeanson reveals that Truffaut borrowed the documents he needed to write this piece directly from Pierre Bost, after showering him with compliments. Bost confirmed this story when I was working on *L'Horloger de Saint-Paul* with him and Aurenche, and he even showed me a letter from Truffaut that read: 'You must have been surprised by the brutal tone of my article. You will understand that I am a young journalist, and to get myself noticed I have to adopt a polemical tone and not necessarily say what I think ... I still have a great deal of admiration for you. It's Aurenche I'm really against.' When I said that he could have used Truffaut's letter to defend himself, he answered, 'No, Truffaut was very impolite to me. I don't want to use the same weapons,' adding, 'I never showed that letter to Aurenche.'

I got closer to Truffaut after *Que la fête commence*,§ which he liked a great deal. As for me, I had been greatly moved by *La Chambre verte*.¶ We spoke and

---

* *The Four Hundred Blows.*
† *Shoot the Pianist.*
‡ 'Une certaine tendance du cinéma française', *Cahiers du cinéma*, 1954.
§ *Let Joy Reign Supreme.*
¶ *The Green Room.* His masterpiece, I think.

wrote to each other a few times: he sent me very complimentary notes after *Une semaine de vacances*, *Coup de torchon* and *Un dimanche à la campagne*. During a lunch I even shyly tried to get him to talk about that ignominious article. He told me he would never write anything like that now, and then we changed the subject. Out of modesty and reticence I never saw our relationship as anything but episodic. Like in a Henry James novel, we talked to each other through Danielle Bio, a very sensitive woman who worshipped Truffaut and had written a book about me. She told me how tactful and thoughtful he was. I keenly read his last interviews, which struck me as more and more intelligent. I very much regret my diffidence.

16 January

I see the first 35mm print of *La Guerre sans nom*. I'm horrified by the poor grading of the special effects (dissolves, wipes). They emphasize the cuts rather than concealing them. I immediately decide to get rid of them all. Another problem: the optical soundtrack is weak, dull, lacking definition. Nothing like what I heard during the sound mixing. But Gérard Lamps, my mixer, had already rejected four test prints. I've already had a few set-tos with the French labs, especially LTC, who don't seem to attach any importance to the printing or the quality of the sound. For example, I've rejected many optical prints and several release prints of *Daddy Nostalgie*, the soundtracks were so crackly and spluttery. In Cannes, M. Roques, one of the heads of LTC, replied with a masterly: 'That's because there aren't enough notes in your music' – showing what idiots he thinks we directors are.

At the first screening I apologize for these shortcomings to viewers who don't seem to have noticed them. They seem overwhelmed by the film. Another satisfaction: nobody complains about the four-hour length. I see a man leaving at a hurried pace, then he turns and comes back and says to me: 'I was in Algeria, I'm a veteran, too. I've just relived my life. I'm going home to weep.'

17 January

After two further fruitless attempts, Lamps accepts the new print of the optical soundtrack.

21 January

Six o'clock in the evening, the first public screening of *La Guerre sans nom*. The event has been organized by SCAM, the association of documentary directors and authors. They clearly hadn't expected such a turnout, and the auditorium is soon full of people who, because of a mistake on the invitation, don't realize that the film is four hours long. Some of them, having accepted dinner invitations, apologize in advance. It's so crowded, we organize a second showing twenty minutes after the first one.

During the intermission Patrick Rotman and I are warmly congratulated by the historians in the audience. Michel Winock tells us he feels as if he's witnessing 'a kind of resurrection of memory, as if it were emerging from the bowels of the earth'. As the second half begins a few people leave, but not before checking there's nothing left to eat or drink. Parisian habits – nothing new!

It's a much better print, and getting rid of the wipes strengthens the dramatic progression. Some of the cuts hadn't gained from being concealed; others were invisible. As for the sound, it's incomparably better than the answer print. The second half, in spite of the very long intermission that broke people's concentration, seems to hold the audience's attention even more. The appearance of Jean Bollon, the president of UNC, a rather right-wing veterans' association, showing off his office and the relics it contains as if it was a museum (photograph of Clémenceau, his father's hat, a German helmet), the mumblings of his acolytes, getting their places and dates wrong, provokes considerable hilarity. This rigid and funny ritual, a victorious example of involuntary satire, had been imposed on me. Bollon wouldn't appear without it. I would never have dared ask him for it.

Seeing it in front of an audience, *La Guerre sans nom* strikes me as truly honest, rigorous, never deliberately exploitative.

Despite all the praise, the discussion that follows is generally disappointing. Many of the speakers are less concerned with voicing an opinion than with talking about themselves, their problems, telling us what they know. Some even leave before we can answer them. The thirty-five debates that are going to be held throughout the whole of France will be more moving, more exciting than this one, despite being held under the aegis of an association of film directors.

Patrick and I were most moved by the heated speech – and praise – of René Vautier, a film-maker who worked with the FLN and directed the first fictional film about the Algerian War, *Avoir 20 ans dans les aures*. A few days before he had sent me a letter saying that the political interviews he had been doing over the years had been stolen recently – proving the current importance of a war that happened thirty years ago, and the hold it continues to exert on French politics.

22 January

Private screenings of *La Guerre sans nom* begin. One was set aside for the *Nouvel Observateur*, a fashionable left-wing weekly whose attitudes during the Algerian war were exemplary. We invited the magazine's general editor, Jean Daniel, and its main political journalists who are putting together a special issue on this war.

They even fixed the date of the screening themselves. Come the day, not a soul. After half an hour we give them a call and are told politely that nobody from the magazine is going to turn up. Fortunately, having predicted this, Eva Simonet, our press attaché, had invited some other journalists..

24–5 January

Among my many activities, I am President of the Lumière Institute created in Lyons by Bernard Chardère, the founder of *Positif*, to celebrate the memory and the work of Louis and Auguste Lumière and explore the history of cinema.

The Institute managed to find a place for itself not in the Lumière Brothers' house, which was scandalously destroyed at the beginning of the seventies to make way for a ghastly bank, but in their father's house beside the hangar where they made their first film, *La Sortie des usines Lumière*, the façade of which still stands. The municipal authorities wanted to tear it down three years ago to make room for a new building project. 'What's the historic interest of this old ruin?' they asked us. We had to fight, explain that these were the remains of the first set of the first film, that Lyons would have a great deal to gain by restoring it. This is typical of Lyons' mayors and councillors, who over the past decades have contemptuously allowed an invaluable heritage to disappear. Almost ten years ago, at the first meeting of the board of directors, I declared that if the Lumière brothers had been called Light and been born in Seattle or Atlanta, they would have been honoured by a museum or monument, and Japanese tourists would be queuing to buy videos or souvenirs. But Lyons is a secretive city ('the city of secret feelings and true loves' as Henri Béraud* put it), always a bit afraid of the arrival of 'too many strangers who aren't from around here' as the local saying has it. Added to this is a rivalry, even a war, with Paris, to which political hostility was added in 1982–3, since Lyons council is fairly right wing. But relations got even worse when, during the 'cohabitation' (the period when Chirac was Prime Minister after the Right won the legislative elections while the socialist Mitterrand was still President), the Minister of Culture went over to the right. Result: the work of the Lumière Brothers is not very well known either in their own city or abroad. The Museum of the Moving Image in London barely mentions them. Does anybody know they were making 3D films in the thirties?

Things have been improving over the past few years, the centenary of the birth of the cinema having helped, and the new council is more willing to assist

---

* A brilliant journalist and novelist who was first left-wing then became right-wing and anti-semitic due to Anglophobia. After the Second World War he was sentenced to death, but was saved by De Gaulle.

63   The Lumière brothers: Auguste and Louis

us. The battle I launched ten years ago to sort out the rights of the Lumière films is reaching an end. The Centre du Cinéma,* after taking expert legal advice, finally admitted that the films were not in the public domain and belonged to the family, which will bring their anarchic exploitation to an end.

This weekend the Institut Lumière held a series of screenings and seminars redefining the contribution made by French screenwriters during the thirties, forties and fifties. I programmed the event with the artistic director, Thierry Frémaux, and wrote an introduction:

This series of screenings and seminars on the French screenwriters, constitutes the first incursion, an initial exploration of a virtually uncharted territory. A territory we thought we knew, but only because of outdated pointers, unreliable milestones, and deceitful signposts. A map, we know, is not the territory and yet in this case, it's as if it were. We still talk in abstractions and theories, describe sites and partial landscapes – sometimes entirely imaginary – and depend on old-fashioned ideas and dictatorial dogmas that die hard. True, it took certain map-makers several centuries to admit the earth was round. Thus, for more than twenty years we've witnessed the trashing of Michel Audiard, who often proved to be a highly inventive dialogue writer, gifted with a wildly zany and genuinely poetic sense of popular lyricism. Had he been recognized sooner, maybe he would have written more films in the vein of *Mortelle randonée* and less of those like *Les Morfalous*.

Similarly, Aurenche, with or without Bost, has been pigeonholed among the literary adaptors, which is to forget films such as *Lettre d'amour*, *L'Auberge rouge*, *Que la fête commence*, *Le Juge et l'assassin*, his publicity shorts, his collaborations with Paul Grimault, as well as a documentary such as *Les Pirates du Rhône*. And that several of his adaptations are essentially original scripts: *Douce*, *Le Mariage de Chiffon*, even *L'Horologer de Saint Paul*. (It's worth noting that this epithet, adaptor, is never stuck on American directors or screenwriters – Dalton Trumbo, for example, – whose work is practically nothing but adaptations.)

As for Henri Jeanson, his case is even more complex than it seems. Behind the brilliant dialogue writer lurked one of the few screenwriters to have put his name on the first anti-fascist manifesto (there was only Prévert and him), to have been indicted for anti-colonialism and pacifism, to have served a prison term under the Occupation. Facts that give an authentic realism to certain lines in *Le Drame de Shanghai*, *Boule de Suif*, *Les Maudits*, not to mention the outstanding *Un revennant*, possibly his masterpiece.

And the forgotten ... When can you find the slightest study or analysis of the contribution of Maurice Aubergé, author of screenplay and dialogue for *Falbalas* and *La Vérité sur Bebé Donge*, two extraordinary scripts? If you were to go through all the revues and film weeklies, would you find his name? I doubt it. The same goes for Bernard Zimmer, [a successful dramatist and translator of Aristophanes], who wrote several outstanding screenplays, among them *Le Coupable*, with its Buñuelian strains, *Pontcarral*.

Where will you find a real filmography for Jean Anouilh, who collaborated anonymously on many films produced by François Chavanne? And Claude Sautet, who doctored numerous films? When will we see studies of Vitrac, Marcel Aymé, Pierre

---

* The institution which administers and regulates the cinema in France.

Véry, Raymond Queneau, René Wheeler (who also directed a fine film, *Premières Armes*), such as American writers as Faulkner, Huxley, Fitzgerald and Ben Hecht have enjoyed?

Without false modesty, we can say that with Jean Pierre Coursodon, we've pointed the way in *30 Ans de Cinéma Américain* (and in a more developed manner in *50 Ans*). It catalysed an entire series of essays, inquiries, anthologies of interviews, from Richard Corliss to Patrick McGilligan's two-volume *Backstory*, as well as the Ben Hecht biography, an exciting contribution that updates the history of cinema.

In France, nothing. Or nothing much.

It's time to get started.

Those three days were very exciting. We heard thrilling lectures on Pierre Véry, Yves Mirande; we rediscovered *Sortilèges*, a magnificent screenplay by Prévert, powerfully and lyrically filmed by Christian Jaque, and *Occupe-toi d'Amélie*, a masterful adaptation of Feydeau, in which Aurenche and Bost mixed theatre with cinema, the audience with the characters in the play, anticipating *The Purple Rose of Cairo* by thirty-five years; Philippe d'Hugues revealed to us that Anouilh had been the uncredited scriptwriter of Albert Valentin's *Marie Martine* (in which Saturnin Fabre creates an unforgettable eccentric), *Battement de coeur* by Decoin and *Je suis une aventurière* by Raymond Bernard, two delicious comedies, and that Jeanson wrote the scripts for *Bonsoir mesdames, bonsoir messieurs*, credited to Robert Desnos, and *L'Aventure est au coin de la rue*, while he was put in prison by the German Occupation.

A very good start. To be continued, in the hope that the films can be shown in France and abroad. I'll have to have a word with David Meeker at the British Film Institute.

27 January

The dubbing of *L 627* takes less than a day. Michel Desrois's direct sound is terrific as ever. One scene, the one in the Métro, will need to be dubbed; the over-realistic use of walkie-talkies, plus a few accidents while filming, have made some of the dialogue barely audible. I also redo a couple of phrases where I don't like the performances, and add the police messages, the announcements and radio conversations for the background soundtrack. Michel Alexandre has written some rich, precise, and funny dialogue. He does some of it himself.

I take a break, not without a degree of apprehension, to have a look at a short film produced by Nils, in which he plays the leading role. A very pleasant surprise. The film, touching, poetic and unexpected, isn't, like most short films, based on one single idea. More on atmosphere. I congratulate Nils, whose behaviour during the shoot was exemplary, and decide to dedicate *L 627* to him. I owe him that.

In the evening I have dinner with my daughter Tiffany, who has been a trainee and has had a rough time of it because of the difficult locations where we were shooting, and especially because of the shortcomings of the first assistant. Because she got the job through him, she never came to me to complain about him. I approve of that attitude, which was also that of the second assistant, Albane Guilhe. Although both were fed up with the consequences: twice the work for them, unjust reprimands, more pressure on me and exhaustion for Albane, who had to leave the shoot to go into hospital. Very animated discussions with Tiffany about whether these problems were enough to merit breaking off a relationship that had reached a standstill. Wasn't there a point when, despite their gratitude to a person who had helped them, they should have let me know and salvaged a few situations in the process?

28 January

After putting it off for some months I finally watch the video of *The Sound Barrier*, a film I had seen at the Normandie cinema when it was first released. I only recall two scenes (the ones in which first Nigel Patrick, then John Justin try to break the sound barrier), and I was afraid to see a film drowning in the clichés of sober heroism and virile friendship. Instead, I discover a complex and sombre picture, articulate about lack of communication, punctuated by useless sacrifices, which, without resorting to unnecessary effects, reveals the motivations of every character, particularly the one played by Ann Todd (the scene where they come to the cinema to tell her about her husband's death is utterly splendid).

Passion – for a job, a principle, an idea – and courage are simultaneously praised and put in their exact perspective, are shown as indispensable values which, nevertheless, provoke destruction, isolation, and incomprehension. Throughout this oscillation between exaltation and lucidity, Lean and Rattigan avoid all the pitfalls of individualistic anti-intellectualism that undermine American films with the same theme.

So, I immediately watched *Madeleine*, released in Paris in the cinema bearing the same name, which my parents wouldn't let me see at the time. I try to understand why the film has such a bad reputation. The first part is remarkable, with a stiflingly claustrophobic atmosphere. The décor of the flat, of Madeleine's room inspires in Lean's direction some extremely violent shots, symbolizing social and sexual conflict.

Dare I say that I prefer these two films – and the Dickens adaptations – to *Brief Encounter* (which disappoints me every time I see it, finding it stylistically limited and too carefully plotted), *Summertime*, and all those epic films – apart from *Lawrence of Arabia*.

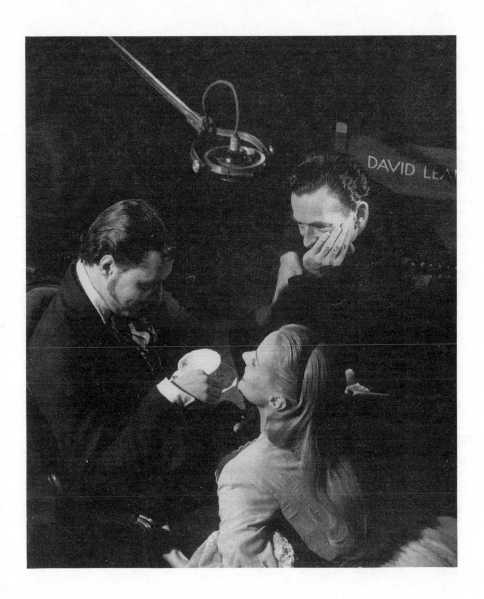

64   *Madeleine*: David Lean in the director's chair

29 January

In the evening I catch *Riff-Raff*, one of Ken Loach's best films, and the best English movie of the past year and a half, along with Mike Leigh's *Life is Sweet*. Added to the emotion – fortunately blended with humour – conveyed by *Riff-Raff* is the pleasure of seeing a film-maker remaining true to his political commitments, refusing to yield to the demands of fashion. Wasn't it Orwell who said: 'The people who swallowed the worst lies of Stalinism are the ones who now object to the idea of socialism' (I'm quoting from memory). One amusing detail – I've been a press attaché for both these directors – Leigh for *Bleak Moments*, which Pierre Rissient and I handled in France; and Loach for *Family Life*.

30 January

I'm awarded a new prize, the Prix des Cinémas d'Art et d'Essai, for *50 ans de cinéma américain*. The other laureate is Pascal Bonitzer, for a very good book on Eric Rohmer. By a funny coincidence, it was Rohmer who brought me into *Cahiers du cinéma* to write about American cinema, and, at the same time, got me to dub the voice of Barbet Schroeder, who was playing the lead in *La Boulangère de Monceau*, and deliver the commentary for the film, the first of his *Moral Tales*. Rohmer rehearsed me at lunchtime, in the local bar of the *Cahiers*. His meticulousness, shyness and politeness made him speak in a meandering and convoluted way; then there would come an abrupt statement, accompanied by a chuckle, which signalled it was a suggestion that one was obliged to take up. I was fascinated by his way of speaking, by his openness and gentility. He constantly said: 'You must always assign an article or a review to the person who likes the subject best. Then you don't get people writing stupid things.' I have always liked and respected Eric Rohmer, and was deeply shocked by the scandalous way he was fired from *Cahiers*, supposedly for ideological reasons. But that, as Kipling would say, is another story.

3–4 February

Recording the music in London. My producer, Frédéric Bourboulon, comes with me, and on the evening of 2 February we turn up at the Dorchester. Sarde has a fetishistic attachment to the place. It's just one of his manias – similar to his refusal to work or even leave the house on the 22nd, or to stay in a room whose digits add up to 13, 21 or 22.

When I first met Philippe it took a superhuman effort to get him to leave the Champs-Elysées, and then only in a taxi even if we were only crossing the avenue. It was like the beginning of Keaton's *The Navigator*. One day, coming back from the Studios de Boulogne, Pierre Rissient and I forced him to take the 52 bus. It must have been the first time – he complained of dizziness, palpitations and nausea until we agreed to let him off.

I won't easily forget his spectacular arrival in Vals les Bains (Ardèche) during the filming of *Le Juge et l'assassin*. He was supposed to be bringing the playback for a song by Jean Roger Caussimon to accompany a scene which I was filming the next morning. We waited for him at Valence station at six o'clock in the evening. No Sarde. Down we trekked to the airport. Not a soul. The next trains, still no sign. Panic among the production team. We called Paris. No answer. Suddenly, at the end of dinner, he turned up at the hotel dining-room, and when I asked him how he got there he answered, 'In a taxi.' 'From Valence? But we didn't see you at the station!' 'No, I got the taxi in Paris.' He'd hailed a taxi on the Rue de Ponthieu and said: 'Grand Hotel des Bains in Vals les Bains.' The production manager, a man from the Midi with a Pagnolesque accent, thought it was a joke until he saw the bill, which came to more than 5,000 francs – in 1975. As he would later repeat over the years: 'I thought there was a mistake. I went out to tell the driver I wasn't buying his car, but then I had a look at the meter, and was flabbergasted!'

These images all come back to me in that luxurious room in the Dorchester. A little green arrow on the ceiling shows the direction of Mecca.

I always go to the recording sessions in a state of joy and apprehension: the joy of hearing in all its complexity a score that I've followed through various stages of its development, but only ever heard on a piano or a synthesizer; of watching certain emotions assume their true colours, ones I've been imagining. I feel less exposed than usual; for once somebody else is in the firing line – but also apprehensive because this moment is a test of sorts: we're finally going to know, from his musical response, whether the first real viewer of the film, the composer, has been moved, whether he's been inspired by the tone and theme of the film – in short, whether you've succeeded in achieving your aims. You can feel it too in the way the musicians react to the arrangements, their astonishment and interest.

I've already made three London sorties with Sarde, for *L'Horloger de Saint-Paul*, *Coup de torchon* and *Le Juge et l'assassin*. (The day before the recording sessions, a dinner at the Hilton with Sarde, the conductor Carlo Savina, the accordion genius Marcel Azzola, the sound engineer, the music publisher, my editor Armand Psenny and myself was interrupted by a bomb scare just before the dessert. We all had to evacuate the restaurant. Because it had happened just before the bill, everybody assumed the music publisher had concocted the threat.)

The real odyssey begins once we leave the hotel, when Sarde tries to give the taxi-driver directions to the studio, all in an English that is as approximate as it is intense. He has the exact address, written on a piece of paper that he's holding in his hand, but, no, that would be too easy. It's much more interesting to come out with incomprehensible and utterly catagorical instructions.

This priceless bilingual outpouring, punctuated by dreadful jokes, loud laughter and sudden fits of rage, continues as far as the Angel Studio – a converted former chapel – and carries on inside with the technicians, the musicians, the conductor, Harry Rabinowitz, an old hand who also conducted Antoine Duhamel's score for *Deathwatch*: 'The music I hear is not ce que j'ai écrit ... my dear Freddy, I don't know what you play, but it is not dans la bonne tonalité, ze good tonalité.' But the Margaret Dumont prize for long suffering has to go to Nat Peck, a former jazz trombonist who is now a 'fixer', and has organized all Sarde's sessions for over twenty years, putting up with contradictory instructions, rapid changes of mood and date with a phlegmatic resignation, a fatalistic calm that makes him a natural descendant of Droopy, or Franklin Pangborn when being tormented by W. C. Fields.

Sarde's perfectionism leads him to seek out the best musicians, even if only to play a few notes. For *L'Horloger de Saint-Paul* he hired a solo pianist to play scales and murder *Für Elise* like a beginner would. He has always insisted on recording in London. As far as he is concerned, the quality of the musicians, their reliability and speed make up for the cost of the journey and additional expenses. But this morning the sound engineer is late and there's a saxophonist missing. A malicious chuckle from Frédéric Bourboulon, who still couldn't believe the price of the rooms at the Dorchester.

But they manage to get everything done with only half an hour overtime, and I'm impressed, all in all, by the speed with which the musicians read, and by their concentration. The first section of 3.31 minutes, the main theme and opening of the film, undergoes a number of changes of tempo and key, embracing dissonances, a tune inspired by an old hymn and played against a muscular percussive rhythm, and the disjointed chords of a slow 'java'. Sarde interrupts the first couple of takes in the middle, isn't very happy with the third one, smiles at the fourth ('My dear Harry, zis is not very bad. But on peut avoir mieux.') The fifth is right. That's where I have to come in, to stop him going through each piece over and over again.

On the first day I only ask for two major changes: in the scene showing the meeting between Lulu and Cécile at her 'place of work', I have him change the pulse and the style of the percussion to intensify the violence, the roughness of the scene. I don't want a regular rhythm, but something closer to sound effects. As for the throbbing chant running beneath Lulu's wife's questions, I get him to cut the melodic development that begins at the start of the following sequence, which made the images look too lyrical. I'm very pleased with the rest. It takes me back ten years, to the first time I heard the score of *Coup de torchon* in Abbey Road. I'm disappointed by one very short passage, but Sarde manages to win me over. In fact, I'll use different music in the sound mix. On the other hand, the music he's almost forced me to use for Lulu's arrival at the brigade's headquarters works admirably well, and seems to give the film a boost.

During the session we have a visit from Joseph Losey's widow, Patricia, and Walter Donohue, my editor from Faber and Faber, who wants to take us to one of the best fish and chip restaurants in London for lunch – unfortunately closed on Mondays – and tries in vain to find a video of Roger Corman's mysterious *Frankenstein Unbound* in that part of town. A double failure, which he will make up for by sending over a parcel of books including Dennis Potter's scripts.

In the evening, a fruitless attempt at Tower Records to find *Frankenstein Unbound*, a Monty Python video containing *The Cheese Shop*, which I've been trying to find for more than two years, and *A Matter of Life and Death* by Powell and Pressburger, which overwhelmed me when I saw it again at the first Dinar festival. Video distribution with its chaotic and puzzling incoherence remains a constant source of astonishment: you can find fantastic obscure and minimalist films, some of them interesting (Corman's *The Undead*); underestimated B movies (Parrish's *Cry Danger*, Mark Stevens' *Cry Vengeance*); dull, little-known comedies, and dated pseudo-classics that have been out of fashion for thirty years. Yet you will seek in vain for very famous titles featuring very big stars, or films that were rehabilitated or rediscovered decades ago: *Gone to Earth* or *The Small Back Room* by Powell and Pressburger, *Call Northside 777*, *Exodus* and all of Preminger's early *film noirs*, *Point Blank*, Parrish's *The Wonderful Country* with Mitchum, *Pride of the Marines* and *The Hanging Tree* by Delmer Daves, the magnificent Wellmans of the thirties (*Heroes for Sale*, *Safe in Hell*), the films of Cassavetes. Some pictures are mutilated, like *Kiss Me Deadly*, whose ending was savagely cut: all the last shots of Mike Hammer and Velma witnessing the apocalyptic conclusion are missing on the video.

Not forgetting the shameful absence of foreign film-makers. Dozens of French, Italian and Japanese masterpieces are completely ignored. Not quite so many in a few months' time, because the Americans, in an unheard-of gesture of imperialist greed, have decided, contrary to the spirit of the Berne Convention (which they have just finally signed), that all foreign films not registered in the Library of Congress before America's endorsement of the Convention (1989) are to be considered public domain. And this despite the fact that these films are distinctly protected by Article 5 of this Convention, of which France has long been a member. A scandalous distortion, a scorn for international law,* an abject attitude that is also found in the agricultural negotiations for the General Agreement on Tariff and Trade (GATT).

* The damages caused by this theft is estimated by lawyers in Brussels to be in the region of 530 million francs, nearly 89 million dollars, since 1989.

American politics is actually duplicating archetypal westerns: the conflict between small farmers and the cattle baron who demands that his herds have free access to the river, which means allowing them to trample through the farmers' fields and crops. When the farmers try to erect fences, the cattle baron screams that they're impinging on his freedom and hires killers to enforce his will. The subject is familiar from Anthony Mann (*The Man from Laramie, The Furies*) to King Vidor's *Man without a Star* – except that American politicians, in betraying their film-makers, and denying the spirit of these films, are joining the camp of the cattle baron. And Europe has yet to find its James Stewart or Kirk Douglas.

4 February

10 a.m.: back to Angel Studio. Unfortunately I won't be able to attend the afternoon session, because FR3 Grenoble, the regional station of the third TV channel, has imperiously demanded an interview about *La Guerre sans nom* at half-past five. We are screening the documentary there this evening for local politicians, members of the Council, and, particularly, for the thirty former conscripts that we interviewed.

I leave the studio frustrated and irritated. It's the first time I've abandoned a recording. I've only heard a first reading of the two last cues. The first of these, using a counter-rhythmical contrast between a throbbing continuo and a lyrical theme – on the soprano sax joined by a B flat clarinet, with the soprano playing in counterpoint – satisfies me immediately. The other leaves me vaguely troubled although I can't, in the two minutes I have, work out the source of my concern. I figure it out on the plane: the speeding up of the tempo, after the last image, happens too soon, breaks the mood and seems to act as a commentary on what went before – which makes me nervous. The music should be a contrapuntal voice in opposition to or in harmony with the harmonic discourse of the *mise-en-scène*. Its function is not to explain or judge. It might even obscure something happening on the screen.

I'll have to wait till we get down to the mixing so that Sarde, after one last, nail-biting deadline, can immediately come up with a brilliant solution, after putting on a stunning, flamboyant, show-biz act, spectacularly designed to make us forget he was late.

In Grenoble I meet Patrick Rotman and my distributors Claude Philippot and Serge Bernstein just in time to get to FR3. There, we pass through corridors as sinister as they are deserted, plastered with notices constantly threatening strike action, to be welcomed by a person, affable but rushed. He's holding in his hand the book containing the complete interviews from the film, and declares that he didn't get to see the film at the press showing. When he asks me if I used professionals in the film, I'm struck by a vague doubt whether he has even read the book, which I camouflage by suggesting that he interview Patrick Rotman as well as myself. This clearly hadn't occurred to him. After a short hesitation he agrees, adding an unforgettable phrase: 'I can't do you both at the same time because I only have one armchair.' This heart-breaking admission about the poverty of the public service provokes a collective hoot of laughter that we hide behind a fit of coughing and a sudden desire to go to the lavatory, especially when we see the armchair in question – a cloth folding chair with a frame that can be dismantled. Unruffled, our host adds: 'Be brief, because we only have four minutes including the clip.' That's what FR3 Grenoble – their regional television station – is willing to give to a film shot entirely in the city and its surroundings, a film that brings back to life the history, the fate of thirty of its citizens during the Algerian War, an entire past that is rooted in the region and never spoken about today.

They'd made me leave the score of my film, setting off in a mad rush just to be interviewed, for three minutes, by someone who doesn't have the courtesy to do the slightest bit of research. Serge suggests filming the thirty conscripts turning up at the cinema, particularly their reactions after the screening. That could provide a moving segment that they would certainly be able to use in Paris. The interviewer looks as exasperated as Disney might have, if he'd been asked to put up the money for a Godard: 'It's happening too late, and we've got nobody to do it anyway. Everything's being monopolized by the Winter Olympics in Albertville. They get absolute priority.'

'And the footage Paris wanted?'

'If they're that interested they could easily send a crew.'

As I write this, the authors and participants of *La Guerre sans nom* have been interviewed in dozens of towns, by Belgian, Italian, German, English and Spanish channels. Everywhere, except in the very city where they live.

In fact, we are only slightly surprised. FR3's reception is part of the ethnographic ritual performed on the film-maker who wants to promote a film in the provinces. Invariably seated in front of the poster of his film, he has to feign magnanimous modesty while listening to people say, 'I haven't had time to see your film', followed by 'and we've only got two minutes anyway', or, more disarmingly, 'What questions should I ask you?' He must, with a smile, put up with boorishness and incompetence; scriptwriter, actor or co-writer are ignored; there are filmographical errors (the number of times they've attributed Bertrand Blier's films to me); people getting the subject wrong: for *La Guerre sans nom* someone began the interview by adding an extra four years to the Algerian War.

As long ago as 1975, at the premiere of *Que la fête commence*, I found myself being asked: 'Bertrand Tavernier, so, you're exploring the French Revolution'. As my film was set thirty-four years before the taking of the Bastille, I burst out laughing, but was quickly drawn up short by a cutting remark from the journalist: 'Be quiet! We're trying to work here!' I can still hear the voice of Jean-Pierre Marielle behind me: 'I'm going to thump this jerk.' I told this story on the radio, in a discussion with Roger Planchon. The head of the station demanded that I apologize publicly to the journalist in question. I refused, and was immediately blacklisted by FR3 (Lyons) for four years.

This arrogance, self-satisfaction and bureaucratic dullness, is carefully maintained by the dictatorship of the national or local politicians – who impose subjects and play musical chairs with the staff every time there's a change of government, or at the first sign of independent thought – and by a lack of funds or vision, by an overly protectionist union system.

It's even more of a pleasure, therefore, to meet vibrant and passionate journalists and directors who dream of real regional television, as I have done recently in Rennes, Lyons, Toulouse, and, most recently, in Pontarlier, where a young journalist went out of her way to film me in a cinema where I was introducing a public screening of *Black Narcissus*, and then during the discussion that followed. Filming a debate with local people strikes me as more exciting, less static than that fixed interview shot in front of the inevitable film poster. I've been asking for that for years. And every time I heard the excuse, 'I'm afraid we don't have any crews after six o'clock', I get furious, especially when I think of all those invigorating discussions after *La Vie et rien autre*, all the stunning confessions that poured from people after seeing *La Guerre sans nom* and which should have been recorded.

So, no TV tonight. I'm cross with myself for not having asked Choquart, who came straight from the Ardèche, to pick up a camera. My editor, the talented and adorable Luce Grunenwaldt, who has put up with my rages, worries and doubts, also went out of her way so that she could finally meet all the people she'd only seen on the screen of her editing machine. She is, like all of us, excited and a little nervous. How will they react to the film, the cuts, the reordering of their accounts?

They all come with their wives. Most of them are in their Sunday best, and meet up with each other with that warm shyness, that stilted joviality that you see at the start of a wedding ceremony. Everyone except Jean Trouilloud, the peasant who was dragged off to war by two 'gendarmes', who died of cancer some weeks ago, and Michel Pétrone, a driver with the Legion who killed himself in very strange circumstances.

What a pleasure it is, what an emotional occasion, to meet them again. I feel I'm on friendly ground. Serge Puygrenier shows me some magnificent photographs that he's just rediscovered, 'In case it might be of use to you.' I try to explain to him that all the lab work is done. In the cinema, there are some local politicians and a lot of veterans.

We can't, unfortunately, stay for the whole screening because we must have dinner with the local journalists. Warm and sympathetic atmosphere. Getting back to the cinema, thirty-five minutes before the end, we're struck by the attention of the audience, the intensity of their reactions to the moments of comedy, as well as to the polemical statement. Suddenly – the terror of every director – the film breaks. Disaster. The lights come on. Luce runs to the projection-room with Laure, her assistant. As no one from the cinema is in evidence, I jump up and announce that the screening isn't over, that the ending is important. While they're still fixing things, unable to bear the tension in the cinema, being face-to-face with our 'actors', Patrick and I take refuge in the foyer, where we are joined by one of them, Bruno Enrietti. Immediate and unspoken reaction on the part of the two film-makers: 'He's leaving. It's not working. It's a disaster.' But Enrietti simply lights a cigarette, and, after taking a drag, says, 'I'm glad of this break. It's too powerful. I couldn't bear it any more.' Not the slightest note of sycophancy in his tone. Just a simple, clear statement that goes straight to our hearts. Another source of satisfaction: nobody uses the break as an excuse to leave the cinema.

Thunderous applause at the end. Nevertheless, we're anxious to hear their reactions. The first people to come up to us are the officers, the ones we were most afraid of, Pierre Achain, Gilbert Gardien, Robert André. They literally fall into our arms: 'We were so scared, but you've done a terrific job, very honest.' Grégoire Alonzo, normally so reserved, almost kisses me, just before Argelès, the communist teacher, and Jean Manin, the Christian trade unionist.

After a photograph for *Paris Match*, which will never be published, we take them all off for a drink. Atmosphere of relief and elation, as at the end of a victorious match. Patrick witnesses a great scene: Bernard Loiseau, officer from the Engineers, takes aside Étienne Boulanger, the militant communist who refused to take up arms and spent two years in jail, and attacks him: 'When you accused yourself of cowardice for not having deserted and joined the FLN, I was really shocked. I couldn't bear that. I think you went a bit far.' But Boulanger finds an unexpected supporter in Jaques Bec, who commanded a *harka* [a batallion of Algerians loyal to the French] in the Aurès, and was more than somewhat right-wing: 'No, he was right to say that. It's *his* truth, and it had to be in the film.' Never, when we undertook to make the film, did we imagine that we would see this French Algerian officer rushing to the support of this insubordinate communist.

The women seem to discover facets of their husbands' lives that they didn't know about. Gaétan Esposito's wife declares that she's learned more during this evening than in twenty years of marriage. 'Obviously,' he answers, 'every time I've tried to talk about it you've told me to be quiet.' 'You talk too much, that's true. All in all, I'd rather find out about it in a film.' Serge Puygrenier's wife, talking about her husband, one of whose legs was amputated, comes out with an astonishing sentence: 'The Algerian war is our everyday life,' and she confesses to me, blushing, 'Serge's love letter moves me even more when you read it.'

Some days later I receive warm and emotional letters. Like this one from Séraphin Berthier:

I want to thank Patrick and you for what you've done for us.

I admit I did have some fears before the screening, fears of manipulation and interpretation. I'm sorry I had those fears, and I apologize. Whatever your personal feelings about this war, you have shown a rare degree of honesty.

Patrick and you have managed, with ease, to bring out something that had, I believe, been buried for thirty years. To say that the memories have been flooding back since the film is certainly an understatement. Calling you *tu* came spontaneously (as one does at emotional moments), and I've rediscovered the raw language of my twenties.

You have allowed us to express ourselves, we, the people who bear the shame of certain individual acts (planned or covered up by the politicians).

I hope your film will have the success it deserves, first and foremost for you and your crew, so that it will open the eyes of the largest possible number of people, and reveal that Manicheeism is not a good philosophy.

I'm bowled over by the last sentence, coming as it does from a man who, at one point in his life, flirted with the OAS [Organisation de l'armée secrète, the illegal military organization that supported French rule in Algeria and even after the end of the war, murdered a lot of people].

5 February

First public showing of *La Guerre sans nom* in Annecy, and first post-screening debate with the audience. Serge has set up around forty of these throughout France. Exhausting work which takes up a huge amount of time, much of it spent travelling. But if we want to promote distribution in the provinces and help the independent cinemas run by film-lovers, we must, as Signoret used to say, 'polish the silverware'. And a film like *La Guerre sans nom* gives rise to passionate debates, and unleashes astonishing confessions. Here are a few samples. In Annecy , a former conscript:

I hesitated before going to see the film. I was afraid we'd be presented as curious animals, that we'd be looked on as something like the old Nazi refugees in South America. On the contrary, I saw what I'd been through, I heard the words, the sentences that belonged to me, I relived my fears. I'd been through everything they talked about. And I've never been able to talk about it, because when I returned, everybody saw me as a fascist. And yet I had witnessed scenes of torture. I was in a terrible state. My mother made me eat and sleep for six months. That's how I managed to survive. And I've kept my mouth shut until this evening.

This last sentence was to be a leitmotiv.

Lyons: a woman is taken ill at the beginning of the film. Epileptic fit. We lay her down in the foyer calling for an ambulance, which arrives forty minutes later. When she recovers she obstinately refuses to be taken to hospital, because her husband will have to follow her: 'I want him to see the film. It's too important for him.' She's given a tranquillizing injection and taken back to her seat. As Rotman said, there's an example of a captive audience.

A young man during the debate: 'Before your film I viewed all the Algerian veterans as revanchist, racist brutes. I've discovered a much more complex and worrying reality, and I'll never think of them that way again.'

An 18-year-old girl in St Etienne: 'My father had never talked to me about his Algerian War. I was so overwhelmed by the film that I started asking him questions. And I discovered a different man. We came a lot closer together.'

An Algerian in Paris: 'I wanted to have a look at "the other camp". I discovered an unexpected world. I was tortured by parachutists. It was hard, but it was war. There's another thing that's even worse than torture. It's the silence after torture, around torture. That silence has been broken. And I listened. Thank you.'

In a cinema in the suburbs I come across Etienne Boulanger's fellow prisoner, the man who shared his cell for two years. And we hear the terrifying, and poignant, testimonies about torture which contradict the stupid letter from a General sent to 'Tavernier and consorts' (sic), which stated that during eight years spent in Algeria he never saw the slightest evidence of torture or barbarity. When we read it out to the audiences, it was a great comic success. Each debate brings its own set of unpublished atrocities: prisoners forced to swallow lye, those whose backs were slashed with razors before being exposed to the sun, ears cut off to be worn as necklaces, children killed, corpses mutilated, and whose heads, after being boiled up, were used as candle-holders.

Inevitably, we also get one or two complaints from people who would rather have seen *their* film than ours. They ask us why we didn't include any *pieds-noirs* [Algerian-born Frenchmen], *harkis* [Algerians who enlisted in the French army], Algerian *maquisards* [members of the underground resistance]. We keep on having to restate the argument of the film, although it is presented at the beginning by a commentary which says that the intention of the film is to be a chronicle of the memories of *one* category of combatants from *one* French city. Why would we bring in *harkis*, Algerian volunteers, and not legionnaires, commanding officers, war correspondents?

As for the Algerian rebels, I can't help detecting a touch of paternalism, of submission to 'political correctness', among the people who wish they had been included. Filming a few of these combatants wouldn't have contributed anything. To contradict or confirm our testimony, we would have had to find those who were at the same place, at the same time. If not, it would soothe the conscience too easily. More important, out of courtesy we would have had to give them equal time. If you're going to talk about the Algerian resistance, you have to study all the different strands, from the FLN to the MNA [Mouvement

National Algérian], from the various currents of Islam to the communists, from the moderates to the extremists. You'd have to talk about their contradictions, which led to incredibly bloody fights. You'd have to attack legends and counter-truths, probe the way in which certain heroes of the revolution were eliminated by the politicians, recall the last-minute converts to the Resistance, and describe the military chiefs stuck in Tunisia. Patrick and I thought only an Algerian director would be able to deal with a subject like that.

These questions, which seem to pre-empt their own answers, make me think of that definitive story that Marcel Ophuls told me: the Museum of Modern Art had just shown the admirable *Le Chagrin et la pitié** for the first time in America. Ophuls was introduced to the audience, and in the first question he was violently attacked by a left-wing feminist: 'Why did you make a film about the occupation of France by the Germans when there are so many more important subjects like women's liberation in the USA, the black movements, the revolutionary struggles in South America?' (Presumably China and Vietnam had already gone out of fashion?)

'Because,' Ophuls answered, 'I am a lazy fuck.'

8 February

I was disappointed with *All the King's Men* by King Hu. Picturesque touches, an amusing setting in a chemist shop, aren't enough to lend consistency to a screenplay that's as banal as it's convoluted, with a redeeming, untrue, incredibly elliptical ending.

Nowadays, directorial brilliance and stylistic daring are to be found in the work of the Taiwanese directors, who are much more in touch with the life and contradictions of their country than King Hu. Edward Yang, in particular, with his masterly, breathless, episodic chronicle *A Brighter Summer Day* (looking like Dos Passos disrupted by Scorsese), and Hou Hsia Hsien, three of whose films I've seen already – sharp, moving and innovative: *My Summer with Grandfather*, *City of Sorrows* and *Dust in the Wind*.

13 February

I hold a screening of *L 627* for my distributor Richard Pezet. He declares that he liked it a lot, that he was thrilled by Didier Bezace, but complains about the length. His reaction worries me because I too felt it was dragging – but *before* the scenes that bothered him. I think I've discovered the reason. Three-quarters of the way through the story, Cécile, the young drug-addict prostitute, Lulu's girlfriend and informer, disappears. Worried, he sets off to look

The Sorrow and the Pity.

for her, and this search suddenly forms a narrative block that contradicts the main thrust of the film. We suddenly find ourselves, forcing our way into a linear plot line which I decide to disjoint by starting the search for Cécile earlier, linking it more closely to the daily work of Lulu and the group. This involves restructuring three reels and cutting more than five minutes.

In fact the film had found its own rhythm, a life of its own, during the shooting, sometimes refusing to follow the construction of the screenplay, much as *Une semaine de vacances*, *Un dimanche à la campagne* and *La Vie et rien autre* imposed different endings from the ones we'd planned.

Richard Pezet also strongly objected to the violence of a scene that he found disturbing and intolerable: the one where the cops rashly break into a sordid squat, finding only two black women, one of whom, in a hysterical state after smoking crack, tries to protect her baby. I fiercely defend the scene, its style and meaning, and absolutely refuse to cut it. Its violence strikes me as moral, true, essential. If there is a problem it comes not from the conception, but the construction of the sequence. The discovery of the place and the women, Lulu's sudden awareness of the situation, are stronger than the clumsy attempts to resolve it. So there's a feeling of excess, of repetition. I decide to simplify it, to bring it to an end sooner: on a close-up of Lulu powerlessly watching the misery of a young cop played by my son Nils, cutting out the search for drugs and the last idiotic actions of the group leader (he was shown stealing a dildo). I only keep the first of two external shots, losing, which is a shame, a terrific rebellious moment on the part of Charlotte, which causes me to cut the first part of the following scene. I think I've cut more than twelve minutes from the five reels. I'm sadly disappointed when Ariane announces that we've only lost 7 minutes 30 seconds.

The eighth attempt to get Jean Daniel or any political journalist from *Le Nouvel Observateur* to come to a screening. They promise and do not show up. I am sure the magazine will make little mention of our film, while dealing extensively with Pierre Schoendoerffer's *Dien Bien Phu*, produced, it has to be said, by a close friend of Jacques Attali, François Mitterrand's right-hand man – which explains why Jack Lang, the Minister of Culture, was at the première, although he didn't have time to come to any of the sixteen screenings of *La Guerre sans nom* to which he had been invited. His wife Monique cancelled the second from last in person: 'We're invited to dinner with the President, and at the moment, you understand, we can't turn him down'. 'At the moment' refers to Mitterrand's drop in popularity in the polls. Ah well. In all my interviews I'll just have to mention that Jack Lang found the time to organize two screenings of *Batman* at the Ministry.

All the politicians wriggle out of coming, apart from Pierre Joxe – who is bowled over by the film. It's a shame; I'd have liked to hear the reactions of Chirac, and Rocard who wrote the first report on the internment camps. I'd have liked the socialists who were rebelling against Guy Mollet to make use of the film and thus rise above these pathetic electoral squabbles. But the ghost of Mitterrand, who was very repressive at the beginning of the war, must be paralysing them. Another missed opportunity.

15–16 February

The military attitude doesn't change: the selection and screening of *La Guerre sans nom* at the Berlin Film Festival provokes an annoyed reaction from the Commander General of the French forces in Germany, doubtless a reader of *Figaro*. Needless to say he hasn't seen the film, any more than the representative of the National Front in Lyons who, while we were still at the editing stage, attacked 'this work by a Stalinist barbarian'. In a one-act play, *Brûlons Voltaire*, Eugene Labiche has already demonstrated, in a devastating counter-attack, the profound stupidity revealed by this kind of attitude: a middle-class woman who has bought a house discovers that the library contains the complete works of Voltaire. Appalled, she decides to burn them, and when the house-seller, a good, honest wine merchant, asks her if she has at least read them, she confidently declares that 'you don't have to have read Voltaire to want to burn him'.

I plunge back into the ritualistic, over-heated life of the film festivals with their imposed ordeals – press conferences, heated exchanges, strings of interviews. Its surprises: a brief and unexpected meeting with Jeremy Thomas, whom I've known since Skolomowski's *The Shout*.

Another source of amazement in a country whose national cinema is moribund: the crowd of autograph-hunters outside the Hotel Kempinski, ordering you to sign their notebooks, visiting cards or very rare stills from films which, you sense, they've clearly never bothered to see. This breed of half-wits (whom Bette Davis in *All about Eve* labels as 'juvenile delinquents') proliferates in Germany, and pesters you at home with countless letters in wobbly handwriting. Not out of any love of the cinema, but just for trading purposes.

Billy Wilder told me that once at the Cannes Festival, two Germans had set upon him and made him sign five cards each. Astonished, he followed them and heard them shouting: 'Great, for three Billy Wilders we can get one Clint Eastwood!'

During the final quarter of an hour of the screening, a few people walk out, including the French ambassador's wife, who spots me immediately. A delicate moment, from which she extricates herself with highly professional elegance – a deluge of compliments, an obligation to prepare for the reception that evening. 'Anyway,' she adds, 'the conscripts are on their way back to France, so everything's fine.'

At that reception I meet Dave Kehr of the *Chicago Tribune*, one of the most knowledgeable, enthusiastic and film-loving critics in America. He tells me he was very moved by the film, its sadness, its absence of self-pity: 'What I saw goes beyond the context of France, it talked to me for four hours about the heartbreaks and contradictions of the Vietnam War.' That morning, at the press conference, a Russian journalist made the same kind of remark to me, swapping Afghanistan for Vietnam.

While the ambassador's wife is introducing me to her husband, I hear a voice that would be unmistakable among a thousand others: Fanny Ardant has just arrived, resplendent and regal in an evening dress with a long train. When she's introduced to the ambassador she suddenly dives under the table 'to clean up a stain without attracting anyone's attention', obviously achieving the opposite. All of Fanny is contained in that scatty, unpredictable and brash gesture. She always drags you into a whirlwind of misunderstandings, a permanent frenzy that she maintains with perpetual distortions of reality, sudden romantic professions of faith. I've seen her read *Anna Karenina* aloud at an airport, and faint a few minutes later. It's hard to spot the line between spontaneity and a taste for game-playing, the desire to astonish and to be astonished. Her absent-mindedness can have hilarious results: questioned by Derek Malcolm at the NFT about the birthplace of the character played by Vittorio Gassman in *Benvenuta*, she heard *Nepal* instead of *Naples*, and set off to the stupefaction of Derek, who was wondering what on earth she was talking about, on a long digression explaining that he wasn't Indian, which sent the interview off-course for many minutes. Seeing her like that, you wonder why people don't write more Katharine Hepburn-like parts for her, rather than all those upper-class women devoted to non-communication and post-Antonioni ramblings.

The next day, David Stratton, who used to run the Sydney Festival and now buys films for Australian television, suggests that I accompany him to interview Hal Roach jr, who is celebrating his hundredth birthday in Berlin. Unfortunately, there's an hour's delay before we're allowed into an ice-cold suite through which television crews and journalists parade. Roach must have difficulty keeping up with all this. He's sitting in an armchair, impeccably dressed. His gestures are lively, but his answers are jerky: he keeps stopping, forgetting what he was going to say. His hearing is very poor, and a 'secretary-assistant-friend' who has the physique for the part (he's just like all those people who look after elderly stars) repeats all the questions for him, corrects his mistakes and puts him back on the right track. I only have the time to hear David's first question and the last, rather silly question from the previous interviewer, from a German who wants to know what advice Mr Roach would give to someone who wanted to live to be as old as he was. Roach answers that he hasn't followed any particular diet, that he's drunk and smoked, and then launches into an interminable, confused speech about breakfast cereals and their beneficial powers, listing the ones he likes and the ones he doesn't.

David immediately brings him back to the subject. He wants to know (and so do I) who was responsible for bringing together Laurel and Hardy. This time Roach doesn't need to have the question repeated. He answers immediately: 'It was Leo McCarey who had the idea of pairing them and the characters. Nobody else. Laurel had already made films, but his eyes didn't catch the light with orthochromatic film. McCarey tried him out with the new panchromatic film and everything was fine. McCarey was an extremely brilliant man, with great ideas. You remember *Putting Pants on Philip*. The film's very funny, but the script is even more so. Every time I feel like laughing I reread it.'

On that last sentence I slip off back to Paris without knowing whether D. W. Griffith worked on the direction of *One Million BC*,* or how Hal Roach, a major producer but a lame director, had the idea of *Turnabout*, a ludicrous and flatly directed comedy, but with a fantastic subject that makes it the ancestor of the 'switch pictures' that are so fashionable at the moment (the most recent examples are *Switch* and *Prelude to a Kiss*). A husband and his wife change sex after being cursed by a fakir. There follows a stream of fairly scabrous events, which Scorsese raved about and insisted on showing to me.

A phone call from Frédéric Bourboulon who reads me the few lines of praise written in *Libération* by Gérard Lefort. 'Incredible', he says, 'Yes,' I reply, 'I wonder if we shouldn't sue.' *Libération*'s systematic demolition of all my films, of all my actions (battles for authors' rights, crusade against the colorization of *The Asphalt Jungle*) has became the butt of jokes in my crew. We've even been having fun on the set by writing on a call sheet a parody of the review we expect to see in a few months. The very good reviews I have had were either written by a political journalist (*La Guerre sans nom*) or by a TV journalist (*Coup de torchon*) – although the film was attributed to René le Henaff (sic).

23 February

Tous les matins du monde sweeps all the main Césars apart from the one for male actor, which goes to Jacques Dutronc for *Van Gogh*. A pity for Jean Pierre Marielle, whom I would have liked to have seen properly rewarded. He really deserves it. I can still hear him six years ago, when Georges Cravenne, the founder of the Césars, asked him to present a César during the ceremony – 'I don't participate in lotteries.' I'm delighted for Corneau, though sorry that the Pialat and the Rivette films didn't get the awards they deserved. However much you distance yourself from these glamorous hand-outs ('The prizes are

---

* When I meet David at the Venice Film Festival, he tells me that in order to give Griffith some kind of work, Roach asked Griffith to look at the rushes.

just a reward for good behaviour,' Guy Marchand used to say), you can't help feeling a degree of frustration at certain injustices like the lack of nominations for Catherine Breillat's powerful, *Sale comme un ange*.

One grotesque and distressing moment comes when Sylvester Stallone is given an honorary César by a sarcastic Roman Polanski. A few days previously, Jack Lang had, in a discouragingly idiotic gesture, made him Knight of Arts and Letters, even going so far as to assert that the name Rambo had been chosen in honour of Rimbaud (Arthur). As Ödon von Horvath said, in a foreword to his beautiful play, *Tales from the Vienna Woods*: 'Nothing gives us the feeling of eternity so much as stupidity'.

The height of irony: I'd be willing to bet that the people who made these ludicrous awards, ludicrous even in box-office terms, haven't the slightest familiarity with the only interesting film that Stallone's directed, the curious *Paradise Alley*.

Some days later a photograph was published showing him in François Mitterrand's kitchen in the Rue de Bièvre, with Danielle Mitterrand on his lap. I hope she got a big fat cheque out of him for the Kurds.

Irwin Winkler told me that Ronald Reagan called Stallone one day to congratulate him on the success of *Rambo II: The Mission* and ask him for an autographed poster. Who would ever have thought that a socialist government would ape Reagan at his most senile.

24 February–14 March

Three weeks of mixing at the SIS Studio. Three weeks of an almost monastic existence, since the mixing requires just as much concentration as the shooting, with the additional exhaustion of being continually shut up in the dark, *all the time*.

We're now using ultra-sophisticated consoles with a memory, turning the studios into branches of NASA, in 'Kubrickian' spaceships. In France, this revolution was launched by Philippe Sarde who, fed up with the lack of initiative by the studio managers, created the auditorium of his dreams in the sitting-room and bedroom of his old flat. I inaugurated it with *'Round Midnight*, mixing during the day while Polanski was finishing *Pirates* at night, marvelling at the staggering technology, which only stopped when Sarde sometimes forgot to pay the electricity bill.

All this sophisticated equipment was designed, they say, not only to make the soundtrack sharper, to give it a real sense of depth, but to simplify our lives, to help us save time. They pointed out the advantages of the high-speed projector, allowing us to rewind ten times quicker, and the memory circuits that could store a great deal of information, several versions of the same scene with full soundtrack, which we could find immediately if we suddenly had doubts or changed our minds.

But I'd mixed *Le Juge et l'assassin* (1975, 2 hours 9, scope) in only one week, and *La Vie et rien autre* (1988, 2 hours 10, scope) in three.

For these machines, with all their countless tracks, require more staff and maintenance, more minute adjustments, which vary from film to film, sound engineer to sound engineer, and can take more than half a day. This was true of *La Passion Béatrice* and *L 627*. Their technological refinement involves new problems, causes mysterious breakdowns, incomprehensible whims, strange disappearances: the machine can't locate a sound, a particular effect. One very fine solo by Herbie Hancock was swallowed up in the guts of the console, reappeared one day only to vanish again. Gérard Lamps spent an hour trying to find a line of dialogue from *La Passion Béatrice*. These accidents bring forth all manner of clever specialists who spout a knowing, esoteric jargon: 'But she seemed to have found her food in the car park ... Have you put out the cutlery? We're going to have to open the window.'

But, more important, this ever greater quest for high fidelity, this desire to expand and energize the possibilities of the soundtrack create new demands – demands for more marked effects, multiplying the possibilities, the choices, and the hesitations. Hence another risk of dictatorship by technology. I understand Rohmer's suspicion of stereo and dolby, which run the risk of reducing the films, distorting their meaning with an excess of often-superficial jarring sounds – the equivalent of the projectiles that were hurled at the audience in the 3D films of William Castle and Lew Landers, a process lampooned by André de Toth in *House of Wax*, used to spectacular effect by Jack Arnold in *It Came from Outer Space* and *The Glass Web*, and was morally transcended by Hitchcock in *Dial M for Murder*, where Grace Kelly, in picking up the famous pair of scissors in 3D *from the auditorium*, thereby made the public her accomplice in murder.

This obsession with high fidelity can create a clinical, brilliant yet antiseptic perfection from which all disorder, everything accidental has been banished – the opposite of the vibrant innovations of Godard or Altman. It isn't a matter of denying the positive aspect of this technical revolution: the suppression of hiss and background noise, the increased depth. I've spent enough time cursing my very talented editor, Armand Psenny, who won't even look at a scene on any kind of horizontal editing-table – Kemm, Steenbeck, CTM – preferring instead his old moviola on which you can hardly see anything and hear even less. But technique must remain a tool, and not become a philosophy. One must simply learn how to use it, and not be enslaved by it, unlike all those films where you wonder – it's the old problem of the chicken and the egg – whether it's the conception which has created the technology or the reverse.

I talked a great deal about these dangers with Gérard Lamps. To preserve the authenticity, the force of Michel Desrois' live sound and avoid any softening of the unaffected violence of the film, he suggested using stereo only when the action of the film went out into the street or the Métro. This will accentuate the feeling of claustrophobia of the interiors, which will remain in mono to increase the sense of suffocation.

He also decides to abandon the dialogue pre-mixes; mixing the dialogue first is an old French habit that I resist every time I make a film. If you fix their timbre, determine their volume, their colour, without actually referring to the sound effects, the music, the footsteps, you risk losing the overall vision. It's as if, when editing, you were to start with all the reverse angle shots before moving on to the action sequences or wide shots.

French films have been mixed by a single technician since the fifties. In 1979, during *Deathwatch*, I discovered that in England a mixer works with one or several assistants to whom he entrusts some of the sound effects or the post-sync material. After running through it for a number of hours they try to record a whole reel at the same time, which gives them the possibility of a more cohesive approach.

I followed this example, and was the first person in France to introduce two sound mixers, with superb results in *Coup de torchon* and *'Round Midnight.*

Today, as soon as we test the first reel of *L 627* with all its different elements, all the tracks, I feel that we're going to preserve the raw and desperate energy of the film – at the same time avoiding two of the particular weaknesses of French soundtracks: mixing the voices too deep (which produces great results in the mixing studios, but creates problems of comprehension in the cinema), and, secondly, treating sounds and atmospheres too naturalistically. Too many films seem essentially designed to be heard in mixing studios. I always fight against recording every single footstep, and would rather lose the sound of people settling into armchairs etc, and fade out a particular atmosphere sound once the emotional impact has been achieved, even at the cost of realism. You have to know how to play with silence, to treat sound like music. In Gérard Lamps I've found a true accomplice, patient, calm and inventive, who's worked with me since *La Passion Béatrice.* (The quality of his sound mix is well captured in the American laser disc.)

I won't go into detail about those three weeks of enthusiasm, passion, anxiety and happiness punctuated by fits of rage against some detail or some shots that struck me as unsuccessful. To redeem myself I tried to bring surprise treats for the crew every day: sugared almonds, *calissons*, extra-strong preserved ginger, Turkish delight, various kinds of sausage, bacon buns. I love giving my collaborators plenty to eat, specially if I'm following a diet. Sabine Azéma always bursts out laughing when she imitates me walking across the Grézaucourt field or through the tunnel with two enormous parcels of Carambar which I handed out to the actors and technicians. In Glasgow, during the shooting of *Deathwatch*, I found a confectioner near the station who made wonderful toffees – huge, hard and sticky. I gave one to my director of photography, Pierre William Glenn, when I wanted to keep him quiet for twenty minutes.

As I have a good memory, I sometimes surprise the editors by pointing out the existence of a missing wild track, or a phrase at the end of a shot that hasn't been edited. I also come up with new ideas in the mixing: moving a sound, a piece of music, cutting a word from a line of dialogue, shifting an effect. As the sound edit has been done digitally, it is up to the computer to identify the sound and put it in the right place. Sometimes it takes a long time, but the results are always impressive. So I decide to get rid of the music in the Métro sequence. Too dense, too complex, it was interfering with the dialogue, changing the tone and the style of the *mise-en-scène*. I keep a few reggae chords which I use in another reel when Lulu sees a passing car.

8 March

For a few days now, I've come back from SIS, to find a number of messages from Simon Mizrahi, as well as from his mother and sister. He's just gone into hospital again and is begging me to come and see him. Simon was press attaché on *Coup de torchon*, *'Round Midnight*, *La Passion Béatrice*, and *Daddy Nostalgie*. Much more than that, I knew him as a passionate film-buff, who made you share not only his enthusiasms – for *Moonfleet*, or *Party Girl* – but his dislikes as well. He had come back from Spain at the beginning of the sixties, illuminated by his experience of being an actor and an assistant to his idol, Nicholas Ray. On *King of Kings* he belonged to a group of film-buffs we called the 'neo-Macmahonians,* and made me share in his battles to rehabilitate or discover unknown or misunderstood directors: Riccardo Freda, Dino Risi, Comencini, Monicelli, the Festa Campanile of *Voci bianche* and *Une Vergine per il principe*, Scola. He managed to bring out many masterpieces, finding distributors and cinemas and subtitling the films himself. Among the American directors he championed were Dwan, Ray, Walsh, Tourneur, Stuart Heisler (I think he even interviewed this talented and mysterious director).

I'd suspected the worst for a year and a half – AIDS. But every time I spoke to him he dodged the question, assuring me that everything was fine. Just like the producer of *Daddy Nostalgie*, Adolphe Viezzi who, almost to the last moment, talked about lung infections, before dying with extraordinary class and courage.

---

* An influential and important movement so named because they had private screenings at the MacMahon cinema. The group was composed of critics and film-buffs, like Pierre Rissient, who had a selective and personal approach to films. Their idols were Raoul Walsh, Otto Preminger, Fritz Lang and Joseph Losey. They were the theoreticians of 'pure cinema'.

It was during the 1991 Venice Festival that I started to get really worried; he started leaving me wild and incoherent messages. It was worse at the European Festival of La Baule. To keep himself going, he would take stimulants which, added to the medication he was taking, sent him soaring.

On Sunday afternoon I go to the Bichat Hospital with Riccardo Freda – Simon published his first interview with him in *Présence du cinéma*. When we arrive in his room we find him surrounded by his mother, his brother and his sister. A terrible shock. His body is emaciated, his cheeks are hollow, his teeth are virtually falling out of his mouth. Tubes are fixed to his arms. Transfusion and perfusion. I have trouble replying to his 'Hello, baby!', and am ashamed by my half-silence. Riccardo, who's also overwhelmed, is more talkative. A smell of death, diarrhoea, eau de cologne. I've brought him some books, fruit juices, newspapers. *Le Canard enchaîné* makes him laugh, but he's cross about the negative review of the last Comencini, which he thought was magnificent. He has lost none of his passion. Moving his arm he dislodges his drip. The nurse makes us go into the corridor so she can put it back in. Screams.

12 March

Normally I don't see a film during the mix but this time I make an exception. I bring Charlotte, Jean Cosmos, the scriptwriter of *La Vie et rien autre*, and his wife to a private screening of *The Life and Death of Colonel Blimp*, which is finally going to be shown in France, and which I'm seeing for the twelfth time. They come out filled with wonder. What a pleasure it is to introduce a film you admire to the young woman you love, to a friend who is dear to you, and share their enthusiasm.

The print is fine, apart from two or three unfortunate errors in the colour grading during the sequence in the Berlin café. The predominant colour changes abruptly, becoming greenish until almost the end of the scene.

13 March

Jean-Michel Frodon asks me for an article on Powell for *Le Monde*, to coincide with the re-releases of *Blimp* and *Peeping Tom*. It takes me three nights to write:

Over the years, the films of Michael Powell and Emeric Pressburger have, like those of Renoir, Ophuls, Ford and Jacques Becker, become faithful and indispensable companions to me, stimulating and provocative, comforting at times of doubt or anxiety, and a joy to introduce to your best friends. Jean-Pierre Melville used to like to relate entire sequences from *The Life and Death of Colonel Blimp*, describing each shot, and pointing out that he had gone to England during the war to see the film. It was with him that I discovered *Peeping Tom* at the Scarlett cinema, rue des Martyrs, a film I managed to get re-released in 1968 – even inviting Powell to Paris and using the opportunity to

65   Michael Powell greeting Jean-Pierre Melville

66   *Que la fête commence*: Michael Powell with Bertrand Tavernier (back to camera)

record the first discussion about his work as a whole. It was the beginning of a long friendship. This invitation and the critical rehabilitation of the film, he later wrote to me, acted as a lifeline during that very dark time in his life. Having been a very important director between 1940 and 1950, he was either forgotten or held up for obloquy.

He was forgotten also in France, or rather completely misunderstood, the chief victim of the *auteur* theory. As a means of defending Hitchcock, François Truffaut had denied other British directors any talent, ruling out – at a stroke – not only Powell, but also Cavalcanti, Mackendrick, Robert Hamer, Launder and Gilliat. This peremptory opinion can be explained, but not justified, by the context of the time, by the wish to champion Hitchcock at any cost, and by an ignorance of certain films like *Blimp*. Truffaut could not have seen the real version because the one that had been released in France had been re-edited and shorn of fifty-four minutes. But this judgement was mimicked religiously, like a dogma, until recent years. Powell's death was not even mentioned during the César ceremony; almost none of his films are shown on French television except *Gone to Earth*, which was shown as part of a homage to David O. Selznick. This is ironic given the great, and justified, dislike of Selznick by Powell.

Things were worse in England. Powell had been rubbed off the map, been put on a blacklist, since *Peeping Tom*, so violent and insulting had been the critical reception: 'abject' and 'revolting' were the most restrained adjectives. Derek Hill even wrote 'that the only sensible thing to do would be to get hold of the film cans and throw them into the nearest sewer'. This shattered Powell's career. His last films, which were either commissions or obscure Australian co-productions, reveal a certain fatigue and lack of spirit – apart from Bartok's *Bluebeard's Castle*, produced by the singer Norman Foster. When he got back on his feet, it was too late: his most cherished project, an adaptation of Shakespeare's *The Tempest* with James Mason, never got past the planning stage. He wrote before his death: 'When I conceived this project on *The Tempest*, I didn't know I was signing my death-warrant where cinema was concerned. I was so enthusiastic about the modernity of the play, this allegory about the cinema, that I lived with it day and night. I was even mad enough to contact English producers . . .'

The irony is not gratuitous. Within British cinema Powell has a place of his own. He refused to follow fashion, didn't associate with any school, even with the rebels and troublemakers like Hamer, Cavalcanti, and Mackendrick. When he became involved in the collective spirit during the war, his approach remained extraordinarily personal – as *Blimp* or the esoteric *A Canterbury Tale* reveal.

The films he made between 1937 and 1951 radiate an amazing originality and freedom of tone. Profoundly rooted in a national culture, they avoid any spirit of insularity, revealing an openness of mind, a curiosity and a breadth of vision that are almost unique. The closed worlds described by so many English films, those apologias for the small family business – those 'chronicles of the lives of herbivores', to quote Michael Frayn – are completely alien to him. His films are much more ambitious, more tumultuous, more vast, shaken by cataclysms, pierced by flashes of lightning, with dazzling and mysterious landscape shots. His intentions go beyond everyday naturalism, and lead to a metaphysical, irrational intensity which bears countless visions. You don't follow a plot, you dive into a universe – and dive back in with delight.

Powell's collaboration with Emeric Pressburger, the talented Hungarian scriptwriter who had already written for Robert Siodmak (the remarkable *Abschied*) and Ophuls proved ideal (the choice of collaborator in itself reveals an already 'European' openness of mind). A national consciousness is conjoined with irony, scepticism with a spirit of adventure, literary intelligence with visual invention.

It makes for adventurous cinema, surprising in its demands, in its unprecedented imagination – which can transform an official state commission on Anglo-American reconciliation into a dream poem of love (the admirable *A Matter of Life and Death*). Its variety is such that you move, sometimes during the same film, from realism to fable, from documentary to fantasy, from real exteriors to the most staggering special effects. The India of *Black Narcissus*, entirely dreamed up in a studio, is still an unparalleled achievement, twenty years ahead of its time; the effects in *A Matter of Life and Death* are truly dazzling, as well as intellectually stimulating (Roger Livesey surveying the village with his camera before literally plunging into David Niven's subconscious seems a good alter-ego of Powell himself). The comparison between two religions, two civilizations and two cultures becomes the only source of the dramatization (*Black Narcissus*), just as the torments of creativity are the chief dramatic focus of *The Red Shoes* and *Peeping Tom*. All Powell's and Pressburger's films privilege intellectuals and researchers, showing them gnawed by doubt, but progressing all the same (*The Small Back Room*), rejecting the ideology of most of the English, and almost all of the American cinema.

All these visual and dramatic risks display a huge trust both in the powers of cinema and the audience's capacity for curiosity. Today's ambitious, personal films keep stressing how ambitious and personal they are; viewers are forewarned when they go see a Rivette, a Pialat, a Corneau, or a film by a more marginal director. Powell and Pressburger's films were distributed by Rank or Alexander Korda, and outwardly nothing distinguished them from the rest of that output – apart from the famous trademark of their production company: a target being struck by an arrow. Their innovations were not self-publicizing.

The strokes of inventive daring in *Blimp* are endless: making a film – basically a propaganda film – in the middle of a war, in which the hero is an English officer who is not very intelligent, who is decent, but limited, who gets things wrong all the time, and whose superiors are hardly any brighter; basing all the turns of the plot on the mistakes, the blindness of this character, who is always behind the times; and, in an extremely elegant gesture, putting the only words celebrating England into the mouth of a German officer ('very foolishly I remember the beauty of the English countryside') – a lucid and disenchanted witness to whom the authors give the moral of the film, and in 1942! The scene, or rather the long take, is sublime, worthy of Lubitsch's *Heaven Can Wait*, whose sophistication, spirit of civilization and devastating irony *Blimp* shares.

Visual innovations, too, like the use of Technicolor half-tones. In his memoirs, Powell recalls the battles he had to wage with Nathalie Kalmus in order to suppress and desaturate certain colours so as to get almost monochromatic sequences illuminated by the brilliance of a red uniform. Thus both the duel scene, and the preparation for it, bring out a whole range of blacks and greys (very difficult to obtain in films today) of incredible delicacy, highlighted by Alfred Junge's pastel sets, accentuating its ceremonial theatricality and the irony with which it is treated.

In counterpoint to the three wars that Colonel Blimp goes through, Powell and Pressburger tell a triple love story, all entirely different in tone (moving from romanticism to a laconic style worthy of Pinter). Each time the heroine is played by Deborah Kerr, as splendid as a militant feminist with whom Blimp (Clive Candy) discovers too late that he is in love, as she is as a nurse during the First World War whom he will marry for her resemblance to her first incarnation, or the woman soldier that he employs as a driver without noticing that she is the image of his wife.

The attention paid to these three women reveals Powell as one of the few film-makers who escape the 'poverty of desire', the distinguishing feature, for Ernest Bevin, of British civilization. His female characters are important, dominant, in fact, admirably written and filmed, with not a trace of machismo. Every shot of *Black Narcissus* and *Blimp* (after seeing these films you realize how Deborah Kerr's talent was very often spoiled in Hollywood), of *I Know Where I'm Going* and *The Small Back Room* reveal a director in love with his actresses, one of the few who dare to discuss sexuality at the risk of breaking the rules of 'good taste'.

It's even the underlying theme of *Peeping Tom*, which Powell described to me with a slight smile as 'an autobiographical film, very tender, almost romantic, the story of a character it was very easy for me to identify with, because *I live cinema*. I don't have a particular style like René Clair, *I am cinema*; I well understood that technician of emotion who could only approach life as a director and suffered atrociously from it, given that I cut and edit everything I see in the street.'

In fact Mark Lewis, the 'peeping Tom' of the title, represents the absolute director, who, like any real film-maker, wants to capture the definitive shot, the one that will calm his anxieties. Abandoning the artifices involved in directing actors, he is finally led to capture the torments of fear, to film 'death live' (my film, *Deathwatch*, was a homage and variation on Powell's), to invent the ultimate tracking shot: the one in which one of the legs of the camera tripod, which has been turned into a knife-blade, pierces the throat of the 'actresses' he is filming, who watch themselves die – the supreme refinement – in a mirror fixed above the camera.

As Hugo said: 'The public highway is clearly badly guarded. It seems that there are poets on the loose. The chief of police is negligently allowing minds to wander freely. We should be on our guard. Intelligences may be bitten.' *Blimp* and *Peeping Tom* are films without leash and muzzle.*

15 March

Whenever I have a moment I go and see Simon at the hospital, either alone or with Riccardo Freda. He's even more striking now. His skin has turned entirely black. I bring him the proofs of *Projections 1*. He seems to like this. And yet I can't tell whether he has the strength to read. In a broken voice he talks passionately about John Boorman's *I Dreamt I Woke Up*, which he saw at Venice and thought was 'brilliant'. He makes a point of asking me to go and see it. It's his latest discovery, along with the telefilm directed by Jerry Lewis. I tell him of my enthusiasm for the Cukor biography by Patrick McGilligan, which he asks to see immediately. Clearly, he tires more quickly, and has greater difficulty concentrating. But you can sense that he wants to talk cinema. His eyes light up when I tell him I've just seen by Mitchell Leisen's *Frenchman's Creek*, an extremely original pirate film – dark, meditative, visually sumptuous, closer to Minnelli than to Curtiz or Walsh. 'It's admirable,' he

---

* I owe this information to Ian Christie's monograph on Powell and Pressburger (British Film Institute, 1985). Recently, I watched the stunning laser-disc of *Tales from Hoffman* and was struck by its influence on the toy-maker section of *Blade Runner*.

manages to articulate. Then he asks me when he'll be able to see *La Guerre sans nom* so he can work on it. Overwhelmed, I haven't the strength to tell him the film's already been released.

16 March

First screening of *L 627* to check the sound mixing. As at the others, I've invited a few friends along: Alain Corneau, Marcel Ophuls (to whom Truffaut used to show all his first cuts), the artistic director of the Institut Lumière, Thierry Frémaux; I watch their reactions as to the length of the film.

I think the mixing's terrific. Very inventive, something daring, it matches the images perfectly. Like Sarde's music. As for the new cut, it now strikes me as clear. The personal quest and professional life of Lulu, once light has been cast on their interaction, seem to echo one another, to rub up against each other. At the end of the screening, Corneau exclaims enthusiastically: 'Whatever you do, don't cut anything. It's great as it is. The fact that it's unusually long is part of the project. That's what gives the film its force, its novelty, its feeling.' Ophuls, who also reacts favourably, says it's my best film, identifying Lulu with Commander Dellaplane, but he's also more nit-picking, challenging certain repetitions in the famous reel six. I try to explain to him that I've repeated certain scenes to make them appear less exceptional. He doesn't seem convinced.

We return to this double conversation the next day. Corneau begs me not to cut anything. Ophuls insists that the first tailing-scene in reel six spoils the one in which they tail the taxi in the Cour de Vincennes: 'You've got your sense of exhaustion, fatigue, of everything starting over and over again, disillusion with the stinginess of the French administration; the characters, their gestures and their behaviour are full of it. And it makes this scene redundant. Don't cut the scenes taking place in the prefabs or in the hotels. But cut that.'

I set about analysing the sequence, highlighting what it tells us about Lulu, his open-mindedness, his rejection of generalities about blacks (he points out the differences between people from Mali, Benin and Zaïre to Vincent, who clearly has learned nothing about it at school). I have the feeling I'm jeopardizing the whole meaning of the film. Ophuls mercilessly sweeps aside my objections, finding these qualities in the rest of the film.

I must say that I'm also resistant because this tailing scene was very hard to film, and it involved re-takes. It's infuriating to tell yourself that you've sweated blood for nothing, that everything's going to end up in the bin. So with a stubbornness and a bit of a bad conscience, I try to keep at least part of it, particularly one magnificent night shot where the Zaïreans leave a café to get into their car.

The result isn't convincing. Another, shorter version is even less persuasive.

Desperate, I cut the whole scene. I use the opportunity to reverse two scenes in the same reel, which works better.

The next screening proves me wrong, and Ophuls right.

19 March

I learn that for the first time in thirty years three ministers – two of whom, Pierre Joxe and Mexandeau have seen our film – have gone to the Arc de Triomphe to celebrate the anniversary of the ceasefire in Algeria. This gesture implies an implicit recognition of the state of war, which has been refused by all governments. And another first: François Mitterrand receives a delegation of former conscripts, who make the same request; he answers: 'It sounds reasonable.'

28 March

Jean-Pierre Lavoignat of *Studio* magazine comes to interview me with Nils, to whom I've dedicated *L 627* as a way of thanking him for having introduced me to Michel Alexandre, and therefore, started off the film. And for a deeper, more personal reason: a few years ago, when he was going through a bad patch, he had taken refuge in drugs. Colo and I had tried to help him, to show him that we weren't going to let him down. Luckily, we met a wonderful Jungian analyst – open, pragmatic, comprehensive, a nice change after the irresponsible attitude of some of his colleagues. I'll never forget the doctor, a real criminal, who told us that our son was living an experience and had to go through it to the end: 'He has to touch the bottom before he resurfaces.' Of course, Nils got out of it mostly through his own will power. Later, he showed me all the places where you could get hold of the stuff without any difficulty: the corridors of the Châtelet Métro station, where a crowd of Zaïrean dealers were selling it openly as if they were in a market; in front of the Lycée Carnot; in the other private schools where we had put him; in famous nightclubs, etc.

In 1985 I was invited to lunch, with Costa-Gavras, by Laurent Fabius, who was then Prime Minister. He wanted to know what were the problems that struck us as being the most serious. So I told him everything I'd discovered through Nils. He interrupted me sharply as if I had asked him to take care of my parking fines: 'I asked you to speak about a *serious* problem.' I left in a mad fury, unable to concentrate for many hours, or sleep the following night. I swore I'd make him pay for that sentence, which showed such incredible ignorance, such a shameful lack of awareness. The same ignorance, the same lack of awareness, shared by many doctors and right-wing politicians, caused the death of so many haemophiliacs, injected with contaminated blood while he was Prime Minister, months after it was discovered to be fatal. What could you expect of a man who declared during the same lunch, looking at us straight in the eyes, 'As long as I'm Prime Minister there won't be any commercial breaks in films shown on TV', then several weeks later imposes, with François Mitterrand, the shameful and stupid Fifth Channel, with commercial breaks, a project which had been in preparation for months in his cabinet. Why lie to us like that? Because he conteptuously thinks we will have forgotten a week after?

During the interview with Lavoignat, Nils explains his fascination with the street, his night-time rambles, the world of the police, which he describes magnificently well, without the slightest self-indulgence. He talks about their liking for showing-off, for sordid jokes; how they use their macho impulses 'so as not to break down in tears'. He claims he was surprised by the ease with which I became part of this world, which was apparently so far away from me, and 'which was never filmed in a touristy way'. He also defines Michel Alexandre's contribution very well.

3 April

Simon Mizrahi has asked me to bring him some Chinese food. In addition I buy some flans and crêmes brulées from Fauchon. While it's very hard for him to eat (on the previous day I had to insist before he would swallow some vegetables or pieces of meat), he pounces on a pot of crêmes brulée and swallows it extraordinarily quickly. He's still a greedy chap. Today his skin has almost returned to its normal colour. But I still have to struggle with myself to take his hand or wipe his face. Illness and death chill my blood. But I get over it. Sometimes.

Fortunately he's getting a lot of visitors. Marie-Noelle Tranchant from *Figaro* came to read him some psalms. Danielle Heymann, the editor of the arts and leisure section of *Le Monde*, is very tender and compassionate. Scola and Comencini are constantly phoning his mother, who is with him today. She doesn't really seem aware of the seriousness of her son's illness. Or else she's refusing to admit the truth – to keep her spirits up and help her son do the same.

6–8 April

Two screenings of *La Guerre sans nom*, a very short space apart, in Marseilles and London, force me to juggle timetables and modes of transport. At seven in the morning, although the long debate on the previous day went on until late, I take the plane to London with Jean-Pierre Guérin, the film's producer. Charlotte, who came straight from Paris, is already waiting for me. Alan Yentob, the controller of BBC 2, who bought *La Guerre sans nom* while it was being edited (I was very touched by his enthusiasm, which did a lot to calm my anxieties), wants to broadcast it over Easter weekend between my two most recent films: *Daddy Nostalgie* and *La Vie et rien autre*. The date and time are very good (but I would rather have had it screened in a cinema, even if it was only for a week), particularly when you think about the way documentaries are treated on French television. The winner of the Fipa d'Or, *Les Messagers de l'ombre*, about the behaviour of French writers in the Occupation, was shown at twenty to one in the morning, the splendid *Les Moissons de fer* hardly any earlier. A *Memory of Justice* by Marcel Ophuls still hasn't been shown. And yet one of the biggest successes of the fifth channel was *La Justice en France* by Daniel Karlin and Philippe Boucher.

Because of this impending broadcast, Alan Yentob has asked me to be present at the press screening, scheduled for ten in the morning. I'd hardly arrived at the hotel, and just had time to kiss Charlotte before I found myself swamped by a series of interviews for the radio, television, the press. With all the debates going on, I feel as if I haven't stopped talking about this film for two months. And on top of that I have to do it in a foreign language.

Fortunately I've had training, specially thanks to the Cannes Festival. When one of your films is selected, Unifrance Film throws you to the foreign television channels, ten minutes for two channels over a period of three hours. You emerge from it a little like Wile E. Coyote in the Chuck Jones cartoons, after the diabolical trap he's laid for the Roadrunner has blown up in his face for the twentieth time.

In London, among the first journalists, I meet again people I really like because of their love and knowledge of the cinema: Philip French and Derek Malcolm.

In the evening Alan Yentob invites us to dinner (Charlotte, Jean-Pierre Guérin, Dominique Bourgois, the wife of the publisher who's in charge of the foreign sales of the film), at an excellent Indian restaurant where, once again, we meet Jeremy Thomas among the other guests.

Jean-Pierre Guérin is the only one who doesn't speak English, but this doesn't stop his valiant efforts to suggest various co-production ideas. Initially, people begin to answer him with a few sentences in French and then, ineluctably, quickly switch back to English. So, there he is all at sea, lost, vainly trying to catch a title or a name. It feels like being part of a very funny scene in *That Uncertain Feeling*, a minor Lubitsch that was massacred by the censors – if you believe what Walter Reisch says in *Backstory II*. To honour his Hungarian or Serbian guests the master of the house had learned a toast in their language. He raised it at the beginning of the meal, causing a brief silence. Then everyone started talking in Hungarian, excluding him and his wife from the conversation.

Dominique Bourgois tries to help Jean-Pierre – he's a lovely man, but fate seems to take a mean delight in laying traps in his path. I knew someone like that, a man called Alfred Eibel. He was erudite and brilliant but, like a magnet, he attracted the most preposterous disasters: at the end of a late private screening Eibel was always the one who would get locked in a building or the toilets; when we were out in a group, he was always the one who would be chosen by a voluble and tenacious foreigner speaking an incomprehensible lingo, by a professional drunk philosopher or an exasperated tourist. When one of his literary idols, Jim Thompson, came to Paris, Eibel wanted to have dinner with him so he could get to know him better. But Thompson made him drink so much that when he woke up the next day, he hadn't a single memory of what had been said during the evening. I had lunch with him one day in a restaurant in the Avenue Victor Hugo. Near me was a young woman who was sitting at the next table and therefore almost opposite Eibel. She wrongly imagined that he was staring at her (in fact, he was waiting for the waiter who was taking an order immediately behind her), and suddenly lifted up her sweater revealing the absence of a bra and two very fine breasts, yelling, 'Since you're so interested, have a look.' I saw him grow crimson like the wolf in a Tex Avery cartoon, his eyes jumping out of their sockets, petrified, his mouth open, as if he'd just had an apoplectic seizure.

I talk to Yentob about two ideas for television programmes that seem to interest Dominique and Jean-Pierre. As President of the Institut Lumière, I would like somebody to do a well-researched documentary on fundamental contributions made by the Lumière Brothers for the centenary of the cinema. Marey and Edison perfected the moving image. The Lumière Brothers invented the cinema. They brought the image out of the studio and threw it into the street, into life and showed it to an audience. Between the Lumières and Edison there lies a difference in vision. The former invented the cinema, the latter imagined television. Kevin Brownlow is the only person I can imagine treating this subject with the proper rigour.

The second, more personal project would consist in rehabilitating about fifteen misunderstood French films which I would choose, and which I would introduce either on my own or with the director, actors or technicians. As an example I quote *Bonne chance*, a fine comedy by Sacha Guitry, an original screenplay written with an astounding freedom: Guitry shoots a scene in a car just to include some dialogue where someone asks how to shoot a scene in a car, or a sequence on a transatlantic liner for a single line: 'The only problem with ships is that they make it difficult to eat asparagus.' And as the ship rolls the sauce really does move back and forth on the plate. This film had been thought to have disappeared, but was rediscovered by René Château in his video collection called 'La Mémoire du cinéma français'.

Alan asks me to send him a complete list with a brief description when I get back to Paris. I tell him that we could adapt this kind of idea to other countries, asking Wenders for German films that he feels have been unjustly ignored;

contact Scorsese or Joe Dante for the States. I'm pleased with the reaction, although a journalist says that he wants to limit buying subtitled European films. Let's wait and see.

The next day in the screening room I recognize some friends, some directors among the journalists: John Boorman, Karel Reisz, Ken Loach. I do my best to introduce the film, clips of which will be shown on video. This means that Alain Choquart's camera work takes a knock, with the faces turning purple or green. I find two or three mistakes in the subtitles, which are otherwise excellent. The BBC press department has set up a cold buffet for afterwards, and I know, by experience, that I will not be able to enjoy it. No sooner do I take a sandwich or a plate of smoked salmon than I'm introduced to a journalist or somebody who wants to shake my hand. I become clumsy and awkward. I don't know what to do with the sandwich, which I crush nervously in my hand (I've often ended up, out of shyness, by putting it in my pocket), or else I drop the contents of my plate or try to swallow it very quickly. It's generally at this point that the radio people turn up to ask their questions. It's probably better just to forget the buffet piled up before your famished eyes.

The reactions seem very warm. John talks about the emotion in the film, its universal aspect. Ken Loach agrees, and adds that what has been said applies perfectly to Ireland. Encumbered by a sandwich, I can only agree, and don't even get to tell him all the good things I think about *Riff-Raff*. By the time I've finished eating, he's already left.

In the afternoon, Jean-Pierre sets off back to Paris, absent-mindedly taking *my* ticket with him – Marseilles–London – instead of his own, which means that he will miss his plane.

In the evening, dinner with John Boorman, Matthew Evans of Faber and Faber and Walter Donohue. The restaurant is elegant and clearly very fashionable. John, accompanied by Isabella, is in great form. *Projections 1* has been very well received, which is not going to make life easy for its successor. He then tries to reassure me, telling me that he's very much liked the sections of my diary which I've sent so far.

The atmosphere of the meal (excellent) is very agreeable. Isabella, whom I've already met in Dublin (as well as Matthew Evans), is charming and very lively, as is Matthew's wife, Caroline. John talks to me about his relationship with Michael Powell, who had sent him a very touching letter about *Hope and Glory*. Then I tell him about the screening of *'Round Midnight*. After gripping me by the arm, Powell had said to me: 'I felt I've understood jazz, I've penetrated deep within the music *thanks to the direction*. Because it *is music*. It's a magnificent film, the glorification of one art form by another work of art.' The same Michael Powell could be merciless, tearing apart a film or a film-maker in a few words. He summed up Michael Balcon in a lightning judgment: 'petty bourgeois'. Of James Ivory he said, 'Nice images, taste. No style.'

John, who has been invited to be a jury member in Cannes, tells us some very funny stories about the Festival. Walter brings the conversation round to *50 ans de cinéma américain*. The ambition of the book, the mass of information that it contains: the fact that we had another look at all the films we talked about in detail, seems to leave him bowled over with admiration: 'How did you find the time to do it, while making two films and preparing *La Guerre sans nom*?' Charlotte, who was very closely involved in the writing of the book, answers with a laugh, 'It's simple, he hardly slept during all that time.'

He asks me a lot of questions about the section devoted to scriptwriters and all the research that it must have involved. It's true that it's still a very unknown area – a little less so thanks to our previous publication, *30 ans de cinéma américain*, thanks also to the works of Pierre Rissient and in the USA, of Richard Corliss, Pat McGilligan and a few others. Quite naturally, I bring up the case of Philip Yordan which has obsessed me for more than twenty years. Pierre Rissient and myself discovered that this prolific screenwriter, much vaunted in French magazines (in the sixties he was practically the only name mentioned), had a large number of ghost writers, specially among blacklisted writers. We gradually managed to discover the real authors of the scripts that he had put his name to, and our essay in *50 ans* was extremely thorough, especially thanks to the help of McGilligan. We had communicated our discoveries to one another, and McGilligan sent me a very recent interview that he'd done with Yordan (mine, published in *Les Cahiers du cinéma*, was a tissue of lies: he'd run rings around the credulous film-buff that I was).

I'm afraid the conversation was getting too esoteric, as often happens when it's monopolized by film-buffs, and we're interrupted by Matthew Evans, who asks us what interest could there possibly be in identifying who really wrote a particular piece of crap. I answer with a smile that he's over-simplifying. Many of these works are excellent (*The Naked Jungle* by Byron Haskin, *House of Strangers* by Mankiewicz, *Day of the Outlaw*, a remarkable and unusual Western by André de Toth), some are real genre classics (*Johnny Guitar* by Ray, *Men in War*, *The Last Frontier* by Anthony Mann, *The Big Combo* by Joseph H. Lewis). Others, finally, have a good reputation (undeservedly, like the horrible *Dillinger* with Lawrence Tierney); *When Strangers Marry* got rave reactions from James Agee and Orson Welles. It seemed natural to me to want to know who had really written these screenplays, if only to repair an injustice.

Ghostwriting was very common in Hollywood. Ben Hecht, for example, worked uncredited on dozens of scripts, doctoring scenes and sharpening up the dialogue. He sometimes supplied brilliant ideas without knowing it: John Ford and Walter Wanger went to consult him on *Stagecoach* without telling him that the film was about to be shot: he suggested turning Claire Trevor into a prostitute, Wayne into a hunted man out for revenge. When he saw the film the plot vaguely reminded him of something. 'Sure it does', Ford told him, 'you wrote it. We couldn't pay you so we thought up this plan ...' But Hecht himself also put his name to a lot of films that he'd only supervised.

But Yordan went further than that. He turned a habit into an economic system, working in a closed circuit, he exploited the political climate, the witch hunts of the fifties. He took under contract screenwriters suspected of being communists or progressives, who were suddenly unable to find work, gave them a much lower salary than they'd been getting, put his name on their scripts or their adaptations and produced the films. His company was called Security Pictures! We might add, to increase the complexity of this character right out of Balzac, that he remained faithful to them long after the end of McCarthyism, and finally enabled them to survive. Several of his 'victims', while complaining about his literary usurpation and his absolute lack of artistic or intellectual ambition, talk about him with a degree of affection.

All these Machiavellian, puzzling, contradictory events, this exploitation of a moment of political hysteria which itself exploited the climate of the cold war, would make a terrific subject for a Brechtian political fable, the absolute antithesis of Walter Bernstein and Martin Ritt's *The Front*. Yordan is the perfect opposite of the character played by Woody Allen. When he put his name to something, he did it for his own advantage!

Don't worry, I didn't go into all this during dinner. I spoke about it briefly and then let the conversation drift towards other subjects of interest. I know that I sometimes tend to monopolize the conversation, to pile on one anecdote after another. An excess of enthusiasm, a need to persuade, to overcome a terrible shyness, as well as a need to protect myself. As an adolescent I was incapable of talking in public. I blushed and stammered. I had to fight against that when I became a press attaché. But even today when I'm asked to do something in front of people, I'm sure I'm going to get it all wrong.

There are two ways of concealing shyness: keeping silent or talking a lot. I chose the second. I try to fight down mounting anxiety and fear with words, which I use as shields. It's a kind of escape, and I'm the first victim of it. It's like a revenge on my college years when, sickly and gauche, I felt crushed and rejected. It helped me to build a front that protects me from journalists, who see no further than the passionate gourmet, the epicurean for whom food is more important than anything else. I know how untrue it is, but they are so happy with that image. They don't bother to go deeper. So I am safe.

Let's get back to Yordan. Something that adds even more to the stature of the character is that he didn't, as people thought, start this kind of practice with the introduction of the blacklist. It gradually came to light that even in his first films he 'hired' anonymous collaborators. Between Pierre Rissient, Pat McGilligan and myself we've discovered a large number of them: Robert Tasker who wrote *Dillinger*, which established Yordan's reputation; a small drugstore owner from whom he bought the story of *When Strangers Marry* for a few hundred dollars, adding two scenes lifted from Tourneur and Val Lewton. Mankiewicz says that he entirely rewrote *House of Strangers*, as the producer Sol C. Siegel confirms. When the Writers Guild insisted on a shared credit, Mankiewicz angrily withdrew his name. As for the play that won him the Pulitzer Prize, *Anna Lucasta*, its story is a splendid, comic imbroglio worthy of Neopolitan farce, that McGilligan has managed to elucidate. Yordan set the action of *Anna Lucasta* (an exact copy, it is said, of *Anna Christie*), in the Polish community in Chicago. When the play was rejected, he employed a young black writer who transposed it to Harlem, adapting the dialogue, of course, to the black language of the time. The play was accepted, brought him huge success and won the Pulitzer Prize. Hollywood bought it and then decided that it was out of the question to produce a film acted entirely by blacks. 'As you like', cried Yordan, and he gave them the first version. When, as times changed, they decided to do a more daring remake, Yordan went back to the version conceived for the stage.

Ben Maddow goes so far as to assert in *Backstory II* that 'Yordan never wrote a sentence in his life'. Not bad for one of Hollywood's most prolific screenwriters, who won an Oscar for *The Broken Lance*, a remake of which he didn't write a single line, based on an original screenplay entirely written by somebody else!

... Back in the restaurant. When we are leaving, Charlotte, seized with admiration for the rich burgundy-coloured coat of Matthew Evans' wife, immediately guesses where it comes from – Vivienne Westwood. She has a sharp eye and often, during *L 627*, surprised the cops with her faculty of observation. Now, she can spot a dealer, or a cop car on a stakeout in seconds. Charlotte talks to me about John in lyrical terms. It must be said that the first film we saw together before our romance really began was *Hope and Glory*.

9 April

I can't help establishing a correlation between the closure of the cinemas and the rise of the extreme right. By more and more shutting themselves away in their homes where they only watch TV, people seem to become more vulnerable to repressive ideologies, more inclined to want to defend and protect themselves. Cinema is a good barometer. François Truffaut told me that he judged a newspaper's *gravitas*, reliability and tone from the quality of its cinema reviews.

13 April

Someone on the Métro tells me about the dismissal of the Touvier case.*
Violent feeling of rage, disgust. I go for an hour's walk to calm down. Without
success. Klaus Barbie was kidnapped and French justice was administered;
when crimes are committed by French people, or by French institutions, we're
witnessing a competition in hypocrisy. People talk about national unity, and
pretend to believe that Vichy was an anti-republican entity that came into
being with the defeat of France and died with the Liberation. But certain laws
voted in with Vichy are still applied today, starting with the Centre du Cinéma,
founded during this period and which, according to this reasoning, should no
longer have any legal existence. But for a long time after the victory you could
see magistrates and police in the same posts they held during the Occupation.
By turning the Vichy administration into an illegal abstraction all these crimes
are rendered parenthetical.

In *Le Monde* I read the astonishing arguments that led to the dismissal of the
case. The three judges wanted to provide a history lesson: Touvier couldn't be
guilty of crimes against humanity because he was only carrying out orders,
which may have been horrible, but were issued by a regime without any
hegemonic, racist or anti-semitic policy of its own, but which just had to obey
the will of the Nazis. Unimaginable! What about the law concerning foreigners
passed in October 1940? And the statute of the Jews as of 18 October? 'It isn't
a surprise, but it's still a shock', the historian Philippe Erlanger wrote in his
diary of the Occupation, adding: 'We're back in the Middle Ages. The stakes
will probably be lit any minute.' Erlanger, who remembered that Laval, in
1935, when he was Prime Minister, had asked him for the Protocol of the
Elders of Zion, added, 'The men of Vichy have returned to a doctrine of
Maurice Barrès, according to which all the ills that have arisen since the
Revolution are due to Jewish and foreign ideologies. It's the belated revenge of
those anti-Dreyfusards who proclaim: 'The Jew was created by God to serve as
a traitor everywhere.'

What about the establishment of the Commissariat for Jewish Affairs, under
the direction of Xavier Vallat – a pre-war embodiment of the anti-semitism of
Action Française – which was passed on to someone even harsher, Darquier
de Pellepoix, greeted one day by Pétain as 'Monsieur Torturer'. And the
militia, with its openly racist programme, was an official product of Vichy!

But the anti-semitic policy of Vichy was concealed for a long time. It is
barely mentioned in the list of crimes of which Pétain was accused during his
trial. On the tombstones of the well-known murdered Jews the word 'Jew' is

---

* Touvier was one of the leaders of the French militia in Lyons during the Second World War; he
participated in a number of crimes and murders, especially of Jews. He was saved and hidden by
right-wing monks and priests.

never mentioned. It is prudishly replaced by 'victims of Nazi barbarism'. It took Marcel Ophuls and *Le Chagrin et la pitié* to reveal the truth about the atrocious round-up at the Vel d'Hiv, ordered and executed by Frenchmen who, in an excess of zeal that wasn't asked for by the occupying forces, added babies and children to the list of deportees. I feel sullied.

14 April

Very strong reactions from historians specializing in the period, from Henri Amouroux to Jean-Pierre Azéma and Robert Paxton, whom our magistrates have clearly never read. They all contest the 'historical explanations'.

A remarkable article in *Le Monde* which, after taking apart the argument, places it in its context, including the strange leniency that the Liberation government showed towards the magistrature, most of whose members had pledged allegiance to Vichy. There was only an inquiry, the results of which are still kept under the seal of secrecy. On the other hand, how can we fail to see a relation between this dismissal and the declaration of ministers and socialist figures, clearly inspired by the Elysée Palace, expressing their regret over the continuing pursuit of Papon, Bousquet or Touvier, at the risk of 're-opening old wounds'.

How could one fail to be outraged when this same legal system, so reluctant when it comes to hunting down people accused of terrible crimes (Touvier was sheltered with impunity in far-right convents and abbeys that *Le Canard enchaîné* had exposed years ago), and so energetic when it came to making sure, on the order of the Chancellery, that haemophiliacs did not have access to the law courts in the case of the contaminated blood. If Anne-Marie Casterêt, a journalist with *L'Événement du jeudi*, had not revealed this criminal scandal, Dr Garetta* would have had more time to enjoy his Légion d'Honneur, which was awarded three years after the truth began to emerge, by special request from the Elysée. True, he would have lost the three million francs' indemnity he was granted after he was forced to resign in the wake of this murderous scandal. Laurent Fabius would not have been able to swear that he had done everything in his power (this was when he thought that drugs were not an important subject) and Georgina Dufoix would not have been able to go on TV and give her famous, shameful, sordid reply, obviously written by some adviser aspiring to be a television scriptwriter: 'I feel responsible, but not guilty.'

---

* Dr Garetta was in charge of the Transfusion Centre and continued distributing contaminated blood, refusing to buy heated products several months after the danger had been proved.

17 April

Showing of *L 627* at the Club Gaumont for the technical crew and some of the seventy actors. A number of them arrive with five or six friends, which annoys me terribly. I find this attitude rude and irresponsible. A private screening is still work, and you can't just invite everybody, especially four months before its release. Such manners used to exasperate me when I was a press attaché, and one day I turned away a journalist who had arrived with his children and their friends without having notified us beforehand: 'When you're invited to dinner, do you turn up with this bunch without telling your hosts beforehand?' I'd also invited a few friends: Jean-Claude Missiaen, Alain Resnais and Sabine Azéma, as well as two or three journalists. The only one missing is J.J. Bernard of *Première*.

I go and say hello to Didier Bezace and Jean-Roger Milo, accompanied, of course, by Nils, Lara Guirao and Cécile Garcia. Smail Melki, who was great as a dealer beaten up by Lulu, and Celyane Guy, a West Indian actress who was so impressive in her scene that nobody wants to believe she's an actress. I wait anxiously for their reactions.

I sit down beside Charlotte, who is seeing the film for the first time. She's as anxious as I am, and yet tries to reassure me.

The first reel appears two frames out of synch. I'm about to go to the projectionist's booth when Frédéric Bourboulon stops me, having just been there, and tells me that the reel must have been put on badly. When the reel is changed everything's better. Some comic effects get laughs, but not as much as at some of the previous screenings. I immediately start panicking: 'Oh God, I must have edited it too short . . . I *knew* we were eight frames too short after the bucket of water . . . One more cock-up.' Charlotte reassures me and murmurs in my ear: 'Listen to how closely they're watching. Just because they're not howling with laughter doesn't mean they don't think it's funny . . .' The colour grading seems bad in some of the scenes, particularly at the end.

Marchetti's main titles are a great success. I wanted them to symbolize a race, an endless chase through the Métro, urban landscapes sketched out in a few lines. Nothing figurative. I was thinking, of course, of the extraordinary graphic inventions of Saul Bass, Maurice Binder. Marchetti, absolutely delighted, told me: 'I've been waiting ten years for something like that.' And what he did was marvellous.

When the lights come up, Charlotte grips me tightly by the arm. She's smiling. A huge show of enthusiasm from Dominique Besnehard, a brilliant casting director, turned agent, who didn't notice the length of the film and missed an appointment. He keeps saying, 'I could have had another two hours of it.' I would like Richard Pezet to hear this.

Didier looks enchanted. He simply says, 'It's magnificent.' I reply, 'So were you.' Celyane Guy makes straight for me: 'Terrific. Very moving. And so accurate. For once black people have been filmed as we are, without paternalism, without trying to flatter us.' I'm relieved by her reaction. And very moved. She hugs me while I tell her how good I think she is.

Smail agrees with her: 'It's morally beyond reproach. It's what I see every day in Belleville. God, it hurts.'

Pascale Vignal, Alain Choquart's wife, who played one of the main characters in *La Vie et rien autre*, is one of the people bowled over by the film. She has trouble speaking and suddenly bursts into tears. Alain consoles her: 'She's been crying like that for the last five minutes.' I've sometimes reacted like that in Cannes after a Godard, and recently after Brisseau's *Céline*.

I go to see Alain Resnais, who's remained seated next to Sabine, who seems to be in the same state as Pascale. Alain talks to me quietly: 'Well, it was a great risk and it's paid off. I knew nothing about the film, and I was constantly surprised. You can never predict the next shot or the next scene. It's a very new way of telling a story. The main actor is terrific, but the whole film's a real actors' showcase.' Sabine kisses me very affectionately and whispers in my ear: 'Charlotte is splendid.' Which Dominique Besnehard had said to me as well.

I get Didier and introduce him to Resnais and Sabine. I try to keep a cool head, to keep post-screening fever under control. But, in spite of all my efforts, I am less pessimistic than usual, which bothers me.

It's hard for me not to be touched when Jean-Roger Milo comes and says, 'You were right to shake me up, to kick me up the arse. You've taught me a lot with this film. You've taught me a lot. Thanks.'

I go for a drink with Didier, Charlotte, Jean-Roger, Nils and Jean-Claude Missiaen, another former press attaché who has moved on to directing, and who won't stop talking about the film – he can quote some lines word for word. Michel Alexandre laps it up, all the more because the two police friends he had brought with him liked it a lot. All Didier's worries seem to have vanished. He does a fine analysis of the film, and jokes with Lara Guirao and Jean-Roger Milo.

Charlotte also seems very happy. Coming out of the cinema, Alain Resnais told her she had acted with the energy, the organic vitality of the best American actresses – and Sabine agreed. Charlotte is a little reassured – for two days at least.

18 April

In the morning, a very nice letter from Jean-Jacques Bernard who had been eating strawberry ice-cream with his kids and forgotten all about the screening.

A little later I get a call from Nils, who tells me I'm a grandfather. His son has just been born and his name's Jordan. It wasn't a difficult labour. In the hours that follow my whole family wants to know what it's like to have a grandson, to be a grandfather. As if it was a disaster.

19 April

Charlotte and I go to see Jordan at the Rothschild Hospital. Maybe it's my age, but although I always find new-born babies very ugly, as does the unfortunate Nils, I'm rather won over by my grandson. I must say that he has very good-looking parents.

Nils hasn't left the side of Valérie – the young and beautiful mother – for three or four days. She had had a difficult pregnancy, partly because of him, with his inveterate Don-Juanism, and had ended up taking refuge in her family to protect herself. I found her full of courage and dignity. Nils came to visit her and looked after her well in the end.

I see both of them in this little room, which has a floral name, but is painted a dull greenish-blue. He's attentive, delicate and sensitive, while she, maternal in an almost animal way, is utterly engrossed in her son. A moment of truce and hope. I must not forget that I myself did not behave very well when Colo was pregnant.

20 April

Screening in the little living-room of Jacques Albunque (a passionate film collector) of *Douce* by Claude Autant-Lara. The strength and richness of the film, with its flashes of tenderness, its romantic inventiveness, is amazing. A lively, sharp intelligence, debunking stupidity and injustice, trusting the viewer – and with a sense of innocence that Lara would lose in the fifties (in favour of a higher level of violence, often handled in a masterly way), or turn into sentimentality (*Le franciscain de Bourges*). The direction has a grace, an elegance, an acuteness from the opening travelling shot, to a soundtrack of Christmas carols, along the roof-tops of Paris, with the Eiffel Tower, still under construction, in the background.

It must be said that Aurenche's script and dialogue – according to Bost, Aurenche wrote almost everything – are a wonderful stimulant for the actors and the director. A marvel of poetry, inventiveness, humour and profundity, the dialogue is always organic to the characters, their class, their professions. Among hundreds of gems, let's choose one, one worthy of Prévert. Douce has fled with the steward of the house. They have taken refuge in a rather sordid little hotel where she sets about enjoying a passionate love affair. Looking at herself in the mirror, she remarks, 'It's odd, I've gone all green.' The steward points out that it's the texture of the mirror, which has mildewed glass. She gives a little shout, the lovely cry of a little girl playing at passion, and not having quite worked it out: 'So now when I'm green I'll know that I'm happy.'

Coming away from her visit to the poor – a scene worthy of Buñuel, cut by the Vichy censors – Marguerite Moreno (extraordinary as the bourgeois dowager) tells them, 'Patience and resignation.' To which Roger Pigault, the steward, replies, 'No. Impatience and rebellion.' Not bad for 1943.

And this advice, Douce will follow – as did the people who made the film. It's a real film of impatience and rebellion.

21 April

Over the past few days I've seen Simon Mizrahi a number of times. Today he asks me to go and find the doctor who's looking after him. The doctor has told him he's getting out and seems to have forgotten about him for three days. I go out and talk to a nurse who tells me that the doctor had seen Simon just a few hours ago! So, he's losing his sense of time. Apparently, he will have permission to return home soon. Is this a sign that he's recovering or getting worse? She won't tell me.

I calm Simon down – he has no memory of this consultation (one day he asked Freda if he could see me, when I'd been there for an hour). He smiles; 'It's just that I have to be at the office next Monday to get back to work and look at a few tapes.' He asks me for the biography of Cukor before going to sleep.

23 April

Phone call from Simon Mizrahi's mother: 'You know, Monsieur Tavernier, I'm beginning to get worried about my son. He doesn't seem to be getting any better. And yet I'm bringing him nice things, all the things he likes. I'm worried, and I'm going to get into an argument with his brother, who won't let me.' I have a lump in my throat.

25 April

My birthday. Very nice presents from Charlotte and Colo. Tiffany and Nils call me to say they'll bring theirs round later. Luce Grunenwaldt gives me a collection of short stories by Richard Ford. Magnificent and terribly desperate.

27 April

Passionate discussion about 'Authors' rights and Maastricht', organized by the film section of SACD. Our guest, Mr Veestrynge, from Brussels, says what's at stake and complains of a certain passivity among French authors, due to a lack of information. Compared with us, the Americans devote huge funds to lobbying, mobilizing up to 200 people to block any regulatory measures, any obstacle to their takeover of the market. In a few days we're voting on a directive about video renting rights supported by France, Spain and Greece. Among the opponents are England, Germany and Holland. The result depends on a vote in favour either from Denmark or Ireland. If we win, author status will be given to film directors, which is what Veestrynge wants to defend and the Americans want to stop.

28 April

In the morning I call John Boorman in Ireland and ask him to put in a word with the responsible Minister. Enrico does the same with Gabriel Axel in Denmark.

30 April–2 May

Pontarlier, a little town in the Doubs famous for its *anis*, Pontanis, a mild derivative of absinthe, and for Dr Grenier, the first member of French parliament during the 3rd Republic who did the unheard-of, converted to Islam and came to the chamber in a *djellaba*, has another claim to glory: the Jacques Becker Ciné Club, which is visited by famous film-makers of all nationalities – from Losey to Scola, Boorman to Kazan, Rossi, Fuller, the Taviani brothers, Alain Tanner.

There is a team behind this success. And a man – Pierre Blondeau. While he may have broken with communism and abandoned the teaching profession, Blondeau has never turned his back on the cinema. A libertarian anarchist, who can recite, in a provençal dialect, a whole tirade from Renoir's *La Marseillaise* lambasting the *capellans* – a name given to priests in the Midi at the time; at Ophuls or Godard retrospectives, inveighing against the smugness of the teaching profession, he overflows with passion and rage as he did at eighteen. He must have been born with a red and black flag and twenty-four frames of Vigo in his heart.

For about fifteen years – the worst thing that could happen to a film-buff – his eyesight has gradually faded. He is now almost blind. But this doesn't stop him going to see films, going to Cannes and the Institut Lumière to discover a film or a director. Simone, his wonderful wife, reads him all the subtitles, describes the action to him, and he works out the rest, talking lyrically about the style of direction, describing the camera movements, analysing the relation between sound and image better than most critics. His passion enables him to 're-invent' the film, and to get it right. He's a clairvoyant.

Whenever I get an invitation from him I accept. This time with Charlotte and Jean Cosmos, who are delighted and amazed to meet Pierre and his group of friends who have decided to show *La Vie et rien autre*, *Daddy Nostalgie*, and *La Guerre sans nom*. After each screening, we meet with the audience. After *La Vie* I introduce Jean Cosmos and also the composer Oswald d'Andrea whose powerful, lyrical score won the César for the best music. Pierre has also asked me to introduce *Black Narcissus*, which is given an enthusiastic reception, and to talk about Michael Powell.

We find the time to visit Gustave Courbet's birthplace in Ornans, a very pretty little town. Apart from some recently restored paintings including a beautiful landscape, it houses some very politically committed correspondence, some paintings by his disciples, various different sketches of the famous 'Artist's Studio' accompanied by a magnificent text describing each figure: '... at one side of the canvas there stands a Jew I saw in England, moving through the bustle of the London streets ... He had an ivory face, a long beard, a turban, and a long black robe that dragged along the ground. Behind him is a priest, wearing a triumphant expression on his reddish face ...'

I'm also keen to show Charlotte the Saltworks at Arc and Senans, conceived, or rather dreamed up and built by Nicolas Ledoux, an impressive example of utopian architecture that was left unfinished. In this factory, designed to process salt, Ledoux wanted to combine here all the social, spiritual and practical functions that would allow a collective to live as an autarchy. There are dormitories and refectories for the workers, with individual kitchen gardens, silos for storing food supplies, an audaciously conceived chapel near the apartments of the governor of the saltworks. One is struck by the audacity of the enterprise, by the generous and conservative philosophy behind it. This inspired building was filmed by my deceased friend Pierre Kast (who did the first documentary on Ledoux) in *La Morte saison des amours*, and then by Marcel Bluwal for his magnificent television adaptation of Molière's *Don Juan* with Michel Piccoli. When I was working with Jean Genet on *Le Langage de la muraille*, I suggested that Trauner should recreate here the Mettray children's prison – Bayne d'enfants.

The only dark note of those three days, on Sunday the second I learned of the death of Simon Mizrahi. He'd gone home two weeks previously, and I'd visited him a number of times. He had struck me as very weak, very tired. He was dozing in a room with the shutters closed, as the light clearly made him feel worse. I'd brought him some books, a tape of *Les Pirates du rail*, a second-rate colonial movie by Christian Jaque, with one sequence where Stroheim indulges in a kind of carnival of props, striking someone with a stick, taking off his gloves, drinking from a gourd, wiping his mouth with a handkerchief, taking a map from a map-holder, unfolding it, looking through his binoculars, putting his sword on the table, drawing his revolver, filing his nails. The memory of this had brought a hint of a smile from Simon. He had managed to say that he would watch the film in two or three days in the office when he got back to work. His whole family was there watching over him with extraordinary gentleness. They had employed a nurse to take him to the bathroom and wash him. This considerate attentiveness overwhelms Freda, who came with me the first time. In the street he had said he wouldn't come back, because he couldn't bear to see this family that he loved so much being bruised and wounded in this desperate struggle. Simon's mother had told me that at the least sign of pessimism her other son shouted at her. Then she had asked Simon, 'When are you going to take me to the opera like you used to?' The next day they'd announced triumphantly that he'd got up and sat in the drawing-room for two hours. The day before he'd even had dinner with his family. To please him, I'd tried to find him some Chinese dishes. After wandering about in Boulogne I'd bought him some Cantonese rice and a mango. And then some crêmes brulées. He was asleep when I got back. His mother has told me yet again that he was still greedy, that he'd asked for some Comte, that his memory was intact and brilliant, that a number of Italian directors had phoned, that she was so lucky to have a son like him, so appreciated by everybody. And suddenly, in that corridor, I had a brief moment of happiness. Of admiration, too.

I had taken his hand and squeezed it, but not for long enough. I had trouble making the gesture and this evening I'm angry with myself for my cowardice. Why was I so afraid when I was near him?

After my last visit I found a message on my answering machine. It was Simon asking me to go and see the Skolimowski film, telling me that it was a masterpiece. He could hardly speak and was breathing with difficulty. It was the last time he spoke to me.

3 May

I read a panning of *La Guerre sans nom* in *National Hébdo*, a newspaper close to the Front National, which 'I skim', in Henri Jeanson's words, *'d'un derrière distrait'* [with a distracted arse]. I have just enough time to notice, amongst a delectable litany of insults, that Patrick Rotman – doubtless because he's too Jewish – has been entirely ignored. I'm accused not only of manipulation and lying, but also of asking questions in a wheedling and underhanded way, while never appearing on the screen, and of having chosen 'a title which is an imposture, since the war in question really took place' – which the film demonstrates. One therefore wonders whether the signatory of the article has seen it. But the height of involuntary humour is reached when I'm accused, in an article *more than three pages long*, of having invaded the media.

4 May

The *Dictionnaire du cinéma* by Jacques Lourcelles – a deceptive title because it's actually about the 3,000 films that he considers important – on which he's been working for years, has finally been published by Laffont. Going through the copy I've just received, I make a thousand discoveries I'd never encountered before, though I do feel that we're going to be polarized over the twenty polemical articles against Resnais, Rohmer, Wenders, Pasolini, Godard; over the defences of Jacques Rozier, Gleb Panfilov, Syberberg, Salah Abou Seif and the Truffaut of *La Chambre vert.* The fact is, the book is intended to be subjective, personal, far from fashionable. It refuses any kind of dogma or doctrine.

To object to the book as a whole because of a few stentorian judgements (which I don't share) would be to forbid any subjective or partial approaches, which exist – in spite of pseudo-objective claims – in most historical books about cinema. It would be to ignore his intelligent analyses (of Guitry, Ory, Pagnol, Walsh, of genres like 'the comedy' which inspires him), the often-pertinent, sharp and stimulating approach to many films; the very intelligent refutations of Bazin's essays on *Citizen Kane*; the passionate defences of directors who are seldom studied, such as Hugo Fregonese (*Apache Drums*), Ritwik Ghatak, Stuart Heisler – although he omits Heisler's exciting *Among the Living*, very superior to *The Monster and the Girl* – Heinosuko Gosho, Mitchell Leisen, Raffaello Matarazzo. His study of Matarazzo's *Treno populare* makes you want to see the film. Expressing something like a rebirth of cinema with the coming of sound, *Treno populare* ingeniously brings together and harmonizes a number of characteristics of the cinema of the time.

Just as exciting are the rehabilitations of *Child of Divorce*, the first Fleischer, French comedies like *Un déjeuner de soleil*, the very amusing *L'Habit vert*, C. B. DeMille's *The Whispering Chorus*, the first two Devaivres, the defences of Dwan, Jacques Tourneur, Powell, Donen, Mizoguchi – all of which make you want to run out to the cinema.

5 May

After seeing the heartbreaking *Le Petit Prince a dit* by Christine Pascal, the first term that comes to mind is tragic limpidity: the clarity of the direction, the way it places the emotional trajectory of the characters in settings that are simple (a swimming pool, a doctor's surgery) or lyrical (vast mountain landscapes, a theatre stage) gives the feelings a density, creates true intimacy with the audience. There is no darkness, no despair in this chronicle of a death foretold, which, paradoxically, brings together a man and a woman; this education in pain which strangely opens out into a need for happiness. No fatalism, no resignation in this acceptance of the inevitable. As in the work of Kawabata, one is watching a quest for light, the rebirth of a kind of poignant, heartrending harmony, present from the opening shots. The little swimming girl coming out of school is filmed with an invisible mastery, an acute compassion, a refusal of self-pity. The characters in *Le Petit Prince a dit* – like Ida Lupino's heroines as defined by Jacques Lourcelles – 'need serenity, not like a luxury, but like a cure indispensable for their survival'.

Christine, whom I introduced as an actress in *L'Horloger de Saint-Paul*, and who was magnificent in *Que la fête commence*, and who I got to write her first screenplay (*Des enfants gâtés*) has already made three films, of which two, *Felicité* and *Zanzibar*, are exciting and very personal. Their harshness of tone, their narcissistic obsessions, the narrowness of their inspiration, their acuteness, gives them a unique place among films by women. Some shots, some scenes, are transfixing in what they say, in the intransigent force of their realization, in their refusal to play on charm. Uncomfortable, scorched and destructive works, they sometimes have trouble finding a centre. By filming always against the grain, Christine was dismembering her subjects, and some critics failed to see the momentary flashes of beauty.

Le Petit Prince a dit marks a step forward. Taking the side of her subject and her characters for the first time, her direction opens itself up to the world. Without ever losing her acuteness, she gains in light, in gentleness and consoling tenderness. 'When the eye is young,' d'Artagnan said severely, 'there are fibres that you must harden, and you are never really generous and good until the moment when the eye has grown hard and the heart remains tender.' Dumas did not know that in this sublime tirade in *The Vicomte de Bragelonne*, he was defining the cinema of Christine Pascal.

6–17 May

I leave for Cannes early this morning. The previous evening a friend of Simon's, Bruno Barde, had told me that his family would like me to deliver an eulogy at his funeral. Unfortunately I can't postpone my trip, because I have to address the people who run the Cinémas d'Art et d'Essai. The date, the sixth, has been fixed for a long time, and when I announce my decision to turn up later, it causes a general panic. Then Bruno asks me to write a piece about Simon. I spend part of the night writing it. I leave it at the café on the corner of the street as arranged.

You can't deliver a funeral oration over a friend's tomb. The words immediately seem hollow and bombastic. I'm unable to give an account of the grief, the terrible grief felt by everyone who knew and loved him.

It is three in the morning. I'm stumbling and groping my way through this text that your friends and relations have extracted from me, and that I'm starting for the tenth time for fear of not being up to it. Of being up to you, because you're watching me, Simon. You're reading over my shoulder, and I feel you're ready to cut out anything maudlin, fawning or smug – as you did when you came to see the first cut of my films or when I put forward ideas for the press kit. Yes, you're there, passionate, impatient. There are so many things to do. So many films to discover or help others discover. Just before you left the hospital to go back to your parents' house, the thing that most concerned you was that I should go and see Comencini's *Marcellino*, which you thought was sublime, as good as the last Skolimowski, 'which must get a release', you said on my answering machine a fortnight ago. How like you that message was, what a testimony to your refusal to capitulate, to yield to a disease that was eating you up, to go on defending, whatever the cost, a film that had excited you.

No, Simon, you've never changed since our first meeting at the beginning of the sixties. It could have been yesterday. You were leaving the shooting of *King of Kings*, and already you were fighting to communicate your admiration, your amazement when you discovered, and I quote, 'after coming down the red stairs of the MacMahon Cinema, the cinemascope Walshian plains, the little Ray houses under the snow'. Indifferent to fashion, you defended Riccardo Freda, Leo McCarey, Jacques Tourneur: I remember a severe row that we had about *The Battle of Marathon* and a reconciliation thanks to our shared love of Delmer Daves. Cinephilia in an ivory tower, the selfish manias of the collector, all that wasn't your style.

Your enthusiasms, your passions – you couldn't keep them to yourself; you had to share them and I've never known what caused you greater joy: discovering a film or helping others to discover it. It doesn't matter. What counts is that during your whole life you never forgot or stopped loving what you had loved, and you made the people around you love it too. How could I forget those long telephone conversations, those abrupt calls from some distant city just to tell me of your sudden love affair with a Boorman or a dramatic television film by Jerry Lewis that you thought had been shamefully misunderstood. In this world of cinema dominated by money, by the box office, I always knew you to be passionate and disinterested – ready to fight for everything that stirred you. So often you showed films, outside of your work, simply because you were fond of them. You never courted fortune or glory or fashion. You never knelt down to Power. On the contrary, you were ready to do anything to defend your ideas and I can still see you insulting an important journalist – at the risk of getting knocked down – because you thought him capable of showing indulgence to Jean-Marie Le Pen.

The list is endless, of all the film-makers who owe you something: their reputation, their rehabilitation, a better knowledge of their work. I'm not going to list all the films that you subtitled or got released, because I'm not here to teach a course in cinema. Rather, I'm here to talk about a man who moved something in the world and the history of the cinema around him, because, as Hugo said, 'he admired like a madman or like a child'. I'm here to talk about a man whose legendary lateness terrified me, with whom I've shared rages and laughter, and who can proudly say to anyone who asked him, as in Sugawara's poem: 'I carry my life.'

Simon, I can't find words that will be consoling to your parents, your brother and your sister who have been so wonderful that I envied you having them near you. Fortunate person with a family like that. And fortunate, too, the parents who have a son like that.

You see, I can't even talk about you in the past tense. You are such a whirlwind presence in my life, in my memories, in Paris, Cannes and Venice, where I can still hear you insulting the projectionist who couldn't get the film in focus. And then there are all those films that owe their existence to you, which bear your mark. As long as there are cinemas to show them, as long as there is even one viewer to see them, you will be there, fiery, alive, eternally present through those images and those sounds. 'How can you die when you can still dream,' said George Schéhadé.

During those last weeks, Simon, I've discovered your courage, your inner strength your serenity. We never talked about God or religion, at least not directly. From a sense of propriety, no doubt, or shyness. But now, I would really like God to exist so that you could introduce Him to your favourite directors, plead their cause and perhaps change His mind, or even persuade Him to show all the films that you haven't had the time or the opportunity to see. There's a task worthy of you. You must be the only person who could see it through.

I also know that you won't hold my absence against me this morning. I started out by defending the cinema that you love. You would surely have encouraged me to do that. So I don't feel I'm betraying you – on the contrary. I feel that you're with me, beside me.

What's the night like, Simon?

Bright.

On the plane an idea occurs to me. Why not put together, in a single volume, all the interviews published in his press files. Some of them are more than ten pages long, particularly the ones with Italian directors like Scola, Comencini, Dino Risi, Mario Monicelli, Francesco Rosi, Ferreri and Fellini, the latter before he had a row with them. It would be a coherent, exciting collection.

This is the first subject I talk about to the Association des Cinémas d'Art de d'Essai. I also suggest that Simon's name be given to a cinema in the Palais, or a space reserved for the journalists to whom he gave so much.

What a joy to be back in Cannes without having been selected, without any of the pressure and anxiety, purged of that feeling of competition that insinuates itself that is insinuated in you, in spite of yourself. Once again I have the pleasure I used to feel when I was a press attaché with Pierre Rissient, when we set out to find films and film-makers, both the ones we were concerned with and others, who were less well known and who hadn't had their films selected.

We have so much fun, Charlotte and I, that we decide to stay on for another five days: spending a moment with friends and acquaintances; following the Blake Edwards retrospective, which enables us to see *The Party* again, discover *Darling Lili* in the director's cut, distinctly shorter – which is extremely rare – than the version distributed by Universal: the film gains a great deal of rhythm, coherence and originality.

I had already seen, more than twenty years ago, a number of films by Mehboob (*Mangala Daughter of India*, *Mother India*), but the selection put forward by Pierre Rissient is a real shock which makes me want to go and look at his films.

A fascinating experience, after this, to see *Bob Roberts* by Tim Robbins, a fictional plot disguised as a documentary denouncing a fascist politician who hides behind a populist programme, and *Cousin Bobby* by Jonathan Demme, a real documentary about a very progressive priest. Two films that are anti-conformist even in their absence of nuances, very atypical of American cinema at the moment, two returns to the source, two reflections on the political commitment of the sixties that makes their directors very likeable.

In Competition we avoid the French films because of the tension provoked by absurd French polemics. The one around *Casanova* by Edouard Niermans is copiously fed by the debilitating and wounding declarations of Alain Delon, who declares that 'he taught the director how to make films', and erased from the screenplay 'everything about Voltaire'. But it would be cruel to compare the detective films that Delon's made and Nierman's bewitching *Angel Dust*, with the historical culture of the eighteenth century and that of Jean-Claude Carrière. In fact, we see it a few days later in Paris, and Delon's interpretation ruins the film by being overly biased towards the character, not really confronting him (unlike Mastroianni in *La Nuit de Varennes*) in his physical and moral decrepitude. Rather than relying on solemn and superficial effects, he should have tried to translate the culture, the spirit and the malice which survived in Casanova in spite of everything, and which he clearly hasn't worked on. It's depressing to see the suicidal ravages that pride, a lack of humour and a lack of humanity can wreak in an actor so gifted, often magnificent (*The Leopard*, *Monsieur Klein*, *Le Veuve Couderc*, *Rocco*, *Notre histoire*), in a man whose behaviour, as I have twice directly witnessed, has often shown astonishing loyalty. We might also be amazed at the selection of *Le Petit Prince a dit*, which will move many Anglo-Saxon critics to whom I've warmly recommended it.

Dazzled, on the other hand, by *Une vie indépendente* by Vitali Kanevski, a terrible and tumultuous torrent, the vertiginous description of a physical and moral hell. Jubilation at *The Player*, in which I find Robert Altman with his vitality intact, pigheaded, anarchic, sarcastic. Once again he's reborn, proving that he hasn't changed or lost his irony, his malice. A revitalizing example at this time of bland consensus. Severely disappointed by *Of Mice and Men* by Gary Sinise, a spick-and-span television film very inferior to the fine *Miles from Home*, turning, without any reticence whatsoever, a dated and over-rated novel into a campaign for commercials.

Bewitched, finally by the admirable *The Quince Tree Sun* by Victor Erice, a stunning essay about creativity, not without humour. The physical problems encountered by a painter (relationship with his tools, with light), become gauges, measurements like the ones with which Borges dotted his inquiries. It might be understandable if people are insensitive to his process, but making a terrible racket and leaving after ten minutes not only reveals a lack of taste, but an abject contempt for any artistic exploration. There were only about fifty of us left at the end. I hurried to congratulate Erice who was white as a sheet.

Charlotte found his wife crying in the toilets. Do people who behave like that realize that they're criminals, that they're acting, to quote Fellini, like a regiment of impatient cretins?

20 May

On my return from Cannes I try to return to this diary, after a fortnight's interruption. But I also have to supervise the press kit on *L 627* (as the first screenings for the monthly magazines start in a few days), check the trailer, take part in the activities of the Institut Lumière, programmes, editing a series of books devoted to French cinema, setting up a big exhibition that will finally do justice to the Lumière brothers, and which will mark the launch of the events celebrating the centenary of the first public cinema screening.

I also have to follow the battles being waged at SACD. We'll win the case in Brussels anyway, because of the directive on leasing rights. This victory makes the British, Dutch and German directors, against the will of their governments, into *authors*, enjoying the protection of moral right. This is a major first in the English-speaking world of cinema and audiovisuals. The American government was not slow to react. It violently denounced the agreement, which opened a breach in the copyright system, and, of course, it is threatening economic reprisals.

At the same time I'm continuing with three projects: *L'appât* written by Colo and based on an exciting and terribly violent news story, but one that would force me to work in Paris again, which is a trial; *Capitaine Conan*, which Jean Cosmos has adapted from the fine novel, formerly well-known (it won the Prix Goncourt in 1934) by Roger Vercel. I've discovered this magnificent screenplay, which will just need to be pruned and restructured for the cinema by Jean, who wrote it for television. He's been trying for years to get a response from the television channel executives, particularly the second channel. In vain. Even after being nominated for a César for *La Vie et rien autre*. After checking around a little, we realize that nobody had even bought the rights to the book, which we do immediately with Frédéric Bourboulon and his company, Little Bear. And we'll get Jean's rights back in a few months. In the meantime, the head of the public channels has been shouting: 'If there are authors in France, I'd like you to give me their names and telephone numbers.'

The third project, *Anywhere But Here*, written by Steve Tesich from a novel by Mona Simpson, had been sent to me by my agent Sam Cohn, who is also Steve's agent, almost three years ago. I'd been bowled over by it, but I'd run into two problems: the action takes place in Los Angeles, and I don't like that city, which always depresses me very quickly, and which has also been filmed a thousand times. But the main problem was that I had to deal with a finished script. I have always been the originator of my films, whether it has meant choosing a source novel or finding an original story. Even when working on another film, I tend to spend long months making notes, thinking about an angle of treatment, a concept for the adaptation that lets me get to the essence of the book I intend to film, to imagine its characters, visualize its setting. Yes, *imagine*, that's the word. What I need is to meander through a story, even before I begin to write. Maybe out of fear of laziness or to postpone the fateful moment. But the important thing for me is to be able to come and go freely within a plot, even if it means forgetting the models, *sending them home*, as Monet used to say, and just letting the images and ideas come, even if they're nowhere to be found in the work you're adapting.

In this way I constructed the screenplay for *L'Horloger de Saint-Paul* around a scene that seemed to me the key moment of the novel. It was only much later that Bost pointed out to me that the scene in question wasn't in Simenon's novel at all. I could have sworn it was! It's this very scene I spoke to the actors about in order to describe the spirit of the film. In fact, I had completely dreamed it up, fantasized about it. But it was Simenon who had got me dreaming, who had transmitted it to me. That scene was as much his as it was mine.

I let my characters grow inside me. But I only start to make their acquaintance when I begin writing the script. I want to get to know them, without robbing them of their mystery, so that they can surprise me later on the set, contradict me, foil my plans and preconceptions. But I want to know them well enough to make them want to confide in me. In return, I can make them share some of my own opinions and secrets. In fact, I need to make them feel at home since I'll be spending two or three years of my life with them. So when I'm given a finished manuscript, I feel useless, helpless. I feel like I'm circling around a house and don't know how to get inside. I can't find the key to the door. Besides, I have the feeling that its occupants can manage to live their lives without any help from me.

That's what happened to me at first with the Tesich screenplay. I ruminated over it for more than a year, after making Colo read it – she'd been enthusiastic. Then my producer, René Cleitman, made Tesich come to Paris and for a few days we worked and exchanged ideas (for what? as Prévert would say). I told him of my fears, my problems, the reservations I had about some scenes that were over-structured, over-written, over-plotty; events that I'd like to cut. I'd wanted to work with Steve for quite a long time – ever since our first meeting after a New York screening of *'Round Midnight*, which he had loved, and also since *Four Friends* by Arthur Penn, *Breaking Away* and *Eyewitness* by Peter Yates, three remarkable and original screenplays.

Since then, I've read all the different versions of *Anywhere But Here*, all good but less and less strong, less and less personal the more involved Disney became in the project. I annotated them all, as well as Mona Simpson's fine

novel, certain passages of which are as poignant as Carson McCullers. Tesich
kept only a part of the book, eliminating lots of characters, the whole provincial
past of the protagonists; his adaptation is brilliant. But while I accept Tesich's
approach, I want to put lines and scenes back in, to bring Wisconsin a little
more to life without ever showing it. I have found the back door and I begin to
settle myself in.

Among the old films I see, the most interesting are three Wellmans produced by Warners between 1930 and 1932: *Night Nurse*, *Safe in Hell*, *The
Hatchet Man*. Everything we wrote in *50 ans de cinéma américain* after the
discovery of *Heroes for Sale*, *Wild Boys of the Road* and *Other Men's Women* is
confirmed. This is one of the most creative, stimulating and misunderstood
periods of this director's life. Each film has a personal, unique tone, particularly *Safe in Hell*, which mixes an exotic atmosphere à la Somerset
Maugham, a symbolic fable and detective story that emerged from *Black Mask*
as if Jean Genet had enjoyed himself rewriting *Rain*. *Night Nurse* is a pared-
down, elliptical melodrama from which Wellman has erased all traces of
sentimentalism, all pity. Even as stupefying a plot as *The Hatchet Man*, in which
Edward G. Robinson plays a Chinese executioner and Loretta Young his
daughter, inspires a staggering first reel (the gang war in Chinatown), and an
ending, both of which are directorial triumphs.

I've always had a great fondness for Edmond T. Gréville, a fringe director
whose work, personal even at its most chaotic, is beginning to be rediscovered,
after long years of championing, a full quarter century after his death.
Refusing to follow fashion, his films reflect a stubborn faithfulness to certain
stylistic methods inherited from the silent cinema, a fascination for Stroheim
and Borzage, an attachment to an old-fashioned form of cosmopolitan romanticism, both sentimental and anarchist, a penchant for lyrical symbolism with
its echos of Griffith (the water-lillies in *L'Île au bout du monde*), and extravagant
moments in the manner of Stroheim and Buñuel, such as a scene in *Quand
sonnera midi*, where a statue of the Virgin Mary is beheaded by a spray of
machine-gun bullets and falls into a flowerbed, or Stroheim's Janus-like face
in *Menaces*, part of which was disfigured in the war and is covered by a mask.

It is a 'cinema of discontinuity', in which Gréville fragments even his best
films (*Pour une nuit d'amour*, *Noose*, *Remous*, *Le Diable souffle*), shattering them
with changes of mood and rhythm, juxtaposing moments of dated formalism
with some highly modern shots, daring visual ideas and dubious verbal puns,
constantly throwing in details that are alien to an often feeble plot. *Menaces* is
particularly revealing in the way it literally changes its manner depending on
the characters: lyrical and Hollywoodian when dealing with Mireille Balin
(who inspired Gréville for the film's most beautiful shot: the camera dollying in
on her face as she locks herself into a phone booth and begins talking, though
we can't hear the replies of the man she loves); expressionist with Stroheim;

pleonastic with Jean Galland, who is wretched in a sterling part; very 'thirties' French cinema with Paul Demange; and amazingly modern with Madeleine Lambert.

Thanks to David Meeker, I discovered *The Romantic Age* (1949), one of the British Grévilles hardest to see. Yet the plot – a young student makes a bet that she can seduce her professor to avenge herself on him – reveals all his themes and obsessions. But when choosing to adapt a novel by Serge Veber, *Collège de jeunes filles*, with its conventional, canny and predictable dramaturgy, Gréville renders it insipid and bloodless. And what makes matters worse, Mai Zetterling plays a depraved, French *ingénue*, complete with disastrous accent that transforms her into a kind of older sister to Inspector Clouseau. It saps the character of any eroticism and sexuality. Despite some clever framing, insert shots typical of Gréville, and two or three nice camera movements, it's impossible to take any sequence seriously. It's preferable to take another look at *Noose*, a highly stylish film noir, *Secret Lives*, a strange tribute to Sternberg, and *Brief Ecstasy* (1937), over which Graham Greene raved: 'Mr Greville knows that the story doesn't matter; it's the atmosphere which counts, and the atmosphere – of starved sexuality – is wantonly and vividly conveyed. Mr Greville learnt in France how to photograph a woman's body – uncompromisingly: every close up of Miss Linden Travers drives the sexuality home.'

I knew Gréville well in the early sixties. He was a pleasant and cordial cinema enthusiast who'd fallen on particularly hard times. Like Michael Powell, he was an exile from the modern cinema. On several occasions I had to lend him money even though I had very little then, and he always paid me back. He was always impeccably dressed. His English three-piece suits were somewhat threadbare, but you'd never hear a complaint out of him. He was constantly announcing projects, very few of which came into being – though by choosing to live on the Côte d'Azure (again, like Powell), in Haut de Cagnes, he effectively cut himself off from the world of cinema and producers.

With three friends – Bernard Martinand, Yves Martin and André Maginot – I had founded a film club called Le Nickel Odéon, where we held successful screenings of several of Gréville's films: *Le Diable souffle*, *L'Envers du paradis*, *Pour une nuit d'amour*. When Gréville died, he was so poor that we had to get up a subscription to pay for a cemetery plot, otherwise he'd have been put in a pauper's grave. Pierre Mazars, a journalist for *Figaro Littéraire*, heard about this and expressed his outrage in an article, which brought us a letter from René Clair, who had given Gréville one of the lead roles in *Sous les toits de Paris*. The letter was full of warmth and sorrow, and included a cheque. It was the only response from the film industry – and this after a career that had begun in the early thirties.

Apart from his films, Gréville wrote a number of books, including the brilliant and wonderfully dadaist *Supprimé par l'ascenseur* (1927) (which can be translated as *Death by Elevator*) and *Chantegrenouille (Frogsong)* (1930). The latter is an extravagant blend of autobiography, prose poem, and frenzied paean to the cinema. Here are two examples:

The next day, a fortnight of intense activity began for me. On the first day, I went to the movies. On the second day, I went to the movies. On the third day I went to the movies. On the fourth day I went to the movies. On the fifth day, I went to the movies. On the sixth day I went to the movies. On the seventh day I went to the movies. On the eighth day I went to the movies. On the ninth day I went to the movies. On the tenth day I went to the movies. On the eleventh day I went to the movies. On the twelfth day I went to the movies. On the thirteenth day I went to the movies. On the fourteenth day I went to the movies. On the fifteenth day, I passed my baccalaureate exams.

Hemmed in among inflexible, immovable words, what could one do? Give me film and a movie camera, that I may sing! Happy is the author who, so he may express his thoughts, can employ slow motion and rapid motion, close-ups, dissolves, the Shüfftan and Hall processes, 26 and 150 lenses, double exposure and optical effects! Tomorrow there will be sound, the day after, 3-D and colour, next week, television, and in a month's time his thoughts may take form on the screen, without the aid of film, but by means of psychic photography. All art will then become pointless, books and paintings will be burned on vast pyres that will turn the skies purple and all will be Cinema, Cinema, Cinema!

At the time of his death, Gréville had drafted more than two-thirds of his memoirs and had asked me to complete them. I had done the rounds of several publishing houses in vain. But I was young, unknown and didn't know how to go about it (I'm no better at it today, to judge from the many projects I still can't get going). Maybe the moment was premature.

At the end of a recently published interview, the critic Serge Daney launched what I took to be an SOS signal: 'If I were friends with Tavernier, I know he'd look after me.' I was never his friend, nor his enemy: he simply didn't exist for me. But these words affected me. Forgetting his shabby, blind savagings of *Coup de torchon* and *Un dimanche à la campagne*, I called him. Our conversation lasted for two-and-a-half hours. Conversation is hardly the word for it: it was more like a breathless, violent, jolting monologue, a heartbreaking farewell to cinema, an outpouring of bitterness and resentment. He ran down everything and everybody, raging against Serge July, 'who never raised a finger when Claude Berri sued me for defamation', against the *Cahiers du cinéma*, which didn't stand by him during the affair, against Michel Ciment, 'who grades your writings like some schoolteacher and with whom I refuse to have any contact'. Nor did he spare Rivette, 'an autist of feelings', or Godard: 'When he can come up with three shots as beautiful as those filmed by Boris Barnet in *By the Bluest of Seas*, he can consider himself happy.' But with me he suddenly became indulgent: 'Jean Michel Frodon asked me why I had attacked you so violently. I said that I didn't attack you, just that I didn't care for some of your films when I saw them. Maybe I'd change my mind now. It's not important ... maybe I was being too harsh. Especially when I see what Jean-Jacques Annaud and Claude Berri are doing. At least you're a film-maker, you think like a film-maker. The others make commercials.'

He assailed them with unusual violence and along with them an entire generation, which he cut down in a hail of curses. 'They sell their images as if they were cabbage leaves ... It's got nothing to do with cinema anymore.' So I'd earned a reprieve, a pardon almost. And then I listened as Billy Wilder, 'that clever carpet-dealer', got it in the neck. I tried to protest, to tell him that comedy wasn't his strong point, that he hadn't been fair to Capra and La Cava. I understood his pressing need, his passion, to shout when death was only a matter of days away, but I was sorry it always had to end in this kind of purge. We agreed to get together very soon, 'But only in the afternoon. I'm not decent before then.' This last remark came matter-of-factly, without self-pity, even with a touch of humour, like something said by a character in a Hawks movie.

21 May

After taking part with Michel Ciment in a broadcast on Ben Hecht, I rushed by taxi to Jean Devaivre's home in Saint Cloud. Seeing his first two films again filled me with curiosity about them, their director and his strange career. He immediately invited me to lunch along with Thierry Frémaux, who had welcomed him in Lyons to the Lumière Institute.

In the hot late-morning sun, the taxi dropped me off on the hill of Saint Cloud, in a tree-lined street pompously masquerading as an avenue. I had the impression of going back thirty years in time when, as a neophyte film critic, I had trailed after directors such as Melville, Fuller, Boetticher, Gréville and Powell to get interviews with them. This feeling was accentuated by the setting, a residential neighbourhood of timeless charm, complete with its tiny railway station and post office that looked like a provincial set designed by Max Douy for a fifties' movie. Because of the broadcast I was late. Worse – the latest mishap in my chronic messiness – I'd lost the street address. In moments such as these, I'm paralysed with shyness. I couldn't even find the courage to accost an Asian man, who cut an odd figure watering a flowerbed. After trying two houses without success, and exploring a deserted garden on the even-numbered side of the road, I crossed over to take my chances with the odd-numbered addresses. My first try was the right one: I was greeted by a man of medium height, stout, but looking younger than he was.

Despite my wanderings, I was the first to arrive. Thierry, who was picking up Charlotte on the way, came a quarter-hour later. It was cool inside. The shutters were half-closed. But the eye immediately picked out several magnificent paintings, including what seemed to be a Veronese. 'Yes, it is a Veronese, an original,' Devaivre told me. 'I'm not much on films, but I know a thing or two about paintings. I've often said to the folks at the Louvre that I could tell the authentic Veroneses from the ones painted by his disciples. And in a matter of minutes.' Charlotte studied another painting: a Rubens.

Seeing *La Ferme des sept péchés* again, I was struck even more than on my first viewing by its innovative tone, its blend of critical harshness and unusual lyricism. Right from the masterly opening sequence. Devaivre seems to set himself apart from the French cinema of the period. A rapid series of shots and short scenes bluntly establishes a number of contradictory viewpoints about the protagonist, the pamphleteer Paul Louis Courier, who is variously described as a miser, a blasphemer, a friend and defender of the poor and the oppressed, a profligate, a menace to public order, a revolutionary, an egotist, and no doubt destined to an early death. While a children's choir intones a sinister, premonitory chant (the shot of them is quite astonishing), the camera, in a wide-angle shot, follows a man walking through a forest. The choir ceases; the camera dollies in on the man, who swings around suddenly, staring into the camera, and with a dramatic half-smile, as if demanding silence, says: 'Don't speak about this in your families. Those are not tales to tell at night. It'd scare your children.' A few seconds later, woodcutters hear several shots. He has just been murdered. An impressive opening, announcing a vibrant and ambiguous movie in which passions seem to well up from nature, filmed with a dark, disquieting lyricism and a sense of breadth often lacking among French film-makers.

The opening of *La Dame de onze heures*, a kind of trailer intercut with shots of phantasmagoric marionettes, provides a no less spectacular prelude to a thriller, though less sombre and more casual. Despite the thematic differences, these two films share a number of characteristics: the spare narrative rhythm, the abundance of unusual stylistic details, the clean, precise, unaffected direction of the actors. Even rarer is the obvious pleasure the director takes in intentionally shattering the story into pieces, fragmenting the dramatic construction by increasing the number of viewpoints and shifts in tone. Sometimes in the same scene in *La Dame*, the camera suddenly becomes subjective, the characters address themselves to the audience. The description of Paul Louis Courier's character, full of passion and courage in the public arena, yet harsh and dour in private life, takes on an amazingly modern density.

After these two fine films, Devaivre's career declined sharply. He abandoned a genuinely baroque temperament for an anonymous craftsmanship devoid of the ambition, breadth, imagination and style of his first films. We heard a first explanation early during the fine lunch, which offered a nice, ostentatious surprise: a bottle of 1947 Burgundy – the year of *La Ferme des sept péchés*. The commercial failure of the film obliged Devaivre to get back on to the beaten track. In his later films, he controlled himself in order to woo producers and backers and never found any money for personal projects. Later that afternoon, he told us about his attempts to mount productions of *The Desert of the Tartars* or *The Collapse of the Maliverna* by Dino Buzzati, and a film on the life of Mozart, written in a musical form.

He seemed astonished that there could still be any interest in him. 'I dropped out of the film world thirty-one years ago,' he kept repeating, 'and I haven't set foot in a cinema since.' Yet what memories he had! Yes, he had re-cut *Boudu Saved from Drowning*, which couldn't find a distributor, and had excised more than twenty minutes without ever seeing Renoir. He also directed three key scenes in *La Main du diable* (1943), replacing Maurice Tourneur, whose assistant he was: 'He was totally distraught because his wife, who had an American passport, had been interned in a detention camp at Vittel. He asked me to replace him for the sequence of the final judgement and the scene when Roquevert sells the hand to Fresnay. I think it's the best thing I ever directed.' At the time, Devaivre went to work for Continental-Film, a production company set up in France by the Germans on the advice of Jean-Paul Le Chanois, the future scriptwriter of *La Dame de onze heures*. Both were members of a Resistance cell, Le Chanois arguing that they were safer hiding in the lion's den. Devaivre worked with Tourneur (on *Cécile est morte*, a Simenon adaptation), Richard Pottier, and André Cavatte, for whom he prepared the shooting script of *Au bonheur des dames*. Then, one day, Jean-Paul La Chanois was arrested. Fifteen minutes later Devaivre left Tourneur, his papers, his pen, the Continentale and fled Paris to escape the Gestapo, made it to England and parachuted back into France where he had several narrow scrapes with death.

Leaping back and forth among his memories, he revealed new vistas on French film history, and regaled us with portraits, anecdotes and trenchant opinions. He clearly preferred Duvivier to Renoir, like many directors of his generation. He described the unusual genesis of the script for *La Ferme*, which had been suggested by an academic, René Méjean, who was living in Paul Louis Courier's house, and his months of research at the Bibliothèque Nationale. When I mentioned the children's chorus of the opening scene, he said that he had wanted to make 'the words well up out of the ground, as if they were emanations of the earth'.

He even showed us his editing room (he wrote, produced and edited most of his films), which was in his garden: piles of cans with barely legible labels. Editing tables, synchronizers, including one for the Soviet kinopanorama, all getting rusty. All this half-buried in the grass. Tons of hopes and memories. I throw a glance at Charlotte: she's as moved as I am.

Just before leaving, Jean Devaivre's wife, who had been his production manager, suddenly joined the discussion as we struggled to make sense of his filmography. 'Listening to you now, I realize that I was the one who prevented Jean from making personal films. The failure of *La Ferme* really scared us. I knew he was ready to start again on other projects, just as daring and risky.

That's all he cared about and I held him back. Yes, I see that I wasted his talent.' The confession was poignant. With considerable tact, Charlotte sets things right: 'I wouldn't call making two first-rate films like *La Dame* and *La Ferme* wasting talent.'

As he accompanied us to our taxi, Jean confided, 'Today I understood that I blew my career. I could have done so much better. I missed out.' We protested: what counts is what we succeed in doing, not what we fail to do. He smiled.

23 May

Triumphant reissue of John Cassavetes' films. I went back to see *Minnie and Moskowitz*; it's one of his warmest, most optimistic films, and the most continually imaginative as well, but a second viewing of *The Killing of a Chinese Bookie* was something of a disappointment. I had a memory of something more plangently charming and less repetitive.

24 May

At the Lumière Institute we've decided to pay tribute to Marcel Ophuls, which hasn't been done before in France. Thierry Frémaux had to deploy all his energy and resourcefulness to dig up certain films, literally abandoned by their producers or buried in theatrical feature film and television catalogues whose owners seem to care not a jot about the responsibilities attendant on the rights they've acquired: i.e. to give the films new commercial life in theatres, restore the negatives, indeed, find out where they are. After great effort, and in spite of the unwillingness of INA, we found all the films. Thierry even managed to lay his hands on a documentary on Matisse which Ophuls himself had believed lost.

I go down to Lyons to introduce the admirable *A Memory of Justice*, which shamefully remains unseen on French television, which preferred to air the painfully demagogic *De Nuremberg à Nuremberg* made by Frédéric Rossif. A huge success. Thierry even has to organize an extra showing. For the discussion, we were joined by a judge whom I admire greatly, Pierre Truche. He was the prosecutor in the Klaus Barbie trial, and was also instrumental in the indictment of Touvier, as well as of Ted Turner in the *Asphalt Jungle* colorization affair. I appreciate the fact that an adversary of Nazism and collaboration is also a defender of film-makers and authors' rights. I'd even go so far as to say that it's normal, that in these three cases it's a question of a battle for dignity against those who trample that dignity.

The discussion was excited and exciting. The Ophuls–Truche exchanges dazzled with their intelligence, brio, and lucidity, further illuminating the topicality of *A Memory of Justice* and *Hotel Terminus*, pointing up the responsibilities of political institutions in attempting to define 'crimes against humanity', and dissecting the attitude of French justice *vis à vis* collaboration and Nazism. I was sorry that no Paris journalists or Lyons politicians had attended. But Ophuls was delighted. The retrospective was also a chance for me to see *A Sense of Loss*, an inquiry into the tragedy of Northern Ireland, also unseen in France. The tone is just as personal and clear-eyed, though it lacks the scope and power of the *Sorrow/Memory/Hotel* trilogy. Still, the same keen sensibility presides, especially in the overwhelming final sequences.

25 May

In my letterbox, an envelope addressed to 'Bernard' Tavernier. Inside, an invitation from the President of the Republic for a dinner with Mrs Mary Robinson, the President of the Republic of Ireland. A few hours later, Charlotte receives a phone call from the chief of protocol at the Elysée Palace. A whole battery of secretaries deal with her and then she is finally put through to a dignified lady, very polite but extremely aggravated. Using a repertory of paraphrases and precautions, she asked Charlotte if I had received the president's invitation. Confirmation only reinforces her agitation. She begins to explain that there has been a dreadful mistake, a mix-up in names: 'That invitation was meant for a deputy named Tavernier. So you must tell Mr Bertrand Tavernier not to come to this dinner ... It would create huge problems. But he mustn't feel annoyed. There will be other invitations.' And she begins to enumerate to Charlotte (who could barely keep from laughing) all the visitors planned in the future: 'There will be the Queen of England ... the Queen of England is truly fine ... even more important than the President of Ireland ...' She excitedly goes on with her overblown descriptions of upcoming festivities, constantly repeating that I mustn't feel annoyed. 'I had the impression,' Charlotte tells me afterwards, 'that I was dealing with some suburban bourgeoise explaining to her provincial cousin that she couldn't be invited to the next "bash", but that there would be bigger and better ones.'

I hadn't known that I had a namesake among the deputies. He certainly hasn't attracted any attention. So I won't be dining with Mary Robinson. A shame! I had met her in Dublin during a homage to John Boorman and had found her highly likeable and intelligent. I naturally thought that my invitation was the result of that occasion.

I devour Jean Perol's magnificent essay 'New Orleans', in the *Cities* collection published by Champs Vallon. As beautiful and accurate in its breathless, autobiographical lyricism as was his earlier essay, 'Tokyo'. I love reading descriptions such as these:

Thus New Orleans, standing on unsteady water-soaked ground that was more often swamp than earth, hemmed in between a body of water more stagnant than neglect and a body of water more torrential than oblivion, had managed, despite soil, climate, fever, repudiation and the winds of war, to gradually build itself, to rise up to become this captivating city as few others have managed to be, to become one of these affectionately unforgettable cities. Frivolous, capering, sorrowful . . .

Reading these two works I felt the same deep emotion that I had experienced with Gilles Lapouge's *Equinoxiales*.

27 May

Thierry Frémaux receives a very warm and friendly note from Marcel Ophuls, whose epistolary manner is usually more acid and devastating. Ophuls is the grand master of vindictive fax messages and mercilessly pungent missives, which he shoots off at the slightest provocation (never forgetting to send copies to friends). That's the way he is and that's just what his enemies hold against him. Ophuls is like a live wire, fiercely thin-skinned, always refusing to put up a show of good will or patience towards what he considers stupid or unjust. He sniffs out arse-kissing, the way a dog sniffs out truffles. True, given the violence of some of his tirades, he at times hits the wrong target or devastates everything around him. He's never been one for dosing his explosives with an eye-dropper. I have to admit I love his outbursts, his kind of often reckless passion, even when I happen to be his victim as president of the SRF.

Thierry and I would even like to publish his correspondence under the title *Letters Nasty and Very Nasty*. It would add up to a frenzied indictment of everything that threatens us, since Ophuls spares nothing and no one. His long, violent faxes contain graphic descriptions of the public services in decline; the scandalous ascendancy of politicos over the audiovisual sector; the lackeys of the Elysée Palace and the toadies of the RPR party, 'whose only mutual characteristic is their monumental incompetence', who facilitate this ascendancy; the corruption of minds and values; the corrupt old-boy system introduced by Mitterrand; attacks against artists' rights, moral rights and the 'final cut'.

Ophuls does not spare himself in this critical undertaking. Shaken by moments of violent self-doubt, he constantly flagellates himself, defending his work, then violently tearing it apart in order to dream of some highly ambitious, romantic and exciting project. How many times have I seen him ready to abandon a project or book. During the weeks preceding the release of *Hotel Terminus*, the recording on his answering machine begged journalists not to come to any private screenings, because the film was null, a failure, devoid of interest. Astonishing, isn't it.' And rare.

I reread Simon Leys, one of the major political writers with V. S. Naipaul and Jean François Revel, who invites comparison with George Orwell (about whom Leys wrote a monograph). His keen, scathing, analytical denunciations of Maoism and the servitude of Western intellectuals faced with this bloody and senile dictatorship in such works as *Ombres chinoises* (*Chinese Shadows*) and *Les Habits neufs du Président Mao* (*President Mao's New Clothes*) have lost none of their topicality. It shouldn't be forgotten that Leys was once accused of being a CIA agent by a number of writers who are today in vogue. I remember the delight I felt when, as a guest on the literary talk show *Apostrophe*, he destroyed, napalmed and reduced to nothing that worthless, loud-mouthed Maoist blue-stocking, Maria Antonietta Macciochi, whose smugness, monstrous errors and criminal ignorance Leys laid bare with a few quotes and revelatory examples. Leys' recent writings (*La Fôret en feu, L'humeur, l'honneur, l'horreur*) adopt a less violently polemical tone, preferring to dwell on Lu Xun and Victor Segalen, analyse the verse of Wang Zihuan, or study the attitude of the Chinese towards their past. But he's lost none of his fierce lucidity and proves it in incisive essays on the Tiananmen Square massacre, Father Ladany's newsletter, *China News Analysis*, or an hilarious riposte to Alain Peyrefitte. He displays the same acid humour in a short novel, *Le Retour de Napoléon* (*The Return of Napoleon*), which certainly would have excited Borges.

29 May

Another phone conversation with Serge Daney, to whom I sent my *50 ans de cinéma américain*. He thanked me and added, 'I had to lay it on the table to read it because I haven't the strength to pick it up.' No self-pity. He told me about a surprise visit from Pierre William Glenn, the director of photography on my first eight films. We set a date to get together soon.

31 May–2 June

A brief trip to Barcelona, followed by a lightning visit to Valencia for a double retrospective of my films organized by the cinémathèques of these two cities. For the occasion, several critics published a collective volume edited by Esteve Montalban and Casimirio Torreiro. It contains an essay by Manuel Vasquez Montalban, a Catalonian writer I admire enormously. His famous creation is the food-loving private detective, Pepe Carvalho – lover of pancakes, pork trotters with garlic mayonnaise, marinated partridge – who stokes his fireplace with volumes of classical literature.

Warm, enthusiastic, generous reception. Enjoyed an exciting walk around Barcelona, in the midst of pre-Olympic Games effervescence; Esteve said the games would put the city in debt for a good ten years. Discovered the Sagrada Familia church, Antonio Gaudí's extravagant reverie, unfinished because of his megalomania, and representative of the expiatory summits attained by this mythomaniacal artist.

Exciting discussion with Catalonian film-buffs and critics, who are struggling against the dictatorship of American distributors, who want to relegate Spanish films to television so that they can have greater control of the cinemas. It's not some secret whim, but a goal trumpeted by official declarations: 'Stop making movies. From now on, we will make them for you because we are better' has become the official message.

7–22 June

Two-week holiday. My first in three years. I decide to go down to the Sacquèdes, a house near Sainte-Maxime that my father had built just before the war. For thirty years, my sisters and I used to spend our holidays here. Out on a stroll that morning, I none the less feel a bit lost and disoriented in this landscape so familiar to me, yet suddenly so unfamiliar. I discover the reason for this uneasy feeling only the next day: on the other side of the valley a golf course had been built, the twelfth at least along the 50 kilometres of coast separating Saint Raphael from Cavalaire. The developers had an entire hill dynamited to make two artificial hillocks and flattened other areas. I'm told each of these golf courses consume as much water as a city of 200,000 inhabitants, and this at a time when everyone's talking about the threat of drought. And, insinuate the mischief-makers (as well as the irreverent *Canard enchaîné* weekly), the golf courses constitute a means by which the Italian Mafia are moving into the *Côte d'Azure*.

A fortnight of walking, swimming and relaxation without seeing a single film or video. A fortnight to enjoy a reading cure. Scripts, of course, which I selected from the cupboard where I pile them up, but also books, such as Dominique Noguez's riotous and exciting *Les Derniers jours du monde*. I also dip generously into my father's eclectic personal library. I came across anthologies of René Char's poetry, stories by Marcel Aymé, as well as Nelson Algren's *Never Come Morning*, Ben Hecht's *A Jew in Love*, and Henri Guillemin's essential, penetrating essays on Rousseau and Lamartine.

Nils and Valerie come down with my grandson, Jordan, with whom I can now spend some time. Overcoming my clumsiness and shyness, I take him in my arms and even give him his bottle. A real cutie. Valerie, ever the mother hen, clucks over him at the slightest cry and pampers him. I am also very touched by Nils, who seems very close to his son. We spend four very calm and gentle days together. Charlotte finally arrives, numb from an Egyptian promo tour for a educational series on the teaching of French that she made six years ago and which is an enduring success. She's just spent three weeks in the dust with the temperature never dropping below 45 degrees in the shade.

News of Serge Daney's death reaches me at Sainte-Maxime. Godard paid him tribute with a beautiful article. I find the deluge of homages disproportionate. Daney was a brilliant but falacious thinker, a victim of his prejudices, sarcastic and dictatorial, who was right even when he was wrong – a typical characteristic of the French intellectual, as Simon Leys has demonstrated. As a film critic, he was often wrong, often with brio, especially during his Maoist phase. He underrated Kubrick, Scorsese, Altman, Coppola, Woody Allen and many others. Contrary to someone like Etiemble, who reckoned a good critic's margin for error was 50 per cent, Daney never became more humble for that. He would define the kind of cinema he loved, but then champion films that were the very opposite, panning those which in fact applied his theories. His obsession with general ideas, with categoric definitions, made his articles resemble Calvinist firebrands or five-year plans. But he was a brilliant analyst on the subject of television, the media and images. He was a pioneer, exploring the subject without reference to anyone. This gave him an intellectual freedom he never really had when writing about cinema. Too much clannishness, too many shadows, rejections. In his truly outstanding series of articles on the Gulf War, he managed to produce a real social and moral X-ray. I kept thinking of Philippe Boucher's 'Journal d'un amateur', a Friday column in *Le Monde*. No small compliment, that. We'd had a kind of reconciliation in the end, and I'd been touched by what he said and wrote about *La Guerre sans nom*. I'm sure he would have appreciated *L 627*.

On 17 June Charlotte leaves to return to Paris, where she has some screen tests to do for Kieślowski. First windfall of *L 627* for her. Eva Simonet, a warm and first-rate press attaché, called to say that the first press screenings, for the monthly periodicals, were going very well.

23 June

First interviews for *L 627* with two journalists from *La Revue du cinéma*, who are visibly uncomfortable with the film's subject matter, the attention lavished on police officers, the high number of black dealers. Their painfully predictable, disheartening and conformist reactions betray an incomprehension of life, a theoretical view of social realities, a rejection of any uncomfortable complexities, a submission to the dictatorship of the politically correct. By their questions and especially in the way they avoid looking at, questioning or listening to Michel Alexandre, I know we are in for a rotten article. I can predict that my directing will be compared unfavourably to the long takes of so-and-so, that my dialogue will be considered too stunning, when in fact it's all true to life. Prefabricated critical opinions.

24 June

I show *A Matter of Life and Death* to Charlotte on the evening of her birthday. She's thrilled, knocked out by it. And once again, I share the same feeling of wonder. What breathtaking audacity in the shifts in tone and style: the film moves from fantasy to realism, from satire to romance, from reverie to documentary literalness. And what narrative nerve, right from the start with a superb tracking shot through the Milky Way, and that opening line: 'This is the Universe! Big, isn't it?'

Fresh re-viewings of this and other Powell–Pressburger films made between 1939 and 1950 provide a better understanding of the limitations of someone like Michael Balcon. Like them, he was concerned with rooting his films in a cultural and national context, but he lacked their keen sense of curiosity about the world at large. And their vision. A little like David Putnam today, Balcon seems to have undervalued the importance of the director, who for him was little more than a narrative technician, a dependable journeyman of variable talent who could easily be recruited from among his film editors – not a creative artist who could leave a personal mark on a film (that would have been as impolite as talking about politics). Hence his uneasiness with Robert Hamer, Alberto Cavalcanti, Alexander Mackendrick, the most imaginative of the Ealing directors. Camouflaged during the war by his energy, stubborness and a sense of commitment that corresponded perfectly to the concerns of an entire nation, his narrow-mindedness, as well as his terror of female characters and any sexual content, condemned him to turning out increasingly vapid comedies, increasingly abstract and hollow war films, which finally were to be his undoing.

25 June

Phone conversation with Carole, the woman cop on whom Charlotte's role was based. She was moved during the screening and cried at the end: 'Not only because it was real or because it's our life. But there was something else. What really hurt was this feeling, this impression of non-communication between people that the film showed so strongly. I was never aware of that before. While I was watching the film I realized that I'd spent years working with colleagues and that there was nothing to show for it. Yet we'd spent whole nights together on stakeouts and were never out of each other's sight. When I add it up, all that's left are two or three buddies, no more. It's as if the others never existed. Discovering all that waste really devastated me. My mum still has the same girlfriends from work. When you make friends in a factory it's for life. Why is it like that? And how did you manage to get all that? It wasn't in the script.'

26 June

Show *A Matter of Life and Death* to Tiffany. Another believer.

27 June

In the evening, Arnaud Desplechin's *La Sentinelle* turns out to be a fabulous, thrilling experience. It has greater breadth and suppleness than his *La Vie des morts*. The reviews I'd read had led me to expect something neo-Carax, another one of those films full of self-important puffery, which tips off the viewer on how to read its poetic ambitions and narrative disruptions, not unlike the way certain cities post signs along the highway publicizing their landmark attractions. I hadn't been prepared for a work of such mysterious density and control, with its curiosity about life and the world. The narrative movement of *La Sentinelle* remains concrete and precise – if we care to pay attention – even when it goes off on some phantasmagoric tangent. Exposition and narrative details are never dramatized. We pick them up in the midst of a social exchange or in a detail from modern life. We chance upon a state secret, a political plot.

Desplechin shows that he can be just as concrete as Balzac when it comes to describing a daily job: the state of mind, the caste mentality of a profession, the financial rapport and work relationships. He also knows how to shift tones, notably in the delightfdul scenes of romantic *marivaudage* with the triumphant Emmanuelle Devos, and he introduces us to a dozen outstanding new actors. The only reservation: a tentative and confusing finale, piling up pseudo-enigmas and overly elliptical explanations, as if Desplechin were suddenly reining in a theme that seems to cry out for an apocalyptic lyricism in the manner of *Kiss Me Deadly*.

28 June

Another three scripts in the post this morning. A fourth arrives later by Federal Express. They're either projects being submitted to me, or treatments on which I'm asked to give an opinion. I choose a few from the huge pile invading my cupboard and make some stunning discoveries. One particularly thick manuscript begins with this unforgettable phrase: 'Son of a Cardinal and a highly talented Cover Girl!' Another script borrows the premise of René Fallet's novel *Soupe aux choux* – aliens from outer space landing in a field – but the tenth line, where the farmer runs to warn his family 'of 450 members' (sic), stops you dead in your tracks. In a similar vein, a couple of actors list, among their hobbies, 'striking gongs and swallowing swords'.

During a stimulating phone conversation, I learn that as a result of *La*

Guerre sans nom, the Algerians are requesting that Patrick Rotman and I make a similar film telling their side of the story. It would mean dredging up a lot of suffering and sacrifice and refuting plenty of untruths: such as the one million martyrs that historians today bring down to 350,000, at least half of whom where killed by other Algerians. Indeed, this Algerian war was really an atrocious double civil war: the nationalists of the MNA (National First Algerian Movement) vs the rebels of the FLN, moderates vs communists, maquisards vs soldiers of the Tunisian army.

30 July

Back to Paris after more than three weeks in the US combining work and holiday. Before giving a green light to René Cleitman to buy the rights to the script *Anywhere But Here* from Disney, I wanted to be sure that Steve Tesich and I were on the same wavelength. Since he lives in Denver, we decided to meet in Beaver Creek; that way I could show Charlotte the magnificent Colorado mountains, which she'd seen only briefly two years before. I brought my notes, my annotated copy of the novel and the different script versions with my own comments. René came with us. I wanted him to meet Dianne Wiest, the brilliant actress seen in Woody Allen's films and Tim Burton's splendid and underrated *Edward Scissorhands*. Steve wrote the lead part for her, which I thought was a great idea.

When you get to know Sam Cohn a bit, you have the feeling that he can't do without New York any more than New York can do without him. They both run at the same rhythm, experience the same moments of excitement and depression. Going to see this cordial, good-hearted and messy human cyclone – who also happens to be my American agent – means exposing yourself to: standing in your stockinged feet while your shoes get shined; getting a shave; meeting brilliant writers and film-makers; leaving with invitations to shows he thinks are something awful but which should be seen; speaking on the phone with Woody Allen; lunching at the Russian Tea Room, where you end up meeting Sam Cohn's other clients, such as Hume Cronyn, in the company of Jessica Tandy, naturally.

That morning he gives us seats to *Guys and Dolls*, a plodding, academic production devoid of any imagination. Like most of what I saw on Broadway. It's as if any personal vision or flights of fancy has been banished in favour of glossy professionalism and cramped naturalism. How old-fashioned and pro-vincial these productions look at a time when we have Roger Planchon, Giorgo Strehler, Patrice Chéreau, Peter Brook, Marcel Maréchal, even alongside postwar glories such as Jean Vilar and the Berliner Ensemble.

Later we have dinner with Sam and Dianne Wiest, whom I found adorable and unsure of herself. She must have felt she was being put through a test for

René Cleitman, which only reinforced her shyness. She only took part in the conversation when the topic turned to Freud and psychoanalysis.

I see her alone the next day, at the hotel. She is much more relaxed and we spend a couple of hours discussing the script, the conception of the role, her relation with Woody Allen and Tim Burton, her theatre work. I feel she could be fantastic.

I also wanted to meet the author of the book, Mona Simpson, who seemed surprised by my interest and declares how much she had enjoyed 'Round Midnight and La Vie et rien d'autre, which she'd seen three times. I talk to her about some suggested cuts and additions in the script, which she admires. She seems to accept my suggestions enthusiastically and approves my attitude to the characters and the style the film ought to have.

Not many videodisks at the RKO store on Broadway, but some interesting cassettes, such as Capra's outstanding Platinum Blonde, and Ramrod, a sombre, rather formalistic André de Toth western, graced with magnificent exteriors and female characters who dominate the action. At the Virgin store, on the other hand, a sale of videodisks. Among other things, I buy the restored version of The Sea Hawk, a few titles in the superb Criterion collection, always full of surprises (Blimp and Black Narcissus presented by Powell and Scorsese, George Sidney's Scaramouche), Letter from an Unknown Woman, the magnificent Umberto D (unavailable in France and Italy), The 49th Parallel, The Seven Samurai. I show René Cleitman the huge number of French films you can find here (including four of my own) which you can't find in France. But nothing was as odd as the double-bill of two amazingly obscure and low-budget westerns, Alan Dwan's The Restless Breed (which has an odd decorative charm) and Edwin L. Marin's The Cariboo Trail, which makes you wonder how it ever ended up on videodisk.

René had planned to come with me to Colorado, but since he was producing a film by Yolande Zauberman that was being shot in the Ukraine, political events and accidents on the set obliged him to get back to Paris immediately.

Beaver Creek is a small ski resort, located at an altitude of 2,000 metres in the Rocky Mountains. Charlotte, an experienced skier, is full of admiration for the beauty and the diversity of ski slopes, the way in which natural resources and the forest are splendidly conserved, unlike France. For two weeks, I work on the script of Anywhere But Here, either alone or with Steve. The rest of the time, we wear ourselves out on intoxicating walks, climbing as high as 3,200 metres. Even at these heights, we come across red-faced, pop-eyed cyclists. Bicycling seems quite popular in Colorado and the local TV station devoted a good deal of coverage to the Tour de France to Steve's delight. These remain the only televized images we have of France. Or of Europe, for that matter – apart from a few shots of the Pope.

Working with Steve is a real pleasure. He is open, alert, amenable, attentive to the feelings of the characters and ready to give them prominence over action. He even looks relieved when I suggest we take things even farther by cutting the narrative twists and dramatic surprises, minimalizing the plot and letting it take a back seat to the characters. I wanted to find the same narrative freedom of *L 627*, *Un dimanche à la campagne*, *Une semaine de vacances*. He is also quick to agree to cutting all the scenes of the teenagers at school, which we'd seen a hundred times in films and which I wouldn't have been able to direct. During lunch, I get him to talk about politics (he wrote a superb, virulent article on the Gulf War for the *Nation*), about his relationship with America, about the situation in his native Yugoslavia, which was a dreadful tragedy for him (he was twelve when he arrived in America). I like what I hear. After a week of work, he goes back to Denver, full of enthusiasm. He takes my copy of the novel, with the scenes and dialogue I wanted to put back into the script, one of my annotated copies of the script, and several pages of notes. I thought he was going to come with me to Los Angeles to show me the places he described, but the idea didn't seem to please him. I ask him to send the new version, scene-by-scene, to Paris. 'Impossible,' he said. 'When I write, I have to go all the way.' I'm a bit disappointed. As I've noted before, I have to see the script being born, think over each scene, come up with ideas, changes that could affect what follows, before anything begins to fall into place and find its definitive form.

During these few days, Steve remains an enigma to us. Charming, thrilling, and enigmatic. At about the same time each day, he'd disappear to join his wife and daughter, who live in the village and whom we never saw. But I'm used to the strange behaviour of American scriptwriters, having been vaccinated by the eccentric habits of my friend David Rayfiel, my marvellous collaborator on *Deathwatch* and *'Round Midnight*.

In the evening, we watch the Republican Convention on television, a monument to smug vulgarity, stupidity and dishonour. Hard to tell which is more irritating: the base attacks on adversaries or the self-satisfaction. I watch an interview with a young black rapper, who raged against the wealthy, the racists, the powerful, the Establishment, the cops, and then declared he was voting for Bush.

I also hear director Allison Anders state that before writing to Wim Wenders, she had rejected anything that seemed old and outdated to her, jazz for example. I feel sorry for her for missing out on the refreshing excitement and the youthful energy you find in the lyrical flights of Thelonius Monk, Bud Powell, Miles Davis. I know plenty of people who have come out with remarks like that, only to then fall into raptures (thanks to Jim Jarmusch) over John Lurie, the modern adaptor of Paul Barbarin and Maxim Saury.

I am astonished to discover the AMC (American Film Classics) network, with its non-stop airing of often rare black and white films, in superb prints and without a single commercial break. We watch at least two a day. At first, I am thrown by the trailers, which give the East Coast times, so I end up missing *Whispering Smith*, a western with Alan Ladd, whose photos I'd seen in the classic French comic strip 'The Little Sheriff' more than thirty-eight years ago, and who I have wanted to see ever since.

Among the notable films of these fifteen days is John Farrow's *The Big Clock*. Its narrative and visual mastery impresses me even more than the first time I saw it. I'm angry with myself for not having praised it enough in *50 ans de cinéma américain*, especially Jonathan Latimer's intelligent adaptation of the Kenneth Fearing novel (translated into French by Boris Vian) and its sharp dialogue. Gordon Wiles's *The Gangster* is another underestimated *film noir*: also superbly written, by Daniel Fuchs from his fine novel, it concerns the last days of a small-time hood (Barry Sullivan in a classic performance) who loses his territory to a more powerful rival organization. No hope, no suspense, in this chronicle of a downfall foretold, which rejects or inverts most of the genre archetypes and conventions. The hero is negative, the action is minimal, overshadowed by the oppressive atmosphere, the only twists being those founded on failure. No vamps or castrating females; for once, women aren't the instruments of the downfall. They have no baleful influence or destructive power; on the contrary, they try to counter the obsessional fantasies and suicidal stubbornness of the men who rush towards their doom. Wiles's stylish direction smoothly dramatizes each set, doing wonders with an undoubtedly small budget.

Mitchell Leisen's *To Each His Own* is one of the underestimated highlights of melodrama, with an admirable performance by Olivia de Havilland. Here's a quintessential model of the genre, which it respects even as it renews and transcends it by avoiding the moral and social stereotypes it derives from. In his best films, Leisen's talent consists of establishing the right distance – a matter of taste, intuition, experimentation – with the material and finding a delicate balance between elements. It's just this brittle quality, along with the sense of perspective, that gives so many of his films (*Hold Back the Dawn, Arise My Love, Frenchman's Creek, No Man of Her Own*) their originality, their dreamy confidentiality. The way he directs his actresses holds its own with Cukor.

On the other hand, because of the late hour and the commercial cuts, I don't have the strength to sit through all of Rudolph Maté's *No Sad Songs for Me*. It's a film written by Howard Koch about which Truffaut and Godard wrote enthusiastic reviews. I'm struck by the restrained tone, the rightness of the performances of Margaret Sullavan, Wendell Corey and Vivecca Lindors, and by the rejection of the classic shot/reverse shot shooting technique. I write to Robert Parrish, who had been supervising editor, to find out if this stylistic decision was taken by Maté, Koch or himself.

I devoured Joseph McBride's fascinating Capra biography, very well documented but highly debatable.* Exploiting the omissions, errors and boastful declarations he's singled out in Capra's memoirs (and which are typical of all autobiographies), McBride takes a very biased, often underhand approach to the director's life and work. He comes up with some quite exciting revelations, but interprets them in a much too methodical way, constantly applying the same pattern, forever suspecting the director of *Mr Smith Goes to Washington* of the worst intentions without providing adequate proof. He goes out of his way to argue that Capra's screenwriters were the true authors of his films, after showing how Capra minimized their contributions. But no more or less than most directors do in their memoirs or interviews. Less so, in fact, than Hawks, with whom McBride conducted a book-length series of interviews in which the question is never even brought up. The influence of Riskin on Capra was considerable, as McBride rightly establishes. But the inverse is also true: without Capra, Riskin's personality faded and he virtually wrote nothing more of interest, least of all of a politically committed nature. Yet McBride arbitrarily hails him as Capra's social conscience. How then do you explain *The Bitter Tea of General Yen* and *Mr Smith Goes to Washington*, which Riskin didn't write? And it's a fact that Sidney Buchman rarely wrote a film that had the force and control of *Mr Smith*.

Rather than go hunting for the flukes and opportunism in all of Capra's choices, it seems to me to be fairer to give him credit for the genuine critical and anarchistic objectives that drove him towards collaborators who were mostly liberal or left-leaning (Swerling, Buchman, Trumbo), and which became confused with populist yearnings.

It is also worth pointing out that the rapport between scriptwriter and director – especially in the case of Riskin, Buchman and Capra – is more mysterious and complex than the relationship described by McBride, who has a tendency to establish creativity percentages, only taking into consideration the tangible proof: the number of scenes, the written words contributed by one or the other – as if they were an ingredient in a food package. He underestimates the changes that were made during shooting, often at the request of Capra. More serious, he forgets what's implicit, latent, secret and invisible in a collaborative effort. Jean Aurenche told me that when he and Pierre Bost worked with Autant Lara, they used to have long discussions about the script in his presence. Autant Lara almost never said anything. And he wrote even less. Yet, the end result was a script that had a tone, content and style entirely different from the kind of scripts they wrote for Jean Delannoy or any other directors. It had become a work by Lara, Aurenche added. Clearly Riskin, after having influenced Capra, had in turn been influenced during later collaborations by what Capra had made of his script and by the manner in which he had shot certain scenes.

* *Frank Capra: The Catastrophe of Success*, Simon and Schuster (US), Faber and Faber (UK), 1992.

In fact, the major criticism that can be made of this exciting, but too often sensation-seeking book is that it exploits the meanderings of an ageing, senile and horribly reactionary Capra – so far from the impulsive, exuberant young man that he must have been at the time of *American Madness* and *Lady for a Day* – for the sake of making a lame, underhand case.

Cut off from French news sources, I have Paris newspapers sent over to me, if only to keep up on the blood contamination trial. What a strange sight, all these mandarins of medicine and politics, refusing or dodging the responsibilities inherent in the long-coveted positions and powers for which they have fought ferociously. The people who have power in France have a tendency to believe it is above every law.

François Mitterrand has just provided another example in his Bastille Day speech by refusing the 'symbolic gesture' of recognizing France's responsibility for the deportation of Jews, notably during the Vel d'Hiv raid which was decided by the French government of the time and carried out by French police. He preferred to indulge in a contemptuous bit of abstract didacticism when everyone was expecting a human commitment, a gesture in the manner of Willy Brandt. A logical attitude, really, when you consider the declarations made by George Kiejman putting a halt to the lawsuits instituted against Touvier and Bosquet 'to preserve the civil peace' – peace, that allowed Dr Garetta to be decorated for 'outstanding services' (without mentioning which ones, which is illegal), in spite of the warnings from the Ministry of Health, and at a time when the blood scandal had already come out in the open.

A moment of comic relief: Michel Noir's lyrically, loony outburst, 'The France of 1992 is not the Argentina of Allende!'

During our entire trip, we only go out to the movies once, to an uncomfortable cinema in Vale (not unlike the kind found in the sticks in France forty-five years ago), to see Tim Burton's *Batman II*. It's a dark, neurotic visually striking work, a compulsive compendium of destructive frustrations. The overall impression is one of iciness, despite Michelle Pfeiffer's unforgettable performance as Catwoman – just the thing to feed millions of male fantasies.

We arrive in Los Angeles and are invited to the home of Irwin Winkler. We've remained friends since *'Round Midnight*, which he produced. He owns a lavish house in Beverly Hills. Every time I cross the electronic threshold, I feel as if I've come home to Tara. All that's missing is Max Steiner's gushing violins.

'Where's the ghost of Howard Hughes?' Charlotte asks me, as she stares in awe at the magnificent pool, the gardens and fruit orchard, the tennis court, the statues by Mayol and paintings by Renoir and Fantin Latour, the salon with its huge bay windows, dominated by a family portrait which slides apart to reveal the windows of a projection booth. We watch two films, including a disappointing Sidney Lumet picture, reclining rather than sitting on the couches, the smallest of which would be hard to fit in a great number of French movie houses. All this luxury keeps Charlotte divided between stupefaction and hilarity, especially when she is presented with some impressive cooking that wouldn't have been beneath Lasserre, Chapel or Bocuse.

Most truly amazing is the relaxed, friendly, familial atmosphere that Margo and Irwin Winkler maintain in this palace, as if all this were only an ephemeral movie set, something dreamed up by a William Cameron Menzies, to be enjoyed so long as we don't wake up. I find the same simplicity, the same absence of snobbery and ostentation, in their kids. Here money does not seem to have have changed or corrupted anything.

We are put up in 'the little house', a modest name for a spacious villa complete with sauna, a veranda looking out on to a kind of tropical forest where you could have shot *Objective Burma*, and two gyms boasting equipment that outclasses the smartest Parisian health club. Yes, this is California, where the two major obsessions, outside of show business, are physical fitness and food – not just diets, but ingredients, cholesterol, proteins and low-calorie dishes. Sure, that's all part of it. We even end up having a 100 per cent TrueMeat hamburger, guaranteed fat-free and shipped directly from New York. But what really monopolizes conversations is talk of new restaurants, cooking innovations (the latest is the new Tex Mex cuisine), the latest exploits of Wolfgang Puck, a legendary restaurateur with several fine restaurants, including 'Spago' (where diners could watch Los Angeles burning during the recent riots), and 'Chinois' (serving a mixture of Chinese and French *nouvelle cuisine*). They have an entire gastronomic vocabulary of their own, and the highest compliment you can make is to heatedly insist that the food in a particular restaurant is really serious. You get an idea of this trendy scene from Robert Towne's *Tequila Sunrise*.

We spend a wonderful weekend at the splendid house the Winklers have built in Malibu – a triumph of American architecture. The modernity of line and design and the conceptual boldness eases the difficulties of daily life and reinforces comfort: lighting, bay windows, admirably distributed light sources, intelligent layout of the kitchen, which doesn't cut the mistress of the house off from her guests, a spaciousness that doesn't exclude numerous little corners where you can be alone. On the beach, you run into Hollywood's past and present: a Raoul Walsh scriptwriter for *White Heat* and *Band of Angels*, or the current president of one of the studios. During lunches with any number of clever, interchangeable studio executives, the talk centres on astronomical figures something like the whole budget of Denmark. 'We'll be hitting the 150 million dollar mark with *Batman II*.' 'You fell short of your initial estimates.' 'Just a bit. We're somewhat disappointed, but we figure on video sales . . .' I need to make another seventeen films after my first fourteen to get to that number.

I sense a crack in the façade this year. The recession is even making itself felt out in Beverly Hills. You can now see the homeless pushing their shopping carts outside the luxury homes. I've never seen so many beggars in Westwood. On several occasions I hear of muggings and hold-ups, even a heist at a Malibu bar that is virtually next door to a police station. 'It's the proximity that attracts them. It presents a challenge. Los Angeles is now much more violent and dangerous than New York.' We keep hearing this refrain. I take some notes with the intention of changing certain scenes in *Anywhere But Here*.

On the same day we see Irwin's latest film, which he both produced and directed, *Night and the City* (a remake of the magnificent Jules Dassin classic), and the new Clint Eastwood, *Unforgiven*, which, with *Josey Wales*, I consider his masterpiece. It's a very well-written reflection on ageing, death and violence, harsh yet compassionate, a splendid western that has what's lacking in most current American cinema: a personal vision and sense of values.

On the way into the screening room where Irwin's film was being shown, I run into Stanley Donen, who seems in fine form. He hasn't aged a bit, and still sees as many films as before (he's one of the few American directors to see a good number of foreign movies). He asks me about *Le Mari de la coiffeuse*, which he's keen on seeing.

I am partly responsible for this remake of *Night and the City*. I had suggested to my former agent, Harry Uffland, who has become a producer, that he entrust the new version to André de Toth, whom I met again at a screening of *'Round Midnight*, and who told me that the film had overwhelmed him and made him cry, adding this unforgettable line: 'And you know, Bertrand, it's tough crying when you've only got one eye.' Indeed, André de Toth was one of Hollywood's quartet of one-eyed directors. Uffland commissioned a script from Richard Price, but during preparations he realized that he'd forgotten to buy the rights from Dassin.

A few years later, Irwin came across the script and had it rewritten for De Niro and Jessica Lange. The result is a film with some of the most brilliant dialogue in recent years, with strong, racy language reminiscent of Clifford Odets' work on *The Sweet Smell of Success*. Whereas Dassin dealt with small-time hoods in fifties London with an inspired sense of lyrical compassion, Price hit on the brilliant idea of transposing and updating the material to contemporary New York and its petty crooks: cash-machine thieves, phoney nuns, and menacing pedlars. Richard Widmark, the shabby hustler in white shoes, always in a hurry, here becomes a fifth-rate attorney, playing with the law in order to twist and trample it. The desperate, breathless, headlong flight of the original film is replaced by a no less desperate and breathless chatter. Whereas Widmark's motto might have been, 'While I'm running, I'm still alive,' De Niro's is, 'While I'm talking, I'm still alive.' I found Irwin's direction had improved since *Guilty by Suspicion*. Without Michael Balhaus to back him up, he had to make a greater personal investment, cut more to the 'ham-bone of Life' as Audiberti said. My only regret, as a nostalgic film-buff, is that there's nothing like the lyrical finale of Dassin's film, with a flight towards death in the early dawn light.

The screening goes well. Stanley is enthusiastic and Charlotte thinks it's one of De Niro's best roles. I'm happy for Irwin.

Lunch the next day with André de Toth. Now ninety-two, he still drives a car and flies a helicopter, but has given up scuba-diving since the day he nearly broke his neck. On the other hand, he has taken up sculpture. Courteous and smart, he astonishes Charlotte with his high spirits and youthful mentality. I ask him about his Hungarian films. 'Some of them aren't bad. *Semmel Weis* for one. It's about the famous doctor, but you have to remember that I shot all six of them between June and November of 1939. When I tell him I really liked one third of *Slattery's Hurricane*, he says, 'In those days, if you could direct fifteen minutes you could be proud of, that was already a success.' He tells me that he is writing his memoirs and my friend, Todd McCarthy, correspondent for *Variety*, has read the first seventeen chapters and is enthusiastic. André gives me the introduction and drops us off at Rodeo Drive. Suddenly, he gets out of the car, opens the boot, pulls out an amazingly heavy sack, tosses it into my arms, then jumps back into the car and, saying he can't double park, drives off before I can thank him. It is one of his sculptures, a bronze work on an onyx base, entitled 'Please listen', which I'd admired in a photo. It is reminiscent of Henry Moore.

That afternoon, I spend two fascinating hours with Ellis St Joseph, the scriptwriter of one of Douglas Sirk's best films, *A Scandal in Paris*. We first met after a screening of *Deathwatch* at Filmex and again a few years later for the release of *Coup de torchon* during a memorable dinner arranged by Pierre Rissient, who had also invited Abraham Polonsky, Ellis's former schoolmate. The two men, who hadn't seen each other in years, outdid one another in wit, literary and political erudition, and engaged in some brilliant oratory one-up-manship to the delight of all present. Polonsky said that he considered Ellis one of the finest American short-story writers, while Ellis revealed that he had made uncredited contributions to several films, including Jean Renoir's *The River*. He had entirely restructured the story with Renoir in the editing room, doing so in secret so as not to hurt Salka Viertel. That's where they came up with the idea of the commentary that gives the film it's narrative spine. He was full of praise for Renoir.

This late afternoon turns out to be just as exhilarating. Neither illness nor a serious operation has weakened his mental faculties, his trenchant manner, his lucidity and youthful spirits. I've transcribed the notes I hastily jotted down during our conversation:

On Sirk: Douglas was clearly an artist. I loved every minute of our collaboration. What annoys me, though, is how some of his exegeses analyse my ideas as though they were his, as if I didn't exist. *A Scandal in Paris* is the only film I ever worked on that was conceived, written and shot with complete artistic freedom. Our only constraint was budgetary. Our only problems came from Arnold Pressburger. Fortunately we formed a tight, united group. One day AP (as we used to call him) wanted to cut a scene that he thought was too macabre and religiously offensive: the one in which George Sanders catches the little monkey Satan in a cementery, where he sees the name of Vidocq on a tombstone and decides to adopt it. He was categoric. I refused and Sirk and Sanders backed me, since they loved the dialogue in the scene. But it was Hans Eisler who came to our rescue. He had an iron-clad contract and told Pressburger: 'I love this scene and it must stay in the final cut. If not, I'll compose a score that will be so dissonant and bold that it'll take twenty years before your film gets shown and then only at the Museum of Modern Art.' Eisler was a fantastic character who loved to eat and was capable of reading Tolstoy's *Resurrection* in one morning and memorizing the whole thing. Did you know that Chaplin asked him to write the score for *Limelight* based on a theme Chaplin had composed? When he heard it, Eisler said, 'Only you can write music like that.'

Thanks to you and Pierre Rissient *A Scandal in Paris* is at last being rediscovered. I can only repeat what Cocteau once said: 'Artists are never ahead of their time. It's the public that's behind the times.'

I would have loved to work with Sirk again. He did ask me once, but I was revolted by the way Hollywood treats you. René Clair said, 'I had to choose between Hitler and America. I finally chose America because it was a little better.' Anyway, when Sirk called me I told him I wanted to finish a novel and a play first. I was stupid. Yet I adored the man. I gave him a small bronze statue with the inscription 'Souvenir of a Chinese carousel'. Remember the carousel in the film?

On theft (producer): A guy like Jerry Wald made an entire career of putting his name on scripts written by others. He especially exploited the Epstein brothers, whom he paid peanuts and who racked up a lot of hits. One day they asked him for a rise and he laughed in their faces. They were furious and complained to Jack Warner, who was shocked and called in Wald to fire him. 'Wait a minute!' he shouted. 'Without me you'd never have known those guys.' Warner thought it over and then made him a producer. That is a very moral story for you. I worked for Wald on *In Our Time*, a title he took credit for. I'd always thought that it came from Chamberlain's famous appeasement speech about Hitler, 'Peace in our time', but he really stole it from Hemingway.

On Virginia Woolf (politics): I was mad about Virginia Woolf's books and I wanted to meet her. She was magnificent, like a Rossetti painting. One day we were having a heated argument about Chamberlain's appeasement speech and the attitude that revolted us. Though I'm rather sceptical and reserved, I got very worked up. She turned to me and said. 'Don't you young people think any more of the eternal verities?' From that day on, I never opened one of her books again.

On writers (collaboration): I wrote *Joan of Paris* and recently I was surprised to read an interview with Charles Bennett in which he listed it as one of his favourite films. His only contribution was nothing more than two very middling scenes, which were borrowed from the scripts he had written for Hitchcock before the war. The rest was my work . . . That is, after they'd watered down or done away with the sexual innuendo and perverse touches.

On writers (film): There are more and more films that are really written by the public.

A Passenger to Bali: The play had been staged by John Huston and performed on radio by Orson Welles, and had just been selected for the Crown Guide of the best world plays, listing me between Scribe (which didn't flatter me) and Strindberg. I wrote the lead role for Robert Morley, but an incident forced him to return to England. Then Walter Huston went after the role and his son had to comply. He was an actor of limited range, good when playing close to himself or one of those deeply American characters, the kind who exude a curious charm that could make you believe that Bush or Reagan have some semblance of sincerity and that they actually believe what they're saying. But he had a rough relationship with the English language and was at a loss with even slightly florid dialogue. I saw him in *Othello* and he took the cake. He was so bad you felt like you were sitting through the eruption of Krakatoa. It was dark for twenty-four hours. And his performance in *A Passenger to Bali* sank the play. He didn't seem to understand what he was saying, didn't know how to play the subtext. He could manage a comic scene, but had no inkling of humour and was incapable of the slightest sense of irony. Robert Morley could have played irony, just like Sacha Guitry or Louis Jouvet. But not Walter Huston. To replace Morley, I had suggested a young actor who excited John Houston. It was Sidney Greenstreet.

On aphorisms: I'm in the process of completing my autobiography. It will be a book of aphorisms, the most naked form of autobiography, since it dispenses with the crutches of history. Here are two: 'Fear inspired my talent. Fear destroyed my talent. Fear of death has revived it.' 'America is reactionary because it has no tradition of revolution. The so-called American Revolution was entirely a British revolt of Englishmen against England.'

August

Back to Sacquèdes. Three weeks of peace and quiet before confronting the horrors of *L 627*'s release. The tensions and anxieties. The tyranny of attendance figures and first-day receipts. What reinforces this tyranny is the fact that the figures, and the film's budget, become part of the scale of values and system of references employed by the press and media. Typically, a taxi driver from Sainte-Maxime who'd just seen *Indochine* could only tell me about how much it had cost and how well it was doing. A few years ago, he might have mentioned the actors, talked about the photography, maybe even the story. Nowadays Catherine Deneuve takes a back seat to the film's budget and gross, and to her own salary. These are values and references, especially for kids in slum suburbs.

When I hear that, I think of a childhood friend, Gilbert Guerero, who lived just down the Sacquèdes road. He was the son of Italian immigrants who were virtually illiterate. He had to go to work at a torpedo factory near Saint Tropez at a very early age. We saw a lot of each other during the holidays because we shared a passion for movies. He made me drool with brilliant accounts about the films he'd seen. With his delicious Provençal accent he described how one of Errol Flynn's men annoyed a German guard by throwing peas at him in Raoul Walsh's *Desperate Journey* (1942), how Gary Cooper tricked the Indian chief – Boris Karloff – by persuading him to chase them only when the needle on the compass he'd given him pointed in another direction. He never made any reference to the cost of a film or even its director, but talked about the script, the acting, the dialogue, the ideas that made him laugh in *Les Cinq sous de lavarede*.

This passion for film and theatre was Gilbert's whole life. In Cavalaire, he founded an amateur theatre troupe, the Tragos, and put on plays by Goldoni, Molière, Vitrac, Victor Haim. Then, with boundless energy, he created France's longest-running amateur theatre festival, with dozens of guest companies. This summer I see a fine production from Spain about Christopher Columbus, freewheeling and flavourful, much more exciting than the dreary Ridley Scott film, and the latest production by the Tragos, a staging of Molière's *L'Avare*, in which Gilbert gives an outstanding performance as Harpagon. I gave him and some of his actors bit parts in *Daddy Nostalgie*.

Phone call from Frédéric, who excitedly reads me Jean-Jacques Bernard's article in *Première*, which he found first-rate. He also tells me that Frédéric Ploquin, journalist for *l'Evènement du jeudi* and co-author, with *Libération*'s Alain Léauthier, of a remarkable book-length study of the police, *Les Flics*, *120,000*, had organized a screening for the Minister of the Interior, Paul Quilès. I call Ploquin. He tells me that Quilès came with his entire cabinet and a number of policemen. The latter reacted positively throughout the screening, laughing and making comments on scenes, visibly approving their veracity. Several came up to Ploquin afterwards to say how accurate they found the film. Quilès seemed baffled and tense and refused to speak to journalists hoping for an interview or an immediate statement. The members of his cabinet followed their boss's lead. Ploquin's impression was that Quilès had discovered a reality whose existence he never even suspected, and in front of policemen who were gleeful. The only way to save face was to deny it.

Fred asks me to call Jean Devaivre, who had just seen *L 627*. He tells me it was the first time he'd set foot in a cinema in thirty-one years. His reaction is at once churlish, enthusiastic and astonishingly perceptive. He keeps insisting that it is the opposite of the kind of films he made, but he caught all the nuances of the direction, quoted the motet Sarde used, praised the realistic truthfulness of the squat sequence with the crack-crazed mother that so scared Richard Pezet. He speaks at length of the performances of Didier Bezace and Charlotte. For the moment, he's the only person to have noticed that the mixing goes from stereo to mono.

26 August

Preview of *L 627* in Evreux. Michel Alexandre and Jean Labbé, president of the exhibitors' federation, are among us. The theatre owner, young and dynamic, has been fighting for the cinema with special programmes and discussions. I congratulate him on the exceptional screening and acoustics.

After the screening, a lively and heated discussion. The reactions are very positive. François Loncle, the Cities Minister, who showed up at the end of the film for the discussion, takes the floor. Though openly admitting he hadn't seen *L 627*, he goes on at length about the film's qualities and limitations, convinced that we had given a much too bleak and pessimistic view of the police. This act leaves me speechless. That's just what I denounced in the film: the politicians who come out with phrases on subjects they've barely heard about.

The next day, good articles in the local press. One policeman, who found the film exceptionally accurate, writes: 'When young people come to me asking to join the police, I tell them to go see *L 627* first. Then we can talk.'

3 September

A masterly portrait of an emotional cripple: Claude Sautet's *Un coeur en hiver* harks back to the bleakness of *Max et les ferrailleurs*. That bleakness has been an undercurrent throughout Sautet's other films, chronicles of indecision and shilly-shallying by male characters trying to manoeuvre their way out of their responsibilities. But here, more so than in *Quelques jours avec moi* or *Mado*, it becomes the motivation, the soul of the story. Headlong flight becomes a system of attack, egotism the driving force. The charm impregnating *César et Rosalie*, meant to hide the dark areas has been relegated to the background; the tone and subject are harsher, the secret melancholy has given way to acute, clear-eyed pessimism. The protagonist, an autist of the heart, portrayed by Daniel Auteuil with total control and conviction, without indulgence or any fudging of the uncomfortable traits, is the kid brother of Max, that cop in *Max et les ferrailleurs* so obsessed with order that he ends up arranging the crimes he wanted to curb. Like Max, the Auteuil character wants to manipulate lives, stir up passions while suppressing his own feelings, disrupt the outside world while cutting himself off from the things of life – the very life sought by women and which these puritanical yet vulnerable tempters try to wreck and sully. Women like Romy Schneider, full of sensuality and passion in *Max*, like the vibrant Emmanuelle Béart, whose range grows with each film, trying to return the blows that have wounded her. Two films so close; two identical separations; a car departing, eyes meeting and turning away. Hard, impossible, to believe in all this waste. The acute harshness of the account and judgement, with a little bit of warmth still remaining.

A deeply personal film, under the control of a demiurge who is happier and more open than his characters, *Un coeur en hiver* made me think of those Bach fugues that Claude Sautet loves to analyse so much. I don't know why, but this pulsation brought to mind *When the Lights are Low*, that hard, black, stripped down piece by Lionel Hampton. Apart from the tremendous André Dussolier,

I loved Jean-Luc Bideau, the most convincing incarnation of Daniel Toscan du Plantier since Daniel Langlet in Catherine Breillat's *Tapage nocturne*.

The selection of Sautet's film at the Venice Film Festival gives me more pleasure than that of *L 627*, which I accepted for our charming Italian distributor Valerio de Paolis. Or rather, what touched me was sharing that pleasure with Sautet. I've known Claude for thirty-three years ('the age of the Christ', as someone says in a Vadim film). I wrote my first review about his *Classe tous risques* and conducted my first interview with him. He was the one who came in person, about the same time as Jean-Pierre Melville, to see my parents and persuade them to let me go into the cinema. Thank you, Claude.

I call Jean Louis Livi, the producer of *Un coeur en hiver*, to congratulate him. He took the opportunity to shower me with compliments and said he was so shaken by *L 627* that he decided to cancel the thriller he was planning because it now seemed totally outdated by mine. This reaction, as well as those of Alain Finkelkraut and Pierre Truche, who tells me that the film put its finger on everything that threatens our democracy, touch me deeply and prepare me philosophically for the harsh trials of the Venice Film Festival.

4 September

Upon arriving in Venice, we ask Nicoletta Billi, our press attaché, if the festival has organized a screening of the print with English subtitles as we had requested. When I was at Venice with *'Round Midnight*, I noted that a good number of British, German, Australian, Danish and Swedish journalists (and some members of the jury) didn't understand Italian. When they can't speak a film's language, they have to put up with a simultaneous translation with headphones – an absolute horror. Nicoletta says nothing has been done. Fred and I make a little scene. In no time, and with much graciousness, Gilles Pontecorvo finds a cinema and arranges the screening. With a smile, I point out that it was the price to pay for having, once again, selected a jury of mostly English-speakers.

The next day, a sudden, angry reaction against *L 627* from Paul Quilès, after several weeks of lethargy during which he refused Ploquin's request for an interview and committed the immense blunder of ordering an investigation into Michel Alexandre. This act demonstrated genuine contempt for someone who is also a creative personality, a writer, as I said the day before to the correspondent from Agence France Presse. His reactions are immediately picked up in huge headlines by the Italian press (IL MINISTRO FRANCESE QUILE CONTRO BERTRAND TAVERNIER): he takes me to task for having based my script on the account of a single police investigator. 'We cannot accept this one version, and I regret that Bertrand Tavernier didn't try to see me. Rather than coming out with unjust and false things, he would have discovered that not everything is like this caricature, and he'd have learned something of my preoccupations and plans . . .' Such comments make you wonder. Forget about the foolhardy and totally false assertions about the number of police I met, the accounts that we recorded, forget about the touching but slightly megalo-maniacal desire to have a fiction film reflect 'his preoccupations and plans', which only reflects a curious concept of creative writing. True, I might have done something like Serge Piolet, who in *Bang Bang*, in the middle of the action, has a paternalistic Guy Lux appear in another setting and declare encouragingly: 'Don't you worry, Sheila baby, Uncle Guy's watching over you.' I could have cut to a minister declaring, 'Don't worry, Lulu my boy, Uncle Paul is thinking about you.' It would have added some spice to the story along with a sense of foresight, since during the preparation and shooting of the film, Paul Quilès was still Minister of the Post and had I tried to see him, he would have been able to do nothing more than show me his latest stamp collections. Unless the disappointment he claims to have felt only betrayed some kind of scriptwriting ambition, which is what the rest of his declaration would seem to suggest.

At the press conference the usual wild and idiotic questions are asked by people who had already thought them up before seeing the film. I have to put up with a history lesson on the French police (leaving out, sad to say, the river patrol) and racist acts in provincial police stations – it reflects a mentality similar to that of Quilès. I am even asked why I made a film promoting drugs. There ought to be a clause in contracts protecting us from questions like that. Michel Alexandre himself gives a simple and effective answer.

Official festival screening at 6.30 p.m. Charlotte looks exquisite and sexy in her short black Paule Ka gown. In the pre-screening lobby confusion, we run into Jack and Monique Lang as well as Gilles Jacob. In the cinema I spot Dennis Hopper, who didn't come to the screening of the English-subtitle print and now has to submit to headphones and a single voice. Screening conditions have distinctly improved since *'Round Midnight*, although the sound is a bit too loud and metallic. My legs feel wobbly and can't move. The audience laughs and reacts positively. There are two or three walkouts, which affect me like knife thrusts. I note that in the Italian subtitles, Torréton's off-screen crack, 'Now we know it's not Fabius' to Bezace's, 'Watch it, he's going left,' is translated as 'Now we know he's no Socialist.' So Fabius isn't known in Italy? I wait for the Minister's reaction, but he is unfazed.

Sustained applause at the end. I kiss Charlotte and embrace Didier. In the lobby, Jack Lang and Marc Nicolas say the film is terrific, that it is like a blow to the stomach. Neither of them have felt the time go by. Lang insists on knowing if everything in the film is true and bombards Michel Alexandre and Didier Bezace with questions. At the Excelsior bar, Lang admits he didn't really understand Quilès' reaction: 'You both have to talk it over. I'll try to arrange a meeting. And we have to organize seminars and discussions about the film's warning sounds.'

A huge surprise the next day: *Libération* wants to interview me. I agree, all the while thinking that I owe the 'favour' less to my film than to Serge Daney's lines on *La Guerre sans nom*. Marie Colmant, who conducts the interview with genuine skill, first begins by saying that she'd been afraid I would say no. I want to answer her as Zero Mostel had done when asked if he would agree to work with Jerome Robbins, who had denounced him during the McCarthy period: 'I don't want to establish a counter-blacklist.' In the morning Eva Simonet, with a smile, hands me a superb review by Danielle Heymann in *Le Monde*, full of warmth and vibrancy that, I hope, will make people want to see the film. The paragraph on Laura Guirao is magnificent.

Eva tells me that many newspapers and TV programmes don't want to interview Didier Bezace because they think he isn't well-known enough, even though they find him terrific in the film. I've noticed that this form of censorship – because it is censorship – doesn't happen with American actors. A half-page is easily devoted to an actor or actress about whom journalists ask me for information before meeting them because 'we don't know anything about them'. I do as I would in Paris: only according an interview if Didier is present. All the more so because Didier has remarkable things to say about the film, and because his acting and directing are exciting and contain sufficient material for a very good article.

Late in the afternoon, we find ourselves with a free hour on our hands. Charlotte and I stroll around Venice. We even catch a few minutes of a Goldoni play being performed by actors on a small square.

During the festival, we had dinner several times with Alain Sarde at Alfredo's and each time he had us roaring with laughter. One priceless routine we never tire of is his account of *Prénom Carmen*, with Isabelle Adjani walking off the film because she wasn't getting enough illumination, and Godard writing to her: 'If you need so much light, it's because you haven't enough of it in you.' Our companions are Fred and his wife Dominique, whose intelligence, devotion and competence I've appreciated (she produces fine radio broadcasts for Radio-France), and Gilles Jacob, who as a punster can teach Patrick Rotman a thing or two. He thrills Charlotte by saying she would have been a perfect actress for Jean Renoir. A remark I find true. She has the kind of robust health and force typical of the thirties actresses. Pierre Trabaud tells her the same thing a few days later: 'What a pleasure it is to see on a screen a woman full of life, humour and passion, the kind of passion that Arletty and Darrieux had. It's a change from the limp ectoplasms you have straggling through films these days.'

6 September

Before returning to Paris, I attend a seminar organized by Gilles Pontecorvo. Jack Lang delivers a smashing speech, denouncing the ascendancy of the US in the audiovisual sector and the battle waged in Brussels by Carla Hill to destroy all cultural defences. It is a call for insurrection.

Having pulled the rug from under my feet, I can only repeat much of the same, and less brilliantly. I mention the struggle of Turkish film-makers weary of being unable to release their films and of trying to introduce a 25 per cent quota in cinemas for Turkish films and the blunt reaction from Bush, who didn't stop to think that obstructing the national film industry gives ammunition to the fundamentalists, who have already violently criticized the number of American films and their blasphemous immorality. Here was imperialism in all its nakedness. No need to use kid gloves, or invent the slightest alibi, as was the case with France or Italy. We're dealing with savages, so let's just get down to it.

Following Fernando Solanas and Francesco Rosi, Dennis Hopper weighs in with an hysterical and moronic speech. Enraged by what he considered elementary anti-Americanism, he launches into a diatribe full of overheated and self-centered nationalist sentiment, declaring his pride as an American and bitterly attacking France with a full arsenal of misconceptions and clichés. He confuses State money with industry money, forgets that French aid mechanisms also benefit American films, both in the art-house and commercial sector. He also has no inkling about what his government is doing in foreign countries, swallowing whole the lie about liberalism. In short, he reveals his ignorance in all its crass self-satisfaction, just the sort of thing to warm Jack Valenti's heart. He doesn't even seem to be aware that the representatives of the Director's Guild are demanding many of the same things we are.

7 September

Screenings of *L 627* for the film's cast and crew. A good occasion to see a number of technicians and actors again: Jean-Claude Calon, Eric Savin, Smail Melki, and Guy-Claude François, who at last is able to come to see the film. His work on the sets was outstanding, as much an integral part of the film as it was for *La Vie et rien d'autre* and *La passion Béatrice*, so much so that everyone thinks we shot in real interiors. He sends me a very touching letter: 'My dear Bertrand. Well, once again I had the feeling of taking part in a major film. Just as *Béatrice* excited my interest in the Middle Ages, and I can no longer walk past a war monument without stopping to read the names, so *L 627* showed me how politics could be more legitimate if it dealt with life more directly. This was a film on which the conditions allowed me and my team to work with unusual harmony and high spirits.'

8 September

Bernard Chardère sends me a ludicrous administrative memo of 1951 dug up by Paul Louis Thirard and which would have delighted Jean Aurenche. Here's an extract:

– Any signs of hermaphroditism, the absence or loss of a penis, are disqualifications for all overseas posts.

– The loss, absence or advanced atrophy of both testicles are disqualifications for all overseas posts; the loss, absence or atrophy of a single testicle, the other remaining of normal appearance, may conform to active and stationary cadre positions.

– Testicular, orificular or intramural ectopia is cause for immediate disqualification from active cadre post. This anomaly may lead to disqualification from stationary cadres positions only in the event that it induces intense and painful attacks.

And it's signed: François Mitterrand, Minister of Colonies.

This sublime text reveals that sexual life must have been more intense and permissive in the colonies than in Metropolitan France. It's something to distract me from the anxieties of the opening.

In the afternoon, during a radio broadcast at Europe 1, Brillet, a plain-clothes police union representative, contradicts his minister and throws his full support behind the film: 'It contains everything we've been denouncing for ten years, everything the politicians refuse to hear. Rather than hand in a moral report at the end of the year, I am going to show *L 627*.' Nils was on the same programme and spoke superbly.

That evening, he, Lara and Michel Alexandre go to Lille for a public discussion organized by an association of police, doctors, educators and magistrates. An order from the Minister of the Interior obliges the police to cancel the discussion at the cinema, but can't prevent a series of talks from taking place around the buffet table. One cop even whispers to Lara: 'The film is completely accurate. The things it shows are what we try not to think about. Or else we'd end up putting a bullet in our brain.'

9 September

Release of *L 627*. I hole up at home and take the phone off the hook. Charlotte shows me an excellent review in *Télérama* for which Fabienne Pascaud did portraits of Cécile Garcia, Lara and Charlotte.

On the France 2 news, Bruno Masure reads a statement by a Paris police chief which praises the film but claims that it describes conditions that are fifteen years out of date. So, I must have dreamt up everything I have seen during the eight months I worked on the script, beginning with the prefabs in which I wrote certain scenes, and the entire District Police Station. It's stupid to spend four million francs on something that hasn't existed for fifteen years . . .

At the end of the news broadcast, a short piece on the new school year, which begins today all over France. To illustrate the topic, the editors selected a scene from *Dead Poets Society*. I can't help pointing out to Bruno Masure how extremely bizarre and embarrassing it is to use American images to report on a French news item. There are a number of well-known French films dealing with education, such as those by Jean-Claude Brisseau. Sadly, brainwashing is taking its toll.

When working with the distributors AMLF and Alain Sarde, the opening-day tradition is to have dinner together during the first evening showing – a pleasant and convivial rite if initial results are good. If not . . . I have a pleasant memory of the opening-day dinner for *Un dimanche à la campagne*. The first audience figures were rather low, with an overwhelming majority of old people, which was not a good sign. Alain Sarde recalled that Pezet said the film would have to be written off as a loss, which didn't brighten the mood. The only one to remain adamantly optimistic was Louis Ducreux. And the future proved him right.

We arrive at the Tse Yang restaurant with Charlotte, where we are pleasantly greeted by Richard Pezet, resplendent in a bright yellow polo jumper. Alain Sarde and Frédéric Bourboulon had already arrived with their wives.

67   *L 627*: The brigade in action

The distribution manager, Jean Claude Borde, is supposed to stop by at ten o'clock with the figures. By 10.45 he still hasn't arrived. I smell disaster. I'm convinced the opening has been awful. My pessimism infects Fred. We'd taken a three million risk with this film and we'd lost. Richard and Alain try in vain to brighten our moods. At 11.10, Jean Claude Borde shows up. I don't dare ask him anything. He gives us a figure that I don't catch. He repeats: 'It's just fine, we've even done better than we expected.' The reactions in the cinemas are good. This film, which was born when I saw a young boy collapse in the gutter of the Rue Myrrha, wound up with a sumptuous vision of Richard Pezet's yellow polo jumper. All is for the best in the best of all possible worlds.

But not for everybody. Next morning, Fred informs me that the police have conducted a series of raids in the streets where we have filmed. I call Michel Alexandre who is as dismayed as I am. The boys at the Ministry have become like Dodo in the film. And I had hoped they might follow the example of Lulu. Nils tells me that the medical post set up by Médecins du Monde in the Rue Myrrha has been constantly disrupted by uniformed police from the local station, who stomped on the clean syringes that the medics intended for the junkies, declaring, 'Let 'em all croak.' Stop them, they've all gone mad.

Translated by Shaun Whiteside
(additional material by Lenny Burger)

Filmography

1 Shadow and Substance

GEORGE MILLER is the director of, among others, the *Mad Max* trilogy and *Lorenzo's Oil*.

DAPHNE PARIS has been a Script Supervisor since 1979, co-wrote the first episode of *The Dismissal*, and was the Second Unit Director on Wim Wenders' *Until the End of the World*.

2 The Burning Question: Cinema after the Millennium?

PAUL SCHRADER is the director of, among others, *Blue Collar*, *Mishima*, and *Light Sleeper*.

FRED ZINNEMANN is the director of, among others, *High Noon*, *From Here to Eternity*, and *Julia*.

MICHAEL VERHOEVEN is the director of, among others, *White Rose* and *The Nasty Girl*.

DAVID BYRNE is the director of, among others, *True Stories* and *Ilé Aiyé* (*The House of Life*), as well as videos connected to his musical work.

JOCELYN MOORHOUSE is the director of *Pavane*, *The Siege of Barton's Bathroom*, and *Proof*.

JOHN BOORMAN is the director of, among others, *Point Blank*, *Excalibur*, and *Hope and Glory*.

PHILIPPE ROUSSELOT has been the director of photography on, among others, *Diva*, *The Emerald Forest*, and *The River Runs Through It*.

DENYS ARCAND is the director of, among others, *La Maudite Galette*, *The Decline of the American Empire* and *Jesus of Montreal*.

ROGER SPOTTISWOODE is the director of, among others, *Under Fire*, *Air America*, and *Turner and Hooch*.

RICHARD LOWENSTEIN is the director of, among others, *Strikebound*, *Dogs in Space*, and *Say a Little Prayer*.

RON SHELTON is the director of *Bull Durham* and *White Men Can't Jump*.

VINCENT WARD is the director of, among others, *Vigil*, *The Navigator* and *Map of the Human Heart*.

MONTE HELLMAN is the director of, among others, *The Shooting*, *Two Lane Blacktop*, and *Cockfighter*.

ARTHUR PENN is the director of, among others, *Bonnie and Clyde*, *Night Moves*, and *Little Big Man*.

NICOLAS ROEG is the director of, among others, *Performance*, *Don't Look Now*, and *Cold Heaven*.

ISTVÁN SZABÓ is the director of, among others, *Mephisto*, *Colonel Redl* and *Meeting Venus*.

3 Movie Lessons

JACO VAN DORMAEL is the director of, among others, *Maedli-la-Bräche*, *De Boot*, and *Toto The Hero*.

PIERRE HODGSON has worked as assistant director to Raul Ruiz, Olivier Assayas and Jean-Pierre Limosin. He is currently writing a feature-length adaptation of one chapter from *Don Quixote* for Joâo Canijo, as well as producing six half-hour documentaries in Northern Ireland for BBC2.

4 Looking for the Serpent

ALISON MACLEAN is the director of, among others, *Rud's Wife*, *Kitchen Sink*, and *Crush*.

GRAHAM FULLER is the Executive Editor of *Interview* magazine. For Faber and Faber he interviewed Michael Mann in *Projections 1*, interviewed Hal Hartley for the edition of *Simple Men* and *Trust*, and is the editor of *Potter on Potter*.

5 Freewheelin'

GUS VAN SANT is the director of, among others, *Mala Noche*, *Drugstore Cowboy*, and *Even Cowgirls Get the Blues*.

DEREK JARMAN is the director of, among others, *Sebastian*, *The Tempest*, and *Edward II*.

6 *Acting on Impulse*

WILLEM DAFOE has appeared in, among others, *The Loveless*, *Wild at Heart*, and *Light Sleeper*.

7 The Early Life of a Screenwriter II

SIDNY GILLIAT is the co-writer of, among others, *The Lady Vanishes*, *Millions Like Us*, and *I See A Dark Stranger*.

KEVIN MACDONALD is the writer of the short film *Dr Reitzer's Fragment*. He is currently writing a biography of his grandfather Emeric Pressburger.

8 Altman on Altman

ROBERT ALTMAN is the director of, among others, *M★A★S★H*, *The Player*, and *Short Cuts*.

9 Bob Roberts

TIM ROBBINS has appeared in, among others, *Bull Durham*, *Jacob's Ladder*, and *The Player*.

10 I Wake Up Dreaming: A Journal for 1992

BERTRAND TAVERNIER's first feature film *L'Horloger de Saint-Paul* (1973) won the Louis Delluc prize. This film was followed by *Que la fête commence* (1975), *Le Juge et l'assassin* (1976), *Des enfants gâtés* (1971), *Deathwatch* (1979), *Une semaine de vacances* (1980), *Coup de torchon* (1981), *Philippe Soupault* (1982), *Mississippi Blues* (1983), *Un dimanche à la campagne* (1984), *'Round Midnight* (1986), *La Passion Béatrice* (1987), *Lyon, regard intérieur* (1988), *La Vie et rien autre* (1989), *Daddy Nostalgie* (1990), and, in 1992, *La Guerre sans nom* and *L 627*.

Faber Film List

New and Forthcoming

Directors series

Kieślowski on Kieślowski

Levinson on Levinson

Malle on Malle

Biographies

Nicholas Ray: An American Journey
Bernard Eisenschitz

Joseph Losey
David Caute

Emeric Pressburger: The Life and Death of a Screenwriter
Kevin Macdonald

A Siegel Film: An Autobiography
Don Siegel

Screenplays

Simple Men and *Trust*
Hal Hartley

Even Cowgirls Get the Blues and *My Own Private Idaho*
Gus Van Sant

The Life and Death of Colonel Blimp
Michael Powell and Emeric Pressburger

And

The Patty Diphusa Stories and Other Writings
Pedro Almodovar

If you would like a complete Faber Film
Books stocklist, please write to the
Promotions Department
Faber and Faber
3 Queen Square
London WC1N 3AU

Projections 1

Projections is a forum for practitioners of the cinema to reflect on the year in cinema and to speculate on the future. The first issue contains:

Bright Dreams, Hard Knocks
a journal by John Boorman

Film Fiction
an essay by Sam Fuller

The Early Life of a Screenwriter
from the Berlin diaries of Emeric Pressburger

Demme on Demme
a comprehensive survey of the career of 1991's Oscar-winning director

Matters of Photogenics
an essay on photographing the human face by Oscar-winning cameraman Nestor Almendros

My Director and I
a conversation between River Phoenix and Gus Van Sant during the shooting of *My Own Private Idaho*.

Surviving Desire
a screenplay by Hal Hartley

Making Some Light
Michael Mann discusses the making of *The Last of the Mohicans*.

There are also contributions from: Denys Arcand, David Byrne, Jane Campion, Costa-Gavras, Terry Gilliam, Mike Figgis, Tony Harrison, Kzysztof Kieślowski, Richard Lowenstein, Louis Malle, Claude Miller, Arthur Penn, Sydney Pollack, Kevin Reynolds, Francesco Rosi, Ken Russell, Ettore Scola, Istvan Szabo, Paolo and Vittorio Taviani, Michael Verhoeven, Paul Verhoeven, Vincent Ward and Zhang Yimou

METRO TARTAN

The finest in independent and world cinema
1993

Man Bites Dog

The prize winning sensation of Cannes 1992 and hailed as the European film phenomenon of the year, Man Bites Dog is a shocking and provocative black comedy, a spoof documentary about a charming and amiable mass murderer and the film crew who gradually become implicated in his horrendous deeds.

Labyrinth of Passion

Director Pedro Almodovar's early foray into the chaos and anarchy of desire. A kaleidoscopic journey into excess. Savage, wild and fun.

Sweet Emma, Dear Bobe

From the director of the Oscar winning "Mephisto". Istvan Szabo's intimate, humane and touching drama of two young girls caught up in Hungary's painful post-communist transition.

Crush

Alison MaClean's debut feature is a disquieting and often disturbing exploration of the dark side of sexual identity and the shifting power of relationships, starring Marcia Gay Harden.

One False Move

Carl Franklin's critically acclaimed film is a powerful, stylish action-thriller that explores the teetering balance between fate, truth and consequences where "one false move" can turn a hero into a tragic victim.
Stars Bill Paxton.

Leolo

Jean-Claude Lauzon's lyrical, funny and sometimes brutal coming of age story. Leolo is a 12 year old boy growing up in Montreal who refuses to accept the grim reality of his madness plagued family by escaping into his own fantasy world.
Canada's Oscar Nomination for Best Foreign Film 1993.

Sleeping Dogs

A psychological thriller set in the heart of Hollywood. A young author collaborates on a fictional book about murder with a strange man he accepts as a room mate only to discover that his tenant is a real killer.
Stars Sharon Stone and Dylan McDermott.

I Was on Mars

The tragi-comic odyssey of a young Polish woman who comes to New York to sample the delights of 'the free world' but who only succeeds in attracting bad luck like a magnet.

Adorable Lies

An ironic and ambivalent love story about a couple torn between fantasy and reality, tangled in a web of adorable lies.
From Cuban director Gerardo Chijona.

The Last Days of Chez Nous

Bruno Ganz and Lisa Harrow star in Gillian Armstrong's powerful and award winning portrayal of an eccentric Australian household and the lives, loves and struggles of its dysfunctional family.

Prince of Shadows

Terence Stamp and Patsy Kensit star in Pilar Miro's dark and tense political thriller about a reluctant Communist party hit man forced to return to his old hunting grounds to kill a traitor. Silver Bear Winner Berlin 1992.

Jamon Jamon

Winner of the Silver Lion at the Venice Film Festival. Bigas Luna's Jamon Jamon is a story about passion and highways, a love triangle with six apexes. An innovative and often outrageous Spanish sex comedy.

Hard Boiled

A wild, kinetic and breathtaking action thriller. Two men on the opposite sides of the law are forced into an uneasy alliance to defeat a Triad warlord and to save the inhabitants of a beseiged hospital. Directed by Hong Kong's premiere action filmmaker John Woo.

La Fille de L'air

Beatrice Dalle stars as an ex-convict forced to take to the skies to rescue her imprisoned lover. The story of an ordinary woman transformed by the strength of her love for one man into a courageous modern-day folk heroine.

Metro Tartan Ltd.,
79 Wardour Street, London W1V 3TH.
Tel: 071 734 8508 Fax: 071 287 2112
TX: 262 433 REF. 3294

TARTAN VIDEO

Excellence and integrity are the cornerstones of the Tartan philosophy. To this end all Tartan's specially remastered releases are available on both high quality VHS and Laserdisc in their original widescreen format.

A beautifully packaged collection of quality films presenting the finest in world and independent cinema including **Altman's "McCabe & Mrs Miller"**, **Visconti's "The Damned"**, **Milius' "Big Wednesday"**, "Trust", "Volere Volare", "**The Icicle Thief**" and "**Le Grand Bouffe**".

A dazzling array of directors including **Bergman, Blier, Kieslowski** and **Tavernier**. Classics such as "**The Seventh Seal**", "**Wild Strawberries**", **Gerard Depardieu** in "**Les Valseuses**" and "**Mon Pere Ce Heros**", **Vanessa Paradis** in "**Noce Blanche**" and "**The Double Life of Veronique**" amongst many others.

In addition look out for such titles as the **Pedro Almodovar** collection including "**Matador**", **Alison Maclean's "Crush"**, "**Simple Men**" and the award winning "**Man Bites Dog**".

Look out for Tartan, the art in art house.

For further information please write to Tartan Video, 79 Wardour Street, London W1 or call 071 734 8508